Jane Carlyle

Jane Carlye, 1848, by Samuel Laurence, National Trust (Chelsea)

Jane Carlyle
Newly Selected
Letters

Edited by
Kenneth J. Fielding and David R. Sorensen

ASHGATE

Published by
Ashgate Publishing Limited
Gower House
Croft Road
Aldershot
Hants GU11 3HR
England

Ashgate Publishing Company
Suite 420
101 Cherry Street
Burlington
VT 05401-4405
USA

Ashgate website: http:// www.ashgate.com

British Library Cataloguing in Publication Data
Carlyle, Jane Welsh, 1801-1866
        Jane Carlyle: Newly Selected Letters. - (The Nineteenth Century Series)
1. Carlyle, Jane Welsh, 1801-1866—Correspondence. 2. Authors' spouses—Scotland—Correspondence. I. Title. II. Fielding, Kenneth J. (Kenneth Joshua), 1924- . III. Sorensen, David R.
826.8

Library of Congress Cataloging in Publication Data
Carlyle, Jane Welsh, 1801-1866
Jane Carlyle: Newly Selected Letters / edited by Kenneth J. Fielding and David R. Sorensen.
    p.   cm. - (the Nineteenth Century Series)
Includes bibliographical references (p.).
1. Carlyle, Jane Welsh, 1801-1866—Correspondence. 2. Authors' spouses—Great Britain—Correspondence. 3. Great Britain—Intellectual life—
19th century. 4. Intellectuals—Great Britain—Correspondence. I. Fielding, K. J. (Kenneth J.). II. Sorensen, David R., 1953- . III. Title. IV. Nineteenth century (Aldershot, England).
PR4419.C5A83 2003
824'.8-dc21
[B]   2003048917

ISBN 0 7546 0137 4

Printed and bound in Great Britain by MPG Books Ltd, Bodmin, Cornwall

Contents

Illustrations   vii

Acknowledgements   ix

Abbreviations   x

Editors' Introduction: Selecting Jane Carlyle's Letters   xi

Select Bibliography   xxxiii

Chronology   xxxv

Editorial Note   xxxviii

1   In Search of Genius, 1819–26   1

2   In these Moors, 1828–34   20

3   This Stirring Life—and a Parting, 1834–42   35

4   Turned Adrift in the World, 1842–45   78

5   Finding a Mission, 1845–47   113

6   Looking out into the Vague, 1847–49   129

7   Unease in Zion, 1850–56   154

8   Two Interludes   198

9   Past Mending, 1857–60   221

10 Spiritual Magnetism, 1861–63   259

11 Like a Dim Nightmare, 1863–64   294

12 The Perfectly Extraordinary Woman, 1865–66   303

Index of Correspondents   319

General Index   320

Nineteenth Century
General Editors' Preface

The aim of the series is to reflect, develop and extend the great burgeoning of interest in the nineteenth century that has been an inevitable feature of recent years, as that former epoch has come more sharply into focus as a locus for our understanding not only of the past but of the contours of our modernity. It centres primarily upon major authors and subjects within Romantic and Victorian literature. It also includes studies of other British writers and issues, where these are matters of current debate: for example, biography and autobiography, journalism, periodical literature, travel writing, book production, gender and non-canonical writing. We are dedicated principally to publishing original monographs and symposia; our policy is to embrace a broad scope in chronology, approach and range of concern, and both to recognize and cut innovatively across such parameters as those suggested by the designations 'Romantic' and 'Victorian.' We welcome new ideas and theories, while valuing traditional scholarship. It is hoped that the world which predates yet so forcibly predicts and engages our own will emerge in parts, in the wider sweep, and in the lively streams of disputation and change that are so manifest an aspect of its intellectual, artistic and social landscape.

Vincent Newey
Joanne Shattock

University of Leicester

Illustrations

Frontispiece Jane Carlyle, 1848, crayon drawing by Samuel Laurence

1 Miniature of Jane Carlyle, 1826, by Kenneth Macleay
2 Jane Carlyle, 1843, by Spiridione Gambardella
3 Dr John Welsh and Grace Welsh, Jane's father and mother
4 *Notre Dame de Chelsea*, by Elizabeth Paulet
5 Anthony Sterling
6 Jane and Geraldine Jewsbury, 1855
7 Lady Harriet Ashburton, sketch by Francis Holl
8 Jane Carlyle, 1850, sketch by Carl Hartmann
9 Giuseppe Mazzini
10 Charles Gavan Duffy
11 Thomas Carlyle, about 1854
12 Jane's cousin, Jeannie Welsh, 1843, by Spiridione Gambardella
13 *A Chelsea Interior*, 1858, by Robert Tait
14 Erasmus Darwin
15 Ellen Twisleton
16 Jane Carlyle, about 1853
17 W. E. Forster, photographed by M. Bowness, Ambleside
18 Robert Tait
19 Jane Carlyle, 28 July 1854
20 Jane and Nero, 31 July 1854
21 Thomas and Lord Ashburton, photographed by Vernon Heath, 1862
22 From Jane Carlyle's letter to Lady Harriet Ashburton, 14 November 1855
23 From Jane Carlyle's letter to Louisa Lady Ashburton, 25 May 1864
24 The Grange, drawing by J. F. Neale, engraved T. Matthews
25 Charlotte Cushman, photographed by Gutekunsi
26 *Punch*, 14 April 1866, showing Carlyle as Rector of Edinburgh University
27 Jane and Louisa Lady Ashburton in the 1860s
28 Jane Carlyle, 1862, by William Jeffray

Permission for the use of these, as noted, is gratefully acknowledged: the Rare Book and Manuscript Library, Columbia University, 3, 4 and 27; Special Collections, Edinburgh University Library [courtesy of Columbia University], 6, 9, 10, 11, 14, 18, 19 and 20; the National Library of Scotland, 22 and 23; the *Carlyle Letters* office at Edinburgh University, 12, 16, 21 and 24; the National Portrait Gallery, 5 and 17; the Scottish National Portrait Gallery, 1 and 28; the National Trust, Carlyle's House, Chelsea, frontispiece, 7 and 13. Numbers 8, 15, 25 and 26 respectively are from *New Letters and Memorials of Jane Welsh Carlyle*, ed. Alexander Carlyle (London, 1903), *Letters of the Hon. Mrs. Ellen Twisleton, Written to Her Family, 1852-1862*, ed. Ellen Twisleton Vaughan (London, 1928), Emma Stebbins, *Charlotte Cushman, Letters and Memories of Her Life* (New York, 1871), and Punch, 14 April 1866.

Jane Carlyle was keenly interested in the extensive photography of their friends, Thomas and sometimes herself. Two albums of photographs particularly devoted to her have been drawn on: Anthony Sterling's at the National Portrait Gallery, London (see Kenneth J. Fielding, 'Captain Anthony Sterling's Photograph Album', *Carlyle Newsletter* (1985, 42-52), and 'Pictures from the Sun', by Robert Tait, probably instigated by Geraldine Jewsbury, Thomas Carlyle Albums, Rare Book and Manuscript Library, Columbia University. Copies were frequently given to friends and family. Jane writes of accompanying Thomas to 'the best photographer in London' (*NLM* 2:269), and Thomas kept the result by him (number 28), though considering her 'photographs are all *old*, and one and all' lacking 'the finer traits. . . . She was so anxious about my poor portrayings, and wholly neglected her own' (*Reminiscences* 194).

Acknowledgements

We are greatly indebted to the following: the Bodleian Library; Chelsea Public Library; Duke University Library; the Norman and Charlotte Strouse Carlyle Collection, University of California, Santa Cruz; the Pierpont Morgan Library; the trustees of the Trevelyan Family papers at the Robinson Library, Newcastle University; the Master and the Fellows of Trinity College, Cambridge; the Alexander Turnbull Library, the National Library of New Zealand, Te Puna Mātauranga o Aotearoa, Wellington; and the Beinecke Rare Book and Manuscript Library, Yale University. The Houghton Library, Harvard University, the Library of Congress, the trustees of the National Library of Scotland, and the Special Collections of Edinburgh University Library have been particularly helpful. The publishers of the *Collected Letters of Thomas and Jane Welsh Carlyle*, and their director, Steve Cohn, have provided essential cooperation and assistance, as have fellow-editors of the *Collected Letters*, to whom we are especially grateful. We are also indebted to David Southern, Managing Editor of the Carlyle Office at Duke University, for his tireless support. Warm acknowledgement has to be made of the unfailing generosity and helpfulness of Professor Ian Campbell. Though the owners of Carlyle papers and manuscripts given for the first time wish to stay strictly private, they nevertheless deserve the greatest thanks for allowing their use. Without this material, the selection would have been very different. At Saint Joseph's University, Philadelphia, we are grateful to Deans Judi Chapman and Brice Wachterhauser for their encouragement and financial support, to the staff of the Honors Program, and to Tom Malone of the University Press for his expert preparation of the manuscript in Camera Ready Copy. At Edinburgh University, we are grateful to Professor Cairns Craig, Anthea Taylor and the Institute for Advanced Studies in the Humanities for a research fellowship that allowed us to complete the project. We owe a debt to many others, including those who organized and attended the Carlyle conferences in Philadelphia and Edinburgh in 2000–01, whose support and encouragement are most gratefully acknowledged.

Abbreviations

Self-evident short forms have often been used for references and titles; fuller forms may be found in the Select Bibliography. Place of publication is London unless stated otherwise.

CCP   Charlotte Cushman Papers, Library of Congress

CL   *Collected Letters of Thomas and Jane Welsh Carlyle* (Durham, NC, 1970-)

Duke   Duke University Library MS

S. M. Ellis   S. M. Ellis, ed. *Unpublished Letters of Lady Bulwer Lytton to A. E. Chalon, R.A.* (1914)

EUL   Edinburgh University Library MS

Froude, *Life*   J.A. Froude, *Thomas Carlyle, A History of the First Forty Years of His Life, 1795-1835; A History of His Life in London, 1834-1881*, 4 vols. (1882; 1884)

Houghton   Houghton Library, Harvard University

Huxley, *JWCLF*   Leonard Huxley, ed. *Jane Welsh Carlyle, Letters to Her Family, 1839-1863* (1924)

Huxley, *LJWC*   Leonard Huxley, ed. 'Letters from Jane Welsh Carlyle', *Cornhill Magazine*, n.s. 61 (1926): 493-510, 622-38.

JWC   Jane Welsh Carlyle

LM   J.A. Froude, ed. *Letters and Memorials of Jane Welsh Carlyle*, 3 vols. (1883)

NLM   A. Carlyle, ed. *New Letters and Memorials of Jane Welsh Carlyle*, 2 vols. (1903)

NLS   National Library of Scotland MS

Strouse   Norman and Charlotte Strouse Carlyle Collection MS, University of California, Santa Cruz

TC   Thomas Carlyle

Works   Carlyle, *Works*, Centenary edition, 30 vols. (1896-99)

Yale   Beinecke Rare Book and Manuscript Library, Yale University MS

Editors' Introduction:
Selecting Jane Carlyle's Letters

As Jane Carlyle's birthday came round after her death in 1866, Thomas Carlyle described in his *Reminiscences* how he sorted through her past letters: 'such a day's *reading* as I perhaps never had in my life before. What a piercing radiancy of meaning to me in those dear records, hastily thrown off, full of misery, yet of bright eternal love; all as if on wings of lightning, tingling through one's very heart of hearts! . . . I have asked myself, Ought all this to be lost, or kept to myself, and the brief time that now belongs to *me*? . . . As to "talent", epistolary and other, these *Letters*, I perceive, equal and surpass whatever of best I know to exist in that kind' (160–1). He went ahead with his compilation of more than six volumes of the private and personal letters of someone who was known to others for being no more than Mrs Carlyle.

Thomas's judgement of Jane has been amply vindicated by the various editions that have since appeared: the *Letters and Memorials*, annotated by Carlyle and edited by Froude (1883); Alexander Carlyle's *New Letters and Memorials* (1903) and *Love Letters* (1909); Leonard Huxley's collection of letters to the Welsh family (1924); an attractive selection by Trudy Bliss (1949); and Alan and Mary McQueen Simpson's *I Too Am Here* (1977). But another selection is now needed to enrich our understanding of Jane Carlyle's achievement. These works are out of print, and fresh discoveries have been made. More recently writers such as Norma Clarke and Aileen Christianson have built on the work of Lawrence and Elizabeth Hanson's *Necessary Evil* and Virginia Surtees' *Jane Carlyle*, seeing Jane as a woman and an artist distinct from her husband. What emerges from the present selection is someone who is not dramatically changed, but who appears in a brighter and sharper focus, with a different emphasis.

A selection is never entirely simple. In the foreword to her volume, Trudy Bliss rightly refused to claim that her book 'represented the whole' of Jane Carlyle's life: 'In making my choice from the formidable quantity of manuscript letters now in Edinburgh, my design has been that Mrs. Carlyle should write her own story'. Her selection was 'impartial', not 'impersonal', made with no wish to repeat the mistakes of those who 'pounced on' new letters 'to prove a point of view'. Yet to talk of 'her own story' implies that there is a *story* to tell, and that an easy selection can be made with careful decision. Decision means interpretation, and we now have almost 2,000 of Jane's letters from which to choose, when a single-volume selection can include only about 250. It follows that Jane Carlyle cannot exactly tell her own story, because her letters are always selected for her and chosen from a preconceived 'point of view'.

The first selection of *Letters and Memorials* usefully illustrates the point. Carlyle meant the three-volume edition to be twice as long, though he excluded the love letters that were edited in two volumes, after protracted delay, by Alexander Carlyle. Froude insisted that Carlyle's proposal should be reduced by cutting his six volumes to three, so limiting the number of letters drawn on to 367, and incidentally saying nothing about the letters' transcendent merits. He was cool in his appreciation, in spite of being deep in them for Thomas's biography and the volumes he called the *Letters and Memorials*, 'prepared ... by Thomas Carlyle' and 'edited by James Anthony Froude'. In fact, these letters were collected, prepared, annotated, explained and transcribed by, or under the direction of, Carlyle, who bequeathed his careful copies to Froude, accompanied by the heartfelt praise in his *Reminiscences*. Froude then published them with no editorial recommendation apart from his brief leaden introduction.

Later selectors need to consider the design and context of *Letters and Memorials*. Froude constructed a very deliberate plot in his biography, and reinforced it by using excerpts from his dutiful three-volume redaction of Carlyle's selected *Letters and Memorials*. We may suppose that he did not mean to be unjust, but he had already firmly committed himself to a particular interpretation of the Carlyles' lives in his first two volumes of Thomas Carlyle's biography (1882). He was already launched on writing the last two, which were published in 1884, and the three-volume *Letters and Memorials* was imminent in 1883. John Clubbe has persuasively demonstrated in his abridgement of Froude's *Life* (1979) that the biography was a feat of immensely skilful organization showing extraordinary powers of condensation. But as Clubbe acknowledges, Froude felt his task compelled him to dramatize the Carlyles' lives, with the result that his wish 'to shape his characters rendered them dramatically vivid, but his artistic technique, given that he was dealing not with legends but with real persons, inevitably led to distortion' (25). It is recognised that Froude intensified them and that, though reasonably faithful to his sources, he was driven to find devices to heighten his effects and to avoid particular interpretative difficulties, especially in relation to the Carlyles' life together.

Froude's plot was heavily influenced by his romantic notion of 'genius', and by a conviction that the Carlyles' marriage was 'a tragedy as stern and real as the story of Oedipus' (*My Relations with Carlyle* 13). His hero was an unruly Titan, whose creative unrest 'he would carry with him, wherever he might go or be, the wild passionate spirit, fevered with burning thoughts, which would make peace impossible' (*Life* 1:342). By its nature, such a force could not be domesticated. As Isaac D'Israeli had pointed out in his popular *The Literary Character: or, the History of Men of Genius* (1799), which was reissued in a new edition by his son Benjamin Disraeli in the same year as the first two volumes of the *Life*, genius demands isolation:'Solitude is the nurse of enthusiasm, and enthusiasm is the true parent of genius. No considerable work was ever composed till its author . . . first retired to the grove . . . to invocate'.[1] In his biography, Froude used the romantic myth to justify his claim that Carlyle should not have married, and classical parallels to highlight the tragic consequences.

But, as he acknowledged in his apologia, *My Relations with Carlyle* (1903), these literary devices enabled him to avoid open discussion of the more basic reports about the Carlyles' marriage told him by Geraldine Jewsbury. Carlyle's literary genius was said to be 'violent and overbearing' and, in Jewsbury's words, the whole explanation of their problems was that he was 'one of those persons who ought never to have married'. Without children, Jane consoled herself by supposing that she was Thomas's intellectual companion. His infatuation with Lady Harriet Ashburton shattered this illusion:'She had once been his idol, she was now a household drudge, and the imaginative homage which had been once hers was given to another'. In Froude's account, having been abused mentally and physically, Jane meant to commit suicide and told Geraldine that she 'definitely' and 'often' resolved to leave Carlyle and 'even to marry another person' (*My Relations* 22-4). Though totally unsupported by evidence, Froude declares that he was convinced that Jewsbury's declaration was right—her 'information was given to me under too solemn circumstances, and was coupled with too many singular details, to allow doubt to be possible'—yet he could not bring himself to expose his hero. As he bitterly remarked, 'It was all left to my discretion, but how was my discretion to be exercised?' (21-5).

Froude's solution was to 'retailor' reality to the pattern of classical tragedy. Thomas was modelled on Oedipus, the king who experienced a moment of vision after enduring a lifetime of blindness, and who tried to understand his life in the wake of his revelation. In Froude's story, 'He awoke only to the consciousness of what he had been, when the knowledge would bring no more than unavailing remorse' (*Life* 1:285). Jane was given the role of an Iphigenia, who sacrificed her intellect and sexuality for the sake of her husband's genius; unable to pursue her love for Edward Irving, she is said to have married Carlyle for ambition rather than love. Froude represents Thomas's triumph as her moment of self-destruction :'The victory was won, but, as of old in Aulis, not without a victim. Miss Welsh had looked forward to being Carlyle's intellectual companion, to sharing his thoughts and helping him with his writings....

The reality was not like the dream. Poor as they were, she had to work as a menial servant. . . . Bravely she went through it all; and she would have gone through it cheerfully if she had been rewarded with ordinary gratitude' (1:365–6). To 'explain' Carlyle's infatuation with Lady Harriet Ashburton, Froude went on to fantastical Spenserian allusions:'She became Gloriana, Queen of Fairyland, and he, with a true vein of chivalry in him, became her rustic Red Cross Knight, who, if he could, would have gladly led his own *Una* into the same enchanting service' (3:342–3).

Compelling and readable as Froude may be, his account makes in effect a bogus use of these mythic and literary devices. He wants to give a dramatic account of his hero's life, without actually saying what happened. He began with a plot, and then selected letters to reinforce it, which he divided between the *Life* and the *Letters and Memorials*. As Moncure Conway, the American abolitionist, liberal theologian and friend of the Carlyles remarked, Froude 'wrote a "biography" so marked by dramatic situations, thrilling scenes, and startling effects, that I discover in momentous chapters the hand that wrote "Nemesis of Faith" and "Shadows of the Clouds."'[2] With few exceptions—Alexander Carlyle being the most notable and notorious—later editors and selectors of Jane Carlyle's letters have largely accepted Froude's version, often without making their own investigations. Their selections were based on his and on the dramatic way he arranged them. John Clubbe's assertion that 'Froude presents not only a convincing but also a fundamentally sound interpretation of the Carlyles, their courtship, their marriage, and their existence together' (*Life* 7) suggests the extent to which mythical interpretation has eclipsed historical truth in the Carlyles' biography.

The present selection rejects drama in favour of prose. A much wider selection of letters and papers is now available, and no simple plot will accommodate the complexities of this almost continuous record. In confining our volume to about 250 letters, the aim is to miniaturize a domestic account rather than mount a Greek tragedy. Froude's version of the Carlyles is only one among several possible interpretations. Concentrating their lives in a swooping plot after the fashion of Oedipus, he supposed that their characters were fixed. Yet the letters often reveal their writers' unpredictable qualities, which contradict his preconceived ideas of Thomas as a brooding Oedipus, Jane as a self-sacrificing Iphigenia, and Lady Harriet as 'Gloriana'.

Froude's version dramatically simplifies the relationship between Thomas, Jane and Lady Harriet, which lasted fourteen years. Jane not only accepted Lady Harriet's hospitality, but also often visited her on her own with apparent relief. There were times when she was bitterly jealous or exasperated, and objected to the exchange of letters between Thomas and

Lady Harriet. But the Ashburtons' little court was at the centre of the Carlyles' lives and friendships. As *The Times* pointed out in its obituary of Lady Harriet, 'the hospitality of Lord and Lady Ashburton has ... been open to all excellence and liberal to all opinions; it has shown the luxury of wealth compatible with simplicity of life, and mental superiority without a taint of pride or affectation'. Jane as well as Thomas took pleasure in belonging to this circle of distinguished men and women.

Lady Harriet herself was neither allegorical nor aloof, though Froude later wrote to Louisa Lady Ashburton that he sometimes thought that she was an 'evil spirit' and Mrs Carlyle a 'half human Elf'.[3] The daughter of the sixth Earl of Sandwich, Lady Harriet was happy to knit woollen scarves for the author of *The French Revolution* and *Cromwell* and his wife, and deliver them personally to their suburban terraced house in unfashionable Chelsea, as well as to invite them to the grandeur of her country home the Grange, and Bath House, Piccadilly. The actual peculiarities of Carlyle's admiration for Lady Harriet, and her acceptance of it with Jane's resulting jealousy, are more interesting than Froude's deceptive juggling devices with Oedipus and the *Faerie Queene*. There was no blood on the floors at Cheyne Row nor dramatic romance. For all its apparently easy allusions, Froude's version diminishes the characters of Jane, Lady Harriet and Carlyle. He has substituted literary archetypes for the actual complexity of their lives. While post-modernists have argued that such tactics are inherent in biography, readers of the Carlyles' letters should read them differently.

A mythical interpretation is neater than laboured reality. On the one hand it is plain that Carlyle liked Lady Harriet's company and being regarded as 'her dear old Prophet'.[4] On her part, 'coming back into the society of Carlyle after the dons of Oxford', she said, was 'like returning from some conventional country to the human race'.[5] On the other hand there is a fantastical air in his letters to her, not all of which were allowed to survive. A few of them are extraordinary. One apparently uncollected and undated note (of the early 1850s?), written just after she had left him, pursues her with: 'You are the Queen of Women! Magnanimous, patient, gentle, brave and beautiful, beyond the daughters of Eve. Oh, if I could fly into Heaven with you,—would I!—The thought of you gilds all darknesses in my existence; makes London fog itself into clouds of red and gold. Thanks, thanks, dear one. / T. C', (NLS Acc. 11388). In another, he writes, 'before the Queen, so bounteous, gracious in all living things ... I kiss the hem of your garment' (*CL* 28:328), yet this is the conclusion of a perfectly practical discussion of where he can find a quiet place in the Grange to write. He thanks the 'noble woman of a thousand' (*CL* 28:167) for an ordinary kindness to a fellow writer.[6]

It is a little strange, however, that Froude's tendency to veer between exaggeration and ironic reticence has usually passed unchallenged by most of the Carlyles' later biographers, who share his reluctance to cloud the dramatic plot with confusing details and questions. And hardly any biographers, for example, have mentioned the 'blue marks' on Jane's wrists, about which she wrote in her *Journal* on 26 June 1856 (see page 220). Had Thomas struck her? Had there been violence? Or was Moncure Conway right to claim that 'if there were any "blue marks" on Mrs. Carlyle's arm caused by Carlyle it was not done to inflict injury but to save her from it' (*Autobiography* 2:197). Even Carlyle's biographers D. A. Wilson, Fred Kaplan and Simon Heffer avoid the subject. Yet it seems that it was chiefly this passage that so upset Carlyle that he was 'remorsefully' led into editing Jane's letters; and it was the same passage that led Froude to question Geraldine Jewsbury, who famously told him her explanation that Carlyle 'ought never to have married' (*My Relations* 21). Though discussed by Froude, his acolyte Waldo Dunn and Alexander Carlyle, the episode remains somewhat mysterious, as are other accusations that Carlyle was 'violent', Biographers have invoked the 'gospel of silence', allowing the unexplained or doctored versions of Jane's *Journal* published by Froude and Alexander Carlyle to stand as conflicting testimony.[7]

Though the exact truth about the bruises can never be known, we can now see from the relatively unbowdlerized *Journal* (1855–56) why Froude and Alexander Carlyle were so eager to meddle with it. It is a painful record of what Jane really felt and thought, and not surprisingly, a rather new picture emerges. It is neither self-flattering nor unreasonable. She writes in the darkest hours of her life, mixing irony and sarcasm with morbid humour and resentment. While she takes pride in her husband, she bitterly regrets that he has found another companion who can inspire and divert him. Yet if ignoring Jane's *Journal* means underestimating the depth of her depression at this time, treating it as the culmination of an unhappy marriage that had darkened her whole life is equally distorting. As always, context is important. This was Jane's lowest moment. Already, with Lady Harriet's illness, the feeling of her oppression was lessening, to be completely lifted with the latter's death in May 1857 and followed by an ecstatic friendship with the new Louisa Lady Ashburton. Typically, Froude leaped over this phase, swiftly taking the Ashburton story from the point of Lady Harriet's death, through the valley of the shadow of *Frederick*, to Jane's last moments in Hyde Park.

In making this selection, we have tried to keep in mind such letters to Thomas as those beginning with 'Dearest Love', 'My *sweet* Love' (29 Aug. 1837; 18 Sept. 1838), or expressing Jane's anguish when she is sometimes parted from him, her cuddling up to his red night cap when he is away in London

(6 Aug. 1831), and her extreme distress when the post fails to bring his letters (14 July 1846). In these moments, she was moved by something else than 'ambition' (Froude, *Life* 1:291). That they loved one another is beyond doubt. It is often assumed that Thomas found it easier to write letters than to show his love, yet the loving and sensual endearments continue to come from Jane at times, in spite of her frustration with him. The temptation is strong to show their marriage as an unrelieved tragedy. But such a pattern is achieved only at the expense of leaving loose ends. The Carlyles' lives were less a classical tragedy than an extensive patchwork rug.

As a professional writer, Froude could not afford to spend time unpicking the rug. He had been legally forced to pay back £1,500 to Carlyle's niece for appropriating the section on Jane Welsh Carlyle for his edition of the *Reminiscences*, published without her knowledge because he knew she would not agree. The biography had to sell to pay for four years' or more work on it. He had no wish to soften Carlyle's image as a 'moral desperado', and was under considerable pressure to make the life and letters controversial. A distinct plot was needed to give his readers what they were seeking, and he gave way to the need as readily as he did in his dramatic and partisan histories and essays. In his defence, it can be said that he is an editor who arrived early and was at the mercy of the materials entrusted to him. Yet the results do not reveal him as entirely reliable. He accepts what he wants, and rejects whatever contradicts his assumptions. The three-volume *Letters and Memorials* shows his shortcomings. Between all his multi-volumes, he almost entirely fails to use Jane's letters to John Forster, John Sterling, the Welsh family, the two Lady Ashburtons, the Wedgwoods, the Speddings, Erasmus Darwin, Francis Jeffrey and many others. He appears to have been denied the use of the 'love letters', and so tells the story of a courtship and marriage in his own words, offering a version often at odds with the evidence. In short, he allowed himself to select according to his preconceptions. Yet, with a few notable exceptions, those who followed him have mainly accepted his interpretation and let it shape their own.

The result of so much being left out is that the accepted view of life at Cheyne Row is too claustrophobic. It was more lively, interesting, and unusual than Froude led readers to believe. What is remarkable is how mentally alert and curious Jane stayed, despite her frequent bouts of ill health. If we focus mainly on her frustrations with Lady Harriet, especially in the mid-1850s, we miss the variety of Jane's friendships and the attraction of her small 'salon' at Chelsea, where famous and sought-after figures regularly came to see her and her husband. The lack of a child was both an advantage and disadvantage. She was free to form other relationships, such as those with her nieces, and younger friends, including Blanche

Stanley (Lady Airlie) and Kate Sterling. By omitting such figures, earlier editors darkened the picture.

An idea of what has been lost, for example, comes with the discovery of her friendship with Ellen Twisleton from Boston, who came into the Carlyles' lives in 1852 after her marriage to the civil servant and educational reformer, Edward Twisleton. She was petite, dark-eyed, intelligent, affectionate, and anxious to win the favour of her husband's old friends. She was well connected, freely welcome in the Ashburton circle, admired by Lord Lansdowne and popular with everyone who met her. Her friendship with Jane Carlyle was warm and intense. Until recently she has been ignored by Jane's biographers, because there are few surviving letters between them. But a little manuscript of about twenty-seven pages, written by Ellen Twisleton and recently found by Kenneth J. Fielding in the Houghton Library at Harvard, records an intimate conversation with Jane sometime soon after the mid-1850s, when she was very ill and bitterly resentful of Lady Harriet. It is a new document putting the old story in a sharper light. The interview was recorded by Ellen as if Jane were speaking to her, and was perhaps revised with Jane's approval (see pp. 198-203).[8]

It mainly covers life at Craigenputtoch where the Carlyles went in 1828 after their marriage: 'the dreariest place on the face of the earth', and 'the most dreadful, lonesome, barest of places'. Life there was complicated by their sharing it with Thomas's brother Alexander, who lived nearby, 'a man of the most outrageous, coarse, violent temper ... nobody can imagine what I went through with that man'. Nor was the atmosphere enlivened by having Thomas's teenage sister Jean to stay, the future exemplary Jean Aitken (mother of Mary Aitken Carlyle), but then 'a coarse rude girl', with 'such a tre-MENDOUS will as I never met with in any other woman but herself; a will just like Carlyle's. . . . She would come to breakfast with her hair in curl-papers, which I never could put up with, & other things of the sort'. If Craigenputtoch was dreary, so too were their lives. Jane says she saw little of Carlyle, who worked through the day, rode alone for two hours, and joined her late in the evening: '"Jane, will ye play me a few of those Scotch tunes"—& I would sit down & play Scotch tunes till he went to bed,—oftenest with tears running down my face, the while I played'.

Jane's narrative in the Houghton manuscript seems to confirm her role as an 'Iphigenia', yet interpretations or modifications are possible, particularly when her account is set against letters written from Craigenputtoch, which give a very different perspective. Her memory has reshaped the story. She recalls her own sacrifice of the 'little jewel of a house' in Comely Bank for her rebuilt house on the wild moors. Miserable and in ill health, we may see Jane as prone to live in the past, to brood on its failures, and allow herself to be carried away by what Proust called the 'shifting and confused gusts of memory'.[9] Perhaps not surprisingly, the Jane of the Twisleton interview resembles the tragic heroine of Froude's *Life*. It was a self-image that she favoured in later years—and Froude knew her personally only from the time he moved to London in 1861—when she enjoyed the company of young and curious listeners. Yet, other aspects of the Twisleton friendship undercut Froude's account, so deeply influenced by Geraldine Jewsbury. Visiting Chelsea in 1855, Ellen Twisleton's sister found 'the everlasting Jewsbury' decidedly unpleasant, jealous and a source of frequent exasperation to Jane, while she saw Lady Ashburton as deserving 'admiration and respect' and that Mrs Brookfield (the source for many stories about Jane) may have been admired by men but was detested by women.[10]

There are other accounts or assessments to consider. We cannot exclude the question of Carlyle's impotence, as alleged by the journalist Frank Harris.[11] His story was that the aged Carlyle had confided to him, while walking in Hyde Park, that the 'body part seemed so little to me....I had no idea it could mean much to her.... Quarter of a century passed before I found out how wrong I was, how mistaken, how criminally blind. ...It was the doctor told me and then it was too late for anything but repentance' (*English Review* 432). Harris backed it up with the assertion that Jane's physician, Dr Richard Quain, had assured him over dinner at the Garrick Club that when he examined her in the 1860s, he had found her '*virgo intacta*'.[12] Harris's tales have to be mentioned, even if rejected as absurd. This is not to suggest that the sexual side of the Carlyles' marriage was unimportant, only that we know little about it. Harris's modern biographer Philippa Pullar has closely analysed the evidence and concluded that it 'seems most unlikely that Carlyle should have confided intimacies to Harris' (*Frank Harris* 56). In his autobiography, *My Life and Loves* (1925), Harris provides a copious imaginary dialogue between Jane and Thomas on their wedding night, and ends with Jane's confession to Quain that Thomas 'never really made me jealous, save for a short time with Lady Ashburnham [meaning Ashburton]'.[13] Pullar argues that the book was written mainly for money when Harris was impotent himself, and that 'most of the sexual scenes are fantasies, a requiem for lost youth and virility'(*Frank Harris* xi).

There is another sidelight on Jane in her short fiction, *The Simple Story of My Own First Love*. It is now possible to read it in the uncut version (Edinburgh, 2001; and *CL* 30). Written in 1852, it is a mainly autobiographical tale about her childhood in Haddington as a nine-year-old, when her love for the young son of an artillery officer is rejected. It is wistfully self-scrutinizing, and perhaps written to advise younger women friends that they should think twice before giving their hearts away too easily. The unfortunate Thomas is again put up to be knocked down, being unable to believe in love, unlike—for example—Thackeray in his recent novel

Esmond, or the late Duke of Wellington, still the subject of admiring scandal for cheerfully dallying with a married Mrs Jones well over fifty years his junior.

It is another reproachful document, like her newfound *Notebook* (1845–52), which again characterizes her husband as corrosively contemptuous of the mutual help of London thieves and prostitutes, 'the scum of Creation' (p. 131; *CL* 30:126). There is also a dummy book, entitled *The School for Husbands* (1852), which records nothing in its totally blank pages (now in the Norman and Charlotte Strouse collection, Santa Cruz, PR4419.C5A16 1852), and may have been Jane's gift to Thomas, if it were not one given to her. Such rather inconclusive documents may make us ask how far her complaints were fair. And perhaps a just and prescriptive judgement is impossible. For we should allow for the way that Jane's side of the story arises (as she well knew) from her nature as well as her circumstances, from her constant inclination to play the sweet and sour part of a woman who feels 'put upon', so that it is a joke—and more than a joke—and because in nearly 10,000 of his letters Thomas never utters a word of counter-criticism.

Another newfound notebook, written about 1834 to 1857 and in private hands, is so far known only from considerable extracts given by Alexander Carlyle (*NLM* 2:109–15) and is referred to by Carlyle as her 'poor little book of *notabilia*' (*Reminiscences* 95). It is a small book, of about 6½ by 4 inches. Jane's jottings can hardly have been meant to help her conversation and letters, but taken together they show an interest in human nature mixed with scepticism, an inclination to make observations on women and marriage, and a liking for proverbs and sayings, odd little scraps of 'mad poetry', notes in French and Italian, from old sagas in translation, conversation, drama and from Carlyle himself. It may be as commonplace as any commonplace book, but it also confirms the self-sketches she gives in her letters of someone constantly under constraint, who finds relief in cynical comments she can make her own. She sees herself as injured by life itself:

> Able to cure all sadness but despair
> Madame de Stael says of marriage, better one slave than
>   two esprits fort
> All my prospects are bounded as these from a window on a
>   dead wall
>   My youth was left behind
>   For someone else to find [To which TC adds:
> 'More than once she repeated this, with a mock sadness that
> went to my heart.']

When an ass climbs a ladder you may find wisdom in a
    woman—
'Before other people never flatter your wife nor slight her'
'He did not speak when he was annoyed or displeased, but
       worked off his volcanic wrath by firing pistols out of the
       back door in rapid succession (Miss Brontë's father)'

None of her miscellaneous writings supports Dickens's belief expressed on her death that 'none of the writing women come near her at all'.[14] Letter-writing is largely a performance art, which was suited to her wit and spontaneity. Apart from her letters, her best piece was 'Much ado About Nothing', written on her return to Haddington in 1850. Whether she could have developed her skill to support a less self-concerned and more sustained performance is difficult to say. Much of the new material in this selection, in fact, is contradictory, and often resistant to the theories and plots that have dominated her biographies. It is only recently that women writers, some of them feminists, have challenged these versions and begun to explore Jane's smouldering resentment of a male-dominated society, in which she was influenced by other women at the time.

She knew of the writings and life-style of Harriet Taylor and John Stuart Mill, of George Henry Lewes and his 'lovebird' Agnes, and their double life with Thornton Hunt in their Bayswater 'Phalanstery'. Jane enjoyed ridiculing the ultra-conservative Sarah Stickney Ellis, author of *Women of England*. In the late 1850s she exchanged letters with the radical Mary Smith of Carlisle, a local feminist journalist and lecturer. She read and carefully commented on Geraldine Jewsbury's novels. Geraldine's letters to Jane are explicit enough, revealing as they do the two women's interest in feminine issues in education, marriage, personal relations and careers, and the way in which Jewsbury absorbs these into her fiction. We would know more about Jewsbury if she had not burnt Jane's letters, or if her own had not been so savagely cut and presumably destroyed by Mrs Alexander Ireland, who 'edited' Geraldine's letters to Jane. Geraldine was erratic in her tendency to exaggeration, and Jane herself blamed her own 'idiotic credulity' in believing 'the testimony of a female Novelist on any *practical* matter!' (JWC to Lady Stanley, 19 August 1860).

We should also allow that such letters show that Jane's problems arose partly from her own nature, intensified by her own apparently desperate state of health, to be exacerbated by resorting to morphia. Geraldine was to have a final word in her remarkable letter to Froude, 22 November 1866, which biographers have still to take fully into account.[15] Until recently it has been known only from the selective version in the *Letters and*

Memorials (2:273-5), and is now taken from *CL* 30 and manuscript. She began the letter by referring to the *Journal* (1855-56), which Froude had sent her, asking about the 'blue marks', but, as many records show, she had also suffered from her 'closest friend's' sharp scorn:

> *Mrs* C was *proud* & proud of her Pride. It was indeed enormous but a quality she admired in *herself & in others*. The only person who ever had any influence over her was her Father—he died when she was 14 [meaning 18]—& she was left to herself. Her mother & she never agreed well when *together*—tho' she adored her at a distance—and worshipped her after she was dead.

Taking up the question whether Jane was not 'disloyal' to Thomas:

> No. Her allegiance was *never* broken. . . . She liked to be worshipped & to have people give their lives souls & spirit to her—I mean those whom she '*allowed* to love her' as she would have put it, but *all* even the only two she *really* cared for, & who had the *power to make her* suffer—broke themselves against a rock, her *will* was as strong as her *Pride* & she *never* did anything in her life w*h* she wd have considered ignominious. The feelings of pity tenderness generosity (false if you will) w*h* softens & bewilders most women—NEVER disturbed her. The clear pitiless common sense w*h* she always kept to never failed her. She was not heartless, for her feelings were *real & strong* but she had a genuine *preference* for *herself*— From earliest girlhood this was her characteristic in all matters when *men* were in question.

We may divert our attention to noting that it is not clear who the other 'only' person was whom she 'really cared for', apart from her father, unless it was Thomas—or perhaps George Rennie. Geraldine ends with remarks that Froude entirely suppressed:

> She did not falter from her purpose of helping & shielding him *but* she became *warped*. 'We have this treasure in earthly vessels'—& the vessels get cracked & broken & disfigured & people do not see or understand the treasure w*h* is thus carried & they *misjudge & measure & criticise* but the Treasure is there, & the broken blackened misformed unshapely *outside appearance* is swallowed up by Death and 'I believe in the forgiveness of Sins and the Life Everlasting Amen!' *G. E. Jewsbury*

Such incoherence may show the sharpness of her pain at the treatment she often suffered from Jane, not leaving it clear who was to be forgiven, husband, wife or herself. But her characterization shows her deep sense of profound contradictions in all three.

Yet earlier Jane wrote warmly of Geraldine's novel *The Half Sisters*, as 'the one of all her novels which I like the best. And it has *bonafide* arguments in it, betwixt her and me, written down almost word for word as we spoke them in our walks together' (to Mary Russell, 28 November 1856). They shared an enthusiasm for the novels of George Sand— condemned by Thomas in a draft called 'Phallus-Worship'—and which she discussed with other friends, including the Bullers, Sand's close admirer Mazzini and Elizabeth Paulet, the attractive and apparently scandalous feminist, to whom Jewsbury jointly dedicated *The Half Sisters* with Jane Carlyle. Sand may also have influenced Jane's other novelist friends, the liberal-minded Susan Hunter and Martha Lamont, to whom Jane sometimes writes belligerently about 'women's rights'.

Thomas himself was not unaware of feminist issues, and liberal-minded women were attracted to him partly because he enjoyed satirizing their views and arguing with them. Early in marriage he wrote to John Carlyle, expressing concern about the dullness of Jane's life with him as a writer: 'I tell her many times there is *much* for her to do, if she were trained to it; her whole Sex to deliver from the bondage to Frivolity Dollhood and Imbecillity into the freedom of Valour and Womanhood' (*CL* 6:183). But as Jane Carlyle realized or felt, there were few outlets for freedom. In linking her to feminism, the intention is not to make her seem relevant by reflecting present concerns. As with many of her friends, the issue was often in mind. She was a good deal less than an actual feminist, but was aware of 'women's rights', choosing her closer friends from those who were usually more outspoken than she was, but ready to maintain her point of view. Inevitably, Froude ignored the matter, which is only now receiving serious attention.

It is easy to underestimate the importance of such 'rights' in Jane's personal life. She was drawn into friendship with Amalie Bölte, a German radical novelist, who introduced Jane to liberal new ideas on marriage on the continent, which in turn provoked her to scathing comments on marriage in general. Though few letters exist between the two, Bölte's 'domestic spy' letters to Varnhagen von Ense (as they were called in the *Saturday Review* in 1860, where Thomas and Jane might read about them) suggest the topicality of the issue at 5 Cheyne Row, when Amalie wrote her reports. Bölte recalls the teasing chauvinistic superiority of Carlyle accompanied by his brother John, when they discussed the status of German women with her. On hearing Bölte argue that women should be given the vote, Thomas teasingly responded: 'First the women—and next the dogs!'

Though she preferred others to express the more extreme views, Jane was prepared to sign the 'Petition for the Reform of the Married Women's Property Law', presented to Parliament on 14 March 1856. She does not refer to the document in her letters, but her fellow signatories remind us of her 'set': Geraldine Jewsbury, a hesitant Mrs Gaskell, Elizabeth Browning, Anna Jameson, Harriet Martineau, Madame Mohl, Anna Blackwell (who sent her poems to Carlyle), and George Eliot, whose name (Marian Evans) was kept low on the list because of the scandal of her liaison with Lewes. The language of the petition, published in Lewes' *Leader* (16 February 1856) and elsewhere, is blunt: 'That since modern civilisation, in indefinitely extending the sphere of occupation for women, has in some measure broken down their pecuniary dependence on men, it is time that legal protection be thrown over the produce of their labour, and that in entering the state of marriage, they no longer pass from freedom into the condition of a slave, all whose earnings belong to his master and not to himself'. It is hard to think of Froude's Iphigenia signing such a petition, or belonging to such a mainly free-thinking set.

The present selection reflects Jane Carlyle as a thinker in her own right, always willing to speak to women less fortunate than herself—even prostitutes. She was interested in the Fraser/Bagley case, brought by a bullying husband who accused his wife of adultery and failed to convince the court or anyone else. She and Thomas dined with the notorious Caroline Norton, and Jane enjoyed shocking her cousins with the story. When Lady Bulwer Lytton sought the Carlyles' help in her case against her callous and brutal husband, both responded warmly and sympathetically. Yet a balanced picture asks that Jane's activities as mistress of 5 Cheyne Row also be given careful consideration. She was intensely concerned to play her part, to take charge of house decorating and building alterations, and to complain at being deserted by Thomas at one moment, while demanding that he leave in another. Jane was hardly the 'delicate' and refined 'lady brought up in luxury' whom Froude idealized, nor did she usually consider herself 'degraded' by housework, cooking or even sewing (*Life* 2:125, 419). She wanted to contribute actively and regularly to their joint career, and to be the wife of her chosen 'man of genius'. The phrase is one that constantly re-echoes through the letters and, however jokingly used, reflects a truth: that she deliberately chose marriage to a rather uncouth and unknown writer whose outstanding ability would remove her from provincial Haddington to the more stimulating society of Edinburgh and London, even if by way of detour via the dreaded Craigenputtoch.

Inevitably disputes have continued about who was more to blame for the dark passages of the marriage, and, as the rest of her letters are published, re-interpretation must follow. We have argued that allowances have to be made on all sides, and that neither personality was as fixed as earlier biographers supposed. Though she believed her life was dull, her own letters suggest the opposite. Following Carlyle's advice, she makes her letters lengthy, careless, 'garrulous and true-hearted', boldly dashing her comments down even on odd pages from the butcher's book (*CL* 1:xvi–xvii). At other times she is an artist whose letters were composed in a seemingly haphazard style, reflecting her desire to offset her public role as dutiful wife of a 'genius' with that of a shrewd, acerbic and biting commentator on the world immediately around her. In a restricted selection, we have tried to present the range of her talents, including 'set pieces' such as excerpts from 'Much ado About Nothing' and 'Budget of a *Femme* incomprise', the complete Twisleton interview, portions of her unexpurgated *Journal (1855-56)* and many previously unpublished letters. To some degree the story takes a different order and shape from earlier selections. More emphasis is given to the later period than to the earlier better known stages of courtship. Jane's distinctly caring relationship with her mother Grace Welsh can now be seen in new letters, which contradict the assumption that her shocked sorrow at the latter's death was because she had been unloving. There is greater representation of the years after Lady Harriet's death. More room is given to Jane's intellectual pursuits, as well as to her relations with other women such as Martha Lamont, George Eliot and Charlotte Cushman. Many previously uncollected letters are included that the Duke-Edinburgh edition has at the moment passed by or not yet reached. Among these, the few to Charlotte Cushman present a special problem.

Apart from being famed as a great actress in England and America, as dominating as Mrs Siddons, Cushman was unusual. She sometimes played men's parts, such as Hamlet or Romeo, and was known for forming strongly 'romantic attachments' to younger women, among whom we can include Geraldine Jewsbury. Others have expressed less equivocal conclusions about this, as Lillian Faderman, *Surpassing the Love of Men* (1981), Lisa Merrill, *When Romeo was a Woman* (1999), and Julia Markus, *Across an Untried Sea: Discovering Lives Hidden in the Shadow of Convention and Time* (2000). Markus overstates the case when she suggests that Jane suppressed her 'real nature', but she is correct in saying that all the Carlyles' main biographers have held back from enquiring into the friendship, or even venturing an opinion.

At first, in the 1840s and 1850s, Jane had refused to meet Charlotte Cushman, in spite of the encouragement of Geraldine Jewsbury. When they at last came together in 1861, Cushman wrote to her niece, on 7 September, that Jane was 'a person whom I had longed for 12 years to know—Mrs Carlyle wife of Thomas Carlyle. We were very near meeting many years ago, but a Miss Jewsbury was then so injudicious in her praise of me, that Mrs Carlyle took a true womanly antagonism to me & would not know me'.[16] In fact, Geraldine's feelings were sometimes passionate and her jealousies fierce (as perhaps Jane's were), resulting in the need to take them into account in assessing all that they say of each other.

Charlotte and Jane were eventually brought together by Sarah Dilberoglue (b. Anderton), whom Jane had known since at least the mid-1850s. She had married a Greek merchant, Stauros Dilberoglue, who had long been a friend of Geraldine and Jane. Though almost unknown in the Carlyles' story—except for passing references—the Dilberoglues were clearly close to Jane, especially in her later years.[17] They call for a short digression because, like Charlotte Cushman, they are representative of many of Jane's women friends, who are more-or-less unknown or at least ignored in the standard biographies. The first meeting of Charlotte and Jane at Sarah's home was intense, immediate, and dramatic, as they show in the letters between them. Cushman wrote happily to her niece Emma that Jane wanted 'to know me better— Well dear, *she* came—*she* saw—& *I* conquered! & now she admires me "very very much" she says! You don't know how this little triumph has made me vain & conceited—& how I thrive upon it'. Jane had promised to see her after she had been to stay with the Ashburtons: 'Was not *this* gracious. I wish you my darling could have seen this unhandsome, clever, very keen, witty, scathing Scotchwoman come down entirely from her proud Eminence to sit at your Aunties side—with her hand entering hers & occasionally giving it a nervous clutch—as though she had found some warmth & nature there—which she failed to find among the grand intellectualities which surround Carlyle to gather up his crumbs—but who invariably come away glamoured by her! I confess darling to being greatly flattered!'

Was this flattery, admiration or something deeper on Jane's part? We have included all four of her known letters to Charlotte Cushman in this selection, since we need to interpret them in relation to the rest of her life. For, even at the risk of seeming to overestimate their importance, the argument cannot be ignored that Jane's life was shaped by a refusal to admit the nature of her love for her fellow-women—in short, a lesbian inclination. As an exception to our usual practice, therefore, we have felt it necessary to go into this detail as well as to give Cushman's replies to Jane at some length. This is partly because they are the best explanation of Jane's letters to her, and—depending on how they are read—they raise vital questions of interpretation. Nonetheless, we feel some compunction about repeating the action of George Lillie Craik, whom neither Jane nor Thomas forgave for reading her secret diary and treading on her private life with his 'swine's feet' (*Reminiscences* 72-3).

Jane's replies to Charlotte Cushman are certainly unusual, even when we compare them with some of Jane's most impulsive and affectionate letters (mostly of the last decade) to other women, such as Louisa Lady Ashburton, Mrs Oliphant and younger women friends. For they show such an ardent desire for affection that she evidently led Cushman to assume that Jane's highly-charged 'Spiritual Magnetism' (JWC to CC, early Sept. 1861) was more a matter of 'animal magnetism', as mesmerism was then currently known. Such letters also reveal her strong pleasure at being recognized as someone important in her own right, or on her 'own basis', as she emphasizes when writing to John Sterling (4 June 1835), Joseph Neuberg (14 June 1854) and others.

Yet, after Jane and Charlotte Cushman's first ecstatic encounter, it can surely be seen that the sequence of letters develops along the lines of Cushman's desperate demands for the relationship to be kept going, in the face of some back-pedalling by Jane. She makes only passing reference to Cushman in her other correspondence; and how their friendship continued is not quite clear, and needs more enquiry. Charlotte seems rather to have lost heart, writing to her niece from Rome on 19 February 1863 that it was not any 'outward influence' that stopped her from 'writing to Mrs Carlyle— On the contrary! My not writing is purely *interior* difficulty! Mrs Carlyle frightens me. She is a chemical test: she criticises her nearest & dearest ...—she cannot help this—& I have not come to be in such relations to her as to wear off this dreadful awe! I have never been sufficiently with her to forget *her* or myself & see only a warm friendship between us! & then somehow I got the idea before I left England—that she had tired of my stupidity because unless I can utterly forget myself—I am unutterably stupid! If I am frightened of people ... I am so full of awe & terror that I had no power of myself to show mySELF. I heard the other day from the Dilberoglues that Mrs Carlyle wondered why she had not heard from me—so I wrote her a little tiny rattling good for nothing note. But darling—if she *wanted* me—she would write to me!'

A letter from Sarah Dilberoglue to Charlotte Cushman and her companion or partner, Emma Stebbins, on 19 June 1866, just before Jane's death, shows Jane reluctance to write, and her preference for using Sarah to communicate. She recommends an old friend, Gavan Duffy, to Charlotte on his visiting Rome, but will not write herself. But, 'whenever', Sarah wrote, she 'was ... to give her kind love to you both, and to say how glad she will be to see you both here again—and to ask you to excuse her not writing. . . . I fancy that the little inevitable notes that something calls for every day are just as much writing as she has strength for. She has had however much more than this—that Rectorship entailed great amounts of correspondence upon her—first the congratulations and then the invitations to Scotland. . . . Carlyle [the 'dear gracious old man'] went by himself, and had not returned when I was at Chelsea a week ago—of course you have received the address. Was it not right and like himself'.

Sarah then gives a vivid sketch of how she had spoken to Thomas, and how she thought that 'if he had been one of the old Vikings, wouldn't his followers have been devoted to him? He has just the faculty in him to have made the chief of some strong race. . . . Other men say things that are more roundly and completely true, and say them in a better manner, too . . . but with Carlyle one can dissent from what he says, and yet feel a respect and affection for him I think one feels for no other writer—I felt this affection before I knew him personally'. If the Cushman letters complicate our received view of Jane, they also contradict the impression of Thomas as an insensitive and despotic husband. Sarah's remarks here are consistent with her earlier descriptions of him. In a letter to Charlotte in 1861, she gives an account of a scene at Cheyne Row, which confirms the respect in which Jane's newer friends held Thomas.

When Charlotte went to Rome, Sarah was left as an intermediary, and mentions how she felt that she had to 'keep going over' to see Jane while she was so ill: 'She was on the sofa when I saw her Friday, but looking a mere shadow. She has trusted me to tell you this that you may understand why she has not written to you. . . . She desired her best love to you, and promises as soon as her brain feels capable of thinking you a letter, to send you one. I have let [her] have mine to read. Tell dear Miss Stebbins I saw our hero Mr. Carlyle under a most beautiful aspect when I was there one day— She would have venerated the great man more than ever I am sure. He came to ask his wife when he was going out to ride, if he might order her some jelly [apparently from the chemist]. He was told "yes"—but some alterations must be made in it. He took his instructions very carefully—had them repeated over twice—looking all the time with his old Norseman face & figure as grandly [un]fit for this task he was undertaking—but he was so anxious—and so tender, and so childlike in being told what he [must] do—it was something to see. Well he went and in about a quarter of an hour the maid came into the room to say that the Master had turned back, not quite feeling sure about his message. Would Mrs Carlyle tell it him again?. . . . The grand old man has had a great deal of unfitting work lately such as being called up in the night to seek a doctor for a dying neighbour. . . . All sorts of neighbourly kindnesses' (19 December 1861).

While these fresh perspectives enrich our understanding of Jane Carlyle, her own letters remain the focal point of this collection. Through her varied styles and voices, she does ultimately achieve a consistent if sometimes uncertain sense of her own self-identity. She is a private writer, acutely aware of her immediate audience, and confidently holding her readers by her skill as an ironist, story-teller, social critic, gossip and confidante. With remarkable compression, she can capture emotion and experience in direct and well-turned phrases. Reassuring Thomas of her love, she tells him that Edward Irving's 'much vaunted friendship for me, is nothing more than a froth of professions' (*CL* 3:281). But when Thomas dares to suggest they live in Haddington, she scolds him for thinking that they could be happy among the 'inane, low-minded people' who make up its society (7:375). Her isolation at Craigenputtoch only sharpens her powers of observation. A visiting barrister, once a 'Scholar, Genius, and Gig man' now lies 'among the pots,—having made his last stand against the world, on a not too solid basis of whisky and water' (7:44).

In letters to her mother, she combines tenderness with humour, pleading with her to abandon remote Thornhill and come to live with them in Chelsea: 'You must absolutely please not to spend another winter in that place ... it seems a sort of suicide which you have no right to commit' (late Dec. 1841). In her descriptions of the celebrities attracted to Cheyne Row, she is undaunted by their reputations. Unexpectedly finding herself alone with Tennyson, she writes: 'I did just as Carlyle would have done had he been there; got out *pipes* and TOBACCO—and *brandy and water* ... he *professed* to be *ashamed* of polluting my room ... but he smoked on all the same—for *three* mortal hours!—talking like an angel—only exactly as if he were talking with a clever *man*' (19:17). Of Emerson she reports to Lady Harriet, 'The man has *two* faces to begin with which are continually changing into one another like "*dissolving views*," the one young, refined, almost beautiful ... the other decidedly old, hatchet-like, crotchety, inconclusive—like an incarnation of one of his own *poems!*' (22:139).

Her outright religious scepticism makes her a formidable adversary. Froude echoes Jewsbury's view that Carlyle's influence undermined his wife's ability to believe, yet her own writing suggests that her education left her 'a pagan' (*The Simple Story* 19). She is always suspicious of the relation between religion and respectability, ridiculing her old admirer the Very Rev. Charles Terrot—the somewhat absurd Bishop of Edinburgh—and even the saintly Thomas Erskine of Linlathen (*CL* 27:282), who earnestly told her that she 'must go to God', since she needed a father's or mother's love 'more than almost anyone' (24:240). She can never 'get up a sentiment for sermons' (25:64), and finds a 'perfect blockhead' in a pulpit in Liverpool, who reveals himself as 'spooney' by saying that we should be merciful when everyone knows that the merciful man only 'gets ... made into mincemeat' (28:238). Yet, at her most desperate, she uses the words of the Psalms in the *Journal* (26 March 1856) to cry out to a God she does not believe in.

Though attracted to political radicalism, she shrewdly sees its limitations. Mazzini's views puzzle her: 'I never saw a mortal man who so completely made himself into "minced meat" for the universe!' (16:185). Nor does the gospel of 'art' impress her much. She is fond of Ruskin but finds his aestheticism bizarre. She reports his mother's remark that he 'goes to sleep with, every night, a different Turner's picture on a chair opposite his bed "that he may have something beautiful to look at on first opening his eyes of a morning"' (23 February 1856).

What this selection shows is that Froude and some of his successors overlook Jane Carlyle's irony, vivacity, and quick intelligence in order to make her fit the role of a heroine in a classical tragedy. Her first forgotten love poem, 'The Wish', serves to expose the short-sightedness of those who wish to see her as a mere literary archetype. In the poem, she writes of herself wanting 'a valley far away . . . With one who cared for none but me', but it ends with some lines, suppressed by Alexander Carlyle in his edition of the *Love Letters*:

> Is this the destiny that I desire? . . .
> 'Tis well there was no evil Fairy here
> To grant immediately what 'ere I chose;
> Or, for my wishing I had paid as dear
> As that poor man who (as the story goes)
> Attach'd a long, black pudding to his spouse's nose—[18]

It is certainly strange as part of a love letter. Yet from the outset, a mainly resilient Jane Carlyle saw that marriage left considerable room for humour and irony—and she spared no one, including herself, in exploring it.

'The whole story must . . . come out' said Froude (*My Relations* 35), well knowing it to be impossible. Yet he was right to say earlier that we should struggle to avoid 'idle tales . . . stereotyped into facts' (*Life* 3:3). Jane's letters speak for her, and they do so in an astonishingly modern idiom. They allow us to read them even now with the conviction that struck Thomas on his first re-reading, when he saw them as an 'electric shower of . . . brilliancy, penetration, recognition, . . . enthusiasm, humour, grace, patience, courage, love' (*Reminiscences* 161).

Notes

1 *The Literary Character of Men of Genius*, ed. Benjamin Disraeli,1882, 110.

2 *Autobiography, Memories and Experiences*, 1904, 2:192. He refers to Froude's novels, *The Nemesis of Faith* (1848) and *Shadows of the Clouds* (1847).

3 See *CL* 26:xv, from NLS Acc. 11388. These letters with these remarks have survived, but in his will Froude asked his executors to destroy all letters and papers he might leave that were by or about the Carlyles. Not unnaturally, those such as Charles Eliot Norton could not 'interpret this in any way favorable to Froude', and regarded the act as 'either like a bit of posthumous malice' or an attempt to destroy 'evidence of his misuse & misinterpretation' (4 March 1895; letter to Mary Carlyle, MS, Ian Campbell; see K. J. Fielding, 'Justice for Carlyle', in *The Carlyles at Home and Abroad*, ed. David R. Sorensen and Rodger L. Tarr, 2004).

4 C. and A. Brookfield, *Mrs. Brookfield and her Circle*, 1906, 2:382.

5 Lord Houghton, *Monographs, Personal and Social*, 1873, 241.

6 The Ashburton Papers, NLS Acc. 11388, currently drawn on in *CL*, give a somewhat fuller picture of the Ashburton-Carlyle relationship, especially in connection with Louisa Lady Ashburton.

7 For what remains of the *Journal* see *CL* 30. It was kept between 21 October 1855 and 5 July 1856. Froude's copy, bequeathed by TC and transcribed by Mary Aitken Carlyle, was used for his 'Extracts from Mrs. Carlyle's Journal' in *LM* 2:254-75. Alexander Carlyle gave most of the latter half, from 15 April 1856, with omissions, in *NLM* 2:87-109. In our text we have used the original MS, the first part of which is NLS 533 and the second part in private hands. The passage in it about the 'blue marks' was left in by TC (who made other cuts), and removed by Alexander or Mary Carlyle. But Froude had his own copy (made by Mary), reproduced by Dunn (opp. 93) followed in our text. See also *Reminiscences*, 446.

8 Ellen's untitled and undated account of life at Craigenputtoch is Houghton Library, Harvard, bMS Am 1408:376; published K. J. Fielding, 'The Cry from Craigenputtoch', *Times Literary Supplement*, 13 Aug. 1999, 13-14. It is a careful copy, making use of Ellen's monogrammed notepaper, sewn into a booklet 3¾ inches by 6 inches, with a folded insert, no doubt written soon after 23 November. It is not mentioned in Jane's *Journal* but seems meant as a curious and deliberate time bomb.

9 *Swann's Way*, trans. C. K. Scott Moncrief and Terence Kilmartin, 1992, 6.

10 Ellen Twisleton's letters were published as *Letters of the Hon. Mrs. Edward Twisleton*, 1928, ed. Ellen Twisleton Vaughan. We have drawn on her original letters in our account and those of her sister Elisabeth Dwight.

11 See Harris, 'Talks with Carlyle', *English Review* 7 (1910-11): 419-34.

12 Philippa Pullar, *Frank Harris*, 1975, 56.

13 *My Life and Loves*, ed. John F. Gallagher, NY, 1963, 1:234.

14 John Forster, *Life of Charles Dickens*, ed. J.W.T. Ley, 1928, 702; cf. *Reminiscences*, 161: 'Not all the *Sands* and *Eliots* and babbling *cohue* of "celebrated scribbling Women" ... in my time, could ... make one such woman'.

15 The letter is now in private hands; see also *CL* 30 and a forthcoming article by Ian Campbell, 'Geraldine Jewsbury: Jane Welsh Carlyle's "best friend"?' in *The Carlyles at Home and Abroad*, ed. Sorensen and Tarr, 2004.

16 The Cushman and Dilberoglue letters quoted here and in the text are in the Library of Congress, Charlotte Cushman papers, volumes 1, 2, and 9, mainly unused by Carlyleans and biographers.

17 We do hear of Stauros through Francis Espinasse, *Literary Recollections*, 1893, 153–4 (and *CL* 21:23), who, like Charlotte Cushman, speaks of him as handsome, cultivated, and 'of singular refinement'. Sarah had played Juliet to Cushman's Romeo in Boston, in 1852, and is said by Cushman to have been her 'hero-worshipper' because of some help she had given her. Stauros had been given a start in business by Geraldine's brother, Frank; he was successful, came to London, and married in 1857. 'Their house', wrote Cushman, 'is away from the world in a quiet nook in Islington'. Their 'life is of the highest & purest. They live to educate & better themselves . . . spiritually & they neither of them go to Church'. Dilberoglue met JWC through Geraldine Jewsbury. He was a friend of Thomas Woolner and other well known artists. See also *CL* 21:46, and a brief obituary, *The Times*, 25 April 1878.

18 Rodger L. Tarr and F. McClelland, eds, *Collected Poems*, 1986, 112–13.

Select Bibliography

This list is highly selective. The place of publication, unless otherwise stated, is London. References to these works in the text are made by author's names or in shorter forms.

Biographies or biographical studies of JWC include Mrs Alexander Ireland, *Life of JWC* (1891), Elizabeth Drew, *Jane Welsh and Jane Carlyle* (1928), L. and E. Hanson, *Necessary Evil* (1952), Virginia Surtees, *Jane Welsh Carlyle* (1986), Norma Clarke, *Ambitious Heights* (1990), and Rosemary Ashton, *Thomas and Jane Carlyle, Portrait of a Marriage* (2002). She also plays a prominent part in biographies of TC by J.A. Froude (1882–84), D.A. Wilson (1923–34), Emery Neff (1932), Julian Symons (1952), Fred Kaplan (NY, 1983), and Simon Heffer (1995). Valuable recollections of JWC with excerpts of letters to and from her are included in Henry Larkin, 'Carlyle and Mrs. Carlyle: A Ten Years' Reminiscence' (*British Quarterly Review*, 74, July 1881, 15–45), Mary Smith, *Autobiography* (1892), Thomas Wemyss Reid, *The Life of the Rt. Hon. W. E. Forster* (1888), David Davidson, *Memories of a Long Life* (Edinburgh, 1890), David Masson, *Memories of London* (1908), Amy Woolner, *Thomas Woolner, R. A., Sculptor and Poet, His Life in Letters* (1917), *Letters of the Hon. Mrs. Edward Twisleton Written to Her Family, 1852–1862,* ed. Ellen Twisleton Vaughan (1928), and *The Alderley Papers; the Letters and Diaries of Lord and Lady Amberley*, ed. Bertrand and Patricia Russell (1937). For Amalie Bölte, see W. Fischer and A. Behrens, *Amaly Böltes Briefe* (Düsseldorf, 1905), also Fielding, introduction *CL* 22:x–xi, and '"Genuine Letters" and "Impossible Phantasms"', *Carlyle Society Papers*, No. 8 (1994–5):1–8. JWC's friendships with other women have been explored by Virginia Woolf, in 'Geraldine and Jane' (*Times Literary Supplement*, 28 February 1929, 149–50), Elizabeth Hardwick, *Seduction and Betrayal* (1974), Lillian Faderman, *Surpassing the Love of Men: Romantic Friendship and Love Between Women from the Renaissance to the Present* (NY, 1981), Virginia Surtees, *Ludovisi Goddess: The Life of Louisa Lady Ashburton* (1984), Lisa Merrill, *When Romeo was a Woman: Charlotte Cushman and her Circle of Female Spectators* (Michigan, 1999), and Julia Markus, *Across an Untried Sea: Discovering Lives Hidden in the Shadow of Convention and Time* (NY, 2000). For JWC and the 'Women's Petition' of 1856, see Lee Holcombe, *Wives and Property, Reform of the Married Women's Property Law in Nineteenth-Century England* (Oxford, 1983).

Too often discussion of the Carlyle marriage and Froude controversy diminishes JWC's character and achievements, but readers unfamiliar with the debate may pursue it in Froude, *My Relations with Carlyle* (1903), A. Carlyle and Sir James Crichton-Browne, *The Nemesis of Froude* (1903), and Waldo H. Dunn, *Froude & Carlyle* (1930). More recent interpretations of the controversy are offered by John Clubbe in his introduction to *Froude's Life of Carlyle* (1979), Fielding, 'Carlyle and Froude: Some New Considerations', in Fielding and R.L. Tarr eds, *Carlyle Past and Present* (1976), 239-69, Phyllis Rose, *Parallel Lives: Five Victorian Marriages* (NY, 1984), and Trev Lynn Broughton, *Men of Letters, Writing Lives. Masculinity and Literary Auto/Biography in the Late Victorian Period* (1999). Froude's editorial blunders in his edition of the *Reminiscences* (1881) are exposed by Fielding in the introduction to the World's Classics new and complete edition of the same work, ed. Fielding and Ian Campbell (Oxford, 1997). An important corrective to psychoanalytical and feminist analysis of JWC's illnesses is given by Janet Oppenheim in her authoritative *'Shattered Nerves'. Doctors, Patients, and Depression in Victorian England* (1991).

The Duke-Edinburgh edition of the *Collected Letters*, ed. Fielding, C.R. Sanders, C. Ryals, J. Clubbe, A. Christianson, I. Campbell, S. McIntosh, D. Sorensen, vols. 1-31, in progress (Durham, NC, 1970-) is the definitive source for JWC's letters and journals, but earlier collections are important for their biases, omissions, and biographical slant. These include *The Letters and Memorials of JWC*, prepared and annotated by TC, ed. Froude (1883), *New Letters and Memorials*, ed. Alexander Carlyle (1903), with an introduction by Sir James Crichton-Browne, and *New Letters of TC*, ed. A. Carlyle (1904), and Leonard Huxley, *JWC: Letters to Her Family* (1924). Other less partisan selections include Townsend Scudder, *Letters of JWC to Joseph Neuberg* (1938), Trudy Bliss, *JWC, A New Selection of her Letters* (1949) and *TC, Letters to His Wife* (1953), and A. and M. McQueen Simpson, *I Too Am Here*, (Cambridge, 1977). Too little attention has been devoted to JWC's literary talents, an exception being Aileen Christianson's 'Jane Welsh Carlyle's Private Writing Career', *History of Scottish Women's Writing*, ed. D. Gifford and D. McMillan (Edinburgh, 1997), 232-45. See also *The Collected Poems of TC and JWC*, ed. R.L. Tarr and Fleming McClelland (Greenwood, Florida, 1986), and *The Simple Story of My Own First Love*, ed. Fielding and Campbell, with A. Christianson (Edinburgh, 2001).

Chronology

1801 Jane Baillie Welsh born at Haddington, 14 July.

1819 Death of Dr John Welsh, her father, 19 September.

1821 Jane and Thomas meet, in late May.

1825 Jane signs deed of disposition of the Haddington house and Craigenputtoch to her mother, with Thomas to have the prospect of Craigenputtoch on Mrs Welsh's death. Jane visits him in September.

1826 Marriage at Templand, 17 October; then residence at Comely Bank, Edinburgh.

1828 Move to Craigenputtoch, May; the Jeffreys visit, early October.

1831 Thomas visits London, August, later joined by Jane, but is unsuccessful in arranging for publication of *Sartor Resartus*.

1832 Thomas's father dies, 22 January. They return to Craigenputtoch, March.

1833 Visit to Edinburgh (January–May); Emerson visits, August.

1834 Move to 5 Cheyne Row; Thomas starts *The French Revolution*.

1835 Mill reports that vol. 1 of the work is accidentally burnt, 6 March. Finished and published, 1837.

1839 Her mother visits; the tiff about wax candles, 21 February; Thomas continues annual lecturing with Revolutions of Modern Europe, 1 May. Jane is anxious about her mother's illness at Liverpool, and ill herself. Problems with Helen Mitchell.

1841 Thomas begins work on *Cromwell*; they take a cottage at Newby, and Jane visits Templand. She is increasingly unwell in the winter, and attentive in writing to her mother, saying that Thomas is 'enough to drive one into suicide'.

1842 By the end of the year, mother and daughter are ill. Her mother dies 25 February, and Jane is desolate. Visits the Bullers at Troston, August; reads Geraldine Jewsbury's *Zoe* and later arranges for its publication (February 1844).

1843   In May she first meets Lady Harriet Baring, who has been preoccupying Thomas. *Past and Present* published; she meets Gavan Duffy and companions, 26 April, and Father Mathew, August.

1844   Death of John Sterling, 18 September. Mrs Charlotte Sterling is insanely jealous of Jane.

1845   Visits Liverpool and Manchester; *Cromwell* is published, August; Jane first visits the Grange.

1846   She abruptly leaves for Seaforth, July.

1847   She begins her *Notebook* (1845-52), 13 April; they holiday in Derbyshire, July; Emerson reappears, October.

1849   Visits Nottingham, Bradford, and Auchtertool, while Thomas tours Ireland; she meets John Stodart; writes 'Much ado' after her return to Haddington.

1851   She and Thomas advise the maltreated Lady Bulwer Lytton; they visit Malvern; Christmas at the Grange.

1853   Jane visits her mother-in-law who is ill, and Dr John Carlyle and his newly married wife, Phoebe. Thomas's mother dies, 25 December.

1854   Phoebe Carlyle dies after childbirth. Geraldine Jewsbury comes to live near Cheyne Row. The Carlyles and Twisletons become friends.

1855   Jane protests at her housekeeping 'Budget', 7 February. The Twisleton sisters write about her, and some time after November, Ellen Twisleton writes down Jane's memories of Craigenputtoch. Jane starts her *Journal* (1855-56) 21 October, despairing at Thomas's constantly visiting 'that eternal Bath House'.

1856   Meets her old *fiancé* George Rennie, 25 April; the 'blue marks' on her wrists, 26 June. Thomas continues *Frederick*, 6 vols. (1856-65).

1857   Lady Harriet Ashburton dies, 4 May.

1858   Robert Tait's 'A Chelsea Interior' shown at the Royal Academy. Lord Ashburton marries Louisa Stewart Mackenzie, 18 November.

1859   Jane and Thomas make a summer visit to Auchtertool.

1860   Jane now devoted to Louisa Lady Ashburton. Nero (Jane's pet dog), George Rennie, and Kate Sterling (Ross) die.

1861   Meets Charlotte Cushman, 28 August.

1862 Ellen Twisleton and the Countess Pepoli die; Jane stays with Mary
      Russell at Thornhill.

1863 Hurts herself severely in Cheapside, London, 2 October; she is taken
      in pain to St Leonards.

1864 Lord Ashburton dies, 23 March. Jane is accompanied to the Russells'
      at Thornhill; she recovers, and returns to Cheyne Row, 1 October.

1865 Thomas finishes *Frederick*; they visit Lady Ashburton, in Devon.

1866 Thomas's Rectorial Address at Edinburgh, 2 April. Jane dies, 21 April.

Editorial Note

Sources for the letters (manuscript, photocopies or printed) are given and, within a few accepted conventions, we have tried to follow them as closely as reasonably possible. We also note that we have been greatly indebted to *The Collected Letters of Thomas and Jane Welsh Carlyle*, to our fellow editors, and the Duke University Press and others, for help and support in verifying the text. Double underlinings are capitalized, raised letters are brought down and italicized, and inverted commas regularized; anything in square brackets is editorial; Scots dialect and foreign words (except French) are glossed; and Jane Carlyle's very peculiar and characteristic spellings are always followed ('misteries', 'colera', 'gohst', etc.) without using *sic*. Dates and readings are decided to the best of our ability. When known, an indication of where letters were sent is given. Elisions are shown in the usual way. Letters to the same correspondent that immediately follow each other are separated by an asterisk without repeating the addressee's name.

The collection arises from the long-held wish to make Jane Carlyle's letters more easily available for enjoyment and discussion, and has been compiled in the slowly lengthening shadow of the *Collected Letters*. When we started we hoped to keep notes and comments to a minimum, but we can now see only too clearly that the more we learn about Jane Carlyle, the more complicated the story. 'Let your letters be as long and careless as you possibly can' (*CL* 2:260), Thomas told her. 'A letter behoves to tell about oneself' (*CL* 2:xviii), she writes. In the compromise between too little and too much, we ask readers' patience.

Chapter One

In Search of Genius, 1819-26

Jane Baillie Welsh's life was almost untroubled until the sudden death of her father from typhus on 19 September 1819, when she was eighteen. Dr Welsh had studied at Edinburgh University and then practised in the prosperous country town of Haddington, east of Edinburgh, where he soon won a high reputation. In 1800 he had married the attractive and temperamental Grace Welsh, who gave birth to their only child a year later. From the first Jane was encouraged by her father to think and act for herself, admire classical heroes and republican virtues, and take pride in the family's legendary ancestors, William Wallace and John Knox. Writing to her friend Eliza Stodart, not without hope for the future, Jane reflected on her first major sorrow, which was to have a lifelong impact. His death, wrote Thomas, 'To her, and thro' her to me, it had always something of a Doomsday in it' (Private MS).

ELIZA STODART   EUL Dc. 4.94
22 George Sq., Edinburgh

Sunday night [26 Sept. 1819]

. . . I do not think that we can possibly be in Dumfriesshire for three or four weeks from this date—nor do I expect to be in town before that time—Indeed it is astonishing how little desire I feel to leave this place even for a short time— The memory of what has been—And the melancholy pleasure in the reflection that I am still near the being that I loved more than all the world besides although he is no longer conscious of my affection are the feelings which constitute the little happiness I now can feel— When you was here I did not know that he was buried in the Ruin of the church—I cannot tell you how it pleased me—last night when the moon was shining so brightly I felt the most anxious wish to visit his grave—and I will not feel satisfied till I have done so— Those Ruins appear to me now to possess a sublimity with which my fancy never before vested them— I feel that I never can leave this place— May God bless you & preserve you from such a loss as mine is the prayer of Your Affectionate friend / Jane Welsh

Jane continued to follow her father's advice, studying French, German and Italian, and tutoring her young aunt Elizabeth and cousin Christina Howden.

[Early 1820]

... *He* used always to tell me that in giving me a good education, he was leaving me the greatest good—of this I have found the truth, and too late I have begun to feel toward him gratitude which only adds to my sorrow for having it no longer in my power to make any returns— The habits of study in which I have been brought up have done much to support me— I never allow myself to be one moment unoccupied— I read the books he wished me to understand—I have engaged in the plan of study he wished me to persue—and to the last moment of my life it shall be my endeavour to act in all things exactly as he would have desired— when I am giving his sister and Christina their lessons I seem to be filling his place—and the recollection of his anxiety and kindness and unwearied exertions for my improvement & for the improvement of those who have so soon forgot him, is sometimes like to break my heart— ... / Yours Affectionately Jane B Welsh

*In 1811 her father had engaged an extra tutor for her in Latin and mathematics, the handsome and talented Edward Irving. They perhaps surprisingly believed they were in love, but next year Irving left to teach at Kirkcaldy, where he rashly became engaged to a minister's daughter, who refused to release him. He then became an assistant minister in Glasgow. In May 1821 Irving and Thomas Carlyle called on Mrs Welsh at Haddington, and Carlyle recalls how he first set eyes on her daughter: 'The Drawing-room seemed to me the finest apartment I had ever sat or stood in ... I remember our all sitting ... in a little parlour ... talking a long time; Irving mainly, and bringing out me, the two ladies listening with not much of speech, but the younger with lively apprehension of all meaning and shades of meaning' (**Reminiscences** 19-20). Soon after, Thomas told his brother Alick, 'I came back so full of joy, that I have done nothing since but dream of it' (**CL** 1:363). Deeply impressed, Thomas immediately exchanged books and letters, and twice called on Jane when she was visiting Edinburgh, pressing his attentions in spite of her mother's disapproval. He was barely scraping a living by miscellaneous writing.*

TC   NLS 529.14
College St, Edinburgh

[29 Dec.1821]

...You say there is no harm in our correspondence and I believe it:
But assuredly there is harm in disobedience and deceit, the only
means through which it can at present be maintained. And is it for
you who profess to be my friend to teach me these? Is it for you
who talk of generosity so well to require of me the sacrifice of my
own esteem to your selfish gratification? What have you done for
me to merit such a sacrifice? What proofs of regard have you given
me, greater than I can command from every fool who comes in my
way? My friend, before you draw so largely on my gratitude do
something for my sake. Render your friendship as honourable in
the eyes of the world to my Father's child as it is already
honourable in her own eyes to Jane Welsh and then you may *exact*
as *your due* favours you have as yet no *claim* to ask. Oh M*r* Carlyle
if you wish me to admire—to love you (admiration and love is
with me that same feeling) use as you ought your precious time,
and the noble powers that god has given you, and waste no hours
or thoughts on *me*— And do not laugh at fame— It is indeed a
name—perhaps an empty name—but yet it is the object of no low
ambition, and ambition is the crime of no low soul—
    I will not write again— Do not urge me least you wear out
my patience and with it my esteem. You may think it unlikely that
should ever happen— As you have sometimes found me weak and
thoughtless you may expect to find me always so— But there are
moments when the weak are strong, and when the thoughtless
think, and such moments are more frequent with me than you
suppose. When you have finished your review of Faustus send it to
me with such a letter as my Mother may read without anger—and
when you have written four and twenty pages of your book bring
them— I have nothing more to say and you will not be satisfied
with this—but I cannot help it— I dare write no longer. I am
nervous as if I were committing a murder, and my ideas, like my
pen, are dancing at such a rate I cannot stay them— God bless
you— Do your duty— Let me do mine—and leave the rest to
destiny / Your sincere Friend Jane Baillie Welsh ....

*Jane Welsh attracted other suitors, including George Rennie, the son of
a wealthy brewer and farmer, a sculptor and future governor of the
Falklands. She felt herself 'engaged', but his family may have wanted*

someone better for him than a small town doctor's daughter. Yet there is another report that she 'was engaged', and rejected him at her father's wish since he could not believe that Rennie would come to anything (EUL Dc. 4.94(2), f.113). She read Rousseau's **Julie, ou la nouvelle Héloïse** *(1761), which celebrated the classical republican virtues admired by her father. Shelley and Byron had revered the work, condemned by Victorians as unchristian and immoral. The story was a romantic version of the medieval tale of Eloisa, who was seduced by her tutor. But instead of going on to take the veil, the heroine Julie takes to good works. Instead of being castrated, like Abelard, Rousseau's St Preux goes into exile. When he returns he joins his former lover and her husband Wolmar as their friend.*

ELIZA STODART   EUL Dc. 4.94
George Sq., Edinburgh

                                        Haddington [Jan. 1822]

. . . I return the two first volumes of Julia with many thanks— It seems to me, that the most proper way of testifying my gratitude to the amiable Jean Jacques for the pleasure he has afforded me, is to do what in me lies to extend the circle of his admirers— I shall begin with you— Do read this book— You will find it tedious in many of its details, and in some of its scenes culpably indelicate; but for splendour of eloquence, refinement of sensibility, and ardour of passion it has no match in the French language. Fear not that by reading Heloise you will be ruined—or undone—or whatever adjective best suits that fallen state into which young women and angels *will* stumble *at a time*— I promise you that you will rise from Heloise with a deeper impression of whatever is most beautiful and most exalted in virtue than is left upon your mind by 'Blairs sermons' 'Pailey's Theology' or the voluminous 'Jeremy Tailor' himself— I never felt my mind more prepared to brave temptation of every sort than when I closed the second volume of this strange book— I believe if the Devil himself had waited upon me in the shape of Lord Byron I would have desired Betty to show him out— Sages say that every work which presents vice in the colours of virtue has a tendency to corrupt the morals— They are without doubt in the right But when they say that Julia Etange is vicious they are in a most egregious mistake— Read the book and ask your heart or rather your judgement if Julia be vicious. I *do not wish to countenance such irregularities among my female*

acquaintances but I must confess were any individual of them
to meet with *such a man*—to struggle as she struggled—to
endure as she endured—to *yield* as she yielded—and to repent
as she repented—I would love that woman better than the
chastest coldest Prude between Johnnygroats House and Land's
end— One serious bad consequence will result to you from
reading Heloise—at least if your soul-strings are screwed up to
the same key as mine— You will never marry! Alas! I told you
that I should die a virgin if I reached twenty *in vain*— Even so
will it prove— This Book this fatal Book has given me an idea of
a love so *pure* (Yes you may laugh! but I repeat it) so pure, so
constant, so disinterested, so exalted—that no love the men of
this world can offer me will ever fill up the picture my
imagination has drawn with the help of Rousseau— No lover
will Jane Welsh ever find like St Preux—no Husband like Wolmar
(I don't mean to insinuate that *I should like both*—) and to no
man will she ever give her heart and pretty hand who bears to
these no resemblance—George Rennie! James Aitken! Robert
McTurk! James Baird!!! Robby Angus!— O Lord O Lord!—where
is the St Preux? Where is the Wolmar?— Bess I am in earnest—I
shall never marry—and after having laughed so at old maids, it
will be so dreadful to be one of the very race at whom I have
pointed the finger of scorn— Virtuous Venerable females! how
my heart smites me for the illjudged ridicule I have cast on their
pure names! . . .

To Carlyle's regret, a further novel, Madame de Staël's **Corinne, or
Italy** *(1807), strengthened Jane's preference for friendship over love and
marriage. This story of a gifted Italian patriot and actress who sacrifices
her career, and eventually her life, for the love of an unworthy
Englishman inspired many other novelists, including Jane Austen, Mary
Shelley, Margaret Fuller, Charlotte Brontë, George Sand, Geraldine
Jewsbury and George Eliot.*

TC   NLS 529.45, 71, 119
3 Moray St, Edinburgh

                                                   [Mid-June 1822]

'Richard is himself again'!—I am sure you will rejoice at the
Phoenix-like renovation of my faculties—they have been in *full
force* ever since I wrote to you. I have learned my German and
Italian lessons as usual—read several hours a-day—and regularly

tortured my fingers with Beethoven's Themes for another
hour—besides all this I have put feathers into a hat—written
four angry notes to my dress-maker— ...

I think I heard you say you did not think very highly of
Corinne— You must read it again—nobody with a heart and
soul can fail to admire it—I never read a book, in my life, that
made such an impression on me. I cried *two whole hours* at
the conclusion, and in all likelihood I might have been crying
to this minute, but for an engagement to a party in the evening,
where prudential considerations required my eyes should be
visible. . . . I beg of you dont laugh much at my translations, or
any of the silly things I send you—and do not think that it is
vanity that tempts me to submit them to your inspection.
Nobody can hold the trash I write, in deeper contempt than I
myself do—indeed I often think I might write better if I had
more conceit.

How much poetry have you written? send me every line of
it— My wish [her poem 'The Wish'] is the most foolish little thing
possible— I would not send it if I had time to write another—
tho' perhaps the next might be as bad—the other lines came into
my head when I was thinking about my wishes . . . . Send me your
wish immediately and believe me your sincere friend / Jane Welsh

*In 1822 Edward Irving left Glasgow to take charge of the Caledonian
Chapel in Hatton Garden and George Rennie went to Italy to study
sculpture. Irving's growing fame and the announcement of his
engagement and wedding in October 1823 depressed Jane. She resented
the company of her over-solicitous mother and inquisitive relatives.
Though she gossiped with Eliza about Carlyle's inelegance—'St. Preux
never kicked the fire-irons, nor made puddings in his teacup' (CL
2:18)—she was coming to rely on him for emotional as well as
intellectual stimulus, seeing him as like her father and much more.*

Haddington—11*th* November [1822]

My dear friend
If ever I succeed in distinguishing myself above the
common herd of little Misses, thine will be the honour of my
success. Repeatedly have your salutary counsels, and little well-
timed flatteries roused me from inactivity when my own reason
was of no avail. Our meeting forms a memorable epoch in my
history; for my acquaintance with you has from its very

commencement powerfully influenced my character & life.
When you saw me for the first time, I was wretched beyond
description—grief at the loss of the only being I ever loved with
my whole soul had weakened my body and mind—distraction of
various kinds had relaxed my habits of industry— I had no
counsellor that could direct me—no friend that understood
me—the pole-star of my life was lost, and the world looked a
dreary blank— Without plan, hope, or aim I had lived two years
when my good angel sent you hither— I had never heard the
language of talent and genius but from my Father's lips— I had
thought that I should never hear it more—you spoke like him—
your eloquence awoke in my soul the slumbering admirations
and ambitions that *His* first kindled there— I wept to think, the
mind he had cultivated with such anxious, unremitting pains was
running to desolation; and I returned with renewed strength and
ardour to the life that he had destined me to lead— But in my
studies I have neither the same pleasures, or the same motives as
formerly— I am *alone*, and no one loves me better for my
industry—this solitude together with distrust of my own talents,
despair of ennobling my character, and the discouragement I
meet with in devoting myself to a literary life would, I believe,
have, oftener than once, thrown me into a state of helpless
despondency; had not your friendship restored me to myself, by
supplying (in as much as they can ever be supplied) the counsels
and incitements I have lost— You see I am not insensible to the
value of your friendship, or likely to through it away; tho' you
have sometimes charged me with inconstancy and caprice— .../
Your very sincere friend / Jane Welsh ...

*

Haddington—Monday [24 March 1823]

...These nonsensical people with their *Heirathsgedanken* and
Heirathsvorschlagen [thoughts and proposals of marriage] will
assuredly drive me mad. Like Carlos ich fürchte die wie die Pest
[I fear them like the plague]—to cause unhappiness to others,
above all to those I esteem, and would do anything within reach
of my duties and abilities to serve, is the cruelest pain I know—
but positively I can not fall in love—and to sacrifice myself out
of pity is a degree of generosity of which I am not capable—
besides matrimony under any circumstances would interfere
schokingly with my plans—

The Philosopher that used to thank the gods he was born a man, and not a woman, must have had more sense than the generality of his calling—truly our fate is very deplorable. As soon as a poor girl takes that decisive step called *coming out*, she is exposed to a host of vexations men know nothing of— We are the weakest portion of the human kind, and nevertheless we have to bear two thirds of the burdens of sorrows our unwise first Parents left behind them. Really it is very unjust!— What I would give to be a prime Minister or a Commander in chief! An old woman that boiled blankets in this town used to say when I was leaping the mill-dam some dozen years ago,'*that providence had sticket* [spoiled] *a fine Callant* [lad]', She understood my character better than anybody I have had to do with since— '*The extreme enviableness of my condition!*' Oh dear me—I wish you had a trial of it for one twelvemonth— . . ./ Yours Faithfully Jane Welsh

Jane's earliest attempts to foster genius in a boy pedlar were baffled: like Rousseau, she was forced to admit her limitations as a tutor.

ELIZA STODART   EUL Dc. 4.94
George Sq., Edinburgh

Haddington Sunday [30 March 1823]

. . . My ideas of talent are so associated with every thing great and noble, that while I admired the boy's ardour and ambition, it never once occurred to me, a Genius might possibly be a knave—and so I spent my leisure time for one whole fortnight in laying plans for his improvement in the arts, and anticipating the splendid career of successful enterprise that lay before him—but about the end of that time I began to suspect my subject might disappoint my lofty expectations—he discovered a mortal aversion to all kinds of vulgar labour—that is genius-like—he had never undergone the operation of baptism—that was quite romantic—but there were other points of his character and history which I could not easily away with—he is greedy, cunning, and ungrateful—this disgusted me—and when I found no power on earth could prevail with him to refrain from lying or to wash his face I lost all patience— My plans had given him so much *eclat* that *my* patronage was no longer necessary and so I left the *patient* in the hands of his new admirers— The Genius was succeeded in my affection by an Irish pack-man with a

broken back—eight years old and a few inches high—a calm,
correct decided character—the very reverse of the artist—he
hops about with a crutch under one arm and a basket on the
other; and with his profits on tape and chapel needles helps to
maintain three sisters younger than himself. . . . / Yours
affectionately for ever & ever / Jane Baillie Welsh . . .

*In the spring of 1824 Carlyle was invited by Irving 'the Orator' to visit
London, where he went in June, and though Jane was asked, she proudly
declined. She was regularly writing to Carlyle, telling him about the
various men competing for her attention. He countered by describing
the pretty Kitty Kirkpatrick whom he knew through the Buller family
whose sons he had tutored. Despondent and tormented by headaches
and admirers, Jane began to think seriously about Thomas. She was a
sharp judge of ability, and saw that his powers were far beyond those of
a translator or journalist. He was her 'genius'.*

TC   NLS 530.220, 228; *CL* 3:191
Mainhill near Ecclefechan

                                            Haddington 20*th* May, 1824

. . . I do not think that in the whole course of our
correspondence so long an interval has ever elapsed before—
never but when we quarreled and this time there is no
quarrel! To add to my perplexities there have I had a letter
from that stupendous ass the Orator telling me such
nonsensical things, and among the rest, that he is full of joy
because Thomas Carlyle is to be with him this month! Can he
mean you? this month! and twenty days of it are already past
and gone! The man must have been delirious when he wrote
such an impossible story. You can never, never mean to be in
London this month! You promised to be here before you went,
in words that it would be impiety to doubt. I have looked
forward to your coming for weeks: You cannot dream of
disappointing me!
        What I would give to be assured this moment that
excessive occupation is the sole cause of your present
neglectfulness that devils are dunning you for the rest of your
book, and that you are merely giving yourself all to Meister just
now that you may the sooner be all for me. Is it not hard? this is
the only comfortable conjecture I can form to explain your
silence and yet I can never believe in it for more than a minute

at a time— Were I but certain that all is really well what a devil
of a rage I would be in with you. Write Write— I will tell you
about *my visit to London then*— I have no heart for it now—
What an idiot I was ever to think that man so estimable—but I
am done with his Preachership now & for ever—

And Byron is dead! I was told it all at once in a room full
of people, My God if they had said that the sun or the moon
was gone out of the heavens it could not have struck me with
the idea of a more awful and dreary blank in the creation than
the words Byron is dead. I have felt quite cold and dejected
ever since. All my thoughts have been fearful and dismal— I
wish you was come. / Yours for ever Affectionately / Jane Welsh

*

4 Myddleton Terrace, Pentonville
                                              [10 June 1824]

Rash, headstrong Man! How nearly have you overthrown in a
single hour, what it has cost me such an immensity of pains
to bring about! My prudent administration has saved our
commonwealth: and just when it begins to wear a
prosperous look you risk the whole success of my
management on dashes with a pen. Thou a Man of Genius!
thou art an ass— Where were your senses while you wrote
that letter? What did you mean I should make of it? Not that I
should show it to my Mother surely! And yet she *must* have
seen it but for an especial providence of God—and if she
had— Woe! Woe! to you and me. Thank God, as I do, that she
was absent when your parcel came so that I was able to
secret the letter; I said there was none—happily her
attention was so engaged with the beautiful Shakespear, that
she did not look at me when I told the falsehood; if she had
she must have noticed my confusion, I felt as if my whole
face was in a flame. Oh my dear friend spare me such horrid
moments in time to come.

I write just now by stealth, trusting that this may reach and
warn you before you have leisure to write me such another
letter— For mercy's sake keep in mind that my peace of mind,
my credit with my Mother, the continuance of our
correspondence everything depends upon your appearing as
my friend and not my Lover. Take no notice of having written
with the books, or of having heard from me since you went

away. I must reserve my *thanks* as well as many other things I have upon my mind, for another letter—at present I have neither opportunity nor composure— God almighty bless you / Yours ever ever / Jane B Welsh

*

Dover, forwarded to Pentonville
West Craigs [Corstorphine, Edinburgh]
10*th* November [1824]

... Enough of my own affairs— Let us turn to yours—what do I think of your new project? At first I cordially disapproved it altogether. The translating of all Schiller's works seemed a stupendous and ungrateful task, which would heavily occupy your time and talents for years; and be attended with no advantage to you, except putting some hundreds of pounds in your pocket: the other part of the plan filled me with horror, and on deliberation, I am still decidedly against it. What fellowship is there in Annandale for *you*? Doubtless you might find 'kind Christian souls' there to love you and wonder at you, but without spirits like your own to *understand* you, —without sympathy your life would be without a soul— Oh mercy never think of establishing yourself in Annandale! All your faults are the effects of your isolated way of life: if you seclude yourself altogether from your fellows, as sure as fate, you will sink in a year or two, into the most surly, misanthropic, self-opinionative, dreadfully disagreeable person alive. It was only the other day, you wrote to me that you began to think there were many more worthy people in the world than you counted on; and already you are projecting to turn your back on them? You will never be so mad! Certainly the recovery of your health must be attended to above all things else; and if that is not to be brought about in the smoke and bustle of a City, why then, you must seek it in the quietness and pure air of the country: But what is to hinder you setting yourself down within a mile or two of London—in some pleasant place where you might ride and garden just as in Annandale; and, at the same time, occasionally enjoy society which would refresh and incite your spirit? My plan perhaps is foolish: yours is certainly not wise.

As to the translating of Schiller, there is much to be said for and against. It would employ without fatiguing your mind; it would increase your command of language, and make

composition more easy to you; it would insure you a certain
and sufficient income, and deliver you from anxieties about
what you are to do, and how you are to live. On the other
hand, you are likely to be disgusted with the undertaking
before you finish it; there is no exercise for your finest
faculties in turning sentences and choosing words; there is no
scope for your genius in transcribing the thoughts and
sentiments of another; on the contrary I should be afraid that
in imitating so long you might cease to be original, and lastly
the task when done,—however well done will gain you only
the praise of a good Translator. . . . / God bless you Dear.— Ever
ever yours / Jane Baillie Welsh . . .

*Thomas's letters from London then Paris sharpened Jane's distaste for
Haddington and her ambition to marry a 'genius'. Yet there were limits
to her idealism. She brusquely dismissed his proposal to live at
Craigenputtoch, the remote farm north of Dumfries left her by her father.
She had already decided that she was 'half-engaged' to Carlyle. Only
practical questions remained.*

NLS 530.265, 275, 303

23 Southampton St, Pentonville
Haddington / 13th January [1825]

. . . I love you— I have told you so a hundred times; and I should
be the most ungrateful, and injudicious of mortals if I did not—
but I am not *in love* with you—that is to say—my love for you
is not a passion which overclouds my judgement; and absorbs
all my regards for myself and others—it is a simple, honest,
serene affection, made up of admiration and sympathy, and
better perhaps, to found domestic enjoyment on than any
other— In short it is a love which *influences*, does not *make*
the destiny of a life. . . .

I do not wish for fortune more than is sufficient for my
wants—my natural wants, and the artificial ones which habit
has rendered nearly as importunate as the other—but I will not
marry to live on less; because in that case every inconvenience
I was subjected to, would remind me of what I had quitted; and
the idea of a sacrifice should have no place in a voluntary
union— Neither have I any wish for grandeur—the glittering
baits of titles and honours are only for children and fools— But
I conceive it a duty which every one owes to society, not to

throw up that station in it which Providence has assigned
him; and having this conviction, I could not marry into a
station inferior to my own with the approval of my
judgement, *which* alone could enable me to brave the
censures of my acquaintance.

   And now let me ask you have you any *certain* livelihood
to maintain me in the manner I have been used to live in? any
fixed place in the rank of society I have been born and bred
in? No! You have projects for attaining both—capabilities for
attaining both—and much more! but as yet you have *not*
attained them. Use the noble gifts which God has given you!
You have prudence (tho' by the way this last proceeding is no
great proof of it)—devise then how you may gain yourself a
moderate but *settled* income; think of some more promising
plan, than farming the most barren spot in the county of
Dumfries-shire— What a thing that would be to be sure! you
and I keeping house at Craigenputtock! I would just as soon
think of building myself a nest on the Bass-rock—nothing but
your ignorance of the place saves you from the imputation of
insanity for admitting such a thought. Depend upon it, you
could not *exist* there a twelvemonth. For my part I would not
spend a month on it with an Angel— Think of something else
then—apply your industry to carry it into exffect, your talents
to gild over the inequality of our births and then—we will
talk of marrying. If all this were realized I *think* I should have
goodsense enough to abate something of my romantic ideal,
and to content myself with stopping short on this side
idolatry— At all events I will marry no one else— This is all
the promise I can or will make. A positive engagement to
marry a certain person at a certain time, at all haps and
hazards, I have always considered the most rediculous thing
on earth: it is either altogether useless or altogether
miserable; if the parties continue faithfully attached to each
other it is a mere ceremony—if otherwise it becomes a galling
fetter reviting [riveting] them to wretchedness and only to be
broken with disgrace. . . .

   It would be more agreeable to etiquette, and perhaps also
to prudence, that I should adopt no middle course in an affair
such as this—that I should not for another instant encourage an
affection I *may* never reward and a hope I *may* never fulfil; but
cast your heart away from me at once since I cannot embrace
the resolution which would give me a right to it for ever. This I

would assuredly do if *you* were like the generality of lovers, or if it were still in my power to be happy independent of your affection but as it is neither etiquette nor prudence can obtain this of me. If there is any change to be made in the terms on which we have so long lived with one another; it must be made by *you* not *me*— I *cannot* make any

All this I have written with my Mother's sanction; if my decision had been more favourable to you, she might have *disapproved* it but would not have *opposed* it. And this I think is more than you could expect, considering how little she knows you.

I shall not be comfortable till I hear from you again so I beg you will not keep me waiting. God bless you ever affectionately / Yours Jane Welsh

*

Care of J. Badams, Birmingham
Haddington 14th February [1825]

My Dearest

You are welcome to Scotland again, since it must be so. I wished you to remain where you were; for London, it seemed to me, had more inducements to retain you than Scotland had to bring you back. But it was for you only to decide as to what you only understand and after all, I am persuaded that you are in the right,—that you are more likely to find health and happiness among the honest unpretending hearts of your *Fatherland*, than in the Great City, with all its Poets and Orators and Bluestockings, which you have left behind you.

Indeed, it would be difficult for you to do anything that could make me doubt the propriety of your judgement. I know not how your spirit has gained such a mastery over mine in spite of pride and stubbornness: but so it is—tho' self-willed as a Mule with others I am tractable and submissive towards *you*; I hearken to your voice as to the dictates of a second conscience, hardly less awful to me, than that which nature has implanted in my breast. How comes it you have this power over me? for it is not the effect of your genius and virtue merely: sometimes, in my serious moods, I believe it is a *charm* with which my Good Angel has fortified my heart against evil— Be that as it may, your influence has brought me nothing but good—

When will you be here? Be sure you write beforehand, for
I hate *surprises*, however agreeable. I am longing to see you
again; to hear your travels history since we parted; and to talk
with you over all our concerns. But how *am* I to meet you
now. Do you know, I think it is more than probable that I will
take to my own room, when you come, and not go out of it as
long as you are in the house. Upon my word, Mr Thomas
Carlyle, I can hardly forgive you for bringing me into this very
shocking predicament— Here I am blushing like an idiot,
whenever your name is mentioned, so that any body, who
looks at me, may read the whole matter in my face—and then
to be *half engaged*—I who have such a natural horror at
engagements! it gives me asthma every time I think of it— And
yet such is the inconsistency of human nature, or of my
particular nature, that I *would* not, if I might, be free.'*Ce que
je fait, je le ferois encore*'. I cannot say this of much else I
have done in my day— You will come, however; and *at all
events*, you will see my Mother and Miss Gilchrist. . . . I looked
to the London project for deliverance; but *that*, I perceive, is to
miscarry this Season, as it did the last: and I am not sorry. Now
that you are gone, I should have little enjoyment in it;
convinced as I am that Edward Irvings much vaunted
friendship for me, is nothing more than a froth of professions. I
will not quarrel with him however. I love him *still*, after all he
has done, and all that he has *not* done,—and I shall love him to
the last—*in memory*: but I have ceased to admire him, to put
trust in him— He has disgusted me. . . . Come! Ever Yours /
Jane Baillie Welsh

*This 'love' for Irving seems meant in a vaguely romantic way, but
complications came up when Carlyle persuaded Mrs Montagu to write
to advise Jane. Anna Montagu, third wife of the liberal and high-
minded Basil Montagu, had once known Burns and was to introduce
Carlyle to Coleridge. She had heard of Jane from both Irving and
Carlyle, and pressed her to be open about her former love for Irving,
and to make up her mind whether she really wanted to marry her
romantic genius:'There must be no Bluebeard's closet in which the
skeleton may one day be discovered' (**CL** 3:356). Jane sent on Mrs
Montagu's letter almost at once, confessing her former passionate love
or affection, but making clear her commitment to Thomas.*

Hoddam Hill, Ecclefechan

Templand Sunday [24 July1825]

My dearest

I thought to write to you from this place with joy; I write with shame and tears. The enclosed letter, which I found lying for me, has distracted my thoughts from the prospect of our meeting—the brightest in my mind for many months, and fixed them on a part of my own conduct which makes me unworthy ever to see you, or be clasped to your true heart again. I cannot come to you cannot be at peace with myself: till I have made the confession which Mrs Montagu so impressively shows me the need of— Let me tell it then out at once; I have deceived you *I* whose truth and frankness you have so often praised have deceived my bosom friend! I told you that I did not care for Edward Irving, took pains to make you believe this— It was false; I loved him—must I say it— *once* passionately loved him— Would to Heaven that this were all! it might not perhaps lower me much in your opinion for he is no unworthy man, and if I showed weakness in loving one whom I knew to be engaged to another, I made amends in persuading him to marry that other and preserve his honour from reproach: but I have concealed and disguised the truth: and for this I have no excuse—none at least that would bear a moment's scrutiny. Woe to me then if your reason be my judge and not your love! I cannot even plead the merit of a *voluntary* disclosure as a claim to your forgiveness. I make it because I *must*, because this extraordinary woman has moved me to honesty whether I would or no— Read her letter and Judge if it was possible for me to resist it.

Write I beseech you instantly, and let me know my fate— This suspense is worse to endure than any certainty. Say if you *can* that I may come to you—that you will take me to your heart after all as your own, your trusted Jane and I will arrange it as soon as ever I am able—say no—that you no longer wish to see me that my image is defaced in your soul and I will think you *not unjust*. Oh that I had your answer never were you so dear as at this moment when I am in danger of losing your affection or what is still more precious to me your respect / Jane B Welsh

Jane's next letter was delayed in the post, and when Thomas was late in replying, she responded passionately: 'O, I do love you, my own Friend, above the whole earth—no human being was ever half so dear to me—none, none: and will you break my heart? ... I will be yours in life in death through all eternity' (CL 3:361). There was no question of his reply:'How could we ever part? Do we not love each other? Does not your fervid trembling spirit cleave to mine? ... Are not my arms about you, is not my breast your pillow? ... No, we will never part' (CL 3:366). She paid a visit to his family in September, and they discussed where they should live after marriage. In anxiety about her health, Jane had thought carefully about her father's bequest to her of Craigenputtoch and the Haddington home; and now she took care of this by a 'Deed,' sometimes called a 'Will'. Neither she nor Thomas wanted her mother to live with them, nor to see her ejected from Haddington: eventually Mrs Welsh agreed to rent a house for them at Comely Bank in Edinburgh, while she moved to her father's home at Templand, Thornhill, Dumfriesshire. Events moved on to the marriage at Templand on 17 October 1826.

CL 7:375-7

Scotsbrig

Haddington, Monday [May 1826]

Well dearest, you are one of the sublimest geniuses that the world ever saw! To imagine for a moment I would not live anywhere on earth rather than in this vile Haddington! What a surprising, *inhuman* scheme! bring me back to Haddington after all my longing to get out of it, back to such an Inferno just when I thought my deliverance sure. Nein, Nein, my will is not so entirely 'cast into fusion' that it should by any possible process be moulded to *this*. Only think Mr. Carlyle, could you, you of all men living—associate with or bear to see your wife associate with the inane, low minded people who make up the society of Haddington. No truly, unless you be an infinitely more tolerant person that I have hitherto taken you for—more tolerant than I should like to think you, you would rather at once curse God & die. The last proposed arrangement then is out of the question. ... And now having as usual demolished your project I come next to set up one of my own, or rather one of my Mother's in its place.

Eh bien! would you have any objection so soon as your task is completed to bring me home to Edin. at once; provided

some kind geni of the lamp was meanwhile to get a house
there all ready furnished for our reception. My good Mother is
extremely desirous that this should be the way of it—that we
should have a comfortable home at our outset in life thro her
means. And I am fully persuaded that she will have more real
enjoyment in doing us this kindness than all the fine gold in the
world could procure her in any other way, I for one have been
inclined to give a grateful assent to the generous proposal. And
will not you my best Beloved do the same? Assuredly you will.
But Whitsunday is at hand; so that if we are to come to Edin.
before winter there is no time to be lost in looking out for the
said house So do *you* lose no moment in transmitting to my
Mother the seal of your sovereignty for it would be folly I
presume to propose your coming & choosing for yourself in
your present press of business. However if we had only some
idea of the whereabouts I have no fear that she & I together
should be able to suit your taste in a habitation. Do you like
Morning side or is there any other situation you like better. It
would certainly be preferable both in respect to comfort &
economy that we should live out of the hubbub of the town, at
least this is my view of the matter, and yours if I mistake not is
the same. Forgive me for wishing to take the labour of the
Commonwealth *this once* into my own hands, it is not out of
any love of rule but merely to save you all sort of trouble &
annoyance. . . . / For ever & ever / Your own / Jane Welsh

MARGARET WELSH   NLS 601.9
Boreland, Southwick, Dumfries

Templand—1*st* October [1826]

. . . It were no news to tell you what a momentous matter I have
been busied with; 'not to know *that* would argue yourself
unknown'— For a marriage is a topic suited to the capacities of
all living; and in this, as in every other known instance has been
made the most of. But for as much breath as has been wasted
on '*my Situation*'; I have my own doubts whether they have
given you any *right* idea of it. They would tell you, I should
suppose, first and foremost, that my intended is *poor* (for *that*
it requires no great depth of sagacity to discover) and, in the
next place, most likely, indulge in some criticisms scarce
flattering, on his birth (the more likely if their own birth
happened to be mean or doubtful) and, if they happened to be

vulgar-fine people with disputed pretensions to good looks, they would, to a certainty set him down as unpolished and ill-looking— But a hundred chances to one, they would not tell you he is among the cleverest men of his day; and not the cleverest only but the most enlightened! that he possesses all the qualities I deem essential in *my* husband,—a warm true heart to love me, a towering intellect to command me, and a spirit of fire to be the guiding star-light of my life— Excellence of this sort always requires some degree of superiority in those who duly appreciate it: in the eyes of the *canaille*—poor soulless wretches!—it is mere foolishness, and it is only the *canaille* who babble about other peoples affairs—

Such then is this future husband of mine; not a *great* man according to the most common sense of the word, but truly great in its natural, proper sense—a scholar, a poet, a philosopher, a wise and noble man, one who holds his patent of nobility from Almighty God, and who's high stature of manhood is not to be measured by the inchrule of Lilliputs!— Will you like him? no matter whether you do or not—since I like him in [the] deepest part of my soul.

I would invite you to my wedding if I meant to invite any one; but, to *my* taste, such ceremonies cannot be *too* private: besides by making *distinction*, among my relatives on the occasion, I should be sure to give offence; and, by God's blessing, I will have no one there who does not feel kindly both towards *him* and *me*— .../And believe me always your sincere friend and dutiful niece Jane Welsh

Margaret Welsh sent this letter to Thomas Carlyle after Jane's death— 'Ah me!' he noted on it, 'God bless thee, Dear One!'

Chapter Two

In these Moors, 1828–34

In Edinburgh Jane was able to meet her husband's friends, including the elegant and kindly Francis Jeffrey, who liked to flirt with her and invited Thomas to write for his **Edinburgh Review**. *Yet the city was expensive, and they decided to economize by moving to Craigenputtoch. Jane's gift of the rent of the farm to her mother had satisfied Mrs Welsh, who generously financed rebuilding the house, and was now less opposed to such a move. Jane was glad to have her mother fairly nearby at Templand, and she assumed that she and Thomas would not stay at Craigenputtoch for long. Thomas's widening friendships had excited them both: a long letter from Goethe had arrived at Comely Bank, and a package with a gift to Jane of a necklace and locket showing the great poet's head set in gold. Thomas's brother Alick ran the farm, Edinburgh friends such as Jeffrey and Henry Inglis visited, and Jane at first seemed content.*

ELIZA STODART   EUL Dc. 4.94
George Sq., Edinburgh

Craigenputtoch 21*st* November [1828]

. . . You would know what I am doing in these moors? Well I am feeding poultry (at long intervals and merely for form's sake), and I am galloping over the country on a bay horse, and baking bread, and improving my mind, and eating, and sleeping, and making, and mending, and in short, wringing whatever good I can, from the ungrateful soil of the world. On the whole, I was never more contented in my life: one enjoys such freedom and quietude here; nor have we purchased this at the expense of other accommodations; for we have a good house to live in, with all the necessaries of life, and even some touch of the superfluities. 'Do you *attempt* to raise any corn?' the people ask us. Bless their hearts! we are planning strawberry-banks, and shrubberies, and beds of roses, with the most perfect assurance that they will grow: as to the corn, it grows to all lengths, without ever consulting the public about the matter. Another question that is asked me, so often as I am abroad, is, how many cows I keep, which question, to my eternal shame as a housewife, I have never yet been enabled to answer; having never ascertained, up to this moment whether there are seven cows or eleven. The fact is I take no delight in cows, and have happily no concern with them. Carlyle and I are not playing farmers here; which were a rash and unnatural attempt. My Brother in law is the Farmer, and fights his own battle, in his own new house, which one of his sisters manages for him. . . .

My Mother dined here ten days ago, and stayed a night,— her *second* and *longest* visit since we came. But she is of necessity much confined at home now, and also imagines the necessity to be greater than it is. You inquire if I will be in Edin*r* this winter. I think the chances are about two to one that I shall. We are pressingly invited to spend some time with the Jeffreys; and Carlyle has agreed to go, provided he gets three papers, promised to the Foreign Review, finished by then. Should he be belated with these he would have me to go without him, but that I shall not dream of doing— It would be poor entertainment for one in Edinr or anywhere else to think one's Husband was here in the desert *alone*—his stockings get all into holes, and perhaps even his tea running down. . . . Do write ever affectionately yours. / J W Carlyle

*

[Dec. 1830]

. . . It is a real hardship that you will not write oftener; it is only thro'*your* letters that any tone of the old time ever reaches me—all the rest of my young companions, if they have not got new faces, having at least got new dialects. And then you have such plenty of interesting matter lying on all hands— If you were in *my* place you would have more excuse who have to produce letters as the silk-worm spins, all out of my own inside.

We have been very solitary for a long while, our only visitors are now and then a stray pack-man. and the last of these pronounced the place 'altogether *heathenish*' so there is no hope of our being favoured with *his* company another time. Nevertheless I keep up my heart. There is nothing like a good fit of pain for taking the conceit out of one. Had I been newly returned from Edin*r*, my thoughts still wandering on the mountain-tops of vanity, it is probable I should have found life here in this grimest of weather almost intolerable; but being newly recovered from a sore-throat I am quite content beside a good fire, with a book or work, and the invaluable capacity of swallowing tho' the desert around looks the very head quarters of winter; and our knocker hangs a useless ornament.

My Grandfather was no worse when my Mother wrote last week; and her luck seemed to be taking a favourable turn; she had got a visitor, than whom *'no sweeter ever crossed a threshold'*— I mean to spend a week with her so soon as I am able to ride: but I am not quite well yet—at least I am still wearing signals of distress—a nightcap and shawl—that partly I confess, from a secret persuasion that these equipments render my appearance more interesting— But Mercy here is dark night come upon me and a box has yet to be packed with which a man has to ride six miles thro' the snow— I will write you at more length another time—and in the mean while this will show my good intentions— God bless you Dear a kiss to your Uncle / in breakneck haste your / affectionate friend / Jane W Carlyle

In August 1831 Carlyle went to London to try to arrange for the publication of **Sartor Resartus.** *The book was submitted to John Murray, but negotiations broke off in September. Jane wrote to Thomas lovingly over every square inch of her next despatch.*

TC   NLS 1774.13
Woburn Buildings, Tavistock Sq.
                                              Saturday [6-9 Aug. 1831]

Best & Dearest
So you are really gone! and I—ich bin allein! [I am alone]—every instant I feel this; yet I am not so miserable as might be supposed—at least not more miserable *here* than I should be in any other place where you were not. It would be infinitely worse to be obliged to make the agreeable among people whom I was all the while wishing annihilated—as I should be constrained (notwithstanding my true tho' perhaps feeble attachment to my species) to wish, with hardly any exception all creatures of the human kind that 'obtruded' themselves on me in my present humour....

I went to bed when the sound of your wheels could no longer be heard; and cried myself into a troubled sleep. The first thing that met my eyes on waking was your night cap lying on my pillow; whereupon I fell a-crying anew, and actually kissed

it I believe, tho' you know I hate *red* nightcaps. New trials
awaited me when I got out of bed and found some article of
your dress in all parts of the room: but the worst of all was
when I sat down to breakfast, and noticed the *one* cup and *one*
everything, and thought how long this must last. My heart was
nearly failing me altogether; my *head* did fail me—and the
whole of that day and part of the following, I had to keep my
bed. Fate seemed minded to spare me the trouble of seeking
myself employment in your absence. To day I am in my usual
middle state—and have been going about 'siding things' as they
say in Liverpool—in East Lothian dialect 'redding up' [putting
in order] or in your 'brief and energetic' dialect 'making an
earthquake.' . . . I have your profil stuck up on the
mantlepiece— Remembrances to John— How I long for your
letter— Bless you Bless you my dear good Husband. I am ever
thine / Jane W. Carlyle

*Jane joined Thomas in October. Her letters to her Liverpool cousin
Helen Welsh, her close friend Isabella McTurk and her London servant
Eliza Miles suggest how the six months' visit sharpened her observation.
In spite of often being ill she felt part of a sophisticated society that
treated them as equals and respected her wit and charm. Irving's
religious zeal and disastrous convictions about 'speaking with tongues'
dismayed them. Already his pieties had embarrassed them with a
parting request at Comely Bank to kneel in prayer. The meeting of the
two couples in December 1832 was equally awkward, and was when
Jane remarked that 'there would have been no tongues had Irving
married me' (Froude,* **Life** *1:162). Thomas's father died on 22 January;
he was immediately the subject of one of Carlyle's* **Reminiscences.** *They
sombrely returned to Dumfriesshire to hear of Goethe's death.*

HELEN WELSH   NLS 601.19
Maryland St, Liverpool

4 Ampton Street / Mecklenburg Square
26*th* October [1831]

. . . I like London very well—and expect I shall like it still
better in a week or two when some of the people my Husband
likes best shall have returned to town. I have been at no public
place yet except once to Drury Lane theatre where we saw
the silliest piece in the world—rather indifferently performed.
but the house especially the beautiful lustre in the centre of it

were well worth looking at— Not so the Ladies who surprised
me by their almost universal ugliness— One day I went with
Mrs Montagu to Epping Forest—about fifteen miles from
town—to visit Doctor Allan a Scotchman who has a lunatic
establishment in the midst of the Forest—a place where any
sane person might be delighted to get admission. the house or
rather houses (for there are two for patients in different stages
of lunacy) are all overhung with roses and grapes and
surrounded with garden ponds and shrubbery without the
smallest appearance of constraint— And the poor creatures
are all so happy. And there Dr such a good humane Man—that
it does not at all produce the painful impression that Asylums
of that sort usually do— I am going back to stay some days—
Dr Allan is an old friend of Carlyle's and his Wife is a very
excellent woman— A far worse Bedlam is poor Edward
Irving's house where people are to be found at all hours
'*speaking with tongues*' that is to say shrieking and howling
in no tongue. I happened to be there one night just when a
Lady was under the inspiration of 'the Spirit'; and the horrible
sounds she made almost threw me who am not of a hysterical
temperament into a fit. I could not help crying all the way
home. Indeed it is truly distressing to see a man of such talents
and such really good and pious dispositions as Mr Irving given
up to an infatuation so absurd—ready to sacrifice to it his
dearest friends, his reputation, all his worldly prospects. Most
people think it is all a humbug—which is quite reasonable in
those who do not *know* him. but a man more sincere in his
professions does not exist.

    We are going out of town for a few days on a visit to Mr
Badams at Enfield— His wife is about my age, very pretty and
lively and clever she is a daughter of Holcroft's whom you may
have heard of— We had Allan Cunningham at tea with us the
other evening. He is a most sufficient poet as I ever met with—
so substantially built both bodily and mentally—looking in all
respects precisely what he is—a cultivated *Scotch* mason.
Procter (Barry Cornwall) we see often—and his wife who is
Mrs Montagu's daughter is my most intimate acquaintance
here. But among all the literary people that come about us the
one I like best is Mr Mill, son of Mill the Utilitarian, but *he* is no
Utilitarian—he belongs rather to the class to which my
Husband belongs and which for want of a fitter name has been
called 'the Mystic school' —

Jeffrey is getting slowly better—he was able to drive this length the other day—and is going a little way into the country till the Parliament meets— I suppose you are all at a stand in your speculations about the Reform Bill in Liverpool as elsewhere— Here every body I see seems quite tired of thinking about it.

We continue to be well pleased with our lodgings— indeed if we had sought all London I believe we could not have settled more to our mind. They even make us excellent porrige now. . . . Your affectionate Cousin / Jane W Carlyle

ISABELLA McTURK   NLS Acc. 12039
Dumfriesshire

[Ampton St, late Oct. 1831]

. . . I have been horrid bad as they say in Glen Eslin since I came here or I should have enjoyed my life extremely— persecuted too with an irruption on my face which might have been transacted more commodiously at Craigenputtoch than amongst strangers. But every thing is for the best, which I have insight enough to recognize even in this dispensation, for if everything went on here to my hearts content how should I reconcile myself to the idea of returning to the desert in Spring. I wish I had a nice large house here and a handsome income—and that you were come on a visit. There was never anybody contrived to live beside me so satisfactorily for *me* and apparently for herself— I remember with admiration how long you could sit silent without the least fidgeting—and then start into the finest spirits whenever the wind of my humour had changed. . . . In truth dear Bella I rather approve of you on the whole, and hope that we shall spend many a fortnight together before we die.

But I must tell you something of my walk and conversation here in this monstrous Babylon— We have got a pretty little trim lodging in the house of an English family (George Irving's was too noisy) where we find ourselves comfortable enough, except that one feels occasionally as if tied up in a sack. Carlyle is put to unheard of shifts for want of a smoking establishment—sometimes he tries the Balcony . . . where with his Highland bonnet . . . he looks precisely like the figures over tobacconists doors. . . . I have made acquaintance with several rather remarkable women, and

many men of some talent and wort.... Jeffrey is quite well
again, and still ... the brightest and kindest of all my
acquaintance— The people I am oftenest with are the
Montagus.... We were at a Musical party there last week—
where we heard Moschelles.... God bless you. Think of me
kindly while I am absent, as I shall do of you....

ELIZA MILES   *NLM* 1:41–4
Ampton St, London
                                    Craigenputtock, 16 June, 1832

...I was fatigued enough by the journey home; still more by
the *trysting* [meeting] that awaited me here; a dismantled
house, no effectual servants, weak health, and, worse than the
seven plagues of Egypt, a necessity of Painters. All these things
were against me. But happily there is a continual tide in
human affairs; and if a little while ago I was near being swept
away, in the hubbub, so now I find myself in a dead calm. All is
again in order about us, and I fold my hands and ask, 'What is
to be done next?' 'The duty nearest hand, and the next will
shew itself in course.' So my Goethe teaches! No one who lays
this precept to heart can ever be at a stand. Impress it on your
'twenty children' (that I think was the number you had fixed
upon), impress it on the whole twenty from the cradle
upwards, and you will spare your sons the vexation of many a
wild-goose chase, and render your daughters forever
impracticable to *ennui*. Shame that such a malady should exist
in a Christian land; should not only exist, but be almost general
throughout the whole female population that is placed above
the necessity of working for daily bread. If I have an antipathy
for any class of people, it is for *fine ladies*. I almost match my
Husband's detestation of partridge-shooting *gentlemen*. Woe to
the fine lady who should find herself set down at
Craigenputtock for the first time in her life, left alone with her
own thoughts, no '*fancy bazaar*' in the same kingdom with
her, no place of amusement within a day's journey; the very
church, her last imaginable resource, seven miles off. I can
fancy with what horror she would look on the ridge of
mountains that seemed to enclose her from all earthly bliss!
with what despair in her accents she would enquire if there
was not even a 'charity sale' within reach. Alas, no! no outlet
whatever for 'ladies work,' not even a Book for a fine

lady's understanding! It is plain she would have nothing for it but to die as speedily as possible, and to relieve the world of the expenses of her maintenance. For my part I am very content. I have everything here my heart desires, that I could have anywhere else, except society, and even that deprivation is not to be considered wholly an evil: if people we like and take pleasure in do not come about us here as in London, it is thankfully to be remembered that here 'the wicked cease from troubling, and the weary are at rest.' If the knocker make no sound for weeks together, it is so much the better for my nerves. My Husband is as good company as reasonable mortal could desire. Every fair morning we ride on horse-back for an hour before breakfast (my precious horse knew me again and neighed loud and long when he found himself in his old place). Then we eat such a surprising breakfast of home-baked bread, and eggs, etc., etc., as might incite anyone that had breakfasted so long in London to write a pastoral. Then Carlyle takes to his writing, while I, like Eve, 'studious of household good,' inspect my house, my garden, my live stock, gather flowers for my drawingroom, and lapfuls of eggs; and finally betake myself also to writing, or reading, or making or mending, or whatever work seems fittest. After dinner, and only then, I lie on the sofa and (to my shame be it spoken) sometimes *sleep*, but oftenest dream waking. In the evening I walk on the moor (how different from Holborn and the Strand!) and read anything that does not exact much attention. Such is my life,—agreeable as yet from its novelty, if for nothing else. Now, would you not like to share it? I am sure you would be happy beside us for a while, and healthy; for I would keep all drugs from your lips, and pour warm milk into you. . . . My health is slowly mending. / Yours affectionately, / JANE CARLYLE.

Jane reported to her mother-in-law the first of many servant troubles which, as well as being a problem, became a vent for her anger, sarcasm and self-dramatizing. The prospect of wintering at Craigenputtoch again was too much, and they set off for an unhappy five months' stay in Edinburgh in January 1833. The city seemed provincial, and, though Jane resumed her friendship with Jeffrey, he was now in politics and soon left for London. She was depressed by her aging mother's visit and by the news that the Church of Scotland had ejected Irving for heresy. Craigenputtoch on return was enlivened only by a visit from Emerson.

MARGARET CARLYLE   NLS 601.24
Scotsbrig
                                              [25 Sept.1832]

My dear Mother

...Carlyle is toiling away at the new article; and tho by no
means content with the way he makes (when is he ever
content?) still as you used to say what is down will not jump out
again. In three weeks or so it will be done and then we come. I
am certainly mended since you were here; but 'deed M*rs* Carle
a's maist ashamed to sayt.' a's still weakly, and take no unusual
fatigue without suffering for it. The toil and trouble I had about
Betty did me a great mischief, which I have scarcely yet got over.
for the rest that explosion has had no unpleasant consequence.
The woman I got in her stead, on an investigation of three
minutes, proves to be quite as clever a servant as she was whom
I investigated for the space of three half years and rode, as I
compute some hundred miles after. Deaf as a doornail the
present individual has nevertheless conducted herself
heretofore quite satisfactorily—except that Carlyle's silk
handkerchief is occasionally in requisition (oftener I sometimes
think than there is any *visible* cause) wiping off particles of
dust; and once by awful oversight a small mouse-*deed* was
permitted to insinuate itself into *his* bowl of porridge! We are
not to keep her however, because of her deafness, which in any
other place where her ears would be called into vigourous
action, would make her the mere effigy of a servant— I get back
the black button who was here when you came, who I know to
be ignorant as a sucking child of almost every thing I require
her to do; but whom I hope to find honest diligent good-
humoured and moderately quick in the uptake.

I had a very kind letter from Mrs Montagu last week,
reproaching me with forgetfulness of her. We have not heard
from or of Jeffrey for a very long time; but he will certainly
write on Wednesday to acknowledge the repayment of his debt
which, is a great load off our mind.

My Mother writes in great alarm about cholera which is at
Penpont, within three miles of her. three persons have died. I
have been expecting nothing else, and my dread of it is not
greater for its being at hand. the Answer to all such terrors is
simply what Carlyle said a year ago to someone who told him in
London cholera is here—'When is death not here?'

ELIZA MILES   Froude, *Life* 2:351-3
Ampton St, London

Craigenputtock: July 15, 1833

...I well remember the fine evening last year when I received
your letter. I was riding alone across our solitary moor when I met
my boy returning from the post-office, and took it from him and
opened it and read it on horseback, too anxious for news about
you to keep it for a more convenient place. Had anyone predicted
to me *then* that the good, kind, trustful letter was to lie
unanswered for a whole year, I should have treated such
prediction as an injurious calumny which there was not the
remotest chance of my justifying! Alas! and it is actually so! For a
whole year I have left my dear little friend in Ampton Street to
form what theory she pleased concerning the state of my mind
towards her; and finally, I suppose, to set me down for heartless
and fickle, and dismiss my remembrance with a sigh; for her
gentle, affectionate nature is incapable, I believe, of more
indignant reproach. And yet, Eliza (it was), neither the one thing
nor the other. I am capable of as strong attachment as yourself
(which is saying much), and if I do not abandon myself to my
attachment as you do, it is only because I am older, have had my
dreams oftener brought into collision with the realities of life, and
learnt from the heart-rending jarring of such collision that 'all is
not gold that glitters,' and that one's only safe dependence is in
oneself—I mean in the good that is in one. As little am I fickle,
which I must beg you to believe on trust; since my past life,
which would bear me out in the boast, is all unknown to you.
What is it, then, you will ask, that makes me fail in so simple a
duty of friendship as the writing of a letter? It is sometimes sheer
indolence, sometimes sickness, sometimes procrastination. My
first impulse, after reading your letter, was to sit down and answer
it by the very next post. Then I thought I will wait the Lord
Advocate's return, that he may frank it. Then troubles thickened
round me: my mother's illness, my grandfather's death, gave me
much fatigue of body and mind. That, again, increased to cruel
height my own persevering ailments. About the new year we
removed to Edinburgh, where we stayed till the beginning of May.
It was a fully more unhealthy winter for me than the previous one
in London. I wrote to no one; had enough to do in striving with
the tempter ever present with me in the shape of headaches,
heartache, and all kinds of aches, that I might not break out into

fiery indignation over my own destiny and all the earth's. Since my home coming I have improved to a wonder, and the days have passed, I scarce know how, in the pleasant hopelessness that long-continued pain sometimes leaves behind.

Nay, I must not wrong myself. I have not been quite idle. I have made a gown which would delight Mrs. Page, it looks so neat and clean; and a bonnet, and loaves of bread innumerable. At present I am reading Italian most of the day with my medical brother-in-law, who is home at present from Rome. It was my husband who, for all his frightening you with some books, raised me from Ariosto today, with the chiding words that it would be altogether shameful if I let his book parcel go without that letter for Miss Miles, which I had talked of writing these six months back.

. . . How is your health? I hope you do not go often to Dr. Fisher's, or at all. The more I see of doctors the more I hold by my old heresy that they are all 'physicians of no value.' My brother-in-law is a paragon of the class, but he is so by—in as much as possible—undoctoring himself. He told me yesterday, 'Could I give you some agreeable occupation to fill your whole mind, it would do more for you than all the medicines in existence.'

I wish I had you here to drink new milk and ride my horse.

We are at home now for the summer and autumn, most likely for the winter also. We think of France next summer, and moving in the interim were scarce worth while. Surely your father might find someone travelling to Edinburgh by sea, who would take charge of you. It is the easiest and cheapest conveyance possible.

Write to me all that you are thinking and wishing, and never doubt my kind feelings towards you. / Your sincere friend / JANE CARLYLE.

As Carlyle turned to writing about the French Revolution, a friend happily gave him access to a fine country-house library at Barjarg, near Thornhill. It gave Jane reading as well.

ELIZA STODART   EUL Dc. 4.94
George Sq., Edinburgh

                                   Craigenputtoch [9 Nov. 1833]

. . . A great God-send has befallen my Husband this Autumn; in which, as in all his other God-sends and Devil-sends I heartily participate. John Hunter (who never saw him)—has been

induced to confide to him the keys of the Barjarg Library (an
extensive and valuable collection) with leave to borrow
therefrom at discretion. You cannot figure what an inestimable
benifit it is, in our situation nearly impracticable on this side; or
what exhalations of gratitude rise from my Husbands soul
towards the Minister of the Trone. I verily believe if he were in
Edinr, he would even go and hear him preach, to show his
sense of the kindness. Two gig-boxfulls of excellent books have
already been brought over and consumed by one party like
reek [smoke]—while I have selected therefrom '*Memoires of
Marie Antoinette*' (by Me Campan) '*Oeuvres de M Roland*' (the
very best woman I ever scraped acquaintance with—)
'*Memoires de Me de Staal*'—a clever spirited little creature
quite superior to the sentimental de Stael Holstein, that I used
to make such work about in my '*wee existence*.' And finally a life
of Cooke the Actor—as a warning against drunkenness. . . .

HENRY INGLIS   NLS 1797.1
2 Henderson Row, Edinburgh
                          Craigenputtoch 23*d* November [1833]

. . . I beseech you, do not estimate my gratitude for your letter,
by the alacrity I have displayed in answering it. It was delightful
to laugh with you again at anything, even a fellow creature's
indigestions; and still more delightful to find I was remembered
by you, while modestly supposing myself forgotten of the
whole earth: I thanked you, then, from the very bottom of my
heart; and would have told you so on the instant but for an
inveterate habit of procrastination I have somehow acquired.
Whatever is to be done, tho' it were but to stitch a button on
my Husband's shirt; I must put off till 'a more convenient
season': and it is inconceivable what woes are thus
originated,—just in that single matter of shirt-buttons, to go no
further. 'Females' that are fulfilling the end of their being,
videlicet, 'bringing up children,' should be attentive to whip at
the very first symptom of this tendency.
       Why did you not come in Autumn, and make amends to
us for the loss of Hunt? '*Craigen-poo-toch*' looked so well this
year, and felt so well, and could have enjoyed your company
after a quite other fashion than thro' the last winter; when '*my
memory was a long train of indigestions,—my prospects
more of the same*.' John Mill had to go to France; so we were

disappointed of him also: and were thankful to Providence for the windfall of a stray American [Emerson], 'come out for to see whatsoever things were wise and of good report,'—from one end of Europe to the other. With such accuracy of investigation did he prosecute this object, that he arrived, by paths unknown, at the door of Craigenpootoch, which was, of course, opened to him with all the pleasure in life. To find the Christian charities inside, and even the Graces seemed to occasion him the most agreeable surprise. Carlyle had been represented to his transatlantic imagination, quite *Teufelsdreckish*,—a man severe—living in complete isolation, and partial barbarism: the Individual before his bodily eyes was shaven and shorn, overflowing with the milk of human kindness, *und mit Weib im Hause* [and with a wife at home]; a blessing which the amiable American estimated highly— himself having *lost it* after an *exceedingly brief* trial [his wife, Ellen Louisa Tucker, had died of tuberculosis, 1831]. He went 'on-on'—and we saw him no more. Our next inmate was a broken-down Barrister, who some years ago enjoyed the threefold reputation of a Scholar, Genius, and Gig Man; but who is now literally lying among the pots,—having made his last stand against the world, on a not too solid basis of whisky and water— He with a pretty pettish wife of the fine Lady sort, but also taking into whisky exhibited to us for one mortal week a specimen of that sort of company which is worse than none; which at Craigenputtoch of all places one is tempted to deny the possibility of. But they also passed on, and again all was silent and continues silent to this hour. Yet here in the midst of this almost fearful silence we are fixed for the winter—resolute to assert the superiority of mind over matter, by neither going out of our wits nor attempting our lives thro' the dismalities of the ensuing season. Would *you but* come at Christmas it were an act of Mercy never to be forgotten! But alas! you are 'an *ornament to Society in every direction*' and society will not part with you, and you will not part with society to console suffering virtue in its Patmos— Yet it is better to be loved than admired—better to have one *friend* than one thousand *acquaintances*— I doubt if there be one individual alive, out of your own family, that loves [you] more truly than Carlyle does; or even than I do, which however is less to the purpose—yet who of your whole acquaintance sees less of you than we? This is not as it should be— I put it to your conscience, whether the '*infinitismal system*' be a whit more rational in the practice of Friendship, than in the practice of Medicine? One meeting in the course of half a dozen years seems to me as great an absurdity as an ounce of salt put into the Pacific Ocean—and the Friend must suffer equally with the Patient under such a treatment. . . .

*To Jane's relief Thomas decided in the spring that they should leave their 'boggy Patmos' (**CL** 7:137); and, while he went to London to look for a new house, she arranged to let Craigenputtoch and ship their belongings.*

TC   *CL* 7:186-8
Ampton St, London
                              Templand Thursday [22 May 1834]

. . . You will now see the history of my not writing on Tuesday yesterday was as busy a day as any—for after the last carts were gone—I had my own duds to pack—and the Macqueens' things to collect into some sort of decent order—and then I had to go in by Barjarg on the road hither and replace the books— My mother staid with me to the last—worked like a Turk—was pettish enough and annoying with contradictory advice—but on the whole helpful. Poor Harry had to draw us both and Hugh yesterday. Since we came here she has been as kind as possible—so you are not to fancy me wretched— We found Walter and one of the Chrystals on our arrival which rather disturbed the repose we were flattering ourselves with and too much in need of— This morning I rose at four (I have got such a habit of early rising) and wonderful to say quite free of headach— Was I wae [sad] to leave the Puttoch? to be sure I was! But I made little greeting [crying]—just a little in our own room all alone immediately before starting. It consoled me greatly to be leaving the poor house not altogether dilapidated but to a certain extent like itself— If we want to return, we are to have our own things back, with a deduction for use— So that in case of a revolution or plague we can again be fitted up there for a few pounds of money— Besides one is sure the place is going to be rightly kept, since they have been at such outlay in furnishing it— Macqueen has hired a decent maid about forty— very cleanly, and acquainted with the keeping of houses. On the whole dear 'let us be thankful.'

And now what is to be said about *your* house? First and
foremost I vote for having nothing to do with M*rs* Austin's—
these arrangements always give dissatisfaction and besides it is
not till August that we could have access to it—and in the mean
time our goods are at Annan and Goody without *home*.That
Brompton one appears far the likeliest speculation—my counsel
is to take that if it can be had on reasonable terms— But if there
be any drawback which I am not aware of & if you have found
no other to your mind, then I am of opinion I should come to
you in Ampton Street or where else you may be, and help you
with my judgement such as it is— In case of a house being
taken I shall sail in the same boat with the furniture and have
the satisfaction of seeing with my own eyes what comes of it in
Liverpool—and be in London in time to receive it—for no body
is so necessary at the unpacking as some one that has been at
the packing. In the other case I shall start when you bid me—by
the next boat but one shall I not? that is Tomorrow fortnight— I
should prefer tomorrow week, only there would be little time to
work on after receiving your answer.And moreover the next is
my *sick week*, when it is probable I shall be more useless than
ordinary, after so much fatigue— How often I called to mind
your kind injunctions to take things quietly and '*save myself*';
and strove to obey you. But these injunctions were all rendered
fruitless—

    That day in Dumfries was such a day as you never saw—
so much hithering and thithering about the house—so much
running after packers—so much hunting for mats &c (I got two
dozen and three which with a few at home were sufficient, for
9*d* each nearly half price from Bryden Spirit Dealer good and
large—) then all 'the victualling' to provide for such a number
of people—all the investigations about Drumpark—it was one
in the morning when we reached home— O Good what I
would give for a long long sleep in your arms. I have never
however neglected nourishing myself with wholesome food
and even a little Brandy and to my care in this particular I
attribute it that I have continued so well. . . .

    Commend me to our 'celebrated' friends and to the poor
Miles—with whom I am most thankful to know you lodged—
And so God bless you my Husband— Be not '*Bloody*' but '*bold
and resolute*'—and your Goody, 'tho' desperate, no coward,' will
strive to be the same and all will work together for good. My
Mother sends her kind love— / Your faithful Wife / Jane Carlyle . . .

Chapter Three

This Stirring Life—and a Parting, 1834-42

'Here is a new prospect', wrote Jane, 'with a vengeance!' and 'for me, the chief enjoyment, I imagine,will be in the society of my own heart's darling' (CL 7:108). Searching for a house,Carlyle came on Edward Irving,'choked, in the despicablest coil of cobwebs' and 'wofully given over to his idols' (CL 7:196). He died in nine months to be mourned by Thomas in letters and the **Reminiscences,** *while Jane was silent. Then, in London,Thomas met George Rennie. On moving into 5 Cheyne Row, he was worried about the hostile reception of* **Sartor Resartus,** *but Jane remained confident in his genius. Her tea-table salon was already attended by such distinguished figures as Mary Somerville, scientist and mathematician; Sarah Austin, the translator and Germanist;John Stuart Mill, editor and Utilitarian philosopher;John Sterling, idiosyncratic liberal clergyman;Count Carlo Pepoli, Bolognese political exile after the 1831 revolution; Harriet Martineau, political and social reformer; Erasmus Darwin, Charles's elder brother, who shared Jane's scepticism; Fanny Wedgwood, Erasmus's first cousin and daughter of Sir James Mackintosh, the Whig historian;Joseph Garnier, tough political exile from Baden; and Godefroy Cavaignac, a dashing radical exiled from France for his part in the 1830 uprising and who could give Carlyle first-hand accounts of revolution. Eliza continued as Jane's confidante:*

ELIZA STODART   EUL Dc. 4.94
George Sq., Edinburgh

[Aug. 1834]

...Well! is it not very strange that I am here? sitting in my own hired house by the side of the Thames as if nothing had happened; with fragments of Haddington, of Comely Bank, of Craigenputtoch interweaved with *cockneycalities* into a very habitable whole? Is it not strange that I should have an everlasting sound in my ears, of men, women, children, omnibuses, carriages glass coaches, streetcoaches, waggons, carts, dog-carts, steeple bells, doorbells, Gentleman-raps,

twopenny-post-raps, footmen-showers-of raps, of the whole
devil to pay, as if plague pestilence, famine, battle, murder
sudden death and wee Eppie Daidle were broken loose to
make me diversion.— And where is the stillness, the eternal
sameness, of the last six years—? Echo answers at
Craigenputtoch! There let them 'dwell with Melancholy' and old
Nanny Macqueen, for this stirring life is more to my mind, and
has besides a beneficial effect on my bowels. Seriously I have
almost entirely discontinued drugs, and look twenty percent
better, every one says, and 'what every one says must be true.'
This being the case, You may infer that I am tolerably content in
my new position; indeed I am more and more persuaded that
there is no complete misery in the world that does not
emanate from the bowels.

We have got an excellent lodgement; of most antique
phisiognomy, quite to our humour; all wainscoated carved and
queer-looking; roomy substantial, commodious, with closets to
satisfy any Bluebeard, a chinacloset in particular that would
hold our whole worldly substance converted into china! Two
weeks ago there was a row of ancient trees in front, but some
crazy-headed Cokneys have uprooted them—behind we have a
garden (so called in the language of flattery) in the worst order,
but boasting of two vines which produced two bunches of
grapes, in the season, which 'might be eaten'; and a walnut-tree
from which I have gathered almost sixpence worth of walnuts.
'This large and comfortable tenement' we have, *without bugs*,
for some two or three pounds more rent than we paid for the
pepper box at Comely bank. This comes of our noble contempt
for fashion—Chelsea being highly unfashionable. The only
practical disadvantage in this circumstance is that we are far
from most of our acquaintance; a disadvantage which I
endeavour to obviate by learning to walk; my success is already
considerable I have several times walked ten miles without
being laid up. Besides we are not wholly isolated. Leigh Hunt
lives a few doors off. The Celebrated Mrs Somerville is at
Chelsea Hospital within five minutes walk, and Mrs Austin is
coming to introduce me to her tomorrow—and within a mile I
have a *circle* of acquaintances—one of these who lives in
prodigious *shine* with wife and family, you may happen to
recollect something about— A grave handsome, man who has
been here repeatedly, and treats me with infinite respect, and
takes immensely to my Husband—a sort of person with whom

one talks about 'the condition of art' in this country—and such like topics of general interest and studies to support the reputation of a rather intellectual and excessively reasonable woman— Can you divine who I mean? impossible—George Rennie! How has it happened? quite simply. I am one of the most amiable women living; tho' like your Uncle 'My virtues are unknown'— I am incapable of cherishing resentment even against a faithless lover, I heard he was there, I wondered what he was like; I sent him my address. He came instantaneously with his Sister Margaret— 'Bess did I feel awkward?' to be sure I did, and looked awkward for I was within an ace of fainting and he looked like one of his own marbles— But neither of us I believed entertained a particle of tenderness for the other nevertheless—it was mere queaziness from the intense sensation of the flight of time which such a meeting occasioned one—fifteen years! only think! He is much improved by age, in appearance, manner, and also I think in character—but he lives in the wretchedest atmosphere of '*Gigmanity*'—his wife is a perfect fool—the whole kin of them are fools— And poor George must either go in with their folly to a certain extent, or break his heart, or blow up his whole household sky-high— Moreover he is still self-willed and vain enough to show me as often as I see him that I made an escape— I go often to Margaret's, who lives in style also, but seems to feel rather out of her element here. Lady Kinloch is close by the Rennies—she was amazed to see me, and is very kind— I am glad she is not '*dead*'

For the rest our society with a few additions and subtractions is much the same that we had when here formerly—only I find it much pleasanter now being in better ease for enjoying it—John Mill, Leigh Hunt and Mrs Austin remain my favourites. I know some Elliots acquaintances of David Aitken [whom Eliza married, 1836] who are very agreeable people.— By the by did Mr Aitken tell you what a frantically affectionate reception I gave him at Craigenputtoch—he looked rather fearful for the consequences to his cloth— I shall never learn to give up these outbreakings of the old woman in me from time to time—the other morning when Mr Terrot [later Bishop of Edinburgh] came in (who is to carry this) I sprang into his arms and I believe almost stifled him with the ardour of my embrace— He returned it however with more sympathy than was to have been anticipated. I have wondered at my audacity ever since. for the thought of such an attempt in a cool moment would have made me quake. For God's sake write and tell me what everybody in Edin*r* is doing—especially my own relations whom methinks I ought to know something — I so seldom hear out of Scotland— My Mother is most scrupelous about putting me to the expence of postage— I shall be down perhaps next year—and then it will be hard if I do not see you— But will you never come here? I declare to Heaven there is nobody except my Mother I should welcome with such delight— After all you are the only right female friend I ever had in the world—the only one I can to all lengths and without the least misgiving talk nonsense to—and that I consider a pretty good test of friendship— . . . your truly attached Friend — Jane W Carlyle . . .

John Sterling had been direct about what he thought of **Sartor Resartus**, *and was to become an extremely close friend of both Carlyles. His* **Life** *was written by Thomas in 1851, and he was now 'visible', for a time, as a 'brilliant human presence, distinguishable, honourable and lovable'* (**Works** 11:268).

JOHN STERLING   NLS 601.32
Herstmonceaux

5 Cheyne Row—Thursday 4 June 1835

You did kindly to send the little separate note: the least bit *'all to myself,'* (as the children say) was sure to give me a livelier pleasure, than any number of sheets in which I had but a secondary interest. For in spite of the honestest efforts to annihilate my *I-ity*, or merge it in what the world doubtless considers my better half; I still find myself a self-subsisting and alas! selfseeking *Me*. Little Felix, in the Wanderjähre [Goethe's *Wilhelm Meister's Wanderjahre*], when, in the midst of an animated scene between Whilelm and Theresa, he pulls Theresa's gown, and calls out, *'Mama Theresa I too am here!'* only speaks out, with the charming trustfulness of a child, what I am perpetually feeling, tho' too sophisticated to pull peoples skirts, or exclaim in so many words; Mr Sterling *'I* too am here.'

    But I must tell you, I find a grave fault in that note about the last fault which I should have dreamt of finding in any utterance of yours: it is not believing but faithless! In the

first place the parenthesis '(if ever)' seems to me a wilful
questioning of the goodness of Providence. Then you say; if in
some weeks I can bring myself to think of you with patience
perhaps &c—now both the 'if' and '*perhaps*' displease me. Only
the most inveterate Sceptic could, with your fineness of
observation, have known me for two weeks, without certifying
himself that my patience is infinite, inexhaustible! that in fact I,
as well as yourself combine 'the wisdom of Solomon with the
patience of Job.'

Far from being offended by your desertation on the
Sartor I think it the best that has been said or sung of him.
even where your criticism does not quite fall in with my
humble views, I still love the spirit of the critic. For instance, I
am loth to believe that I have married a Pagan,—but I approve
entirely of the warmth with which you warn your Friend
against the delusion of burning pastils before a statue of
Jupiter and such like extravagancies. I suppose it is excessively
heterodox and in a catholic country I should be burnt for it,
but to you I may safely confess that I care almost nothing
about what a man believes, in comparison with *how* he
believes. If his belief be correct, it is so much the better for
himself; but its intensity, its efficacy is the ground on which I
love and trust him. Thus you see I am capable of appreciating
your fervour in behalf of the thirtynine articles, without being
afflicted because my Husband is accused of contumacy against
them. . . . / Affectionately yours / Jane W Carlyle

*Jane mocked Thomas's collection of 'lady-admirers' but she had her
own followers including Cavaignac, Count Pepoli and Edward Sterling
(father of Anthony and John) who was connected with* **The Times**. *She
enjoyed gossip about John Mill's scandalous (but probably platonic)
affair with Harriet Taylor, a champion of women's rights, 'half
angelical' and 'half demoniacal' (CL 8:291). And it may have been at
Harriet's Kingston cottage that a careless servant lit fires with the sole
copy of Carlyle's* **The French Revolution**, *trustingly lent to Mill. On the
evening of 6 March 1835, Mill and Harriet Taylor arrived with the news
at Cheyne Row. The work was rewritten and finished by January 1837:
'Jeannie alone', wrote Thomas, 'burnt like a steady lamp beside me'
(**Reminiscences** 92). Knowing his powers, Jane then encouraged him
to give a series of public lectures on German literature, for necessary
cash as well as reputation.*

ELIZA STODART   EUL Dc. 4.94
George Sq., Edinburgh

                                                   [29 Feb.1836]

...Well! believe it or no, as you like and can; I love you still with
all the *ardour of my young enthusiasm*—much more heartily
and trustfully than I am apt to love nowadays with my
middleaged discretion. Yet I have set myself very seriously to
the business of loving since I came here—conscious that my
long sojourn in the wilderness had developed certain
misanthropical tendencies in me that were leading me rather
devilward,—into the region of hatred and all uncharitableness!
With a good deal of effort I have got up a sentiment for several
men which has a good right to go by the name of friendship in
these days. I have even executed two or three *innocent
flirtations* with good effect, and on the whole live in great
amity with my fellow creatures. They call me '*sweet*,' and
'*gentle*'; and some of the men go the length of calling me
'*ENDEARING*' and I laugh in my sleeve and think oh Lord! if you
but knew what a brimstone of a creature I am behind all this
beautiful amiability! But my *sentiment* for *you* dearest, is not
'*got up*,' but grown up with me out of my sunny childhood, and
wears always a sunny healthful look that these half-literary half-
sentimental intimacies contracted after thirty can never match.
...And so I sit here in no 5 Cheyne Row and make grave
pantomime, and grave speech in acknowledgement of all the
wisdom I hear uttered by the celebrated men and women of the
age; thinking my own thought all the while which is often this
or something like this— 'Was not sitting under a hay-stack in a
summers day with Bess and George Rennie—or even weeping
childlike purely affectionate tears at the sound of *the Castle
bugles*; when in reply to my demand to be allowed to marry,
they sent me two halfcrowns and some barley-sugar; worth a
whole eternity of this idle speculation and barren logic'? But
the people here are good people, and with many noble gifts in
them, and to me they have been quite incomprehensibly kind so
that I ought not to feel discontent with THEM because the magic
of the *imagination* in me has got impaired by years, and no
spectacles that *reason* can invent does any thing at making the
world so green and glorious for me as it once was. My chief
intimates are a family of Sterlings—The Father known by the
name of '*the Thunderer of the Times*'—a clever, tumultuous,

vapid sort of half-Irishman,—the Mother a kind sincere wellenough cultivated most motherly Scotch woman—the Son!—An angel of Heaven! *ostensibly* a Clergyman of the church of England, and author of Arthur Coningsby a highly original Novel; He has also a wife, very fat, and good natured and fine ladyish in the *best* sense of the term. These people, as the elder Sterling told Susan Hunter when she was here, '*all adore me*'! Certainly they load me with kindnesses and treat me as if I were a sort of necessary to their existence: the very footman and Ladysmaid 'have been quite anxious' if I have staid away half a week. Mrs Sterlings portrait in oil hangs over my Mantle-piece—and the whole thing is in the most flourishing condition—if it do but last; then I have an Italian Conte [Pepoli], one of the first poets of Italy, the handsomest and bestmannered of men, who comes twice a week or so and makes my thoughts melodious for the rest of the day. He was my Mothers chief indeed I think *only* favorite here among all our people; which was curious as they had no medium of communication but their eyes! For my part I speak Italian now like a nightingale. and *will* I am told soon write it '*better* than any native Signora'! ... My Husband is pretty well—almost thro the second volume of his illfated book—thinks of your Uncle and you with grateful affection—is on the whole the cleverest man I meet with still and the truest. ... Write to me soon tho I do not deserve it—and love me always—your own Jane Welsh

JOHN STERLING NLS 601.41
Near Bordeaux

1*st* February [1837]

... For the present we are all in sad taking with Influenza. People speak about it more than they did about Cholera; I do not know whether they die more from it. Miss Wilson not having come to close quarters with it, has her mind sufficiently at leisure to make philosophical speculations about its gender! She primly promulgates her opinion that Influenza is masculine; my Husband, for the sake of argument, I presume (for I see not what other interest he has in it) protests that Influenza is feminine; for me who have been laid up with it for two weeks and upwards, making lamentations of Jeremiah (not without reason) I am not prejudiced either way, but content myself with sincerely wishing it were neuter. One great comfort, however

under all afflictions, is that *The French Revolution* is happily
concluded; at least it will be comfort when one is delivered
from the tag-ragery of printer's devils that at present drive one
from post to pillar. Quelle vie! Let no woman who values peace
of soul ever dream of marrying an Author!—that is to say if he
be an honest one, who makes a conscience of *doing* the thing
he pretends to do. But this I observe to you in confidence:
should I state such a sentiment openly, I might happen to get
myself torn in pieces, by the host of my Husband's lady-
admirers, who already I suspect, think me too happy in not
knowing my happiness. — You cannot fancy what way he is
making with the fair Intellectuals here! There is Harriet
Martineau presents him her ear-trumpet with a pretty blushing
air of coquetry which would almost convince one out of belief
in her indentity! And *Mrs* Pierce Butler [Fanny Kemble], bolts in
upon his studies (out of the atmosphere as it were) in riding-
habit cap and whip (but no shadow of a horse, only a
carriage—the whip, I suppose, being to whip the cushions with,
for the purpose of keeping her hand in practice). My
inexperienced Scotch Domestic remaining entirely in a nonplus
whether she had let in '*A Leddy or a gentleman*'! And then
there is a young American Beauty—such a Beauty! '*snow-and-
rose-bloom*' thro' out,—not as to clothes merely but complexion
also—large and soft, and without one idea, you would say, to rub
upon another! and this charming creature *publicly* declares
herself his '*ardent admirer*'; and I heard her with my own ears
call out quite passionately at parting with him 'Oh M*r* Carlyle I
want to see you—to talk a long long time about—*Sartor*'!!—
Sartor of all things in this world! what *could* such a young Lady
have got to say about Sartor, can you imagine? And M*rs* Marsh
the moving Authoress of the Old Man's tales reads *Sartor* when
she is ill in bed; from which one thing at least may be clearly
infered that her illness is not of the head. In short my dear
Friend; the singular Author of Sartor appears to me at this
moment to be rather in a perilous position; in as much as (with
the innocence of a sucking dove, to outward appearance) he is
leading honourable women not a few entirely off their feet—
And who can say that he will keep his own!— After all, in sober
earnest, is it not curious that my Husbands writings should be
only completely understood and adequately appreciated by
women and mad people? I do not know very well *what* to infer
from the fact—

Having got rather into the sphere of scandal, I may mention before leaving it that John Mill and Mrs Taylor get on as charmingly as ever. I saw them together very lately looking most exstatically '*Moony*' at one another, and sublimely superior to all the rest of the world! Mr Spedding is often to be heard of at Miss Wilson's—(not that I fancy anything amiss in that quarter)—only I mention him because he is your friend—for my part I cannot help feeling him to be exceedingly—sensible!— Mr Morris [F.D. Maurice] we rarely see—nor do I greatly regret his absence; for to tell you the truth, I am never in his company without being attacked with a sort of paroxysm of mental cramp! he keeps one always with his wire-drawings and paradoxes as if one were dancing on the points of one's toes (spiritually speaking)— And then he *will* help the kettle and never fails to pour it all over the milk pot and sugar bason!—

Henry Taylor draws off into the upper regions of Gigmanity—the rest I think are all as you left them.

Your Mother was here last night looking young and beautiful, with a new bonnet from Howel and James's— Your brother is a great favorite with Carlyle—and with me also—only one dare not fly into his arms as one does into yours—

Will you give my affectionate regards to your wife, and a kiss for me to each of the children— Ask your wife to write a postscript in your next letter, I deserve some such sign of recollection from her, in return for all the kind thoughts I cherish of her— I wish to heaven you were all back again—you make a terrible chasm in our world which does not look as if it were ever going to get closed in— You will write to me? You will be good enough to write to me in spite of all?— There is *nothing* that I do not fancy you good enough for; so I shall confidently expect a letter— God bless you and all that belongs to you— I am—ever affectionately yours / Jane W Carlyle

JOHN WELSH   NLS 601.42
Maryland St, Liverpool

5 Cheyne Row 4*th* March [1837]

Dearest Uncle of me

. . . But with respect to this influenza Uncle, what think you of it? above all HOW is it, and WHY is it? For my part with all my cleverness I cannot make it out. Sometimes I am half persuaded that there is (in cokney dialect) '*a DO at the bottom on it*'; medical men all over the world having merely entered into a tacit agreement to call all sorts of maladies people are liable to, in cold weather, by one name, so that one sort of treatment may serve for all, and their practice be thereby greatly simplified. In more candid moments, however, I cannot help thinking that it has something to do with the '*diffusion of useful knowledge*':—if not a part of that knowledge, at least that it is meant as a counterpoise, so that our minds may be preserved in some equilibrium; between the consciousness of our enormous acquirements on the one hand, and on the other the *generally diffused* experience, that all the acquirements in the world are not worth a rush to one compared with the blessedness of having a head clear of snifters! However it be; I am thankful to Heaven, that I was the chosen victim in this house, instead of my Husband. For had he been laid up at present, there would have been the very devil to pay. He has TWO Printers on his book that it may if possible be got published in April; and it will hardly be well off his hands when he is to deliver a course of lectures on German Literature to 'Lords and Gentlemen' and 'honourable women not a few.' You wonder how he is to get thro' such a thing; so do I—very sincerely, the more, as he purposes to speak these lectures extempore, Heaven bless the mark! having indeed no leisure to prepare them, before the time at which they will be wanted. One of his Lady-admirers (by the way he is getting a vast number of Lady admirers) was saying the other day that the grand danger to be feared for him was, that he should commence with '*Gentlemen and Ladies*' instead of '*Ladies and Gentlemen*,' a transmutation which would ruin him at the very outset. He vows however that he will say neither the one thing nor the other; and I believe him very secure on that side. Indeed I should as soon look to see gold pieces or penny loaves drop out of his mouth, as to hear from it any such hum-drum unrepublican-like commonplace. If he finds it necessary to address his audience by any particular designation it will be thus '*Men and Women*'! Or perhaps in my Penfillan Grandfather's style '*Fool-creatures come here for diversion.*' On the whole if his hearers be reasonable, and are content that there be good sense in the things he says without requiring that he should furnish them with brains to find it out; I have no doubt but his success will be emminent. The exhibition is to take place in *Willis's Rooms*: 'to begin at three and end at four

precisely' and to be continued every Monday and Friday thro'
the first three weeks of May—*'begin precisely,'* it may; with
proper precaution on my part, to put all the clocks and
watches in the house half an hour before the time; but as to
the *'ending precisely'*!—*that* is all to be tried for! There are
several things in this world which once set a-going, it is not
easy to stop; and *the Book* is one of them. I have been thinking
that perhaps the readiest way of—bringing him to a *cetera
desunt* [the rest is missing]—(*conclusion* is out of the
question) would be just as the clock strikes four to have a
lighted cigar laid on the table before him—we shall see! The
French Revolution done, and the Lectures done; he is going
somewhere (to Scotland most probably) to rest himself a
while—to lie about the roots of hedges and speak to no man,
woman, or child, except in monosyllables! a reasonable project
enough considering the worry he has been kept in for almost
three years back. For my part having neither published nor
lectured, I feel no call to refresh myself by such temporary
descent from my orbit under the waves, and in Shakespearean
dialect, I had such a *'bellyful'* of travelling last year as is likely
to quell my appetite in that way for some time to come. If *I*
had been consulted in the getting up of *the Litany*, there
would have been particular mention made of steamboats
mailcoaches and heavy-coaches among those things from
which we pray to be delivered; and more emphatic mention
made of 'such as travel by land or sea.' . . . God bless you all my
dearest Uncle—Yours Jane W Carlyle—

*In August Thomas left on holiday for his mother's home at Scotsbrig
while Jane set out for Oxford with the elder Sterlings. At the Bodleian
Library, with her usual spirit, she asked about Cromwell, whose name
was ill-received in the old centre of the Royalist cause and at a time of
Anglo-Catholic fervour. Perhaps favoured by Edward Sterling, the
formerly liberal Thackeray wrote a review of* **The French Revolution**
as his first contribution for **The Times***.*

TC
Scotsbrig

CL 9:271–5

[3 Aug. 1837]

. . .Apropos of the *French Revolution*; I have read Thackery's article
in proof—and as Tommy Burns said of Eliza Stodart's leg—'it's nae
great tings'! so small a *ting* indeed that *one* barrel of the Inevitable-

Gun may be decidedly said to have missed fire— He cannot boast of having, in any good sense,'*served Thackery*' however he may have '*served Carlyle*.'When you consider that this is Thackery's *coup d'essai*, in his new part of political renegade, you will however make some allowance for the strange mixture of bluster and platitude which you will find in his two Columns, and rather pity the poor white man, wishing with Mrs Sterling so often as his name comes up that 'he would but stick to his sketchings.'

One fact worth knowing one learns from this source viz: that *the Metropolis* is entirely occupied with our work—a rather hopeful sign of the Metropolis in these wishy-washy times— don't you think it is?—but I will send the paper when it is published— Cavaignac, contrary to your prediction, has written you an immense [?] long letter which he sent last week to go by *Madame ma mere*, that so it might *couter you rien* along with it was a note to me, requesting or rather, *kurt und gut* [short and to the point], *requiring* that I should *order* your bookseller to send a copy of your book to Marast in such a street of such a square who 'proposed reviewing it in *the National*'. Now I was quite at a loss to know whether you would consider *a Review in the National (still only proposed)* worth TWO copies of the book, one as I understood having been sent by Fraser already for that purpose—I rather thought not—but as you were not there to tell me, I did what seemed best to myself. I made Mr Darwin drive me up to Frasers where I stated the case in all plainness to the *versifier of Teufelsdreck*, desiring simply that Mr Fraser would use his own discretion in the matter, as he could judge better than I 'whether it was or was not compromising the dignity of the book to give away another copy of it for the sake of even a *clever* notice in the National.' *Our* Poet Laureat seemed tickled with this putting of the question. What they decided on I have had no opportunity of hearing.

 . . . I will write again whenever I am settled *any where* that you may know how to address me. If I cannot get *two* franks tomorrow I must keep Cavaignac's letter till another opportunity—it is [very] *clever and long* but of no moment otherwise. God for ever bless you my dear Husband—I wish you were with me again—kindest [love] to all and devout imaginations of kisses—to the children / your Jane

*

Bliss, *JWC* 67-72

Folley Arms, / Great Malvern
Worcestershire. / Friday, August 11th / 1837.

... *The Angel* Inn, where we staid at Oxford, gave me a rather
unpleasant impression of the *tone* of that place (for travellers
always get very decided and of course infallible impressions of
places from the Inns where they eat or sleep)—not that the
bread butter et cetera was not first rate, and the silver forks in
'good' style: what disgusted me was to observe in every bed
room, *laid before the looking glass, a bible* and *book of
prayers* with a small hassock underneath (and this preparation I
was told was universal thro' all the Inns at Oxford) *my*
particular hassock (of green cloth) had a drawing printed on it,
which I was at pains to examine—it represented a sportsman
(for consistency's sake let us hope *a parson*) in the midst of a
stubble field taking aim at three birds which he could not fail to
hit, the tips of their wings being touching the muzzle of his gun!
Moreover the Waiters, all large elderly men, had a sort of 'mazed
abstractedness and sad gravity of look which gave one a notion
they must have some time or other been unsuccessful
graduates: while the maids *my-ladied* us at such a rate, and
made their reverences so profoundly that the free Breton-blood
rushed to my face in very shame for them— From all which I
inferred that Oxford was a place much under the domination of
Cant—Cant in its two most killing shapes, of *Religion* that *keeps
its hassock* and *Respectability* that *keeps its gig.*
     The Colleges however, which we saw the best part of
during Tuesday forenoon under the guidance of Jacobson,
interested me beyond measure—not only as being a splendid
memorial of past ages but as shaping for me into actual stone
and mortar, and painted glass, and illuminated manuscripts and
square-capp'd blackgowned figures et cetera, the vague
notions I had gathered in my girlhood, out of novels and
histories, of a Great English University.— But nothing of all
that I saw gave me so lively an emotion of pleasure as—a very
small thing indeed—neither more nor less than *Guy Fox's
Lantern* preserved under a glass case! and what gave Mr.
Sterling the liveliest emotion of *dis*pleasure, was a question I
addressed, with no ill intention but in pure unsophisticated
curiosity, to the gentleman who showed us the Bodleian
Picture Gallery, viz: 'how came it that I saw no picture of

Oliver Cromwell there, seeing that they had raked together so
many insignificant persons of his time?' A broad stare was all
the answer I received to this natural enquiry, from which the
gentleman's features did not relax so long as I remained in his
company. I hope he is now more at ease. There were also many
gloriously illuminated manuscripts shown me, which I could
have spent much more time in looking at than Mr. Sterling
would allow—especially a Plato and Tacitus—and a greek
testament bound in solid silver having a carved ivory Monk in
relief on one side and on the other a Greek inscription
purporting 'the Maker thereof particularly wished God would
bless himself and his family.'— And there was Queen
Elizabeth's Latin exercise-book (putting me very much in mind
of my own) along side of Tippo Saib's gold-lettered *Koran*! But
I should need more sheets than one to enumerate all the
curiosities and niceties I saw.

With all its magnificence it seems to me that the Bodleian
Library must be a most perverse place to study in; for this
reason above all, that the numerous private libraries left to it
in donation, of which it is chiefly composed, are and *must* be
kept *apart* and *entire*; so that instead of *one* great Library
arranged under general heads, you have as it were a great many
little libraries arranged under one general roof. They told me
the inconvenience of this was obviated by the perfection of
the *catalogues* to which I can only say the perfection of the
catalogues must be much beyond the perfection of the
Librarians....

I have stood the travelling better than I expected
hitherto—going at ones own time in ones own carriage with
an officious Stephen to look after ones odds and ends, and
officious Landlords to serve up tender roast chickens and
'exquisite sherry' is a very different sort of thing from dashing
over the country in disarray, in doubt and destitution at the
blast of a mail coach horn— But I *must* stop. God bless you my
beloved. Write instantly on receipt of this—to my present
Address—and tell me if you think of coming back—I do not
want to hurry you—but—it is so long that we have not seen
each other—at least to me it seems long— Love to all— Again
God bless my—Genius—Jane Carlyle....

*

NLS 601.[43]

[29 Aug. 1837]

Dearest Love

...I now perceive the use my company is of to them both [the Sterlings], better then I did when we set out—I furnish, as it were, the sugar and ginger which makes the alkali of the one and the tartaric acid of the other effervesce into a somewhat more agreeable draught for 'the *effervescing* of these people'!— To say the least '*it is very absurd*'! But I shall keep all my stock of *biographic notices* to enliven our winter evenings. Meanwhile you are to know that we left Malvern for Clifton a week ago, all of us with very dry eyes. Mr S on finding that certain Lords who smiled decietful at the Carlton Club, were absolutely inaccessible at the Foley Arms, suddenly discovered that '*your beautiful scenery was a great humbug, as you had only to strip the soil a foot deep and it would be a vile black mass.*' Mrs Sterling in her querulous qualifying about it and about it way—doubted whether it was 'wholesome to overlook such a flat' 'not but what it was very well to have seen it *for once*—or if there was *any necessity* for living there—of course one would not object but &c &c'—and for me—poverina [poor little thing]—from the first moment I set my eyes on the place, I foresaw that it would prove a failure—that it would neither make me a convert to *nature*, nor find me in a new nervous system—every day of our stay there I arose with a headache— and my nights were unspeakable; every day I felt more emphatically that *nature* was an intolerable bore— Do not misconstrue me—genuine unsophisticated nature I grant you is all very amiable and harmless—but beautiful nature which Man has *exploited* as a Reviewer does a work of genius—making it a peg to hang his own conceits upon, to enact his *Triomphe der Empfindsamkeit* [triumph of sensibility] in—beautiful nature which you look out upon from pea-green arbours—which you dawdle about in on the backs of donkies—and where you are haunted with an everlasting smell of roast meat—all that I do declare to be the greatest of bores—and I would rather spend my days amidst downright acknowledged brick houses and paved streets than any such fool's paradises. So entirely *unheimlich* [dismal] I felt myself that the day I got your letter I cried over it for two or three hours. In other more favourable circumstances I should have recognised the tone of sadness that

ran all thro' it, as the simple effect of a tiresome Journey and a
doze of physic at the end, but read at Malvern with headach and
sleeplessness and ennui for interpreters!— Alas what could I do
but fling myself on my bed and cry myself sick. I said to myself
you were no better than when you left me and all this absence
was gone for nothing. I wanted to kiss you into something like
cheerfulness and the length of a kingdom was betwixt us—and
if it had not—the probabilities are that *with the best intentions*
I should have quarrelled with you rather. Poor men and women!
what a time they have in this world—by destiny and their own
deserving— But as M*r* Bradfute used to say 'tell us something
we do not know.' Well then it is an absolute fact that his
Whirlwindship and I road to the top of Malvern hill, each on a
live donky! Just figure it! With a Welch lad whipping us up from
behind; for they were the slowest of donkies tho' named in
defiance of all probability *Fly* and *Lively*. 'The Devil confound
your donkies,' exclaimed my vicacious companion (who might
really I think '*but for the honour of the thing*,' and perhaps
some small diminution of the danger of bursting his lungs, have
as well walked) 'they are so stupidly stubborn that you might as
well beat on a stick'! 'And isn't it a good thing they be stubborn
Sir' said the lad 'as being, ye see, that they have no sense. if they
warnt 'stubborn' they might be for taking down the steep and
we wants no accidents Sir.' 'Now' said I, 'for the first time in my
life I perceive why Conservatives are so stupidly stubborn;
stubbornness, it seems, is a succedaneum for *sense*.' A flash of
indignation—then in a soft tone 'Do you know Mrs Carlyle you
would be a vast deal more amiable if you were not so *damnably*
clever'! This a fair specimen of our talk at Malvern from dewy
morn to balmy eve. . . .

*A new maid from Kirkcaldy, Helen Mitchell, who came at Christmas
was to be a great source of drama for Jane for the next ten years. New
lectures on European literature eased the financial situation, not
much improved by* **The French Revolution**, *'and brought in . . .
perhaps £200, for a month's labour'* (**Reminiscences** 97). *At the end of
the summer of 1838, Thomas was off to Scotland while Jane stayed at
home, where Leigh Hunt introduced her to a set mainly of Unitarians.
Preferring her own brand of scepticism, Jane was privately sarcastic
about them and uneasy about meeting Dr Southwood Smith,
Bentham's disciple whom she was horrified to remember as lecturing
publicly over his friend's corpse, and perhaps for discreetly living with*

the portrait painter Margaret Gillies. Thomas's renown—Jane followed custom in referring to him just as 'Carlyle'—brought him invitations to aristocratic circles, including those of William Baring (Lord Ashburton from 1840) and his wife Lady Harriet, the Earl of Sandwich's eldest daughter.

Jane gave a soirée herself which led to a tiff with her mother for spending too much on cakes and expensive wax candles (21 Feb. 1839); and the candles were put aside not to be lit till the night of her death in April 1866. More happily, she wrote to her mother about a dinner she gave for two French political rivals, Alexis François Rio and Louis Chassaignac de Latrade, at which they were joined by Mrs Macready, the wife of their friend the actor-manager, William. Rio was surprised to find himself in such radical company, but was attracted by Carlyle's geniality and idealism. On his next visit Jane uncharacteristically gave him 'charming details of their six years of solitude in Dumfriesshire ... immediately after their marriage' (CL 11:69). The lectures for 1839 were 'On the Revolutions of Modern Europe'.

TC
Scotsbrig

NLS 601.51

[18 Sept. 1838]

My *sweet* Love

...I had a very surprising *treat* the other evening— Leigh Hunt wrote me a gracious little note inviting me to come and hear his play read—and '*stand by him with some new friends'*— The said new friends turning out to be of the Taylor set Margaret Gillies' and her Sister &c &c— One man was introduced to me very particularly—but Baron Alsdorf being blethering [chattering] about his letter to you at the moment I missed the name— The introduction seemed going to turn out much like Cavaignac's and Mrs Grote's till towards the close of the business that the man and I suddenly found ourselves in the middle of the room together, apparently selected by destiny to represent the two extremes of human opinion on the question of whether *Conventionality* was or was not the strongest thing in this world— I spoke with that faith in human nature and in the force of truth which thank God I have never lost and which my observations in the *Lecture time* gave new vigour to—and the man spoke it seemed to me with a poor rascally disbelief in all that, made rabid by the fact that himself had never been believed in by any man or body of men— It

was one of the curiousest *shines* [parties] that I ever played a
part in—and I cannot imagine yet where I got the courage to
stand and debate there long and loud among so many people,
with an elderly gentleman in breeches and evidently (in his
own estimation and Miss Margaret Gillies, at least) a man of
mark— 'Dr' —said somebody— D*r* what I asked little Lawrence
who stood by me—'don't you know him? D*r* Southwood
Smith'—My dear never do you get acquainted with Dr
Southwood Smith if you can help it—he is a bad man or I am
no physiognomist— As for the play it is plain as a pike staff
why Macready would not play it—it is something far worse
than '*immoral*' —'*anticonventional*' —it is mortal dull—a
beautiful insipidity reigns thro'out—and for the regenerating
truths it is calculated to teach the conventional heart—they
would need to be *shot at it* (as we do our truths) from the
mouth of a cannon, not timourosly *pleadingly tendered* to it
before it were fair to expect that they should take the least
effect— ....

I heard of two reviews of your poor beast [*Sartor*] one of
which I send....The other is to the same flaming tune—in the
Monthly— There *have* also been various newspaper criticisms.
say what you will—

And so God bless you Dear and put home-tendencies into
your head and feet— My love to all—even the most minute
child— Write as soon as possible / Your povera piccola
[poor little one] / Jane W Carlyle

*Mrs Welsh had been to stay in February 1839, when she enjoyed her
visit, and went on to Liverpool, where her brother John was unwell. Jane
wrote to entertain them.*

GRACE WELSH   *NLM* 1:72-8
Maryland St, Liverpool
                                        Chelsea, Sunday, 7 April, 1839

Dearest Mother—It is a week past on Thursday since you went
away, and really that one week looks longer than all the time
you were here. Parting is one of the few hardships in the
world which one does *not* 'use to'; indeed the last time seems
always the worst. It was quite heart-breaking leaving you in
that tremendous apparatus [the Liverpool train], given up as it
were to an irresistible destiny; to be shot away from one like

an arrow into space! I cried all the way home; and then sat down so *dowie* [sad] by the fire, indisposed to speak to any son or daughter of Adam. But Helen was determined I should not despond for lack of a little of her Job's comfort; so she broke the silence by an announcement that we were 'out of baith dips and moulds' [candles]. . . . Then as if on purpose to keep alive my regrets, ever so many things have turned up, since you went, that I should have liked you to have been present at. The very next evening came the French Catholic Rio, that Carlyle had described to us as such a striking man. He pleased me much, tho' resembling the description in no one particular except the duskiness of his complexion. I had fancied him a stern, bigoted enthusiast, whereas he is a sort of French John Sterling; if possible even more voluble and transparent; and his Catholicism sits on him just about as lightly as John's Church-of-Englandism sits on him. I happened to ask him if he knew Cavaignac; 'Ah, who does *not* know Cavaignac by name? But *I*, you know, am a victim of *his* party, as *he* is a victim of Louis Philippe. Does Cavaignac come here?' 'Yes, we have known him long.' 'Good gracious! How strange it would be for us to meet in the same room! How I should like it!' 'Well,' I said, 'he is to dine here on Monday.' 'I will come; good gracious, it will be so strange': and he seemed amazingly charmed with his prospect. Not so Carlyle, who began, before he was well out at the door, 'Mercy Jane, are you distracted?' 'What *can* you do with these two men?' etc., etc. I assured him it would go off without bloodshed, and began to think of my *dinner*. In addition to the boiled leg of mutton already projected for the sake of the capers, I decided on a beefsteak pie; and, that care off my mind, I trusted in Providence that the men would not come to an explosion.

The dinner, however, could hardly be called a 'successful one.' Rio appeared on the scene at half-past three, as if he could not have enough of it. Latrade came as the clock struck four. But Cavaignac— Alas! Two of his friends were on terms about blowing each other's brains out, and Cavaignac was gone to bring them to reason; and not till they were brought to reason would he arrive to eat his dinner. Now, whether the men would be brought to reason before the dinner was quite spoiled, was a delicate question that Latrade himself could not answer. So, one half hour being gone, and still no appearance of him, I was on the point of suggesting that we should wait no longer, when a carriage drove up and deposited Mrs. Macready and Macready's Sister. Was ever beefsteak pie in such a cruel predicament! There was no help, however, but to do the amiable, which was not ill to do even in these trying circumstances, the visitors were such attractive sort of people. ...An hour and half after the dinner had been all ready we proceeded to eat it,—Rio, Latrade, and we. And when it was just going off the table cold, Cavaignac came, his hands full of papers and his head full of the Devil knows what; but not one reasonable word would he speak the whole night. Rio said nothing to his dispraise, but I am sure he thought in his own mind, 'Good Gracious! I had better never be in the same room with him again!'

But there has been another Frenchman here that I would have given a gold guinea that you had seen: To-day gone a week the sound of a whirlwind rushed thro' the street, and there stopt with a prancing of steeds and footman thunder at this door, an equipage, all resplendent with skye-blue and silver, discoverable thro' the blinds, like a piece of the Coronation Procession, from whence emanated Count d'Orsay! ushered in by the small Chorley. Chorley looked 'so much alarmed that he was quite alarming'; his face was all the colours of the rainbow, the under-jaw of him went zig-zag; indeed, from head to foot he was all over one universal quaver, partly, I suppose, from the soul-bewildering honour of having been borne hither in that chariot of the sun; partly from apprehension of the effect which his man of Genius and his man of Fashion were about to produce on one another. Happily it was not one of my nervous days, so that I could contemplate the whole thing from my *prie-Dieu* without being infected by his agitation, and a sight it was to make one think the millenium actually at hand, when the lion and the lamb, and all incompatible things should consort together. Carlyle in his grey plaid suit, and his tub-chair, looking blandly at the Prince of Dandies; and the Prince of Dandies on an opposite chair, all resplendent as a diamond-beetle, looking blandly at *him*. D'Orsay is a really handsome man, after one has heard him speak and found that he has both wit and sense; but at first sight his beauty is of that rather disgusting sort which seems to be like genius, 'of no sex.' And this impression is greatly helped by the fantastical finery of his dress: sky-blue satin cravat, yards of gold chain, white French gloves, light

drab great-coat lined with velvet of the same colour, invisible
inexpressibles, skin-coloured and fitting like a glove, etc., etc.
All this, as John says, is *very* absurd'; but his manners are
manly and unaffected and he convinces one, shortly, that in the
face of all probability he is a devilish clever fellow. Looking at
Shelley's bust, he said 'I dislike it very much; there is a sort of
faces *who* seem to wish to swallow their chins and this is one
of them.' He went to Macready after the first performance of
Richelieu, and Macready asked him, 'What would you suggest?'
'A little more fulness in your petticoat!' answered d'Orsay.
Could contempt for the piece have been more politely
expressed? He was no sooner gone than Helen burst into the
room to condole with me that Mrs. Welsh had not seen him—
such a '*most* beautiful man and most beautiful carriage! The
Queen's was no show i' the worl' compared wi' that!
Everything was so grand and so preceese! But it will be
something for next time.' . . . Carlyle sends his kind love. He has
been saying up to last night, 'One misses her much.' God bless
you. / Your affectionate / JANE CARLYLE

*Carlyle's new lecture series on revolutions began 1 May. Jane was
prompt to report his success.*

Private MS
Friday— [3 May 1839]

Dearest Mother
     By an oversight of Helens my letter did not go off till after
lecture, as you would see by the writing round the
seal, which I wrote from our *green room*—on rejoining the
Matyr-Performer and finding him alive and whole— Indeed he
got thro much more smoothly than on any former first
appearance, not to *his own* satisfaction of course—but I think
he was the only dissatisfied person present. The audience was
as usual very *distinguished*, even to the blocking up of the
whole of Edward Street with equipages— All our last years
beauties reappered in their old seats and the thing had taken
altogether more the air of a regular church-congregation than
of an accidental play-house-gathering— In point of number also
there was no falling off—a thing to be considered still more
than the *distinction*— A Cangaroo's money being notoriously
as good as a lord Duke's—

On the whole we have reason to 'thank heaven and write
to our friends' as heretofore— I would not have written to *you*
however till the thing had advanced a little further, and above
[all] till the aching in my head (which has hardly intermitted
thro' the week) had left me to the full play of my charming
faculties....I ... forgot when you were here—that if my cousins
have any such *good* old clothes to give away, as used to be sent
to Templand they would be a godsend to [Leigh] Hunts little
girls who to judge from appearances, seem to be clothed by the
ravens, more than in any regular way— And now Dearest this is
all I am going to write to you today—for I am not in writing
trim I hope to hear presently that my Uncle is doing well— ...
Do not be uneasy about me—there is a natural Cause for my
fecklessness this week besides the worry on my nerves—
Carlyle is Adamizing in the garden— His love is with you
always— Your affectionate Jane

MARGARET CARLYLE   NLS 601.54
Scotsbrig
                                                       [5 May 1839]

My dear Mother
     Our second lecture '*transpired*' yesterday, and with
surprising success—literally surprising—for he was imputing
the profound attention with which the audience listened, to an
awful sympathizing expectation on their part of his momentary,
complete break-down, when all at once they broke out into
loud plaudits, and he thought they must all have gone clean out
of their wits!— But, as does not happen always, the majority
were in this instance in the right, and it was *he* that was out of
his wits to fancy himself making a stupid lecture, when the fact
is, he really *cannot* be stupid if it were to save his life— ...The
most practical good feature in the business, was a considerable
increase of hearers—even since last day—the audience seems to
me much larger than last year, and even more distinguished—
The whole street was blocked up with 'fine yellow (and all
other imaginable coloured) deliveries'—and this is more than
merely a dangerous flattery to one's vanity—the fashionable
people here being (unlike our Scotch *gigmen* and *gigwomen*)
the most open to light (above all to *his* light) of any sorts of
people one has to do with— Even John Knox, tho' they must
have been very angry at him for demolishing so much beautiful

architecture, which is quite a passion with the English, they were quite willing to let good be said of, so that it was indisputably true—nay it was in reference to Knox that they first applauded yesterday— Perhaps his being a Countryman of their favorite Lecturer's might have something to do with it!— but we will hope better things tho we thus speak—

You will find nothing about *us* in the Examiner of this week— Leigh Hunt who writes the notices there did not arrive at the first Lecture in time to make any report of it— having come in an Omnibus which took it in its head to run a race with another Omnibus after a rather novel fashion, that is to say, each trying which should be *hindmost*. We go to Lecture this year very commodiously in what is called a *Fly* (a little chaise with one horse) furnished us from a Livery stable hard by at a very moderate rate— Yesterday the Woman who keeps these stables sent us a *flunky* more than bargain, in consideration that I was 'such a very nice Lady'—showing therein a spirit above slavery and even above *Livery*— Indeed as a foolish old woman at Dumfries used to say 'every body is kind to *me*' and I take their kindness and am grateful for it without inquiring too closely into their motives— Perhaps I am a genius too as well as my Husband—indeed I really begin to think so—especially since yesterday that I *wrote down* a parrot! which was driving us quite desperate with its screaching. Some new neighbours that came a month or two ago brought with them an accumulation of all the things to be guarded against in a London neighbourhood—viz a pianoforte, a lap-dog and a Parrot—the two first can be born with as they carry on the glory within doors but the Parrot since the fine weather has been holding forth in the Garden under our open windows— Yesterday it was more than usually obstreperous— so that Carlyle at last fairly sprang to his feet declaring he could 'neither think nor live'— Now it was absolutely necessary that he should do both—so, forthwith, on the inspiration of conjugal sympathy I wrote a note to the Parrot's mistress (name unknown) and in five minutes after Pretty Polly was carried within and is now screeching from some subterranean depth whence she is hardly audible. . . . affectionately yours / Jane Carlyle

The lectures had ended. Mrs Welsh had been ill in Liverpool.

GRACE WELSH   Private MS
Maryland St, Liverpool
                                    Wednesday morning [22 May 1839]

My dearest Mother
    These letters which I have been receiving from Liverpool
of late weeks, I may say of late months, are the most
disappointing, alarming sort of things I ever had to do within
the way of correspondence— When I open one of them and
see the extraordinary proportion of *white* paper contained in
it, and the air of breathless haste there is; over what writing
there is my heart takes to beating in a way that makes me
unwell for the rest of the day— I make such a point of always
filling my own letters, unless in cases of direst necessity, that I
am apt to suppose it must be direst necessity that hinders you
or any one who loves me from doing the same by myself— I
do not find fault with Margaret's letter . . . but I *would* like dear
Mother to get a leisurely letter from yourself once more in this
world— I do hardly expect it however now, until you are back
at Templand where I wish you were, since you are not with
me, and are not well— Let people be ever so kind to one it is
always miserable to be ill *from home*— Your illness did not
surprise me, I rather wondered it had kept off so long but it
did not disquiet me the less on that account. . . .
    . . . Carlyle dined with Count d'Orsay the other day at
Gore House . . . . From the specimens Carlyle gives me of his
wit and manners *at home*, I am sure he must be a fine fellow—
he pours Claret into a tumbler and holds the decanter in one
hand while he drinks the tumbler empty—and talking of his
repugnance to *emetics* he said 'if *he* should take one: he was
sure he would *bring his feet out at his mouth*'— When
D'Orsay talks of Carlyle in public he calls him 'his Cher
Carlyle' to the great amusement of those who know them
both— 'Mi Ladi' [Lady Blessington], C thought no great
things—ill off for eye brows—beautifully washed and combed
but fundamentally vulgar looking—full of good-nature and
Irish fun—an 'elderly Wild Irish Girl' in fact—but could at no
age have been a fascinating woman for *him*— Walter Savage
Landor was staying with them, and came here for two hours
one morning . . . so emphatic and exaggerative and voluble—
that one feels as if his talk would drown one before
long—when he means to say that such a one is dullish he calls

him 'a stupid beast'—and such another who is rather amiable is 'something between Man and the Deity'— Now that I have seen him I quite understand his placing Milnes's Poems above Paradise lost—

...Carlyle still talks of going to America to make a fortune in Autumn but I hope he will stay at home and begin a book. ...

My head is very bad or I should have done better

In August Jane was glad to visit her mother. At home she then went through a difficult winter, wracked with colds, flu and headaches, but kept up her good humour and her range of friends. Among them was the handsome Italian revolutionary, Mazzini, introduced by Mill, whom Jane saw as a modern St Preux. He told his mother that Jane was 'an exceptional woman ... with qualities of mind and heart' (CL 12:82). Jane was also friendly with the entertaining John Forster, Dickens's future biographer. Geraldine Jewsbury wrote to Carlyle from Manchester in April 1840 about his religious views, and at first he was more receptive to her than Jane was, who disliked her cigar-smoking, feminism and apparent obsession with finding a man. Yet Geraldine's sincere friendship soon appealed to them both.

HELEN WELSH   Huxley, *JWCLF* 2
Maryland St, Liverpool

5 Cheyne Row / Sunday [22 Sept., 1839]

...After the first of January, when the penny-post bill comes into action, I shall surely send 'Sibilline leaves' all over the world, and you shall get your share of them. But in the meanwhile (our members being all serving their country in the moors a-shooting of innocent grouse) it is a questionable kindness to take fourteen pence out of your purse for any good I can do you by writing. For the consolation of my own conscience, however, I must articulate my thanks for your irish collar—must give some explanation of our crow's-flight southward—must assure you that my cousinly feelings towards you have by no means been steeped out of me by my wet sojourn in Scotland, but have been preserved quite snug in a warm corner of my heart to bloom luxuriantly, I trust to the end of time—that is to say—of *my* time. There was in the Liverpool letters, which came while I was at Templand, indications of a beautiful delusion in the cousinly mind on the subject of my '*improvement*'—tho' in what, if not in the virtue

of patience, I was at a loss to conceive. For my looking-glass
assured me that I was growing thinner and yellower every
day—and headaches, rheumatism, ennui and desperation were
my portion every day and all. How could it be otherwise—it
rained without ceasing, my occupation was gone, and there
was no human speech to be got out of Mundells Macveahs
[neighbours] and the like—but only inhuman clatter. I cannot
conceive how my mother manages to exist in that place, yet
she appears to find it quite satisfactory, nay to think it a sort of
fairyland where everybody *must* thrive, unless thro' own
perversity, and wilful resistance to its 'improving' influences.

When the time came for returning Southward all heart
for other visiting was entirely cut out of me. . . . So we made
our excuses like a couple of liver-hearted travellers, as it must
be admitted we are, and tempted by my Brother-in-law John's
experience who had just come down by the Preston Railroad
we renounced Liverpool also, and putting ourselves into a
coach at Carlyle Carlisle (is that it?), found ourselves in
London twenty hours after. At twelve on Tuesday we started
from Scotsbrig in our gig—at half after one on Wednesday we
were in London. This was losing no time. Our little maid had
arrived according to orders the night before, and opened the
door to us with a half glad 'half Magdeline' aspect. There was
nothing a-missing—but a pair of scissors had been put in.
Darwin, who had my sheets and silver spoons in keeping, was
out of town, which caused a serious destitution at first. But
we have got all back now except the sugar tongs and my
work box, and are restored to tolerable order. Helen goes on
well hitherto, and I only pray that she may not bethink her
some fine day that her *'resolution deserves a dram.'* Miss
Fergus has become 'La contessa Pepoli' two days before our
arrival, and is now domesticated with her angelic Conte
within a quarter of an hour's walk of me. They both look well
content; if the romance of the thing could but hold out! She
will be an acquisition to *me*, and I hope her bold step (not to
say rash) may be justified by a better future than onlookers
predict for her. Old Sterling who had been to see her, said to
me to-day 'Heavenly Father! what a wreck she is! She is fifty
by Jove!' But love has no arithmetic. Cavaignac says 'Voilà un
homme condamné à rendre sa femme heureuse! J'espère qu'il
se donnera cette justification!' I hope so too. Mr. Darwin says
'*Ah!*'—and perhaps that is the best that can be said of the

matter. London is very dead at this season—but one gets the more good of the people that *are* in it. . . . Ever, dear Helen, / Your affectionate cousin, / JANE CARLYLE. . . .

GRACE WELSH   Private MS
Templand, Thornhill

December 30th [1839]

My dear Mother
    The box is come—all safe and the manifold contents—
after due examination and lyrical recognition are deposited in
the proper places The gown on my body, Helen's shawl on her
shoulders and one of Carlyle's handkerchiefs in his pocket—
Thanks from all— We are all as we may well be exceedingly
pleased with our Christmas— The gown at first sight gave me
some qualms— The showiness of the pattern was not in my way
and how was it possible that a gown made at Thornhill could
satisfy *me* accustomed as I have been of late weeks to see
myself fitted like a doll by Madame Chardonnel—the paragon of
french dress-makers—but when I tried it on all apprehensions
as to the make were lost in admiration of your great genius in
getting people to work for an imaginary figure with such
exactness— A little '*confining' at the waist* (as they call it) was
the whole alteration it required to make it fit as well as if it had
come from Chardonnel herself. . . .
    Carlyle was greatly pleased with his handkerchiefs—being
(what with London pick-pockets and the great Universal pick-
pocket *Time*) nearly reduced to cobwebs in that department—
. . . By sending me the mittens you have lost a pair of the
same!—I saw them all the fashion here . . . and got a pair to
send along with a pair of the '*eternal'* ones— but when I saw
the same dangling so prettily at the end of my sleeves I
perceived I had narrowly escaped sending coals to Newcastle
My poor little parcel should have gone before the arrival of
yours for I have hardly the heart to send it now—besides I
wanted it to get to you on newyears day that it might have that
worth as an *omen* which it has not in itself— It will be on the
road tomorrow if there is faith in Fraser—and will reach you in
a week, I hope. I send the first two vols of C's Miscellany to
console you for your missing articles—the lost articles are not
however contained in these but in the third and fourth vols
which I have not to send—all that came from America having

been sold off instantly and the new edition not yet gone to press—but you will get them some time or other. Do read 'Chartism' till you *quite take it in*—and tell me if it is not capital sense....

Helen has *stood* the new year quite bravely hitherto— ... She is so good a servant otherwise and I with my weak health so very much need a good servant at present, and a good natured one to boot.

—The work is got all so out of its natural routine—and the days are so short—and the washing cannot be got dried out of doors—I sometimes think of abdicating the charge and wrapping myself in a blanket and going to bed once for all—but that would not be fulfilling my destiny (as the phrase is)—and it would be but a shabby sort of exit—'died under the pressure of moral difficulties' John Sterling is going to Maidera—Darwin looks as if he needed to go too—very pale and depressed indeed— The nice little sister in law has got a nice little son—

—I see few people.... My intellect is in a fine way—and my penmanship! ! but the worse I write the better you write so never mind— So God keep you— Ever your affectionate Jane Carlyle

Grace Welsh had an easier time in 1840.

MARGARET CARLYLE   NLS 601.63
Scotsbrig
                                                   [27 Oct. 1840]

...What do I do with my time you wonder? With such '*a right easy seat of it*' one might fancy I should be glad to write a letter now and then just to keep the devil from my elbow— But Alicks Jenny and all of you were never more mistaken than when you imagine a woman needs half a dozen squeeling children to keep her uneasy—she can manage to keep herself uneasy in a hundred ways without *that*. For my part I am always as busy as possible—on that side at least I hold out no encouragement to the Devil—and yet, suppose you were to look thro' a microscope—you might be puzzled to discover a trace of what I do—nevertheless depend upon my doings are not lost—but invisible to human eyes they 'sail down the stream of time into the ocean of eternity' and who knows but I may find them after many days.

At present I have got a rather heavy burden on my
shoulders. the guarding of a human being from the perdition of
strong liquors. My poor little Helen has been gradually getting
more and more into the habit of tippling—until some fortnight
ago she rushed down into a fit of the most decided drunkeness
that I ever happened to witness— Figure the *Head of the
Mystic School* and a delicate female like myself up till after three
in the morning, trying to get the maddened creature to bed, not
daring to leave her at large for fear she should set fire to the
house or cut her own throat— Finally we got her *bolted* into
the back kitchen in a corner of which she had established
herself all coiled up and *fuffing* [spitting like a cat] like a young
tiger about to make a spring—or like the *Bride of Lammermuir*
(if you ever read that profane book)—next day she looked black
with shame and despair and the day following, overcome by her
tears, and promises, and self-upbraidings I forgave her again very
much to my own surprise— About *half an hour* after this
forgiveness had been accorded I called to her to make me some
batter—it was long of coming—and I rung the bell—no answer.
I went down to the kitchen to see the meaning of all this
delay—and the meaning was very clear, my penitent was lying
on the floor dead drunk—spread out like the three legs of Man
[Isle of Man]—with a chair upset beside her and in the midst of
a perfect chaos of dirty dishes and fragments of broken
crockery—the whole scene was a lively epitome of a place that
shall be nameless— And this happened at ten in the morning!—
All that day she remained lying on the floor insensible—or
occasionally sitting up like a little bundle of dirt—executing a
sort of *whinner* [neighing]— We could not imagine how she
came to be so long of sobering—but it turned out she had a
whole bottle of whiskey hidden within reach, to which she
crawled *till it was finished* thro'out the day— After this, of
course I was *determined* that she should leave— My friends
here set to work with all zeal to find me a servant—and a very
promising young woman came to stay with me until a
permanent character should turn up— This last scene
'*transpired*' on the Wednesday on the Monday she was to sail for
Kirkaldy— All the intervening days—I held out against her pale
face, her tears, her despair—but I suffered terribly for I am really
much attached to the poor wretch who has no fault under
heaven but this one— On the Sunday night I called her up to
pay her her wages and to inquire into her future prospects—her

future prospects! it was enough to break any body's heart to hear how she talked of them— It was all over for her on this earth, plainly, if I drove her away from me who alone have any influence with her— Beside me she would struggle—away from me she saw no possibility of resisting what she had come to regard as her Fate— You may guess the sequel—I forgave her a third time—and a last time— I *could* not deny this *one* more chance—the creature is so good otherwise— Since then she has abstained from drink, I believe, in *every* shape—finding abstinence, like old Samuel Johnson, easier than temperance— but how long she may be strong enough to persevere in this rigid course, in which lies her only hope—God knows. I am not very sanguine—meanwhile I feel as if I had adopted a child— I find it necessary to take such an incessant charge of her—bodily and mentally—and my own body and soul generally keep me in work enough without any such additional responsibility.

Carlyle is reading voraciously great folios preparatory to writing a new book—for the rest he growls away much in the old style—but one gets to feel a certain indifference to his growling—if one did not, it would be the worse for one— I think he committed a great error in sending away his horse—it distinctly did him good—and would have done him much more good if he could have 'damned the expence'— Even in an economical point of view he would have gained more in the long run by increased ability to work than he spent in making himself healthier. . . . / affectionately yours / Jane W Carlyle

In 1841, desperate to get away from London, Thomas ineffectually arranged a summer break for them near Annan. They set out separately, but met and stayed at a desolate, flea-ridden cottage at Newby. In Dumfries they parted for the last time with Jane's mother 'unusually beautiful, but strangely sad too—eyes bright, but with many tears behind them. . . . We watched her, sorrowful both of us . . . stepping tall and graceful . . . casting no glance back . . . and she was gone for ever' (**Reminiscences** 121-2).

TC   *CL* 13:171-2
Scotsbrig
                                                         [6 July 1841]

. . . Cavaignac walked in very much to my astonishment on Friday evening—he had crossed (*he said*) that morning— He had an engagement with Leader [a radical MP] at eight and his cab waited for him—so I had not very much talk with him He regretted having so nearly missed you (naturally[)]—mumbled odd things about the book [*Heroes*] having reached him and *not* reached him! And that I must 'give him another copy and he would *write* something on it for the newspaper'— The old man in short, in every respect except that he looks older, more weather-beaten, and less distingué than when he lived in England— John Sterling is said to be coming up on Wednesday— What a pity you have missed them both—

Mazzini has written a long and eloquent article on you which he brought to me to be read the other day before offering it to Kemble 'as a guarantee he said' for its giving you no offence, for tho he had said the same things to you a hundred times in speech, you might think them less friendly in print— and if *I* said imprimatur he would feel secure on that head— The first part is the most glowing transcendant praise— Every good quality and every great faculty under Heaven are abundantly allowed but then he says 'our task becomes less pleasant' and he points out your grand want—a *vital* one vitiating all the good and beautiful rest—very want of the *sentiment collectif* and then away he goes full sail into *progres humanitarianism* and 'all that sort of thing'— I told him—that I was certain you would care 'the least in the world' for being publicly taxed with wanting the '*sentiment collectif* that you did not I was sure consider it a thing worth any ones while to have, so long as you were so praised for your *profundity* your *sincerity* your sympathy (of the *individu*) &c &c—and so the article was to be offered at least I hope they will print it for it is admirable *from his point of view*— By the way he remarks that Monsieur Carlyle in inculcating the necessity of *retenir la langue* means it only for those who do not hold *his* views—that the talent of *silence* in fact however much he may commend it is not *his*—that such a spirit cannot be compressed into silence, cannot *love* silence otherwise than '*platoniquement comme on peut dire*'—very good!—

There is another proof sheet lying here which I have revized myself—it needed hardly any correction, the spelling of one word and the effacing of a black shake. We are washing the paint of *your* room to day for want of being able to get on with any thing else— I have no paper you perceive There is a packet came from Fraser's for you but I am too honest to lay

hands on *it*— Oh such a headach I had the day after you
went—the regular old fainting sort—I attributed it to my *thrift*
in having taken your left butter-milk to my supper for I awoke
at three so ill and with such a horror not platonic but practical
of the idea of butter milk!—— God keep you till I come / Ever
yours to command / Jane C.

JOHN FORSTER   NLS 601.74
Lincoln's Inn Fields, London

[10 July 1841]

...You are dreaming perhaps that I am gone away without
sending the address—but no fear of that, or perhaps I should
say, no *hope* of it! The fact is I am still here, feeling more like a
Gohst that cannot get itself *laid* than anything else in prose or
verse! I begin to be ashamed of showing my face even to the
unknown persons who pass me by in the streets— I fancy
them all saying to themselves 'Christ Almighty! what is that
woman still doing above ground?' What indeed but waiting for
the crowing of the cock!—and no cock will crow! 'Did you
ever know anything in the least like it?' (as my good Mother
says).— He went according to the programme, and since his
arrival has written me three letters, each promising that the
next should contain 'some thing definite,' and the whole three
proceeding in a rapidly increasing ratio towards 'confusion
worse confounded'— Today's beats the world! If you only read
it you would not know whether to laugh or cry over it!—five
pages of infinitismal details about houses issuing like one of
our friend Oliver's parliamentary speeches in simple *zero*! 'And
now,' he says, 'comes the practical question what are YOU to do?'
God knows! unless I set about getting a divorce, and marry
again, some man with *common sense* instead of *Genius*!
    Perhaps—indeed positively—if he do not forbid—I will
cut the matter short at once, by putting myself and my maid on
the Railway next week and going straight to the Mother that
bore me—some thirty miles *beyond* that *Annan* of his—having
placed *her* [Helen Mitchell] in safe keeping, for she cannot be
trusted in her own—*you remember*!— I could then join this
much-agitated *Calebs in search of a house* and *make* him find
one, or else resign himself with a good grace to live in the open
air!— Will not this be my best course think you? 'He that
considers everything will never decide on anything' and *this*

man considers *everything* and some things more—

Meanwhile ... there is something *sunshiny* about you, that cheers my gloom,—for little as you may suspect it I am in a state of almost continual blue-devils— ... Ever affectionately yours / Jane Carlyle

GRACE WELSH   Private MS
Templand, Thornhill

[about mid-July 1841]

Dearest Mother

After waiting so long you may expect to be told something definite respecting our plans; but if you do, I can tell you you little know the pig you have got by the ear— *Our* plans! Lord bless you, we never have any, till within twenty four hours of doing the thing—and very often a thing that never entered into our plans! There is no gainsaying on *my* side at present— I think and feel with you of course that if we are to go anywhere for the summer the place that is nearest to *you* would be the most suitable.... In the meanwhile I am resolved not to worry myself any further....

Carlyle is dining today with the beautiful Mrs Stanley ... and you know the results for ME.... He is in a position now to do exactly as he likes in such matters without giving offence to any one—and still he accepts invitations declaring them to be fatal to him all the while— In short he does not manage his life at all well, and he will not let me manage it for him and this world is a perplexed sort of affair! God bless you dearest pray write immediately and tell me that you are stronger.

HELEN WELSH   Huxley, *JWCLF* 5-6
Maryland St, Liverpool

Monday [11*th* Oct. 1841]

... Happily when I do write I have no ill news to tell you. Since my return to London I have been gradually recovering from the nervous excitement occasioned by the winds and waves and '*industrious fleas*' and other unimaginable horrors of my husband's 'realised ideal' 'a cottage by the sea-shore!' It went hard with me at Newby—another month of it and I must have lost my wits or taken to drinking—or died of ennui and flea-bites—but my escape was effected just in time to spare the world the cruel shock of such untimely loss of one of its

brightest ornaments. And surely my husband will never tempt
Providence in so daring a manner again! Since we have been
here, the scales one would say, have fallen from his eyes, and he
has awaked to some sense of the quiet and comfort of No. 5
Cheyne Row in comparison with all the other places he has
tried and found wanting—'it must be confessed his bedroom
here *is* the very freest from noise he ever slept in'—and several
other things have been to be 'confessed,' which hitherto he has
most sceptically denied. . . . You cannot imagine what an
amelioration of my earthly lot it were to be delivered, tho' only
for *one* year, from his hitherto unceasing speculations about
'*flying* presently,' he knows not whither; but to some 'remote
region,' or 'solitary shore of the sea,' or even 'solitary island in
the sea'—where, the beauty of it is, in six months' time he
would be ready to cut his throat. With some people the
difficulty of realising their desires is small, compared with the
difficulty of ascertaining for themselves what their real desires
are. And my husband belongs to this perplexing and perplexed
section of humanity. . . .

*Jane's letters to her mother show that she was uneasy at leaving her
at Templand to face the winter. An old servant, Mary Mills, had left to
marry, and she was largely alone.*

GRACE WELSH   Private MS
Templand, Thornhill
                                              [end of Nov. 1841]

Dearest
        Thank you for putting me out of pain, so soon as you were
so yourself— I heartily congratulate you on being as the English
say, '*settled with a servant,*' and one that you like the *looks* of. .
. . I am persuaded that '*you will find a little* HEVEN (as Helen
wrote to me at Templand) after what you have been yoosed to'!
. . .
        I wish you would send to Edin*r* to *Duncan & Flockart* for
some milk of roses—there is really no 'white lead' in it—and
nothing of all the things I have tried is so very soothing for the
skin. . . . I will send you in this letter a little of my ointment— it
is perfectly innoxious. . . —even Carlyle anoints his chapped
lips with it now tho so sceptical of all medical appliances. . . .
Never touch your face with water—till you get the milk of

roses wipe it softly with violet powder of which I will also
send you a little in case you have none— Blessings on Rowland
Hills penny-postage!

I had a very bad turn last week—two nights and a day of
something horribly violent that kept me on the flat of my
back—we may call it british cholera at a venture— I believe the
fact was—I had been *poisoned*—with mephitick air— I had
been to a soirée at Sir Robert Inglis's, where the people were
standing as thick as cornstalks in a field—and no ventilation. . . .
But for the suffocation . . . I should have been well amused,
there was a nice party of ourselves went from the Wedgwoods
where we dined—Mr & Mrs Wedgwood—Mr and Mrs Henry
Wedgwood—Darwin and Mrs Charles Darwin—C and myself—
and I saw for the first time a great many of the eminent
Professional people who lie out of our usual beat—Dr
Chambers was there among the rest—a great coarse looking
elephant of a man whom I would not suffer to prescribe for a
pain in my little finger. . . .

Surely this is enough for one time— Do be *quiet*—and
write to me that your face is no longer made worse by
agitations / Your own / J W

*Mazzini added a postscript, describing Jane, 'though not as we wish
. . . not worse than she was when she came back from you to London'.
He would write if she grew worse, 'so that she can be scolded . . . from a
more powerful view than mine'. But Jane was able to keep sending
newsy letters, and in one reported that Thomas would not be applying
for a professorship at Edinburgh, that 'City of the Dead', and 'it is only
now when London and the world has discovered his talent that they
are fain to admit it'* (**CL** 13:324).

[19 Dec. 1841]

. . . I had a call from Mrs Montagu the other day, who made the
most gracious enquiries about you— She looks the very same as
ever only that her nose and mouth nearly meet—but every *pin*
and every snick was in the old place. . . .

I have had a good many volunteered visitors this week—
the Scotts of Woolich one day at dinner— Thackery and Darwin
one evening— Our Temperance cousin Dunlop, Wull's brother,
another evening— Craik '*promiscuously*' another evening—and
next week I am to have 'a coachful' of Wedgwoods on Tuesday—

and *Mrs* Jameson with a stranger Lady—and the young poet
Browning the end of the week— Enough of company tho' I
cannot go out

You may tell Mr Ramage the Queen is to be god-Mother to
Mrs J Marshalls bambino— We were invited to dine at the
Monteagles last week but *tossed up a halfpenny* for it!! and
tails being NO, and the thing turned up, we sent an apology! ...

How lazy these Liverpool Angels are! all except little Mary.
...Do write immediately—it is so easily done if you will but
take out your pen in the idea of writing merely two lines—

I am deep in the laborious operation of *wadding* my
dressing gown for the winter; and here is the winter before I am
prepared!—*foolish virgin* that I always am!

God keep you in these cold cheerless days Ever your
affectionate / Jane Pen

*A letter from Thornhill addressed by her mother's doctor aroused
something like panic.*

Saturday [late Dec. 1841]

...I can assure you I had a horrible moment! it was all that I
could do to break the seal!—and then when I saw the long
well-written letter inside, in your own handwriting, I was
relieved indeed, but angry at the fright you had given me!
Perhaps however the preparatory fright made me take a better
view of your actual state than I should otherwise have done—
having expected to find you seriously ill—I was almost thankful
to find you only horridly uncomfortable!— Blockhead of a girl!
you will never be able to make anything of her— She has not
the make of a good servant— Out of doors, among animals, she
might plaister [muddle] on well enough ... but indoors, beside
you, she will feel herself always in a compulsory state ...
because it is your bidding....The best way of any were to lock
up the house as I said before— ...You must absolutely please
not to spend another winter in that place— The idea of it is
altogether intolerably to me, it seems a sort of suicide which
you have no right to commit—if you cannot bring yourself to
be *regularly* during the winter months out of your own
house—have something that you can call your own house,
somewhere else than there— I cannot tell you the uneasiness of
mind I have had about you this winter— *Alone* there with your

delicate health, and social disposition!—while I would be so much the better of you here!— My uncle and *those* girls so much the better for you in Liverpool! An inhabited world all around you, and people that would be glad of you every where that you are known! indeed indeed dearest Mother this must not go on—there is no obligation human or divine that you should sit on that hill top all winter—or indeed at any season of the year and I cannot endure that it should go on.... Pray lay what I am saying to heart and let us see if some better life cannot come of it for you!

I have been out of sorts for some days—but a good hearty headach yesterday has rather cleared me up again— Carlyle is very busy at his new book [*Cromwell*]—and has been nearly driven distracted by—the *cock* I told you of!—it has indeed been a horrible nuisance....

We made out the visit to Forster and the play—almost worth the horrible headach I had in consequence! The Play was the Merchant of Venice and never did I see such acting as Macreadys Shylock that night—he seemed *inspired*—I could not have conceived such acting possible for him!— We went to him afterwards to his dressing room to express our *enthusiasm* and he *blushed* at Carlyles praises like a young girl!— I was glad that Carlyle *could* give him such hearty applause for you may remember he hurt his feelings horribly by something he said in his lectures in Macready's hearing— about a Manager of a theatre being 'the most despised and insignificant of all created beings.'— Poor Macready has behaved nobly to him since and there might be something more than flattery in what Forster said of his being animated that night to the highest efforts of his Genius from knowing that Carlyle was to be there, and the natural wish to redeem himself in his estimation. He is a *good* man any how and deserves the success he is meeting with.... God keep you ... your own / Jane W C

*

Thursday [30 Dec. 1841]

Dearest

I meant to write a long letter to be read by you on new years morning—but I must content myself with a short one— for my head is aching—and the ideas will not flow—it is my

own fault however so you need [not] bestow too much pity on
me— I went with the Macreadys to Drury Lane the second
night of the opening of that theatre and the gass and the late
hour and the excitement &c &c what else could come of all that
but just a headach for the next two or three days—

Moreover C is beginning to write at a new book and the
restlessness of his mind is acting as usual on his body—
interfering with his sleep and troubling every moment of his
existence—last night he was *up smoking* and today he is in a
state of desperation uttering things enough to drive one into
committing suicide if one did not know his way. Even
knowing his way it is not easy to keep ones heart up under
the long prospect of all the torments that will have to be
endured by BOTH OF US before that book gets itself written—
Truly he writes with his heart's-blood the Public may well feel
grateful to *him*. . . .

*

Monday morning [3 Jan. 1842]

. . . Oh Mother Mother Mother— why are you *always* sending
me money & to such an uncoscionable amount? Surely you
had sent us presents enough to make one *wae* [vexed]
without that five pound note, if it were not for fear of vexing
you I would return it with a protest— I beg however that you
will not give me any more money for the next two years—for
if you do, I warn you before hand, that I absolutely must and
will return it— you call the purse ill-done. I do not see how it
could possibly be done better—and with it and the beautiful
lace and the collar which I also think beautiful I conceived my
new years day richly hanselled before I came upon that
note!— Carlyle seemed to *think shame* of his new gifts— 'If I
were like any other man' he said, 'it would have been I that
would have sent *her* a new year's gift instead of her sending
me one—but I never know what to give anybody or how to set
about it'!!! It is a truth; and also a pity. He is kind and
generous as any one; any one in life-and-death moments of
existence but existence not being made up of such
moments—his kindness and generosity lies for the most part
perdu— Better however like him to make no presents at all
than like John to make disgustingly mean ones. — Only fancy
him with his thousand-a year—presenting *us* in common this

Christmas with a print of Milton, *value five shillings*!— He
dines here regularly every Sunday—occasioning a considerable
trouble besides expence—there must always be a better
dinner than we should have for ourselves— Carlyle is
displeased if there is not—and there must be a fire kept up in
the low room that they may smoke and drink brandy negus by
themselves. . . . Yet he did not give Helen a sixpence on new
year day, while Darwin who is always obliging us instead of
being obliged, presented her as he always does with half a
sovereign! I gave her *your* gown on new years morning—
having *kept it up* all this while— So that the ribbon was a
piece of *superfluity*— Still I was glad that *you* should seem to
her so mindfull. . . .

Mrs Sterling is not '*suited*' yet; the man Brown is going to
marry is ten years younger than herself— I think old Sterling is
worse about it than his wife— When Brown announced her
marriage to him he fell upon her neck and wept!!— She will be
a terrible loss for she has managed *his* temper these sixteeen
years as well as the things of the house— Would to heaven that
you were *suited*—or would come away!— You might get a
servant in Liverpool on the way back— I do think there are nice
servants in Liverpool if they knew how to guide them. How lazy
all these girls are!— I have written to one and another of them
lately—really trying to keep up a cousinly correspondence
with—*the family* but nothing of the sort can be expected— I
had prepared little presents for the young ones this new year,
and felt so provoked at their neglect of me that I *bestowed them
else where*! . . . Do you know how many z s you put into M.'s
[Mazzini's] name on the parcel?—just *six*! We had such a laugh
over it—increased by my observing that when you wrote it you
had been 'very cold'—

Where in the world do you *get* such beautiful things? A
prettier handkerchief I never saw than that of C's nor a prettier
tablecloth— God bless you dear Mother— You said nothing of
your *rose* in the last two letters—how is it? / yours ever JC

*

Saturday [early 1842]

Dearest Mother
        I am most thankful to have your note and also D*r*
Russel's—whom I can believe in more implicitly than in

yourself ... — I find from what he writes that it was just as I
supposed—that you have been quite laid up while you were
putting so fair a face upon it— ...

For me, I am also getting better—but my affair has proved
to be a smart influenza—and has kept me down longer than I
expected....

Mrs Sterlings new maid leaves at the end of her month
.... Darwins Sarah ... has given warning ... because she was
desired to bring up the dinner one day that Carlyle dined with
him *by chance*!! it 'being in the agreement that William was to
wait *when* there was *company*'!! 'I simply *will not* bring up
the dinner when there is company ... if I am desired to do it
again I *will go*' 'Go now' said Darwin—not another word—and
she goes—after having been *nursed* by him thro' half a years
illness! human nature is very ungrateful—God keep you / your
own JC

*

Monday [early 1842]

My darling Mother
     Heaven bless you for your kind exertions to keep me easy!
Your two notes came today together! Yesterday alas was Sunday,
when one may not have any communication with those at a
distance—and for the same reason that yesterday was Sunday
you will be a day longer in hearing from me than you ought to
be— I am much more comfortable than when I wrote last for
my headach which had been incessant for ten days is gone—
and I am able to come down stairs about eleven—and it is an
immense thing to be down stairs, tho' I should not get further
for ever so long.— The weather here is extremely sharp again,
and I have still a good deal of cold—but with care, and I mean
to give it plenty I expect to get the better of it without any more
confounded dozes—
     How I hate to think of you confined to your room there,
feeling as I do my own room here so dreary—which still must
be less dreary than yours for I have C to come inti it two or
three times in the day and ask 'how are you now Jane'? and
then off to his Cromwell again—it is still something,—tho' not
much for somehow these hasty visits, with difficulty spared
from more important business, flurry rather than cheer me—for
the rest, tho *I* am within reach of friends both male and female

it does not help me much—Male friends by the rules of english
society must not come to comfort me *in my bed* however much
they might feel disposed to take that trouble—and female
friends have so many demands on them at home— M*rs* Sterling
and Elizabeth Pepoli are the only two of mine that take any
charge of me when I am sick—and this last time I have been
without even them—poor Elizabeth has been laid up herself—
When I sent last night to inquire for her she was still in bed—
and her amiable spouse holding a dinner party! 'making himself
so happy' Helen said—'his laugh was never done'....

As for Mrs Sterling tho' not ill—she is no longer as she
used to be—since *he* quitted the Times, in giving up a large part
of his income, her life seems to me to be gone all to sixes and
sevens— She no longer seems to feel any hearty interest in
anything except in the little details of her own household....
They have no carriage any longer and she dare seldom treat
herself to a cab, so that it is only in fine *walking* weather that
she can get to see me— She went to Guys Hospital to call for
the Maurices . . . and how do you think she went—at this
season of the year? *Walked* to Chelsea and down the river in a
steam boat! and returned by Omnibus—and such a result of
such an economical proceeding! She had her pocket picked of
five sovereigns!! at least she says she is sure she did not drop
her purse and that it was taken out of her pocket in the
Omnibus—nay she is sure of the person that took it! 'A very
gentlemany man, better dressed than either her husband or
mine who sat opposite her.' . . .

But oh dear— C is ready to go off—and I must take the
opportunity of sending this with him—in case of having to go
to the door in Helen's absence which would *look* absurd 'to a
degree' —

God bless you continue to write so often as I will / your
own / J C

JOHN STERLING   NLS 601.80
Falmouth

[19 Jan. 1842]

... [Forster] has been taking counsel with me, *me* of all people
that could have been pitched upon! how to give new life to a
dying Review—the *Foreign* namely— It has passed into the
hands of new publishers Chapman and Hall active and

moneyied men, who are intent on raising a corps of new worthy contributors who are somehow (I do not understand that part of it) to kill and devour the old Editor, a Dr Worthington, who has been for a long time 'sitting on it as an Incubus'— ...

Now in casting our eyes about for men of genius—fit to infuse new life into dead matter there naturally slid over my lips *your* name— 'John Sterling if the Review could but be helped by a fifty-page-article in rhyme!' 'Why not in *prose?*' said Forster 'Ah! that is another question! To persuade *him* to write prose would not be so easy'— 'At all events said Forster with a burst of enthusiasm he *can* and shall and *must* be applied to'— And accordingly he took your address for that purpose. Having consulted with the publishers for whom he is acting gratuitously as Prime Minister, for the mere love of *humanity* and his own inward glory; he finds that it were the most promising way of setting about the thing to apply to you thro some personal friend—and does *me* the honour of taking me for such—in which I hope he is not mistaken.

Today I have a letter from him from which I extract the most important paragraph ... 'Will you propose the article on Dante to Mazzini—and I want YOU to write and ask JOHN Sterling' (indication of celebrity) 'to write an article for the Foreign Quarterly; placing *no* restraint on his opinions in any way. If he will but consent to do anything he may be as radical as he was in his last contribution to conservatism;—you have if your kindness will take it full authority from me!'— This Dr Worthington, it appears is to be got rid of and speedily as possible. If these two articles are supplied it is supposed that they will go far towards knocking him on the head: a matter of much desirability. That done, Carlyle must help these active and excellent Publishers to a *good* man.' ...

So there you have my story! can you do anything with it?— Even if it were only for my private consolation, I should like to see some PROSE from you once more in this world— think and answer .... Remember me in all kindness to your wife—and believe me ever affectionately / yours 'til deth' / Jane Carlyle. ...

Jane wrote her mother unaware that it was for the last time. She died on 25 February.

GRACE WELSH   Froude, *Life* 3:233
Thornhill

5 Cheyne Row: Feb. 23, 1842.

I am continuing to mend. If I could only get a good sleep, I should be quite recovered; but, alas! we are gone to the devil again in the sleeping department. That dreadful woman next door, instead of putting away the cock which we so pathetically appealed against, has produced another. The servant has ceased to take charge of them. They are stuffed with ever so many hens into a small hencoop every night, and left out of doors the night long. Of course they are not comfortable, and of course they crow and screech not only from daylight, but from midnight, and so near that it goes through one's head every time like a sword....

... Carlyle swears he will shoot them, and orders me to borrow Mazzini's gun. Shoot them with all my heart if the consequences were merely having to go to a police office and pay the damage. But the woman would only be irritated thereby into getting fifty instead of two. If there is to be any shooting, however, I will do it myself. It will sound better my shooting them on principle than his doing it in a passion.

This despicable nuisance is not at all unlikely to drive us out of the house after all, just when he had reconciled himself to stay in it. How one is vexed with little things in this life! The great evils one triumphs over bravely, but the little eat away one's heart.

A report came from Dr James Russell at Thornhill, alarmed at the stroke which had cut down Mrs Welsh. Jane set out at once, but at Liverpool she was told that her mother had died, and fell desperately ill herself. It was left to Carlyle to travel to Liverpool and then Templand to sort out all Mrs Welsh's affairs, while Jane fought a desolation almost as great as the loss of her father.

Chapter Four

Turned Adrift in the World, 1842-45

Jane recovered slowly, while Carlyle spent nearly three months consoling her and clearing up her mother's affairs at Thornhill. She gradually improved, supported by close friends and relatives. Her young cousin Jeannie Welsh became a favourite, and Jane often wrote to her and Mary Russell, the doctor's wife at Thornhill.

ELIZA AITKEN   EUL Dc. 4.94
Minto Manse, Hawick

                                          [3 June 1842]

...I *know* that I wrote *part* of a letter to you some weeks ago—immediately after receiving your last—but whether I finished it, and sent it off or whether it shared the fate of many others of my late undertakings and came to an untimely close, I cannot remember, tho' it were to save my life!— From this you may infer that my memory is tolerably bad—indeed all about me has been tolerably bad this long while—and I do not feel as if I could ever gather myself up into the old state again in this world.— Parted as I had been from my Mother so many years and with so many new objects of interest about me it was not to have been foreseen that her loss could have so completely changed the whole face of my existence—indeed I had never thought about losing her—her life seemed always better than my own,—What I had thought about, and always the longer the more anxiously, was getting her beside me again that I might show her more love and care in her old age than in the thoughtlessness of my heart I had done heretofore— And she had promised me not to keep me unquiet by passing any more winters in that lonely place— Had just promised me that 'if it pleased God we should meet this summer, it should be all arranged according to my wish'— So many fine schemes I had in my head for her future comfort!—too late—for her death was already on her and I did not know it— She had taken every pains and forced those about her to take every pains to keep me in ignorance of her state—'a journey at that season would be so dangerous for me.'— All her last weeks seemed one continued thought about *me*—to ward off anxiety from me while she lived and to soften the shock for me should she die—in a letter she wrote to D*r* Russel—after many directions about what was to be done for me if I *must* be sent for she concluded with these words which stick for ever in my heart—'for Jeannie must be saved in *every* way—or there is much to be dreaded'— And when the first stroke came upon her, Margaret Macqueen being by—she uttered no thought for her own future only in sinking down exclaimed 'I am dying Margaret! Oh my poor Jeannie'— On the Saturday I received a letter from her—tender and cheerful as all her late letters had been— She had written the day before she said and had nothing new to tell me—but as there was no post in London on Sunday if I was kept waiting till Monday I 'would be making myself uneasy again'!—and at the time I read that letter she was already dead!— On the Monday came no letter from her as promised—but one from the D*r* stating her to be dangerously ill—yet not precluding all hope—for he feared the blow for me altho at the time he wrote he had no hope himself— Of course I set out by the next Railway train—not despairing— Oh no—or I *could* not have gone— I thought I had little hope—but when all hope was taken from me I found that I had had much. You know the rest—I travelled all night in the cruellest suspense and arriving in Liverpool in the morning was told that my uncle and Walter were already gone—to her funeral!— Oh Bess is it not a wonder that I kept my senses— I am better in health now—but still very feeble and nervous—and so sad!— Oh there is such a perpetual weight on my heart as I cannot describe to you—I feel as helpless and desolate as a little child turned adrift in the world! *I* who have so many friends!—but what are friends?— What is a husband even compared with ones Mother?— Of *her* love one is always so sure!—it is the only love that nothing— not even misconduct on our part can take away from us—. If the letter I began went to you, I have said all this before—for it is the only sort of thing I have to say to anyone—and accordingly I write none at all except to the few whose sympathy I have perfect confidence in—

When shall I see you again? here I mean—for I do not think I shall ever have the heart to set foot in Scotland any more— Alas Alas What a changed Scotland for me—a place of graves —

My Sweet little Cousin Jeannie is still here with me—a comfort so far any companionship *can be* a comfort to me—

Write to me dear Eliza and do not mind my silences That I have thought of you much during *this time* is a sufficient proof of the constancy of regard / Ever your affectionate cousin/ Jane Carlyle

MARGARET WELSH   NLS 601.85
Maryland St, Liverpool
                                                Friday [15 July 1842]

...It was a good thought in you to send me the little purse— and I feel very grateful to you for it— This last birthday was very sad for me as you may easily suppose—very unlike what it was last year and former years—and I needed all the heartening kind souls could give me—but by your kindness and that of others the day was got over with less of a foresaken feeling than could have been anticipated. Only think of my husband too having given me a little present! he who never attends to such *nonsenses* as birthdays—and who dislikes nothing in the world so much as going into a shop to buy anything—even his own trowsers and coats; so that to the consternation of Cockney-tailors *I* am obliged to go about them— Well he actually risked himself in a Jewlers shop and bought me a very nice smelling-bottle!— I cannot tell you how *wae* [sad] his little gift made me as well as glad—it was the first thing of the kind he ever gave me in his life—in *great* matters he is always kind and considerate, but these *little* attentions which we women attach so much importance to he was never in the habit of rendering to any one—his up-bringing and the severe turn of mind he has from nature had alike indisposed him towards them—and now the desire to replace to me the irreplaceable makes him as good in *little* things as he used to be in great— ...God bless you all— Ever your affectionate Cousin / Jane Carlyle

In August Jane was invited to stay with Charles and Isabella Buller at Troston in Suffolk, where Carlyle briefly joined them and toured the Cromwell country. In spite of Thomas's disapproval of 'Young Italy', Jane supported Mazzini's Italian School. Her friend Gambardella abandoned a portrait of Carlyle, and left for Liverpool to paint her uncle John Welsh and Jeannie, while Jane was faced with the challenge of reading Geraldine Jewsbury's **Zoe***. Geraldine had carried on with the novel in 1841, after starting it with Jane and the lively Elizabeth Paulet, wife of the Swiss consul at Liverpool. Mrs Paulet lived in some style, admired Carlyle, fêted Emerson on his visit in 1848, had literary ambitions and was to write her own feminist three-decker,* **Dharma; or Three Phases of Love** *(1865), well after she had lost Jane's good opinion. She was a lively caricaturist, amused by Jane's fascination for her admirers (see illustration 4). Jane liked Geraldine's attacks on masculine domination and gave her a detailed criticism of* **Zoe***, mixing vigorous praise with protest at the 'indecent' passages.*

JEANNIE WELSH   NLS 1891.16, 100
Maryland St, Liverpool

[6 Sept. 1842]

Dearest Babbie
    Another 'few lines' in expectancy of 'a more convenient season'— My last note to you was like to have been my farewell speech, I felt so ill on laying down my pen—that I proceeded to lay *myself* down and was not out of bed for all that day— I was not missed till Mr Buller wanted me to play chess before dinner— Carlyle had gone to Thetford, as I told you—lost his way of course—and of course kept the dinner waiting an hour and arrived when it was finished—having walked innumerable miles—so I had the additional discomfort of feeling that we were a most detestable *pair* of visitors—the one taken to bed— the other *lost* at the dinner hour!— He came safe however and was very sorry for me— At night being still no better Mrs Buller asked if I would let her give me something—*anything* I said not excepting even prusic acid—for I could not well have been made worse— She poured me something into a glass out of two different vials—I swallowed it and—*in one instant* I was well!!— I winked—*listened* to find where the horrid pain was gone but could hear no more tell of it! ...

*

Wednesday [16 Nov. 1842]

...First of *the* [Italian Free School] *Anniversary:* 'the moral satisfaction was complete, the *financial* rather disappointing.' *Thirteen* pounds was the sum collected including the immortal

five—from which deduct the expences, and there would
remain, I am afraid, zero, or perhaps even a *deficit*—the *supper*
of itself must have gone with a half—*forty five* gallons of beer,
fifty pounds of macaroni, and roast beef of unascertained
quantity!—to be sure there were two hundred and fifty sat
down to what the Dumfries courier would call 'the festive
board,' and the fine times of miraculous loaves and fishes are
long gone by: tho' god knows if ever there was a time when
men had more need of them! think of the boiled dead dog!—
The supper transacted itself into a tavern hard by, at the close of
the business—leaving the schoolroom to more poetical
purposes—to distribution of prizes—speeches of 'the *founders*'
(*anglice* the Committee) and 'what shall I say, strange things
upon *my honour*'! You may be sure that old Pestrucci [director
of the school] would not let slip so fine an occasion of
gratifying his melodramatic propensities and accordingly a
series of scenas were most unexpectedly introduced which the
audience must have been charmed to find themselves '*assisting
at*'—*for nothing*—I mean *gratis*— Of the first, poor
unsuspecting, horror-struck Mazzini was made at once the hero
and the victim!— When all had spoken who were to speak, he
came forward—very shame-faced as you may fancy—and
'unveiling himself as the original founder' . . . he made a most
moving address to the school as *learners* and as *patriots*—
When he had finished, amidst shouting like to bring down the
ceiling there stepped forth from the pupils benches the *least*
boy—some twelve years old—who advanced blushing, and laid
a bouquet at his feet! then putting his little hand in his breast, he
pulled out a little paper, and proceeded to read a little sonnet to
his (Mazzinis) honour and glory!—just fancy this!—and consider
the sort of Man! and admire him that he did not turn round and
brain old Pestrucci on the spot—from whose goosehead of
course this *coup de theatre* must have emanated! . . .
      Did I tell you the Fate of Gambardellas picture of
Carlyle?—I think not—at C's desire I stept in to see it one day in
passing to the Sterlings— Speridion (his other name is quite too
long for writing) almost without opening his lips set it up
before me— He had put in a small triangular light just at the
joining of the nose and brow which gave it the appearance of
smelling something to which *assafoetida* was a joke, and
another very broad, circular one in the middle of the under
lip—which I cannot describe unless you can fancy such an

unheard of thing as a lip just *ignited* by a lucifer-match!— I
looked at it for a moment with all the gravity I could muster, and
then looked at the painter— Our eyes met, and *both* exploded
into laughter—'The fact is' said G. 'that poor man can *not* sit!
and will never get himself painted in this world—unless from
memory by some one who has studied his face' (in this last
observation I believe there was a deal of sound sense)— 'But we
must not tell him so'—he continued—'it would vex him, and
the poor man has done the best he could! just let it pass for *my*
want of talent, and I will do him a picture of *you* to make up to
him for his lost time!'...There is C tramping in his boots
overhead so I must seal and be ready—bless you darling—
dispense my love *liberally* yet according to desert— ....

HELEN WELSH   NLS 602.97
Maryland St, Liverpool
                                                  [20 Dec. 1842]

...I am glad you have been to Seaforth, for I am sure M*rs* Paulet
will prove an agreeable addition to your acquaintance I do not
know how she may appear to Miss Pen Sketchly or others
whom she *dislikes*—nor do I find it anything against her that
she is disliked by those she dislikes—it proves her at least to be
no hypocrite—but when there has been as in your case '*a
mutual sympathy*' I predict the friendship will go on bravely—
Geraldine writes to me— 'Jeannie and her Sister were here also
& remained all night— I cannot tell you how much I take to
them both—the elder one has not so much of *you*' (*Pity!*) 'as
Jeannie has; but there is something extremely charming about
her— M*rs* Paulet likes them very much indeed and so does
Monsr. in short it seems altogether a highly satisfactory
arrangement' Since I began writing I have had Jeannie's dear
long letter, for which give her a kiss for me in the meantime—
and I have had also a visit from my old Doctor ... —so you must
make allowance for this *bit* of a letter—at all events
mademoiselle it is better than *none*—which I get from you—
My Doctor confirms the blue-pill system and also the walking
'*without minding the pain*'—but he seemed to think I needed
a *sermon* more than a *prescription* and so gave me the best I
have heard this many a long day.... God bless you my dear
Cousin—love me for God sake—and believe always your /
affectionate sister Jane Carlyle

JEANNIE WELSH   NLS 1891.82, 134
Maryland St, Liverpool

Wednesday [21 Dec. 1842]

... For the last week or two we have breakfasted later than
usual, C. seldom coming down before half after nine—*tant
mieux*, so far as that goes—by the time the table has been
cleared for writing and oneself emerged out of dressing-gown
into fit-to-be-seen-in gown eleven has probably struck— Say
that I then fall to writing—first comes Helen 'what about the
dinner Mum?'—'*Chops*'—that at least is quickly settled—but
then perhaps comes Carlyle to say 'Jane, these cloth-boots of
mine are in imminent need of some repair,' or 'Jane these cloth
trowsers of mine must have a new hem at the bottom'—or
'Jane, some thing or other' alike inconvenient at that particular
moment— Or perhaps Elizabeth Pepoli comes (she comes
very often at present) 'to catch me before I go out'—or
perhaps the Postman brings some note or letter that makes it
imperative for me to turn my writing into another channel
than the premeditated one of Babbie.—There is hardly a day
that one or other of these *perhapses* does not come to pass—
then, if *all* the forenoon were at my own disposal, as it used to
be, Babbie might still get her letter—but at *one* o'clock—I am
forced to go out—every day, unless it rains—which at present
it seems resolute not to do—now that this odious walking
forms part of my *medical* treatment there is no evading of it
without getting myself into worse trouble— If, after coming
in, there be a leisure half hour or so before dinner I am too
much fagged to turn it to any earthly account—and in the
evening I have neither privacy nor strength for writing— I am
always wearied and *sick* in the evenings—the effect I suppose
of the walking and the blue-pills ...
    I received yesterday by rail-way a bundle of Manuscript
from Geraldine and Mrs Paulet—of which I am to give my
opinion—partly from a sort of *vague apprehension*, partly for
another reason I have not yet untied the parcel—this other
reason is, that Carlyle has also a considerable bundle of M.S. *not*
about Cromwell at all!—but about that old Abbot of St Edmonds
Bury!! —which he 'rather wishes me to read and give him my
views about'—and until I have *studied* that which will be no
light matter, I must abstain, for *decency's sake* from showing any
curiosity about the other literary production in which I have

only a *friend's* interest— My Dear, tho we are not trained here
as in China to 'the three-thousand punctualities'—we are always
needing to look to our doings that we may not stumble over
some nicety or other— . . .

Helen's letter has come since I began writing give her my
thanks and three kisses for it—a kiss for every sheet— Oh dear
how I wish we were all together— . . .

*

Sunday [25 Dec. 1842]

. . . I have read the Seaforth novel and, as was to have been
anticipated, with a feeling little short of *terror*! So much
power of genius rushing so recklessly into unknown space!
Geraldine, in particular, shows herself here a far more
profound and daring speculator than even I had fancied her. I
do not believe there is a woman alive at the present day, not
even George Sand herself, that could have written some of the
best passages in this book—or would have had the courage to
write them if she had had the ability,—but they must not
publish it, 'decency forbids'! (as they write at the street
corners)— I do not mean decency in the vulgar sense of the
word—even in *that* sense they are not always *decent*!—but
then their *indecency* looks so purely *scientific*, and so
essential for the full development of the story that one
cannot, at least I cannot get up a feeling of outraged modesty
about it—nay I should feel as if *I* were the indecent person
should I find anything to blush at in what *they* seem to have
written just FOR FACTS SAKE without a consciousness of wrong—
but there is an indecency or want of reserve (let us call it) in
the spiritual department—an exposure of their whole minds
naked as before the fall—without so much as a fig-leaf of
conformity remaining—which no respectable public could
stand—which even the freest spirits among us would call
'coming it too strong'!— I wish a clear day would dawn for me
that I might give them a full and faithful deliverance upon it—
for it is a difficult task they have put on me to criticise such an
extraordinary jumble of sense-and-nonsense, insight beyond
the stars, and blindness before their own nose! One thing I feel
no doubt about that this Geraldine will either 'make a spoon
or spoil a horn'—she is far too clever to do *nothing* in her day
and generation— . . .

Among many London friends, Fanny Wedgwood was a cheerful support, with whom Jane could share her daily problems, such as persuading Carlyle to dine without her at the boring Henry Taylor's when dressed as if he were 'just setting out for the thirty years' war':

FRANCES WEDGWOOD   Wedgwood Papers,
London   Keele University Library
                                        [Jan. 1843]

Drama in one Scene

(... Mrs C ... —is seated at an oval table—strewn with litter—of coloured papers—leather—old books—&c—looking excessively bothered; as well she may—being in the thick of *binding* a copy of Pope's works in *seven* volumes!)

Mr C: Oh dear *dear* me!

Mrs C. Don't you think you are going to make yourself late too *late*?

Mr C: I shall be time enough for any good I shall get! *Certainly* I am a most unfortunate man! My dear, are you not sorry for me?

Mrs C: No—

Mr C. Well! I can assure you however, I am heartily sorry for *myself*!

Mrs C: I am sure you are going to be too late—

Mr C: (looking at his watch) hang it! So I am!—but there is something I should like you to do for me—in fact you *must* do it— Write to Mrs Wedgwood *how I am situated*—out today—shall be all shattered to pieces in consequence—and absolutely unequal to any thing more this week: but that we will come and dine some Monday (not the first—any other) and go all to Wilson's Scotch Songs afterwards!!

Mrs. C: And who do you mean by *we*!

Mr C: *You* and Myself. You will write *that* will you?

Mrs C: Me! me with 'my *interior*' (as you will call it) in an everlasting worry of blue pills—much good Scotch Songs in a cold winter night would do me!

Mr C You will write what I bid you?

Mrs C No—I will engage for you—but not for myself— Dear me you will be an hour too late!

Mr C. I am afraid I shall (exit running)

Hester Sterling died and, within a day or two, her younger son John's wife, Susannah.

JEANNIE WELSH   NLS 1891.253
Maryland St, Liverpool

Tuesday [25 April 1843]

...I was hurried off yesterday at the early hour of twelve
o'clock before I had got well begun— In fact I begin to be sick
of the extraordinary occupation that has been appointed me
for these last ten days, viz.: dry-nursing my great, big,
obstreperous infant of an old Sterling! Actually I have not had
five minutes speech with Mazzini for the last week! At first I
went to him from the impulse of my own compassion—then I
ceased to go; really thinking that at least until the funeral was
over they would be better without visitors— On Tuesday
forenoon I was desirous of having a mouthful of quiet talk
with Elizabeth [Pepoli] whom I had not got a sight of for many
days— I had not been seated more than ten minutes when we
were startled by the sound of Carlyle's voice in the lobby
enquiring for me— I thought the house must have taken fire,
such an occurrance as C's coming to seek me anywhere was
so unprecedented— 'My Dear' says he opening the drawing
room door 'here has old Sterling been to seek you *roaring and
greeting*! [weeping] and I have had to bring him after you! You
must go away in the carriage with him somewhere and keep
him quiet'! I departed with a sigh on my difficult mission—
and we drove—all thro *the streets*! crying the whole way (that
is to say *he* was crying.) and I bottled up beside him in his
very small carriage—looking I am sure the very picture of
what Harriet Martineau defined Queen Victory to be 'a young
woman in prodigiously difficult circumstances'! On
Wednesday Mazzini had just come in and we had just placed
our two pairs of feet on the fender when the little carriage
drove up again and in *rushed* the old man exclaiming 'Oh my
friend—my dear dear friend comfort me! Sooth me!' I was on
the point of lifting up the poker to kill him—when he
disarmed my wrath by adding—'I have a NEW disaster! John's
wife has been carried off by inflamation'!— You know *I* never
felt any affection for Mrs John but the news of her death under
such circumstances was truly shocking—and I became quite
sick— 'Oh come with me says he come and let us walk a few

turns in the pure air of Battersea Bridge'!!— 'I am *unable* to
walk at this moment' says I— 'Then I wont go—I must not
seperate myself from you! We will drive since you cannot
walk—only for the love of God let me stay by your side'!!—
Mazzini was *standing* all the while—*staring* as you can
fancy—the sound of his voice was not heard any more! So off
we set again—*thro the Streets*! Thursday ditto—friday ditto—
Saturday ditto—on Sunday he came with Mrs Anthony.
. . . And yesterday he came again while I was writing to *you*—
But I begin to see he is merely prolonging his wailing in the
view of exploiting my compassion and getting better
treatment from me than he has been used to— His real sorrow
is already pretty well cured!! Already!— Yes it will be just as
his son Anthony told me—'You will see that in a few weeks he
will be back to his Carlton Club and all his old haunts and the
past will be for him as if it had never been'— I thought
Anthony cruel to say so but he knew his Father better than
even I did— In the depth of his despair he proposed to me to
go away with him to the Isle of Wight or some secluded place
for a few weeks—and I in my simplicity actually did not
positively refuse and Carlyle in his simplicity—said 'yes it
would be well done'— But my last drive with him has given
me other thoughts— And now I am going to say a horrible
thing which I entreat of you not to read aloud—'Upon *my*
honour' Babbie I do not think I should be—'what shall I say'—
safe travelling alone with him old as he is!! Plainly for all so
old as *I* am, I have not yet arrived at a thorough understanding
of human nature for it is always revealing itself to me under
new and *a priori* incredible phases. . . .

*Carlyle had been taken up by the Ashburtons some time after
meeting them in 1839. Jane soon found that she had much in
common—perhaps too much—with Lady Harriet Ashburton, known
for being witty, outspoken, sarcastic and imperious. Her mother, the
dowager Lady Sandwich, had been a socialite who, after briefly
mourning her husband, had pursued a life of pleasure. In Paris she
lived in a mansion once occupied by Talleyrand and Philippe Egalité.
Her youngest daughter, Lady Caroline, had married Count Alexandre
Walewski, the illegitimate son of Napoleon I and Marie Walewski, and
was later said to have had an affair with the Duke of Orleans. Lady
Harriet had had to compete for attention; and, after an early marriage
and the death of an infant son, became a society hostess. She was*

'liberal to all opinions', as **The Times** *was to say, uniting 'the luxury of wealth with the simplicity of life and mental superiority ... without pride or affectation'. In being charmed by her, as she by him, Carlyle was following the example of Mill, Charles Buller and many others. The attraction soon became an infatuation.*

JEANNIE WELSH   NLS 1891.292
Maryland St, Liverpool

[27 May 1843]

Private

...I have always ommitted to tell you how marvellously that *liason* has gone on. Geraldine seemed horribly *jealous* about it—nay almost *'scandalized'*—while she was here—for my part, I am singularly inaccessible to jealousy, and am pleased rather that he has found *one* agreeable house to which he likes to go and goes regularly—one evening in the week at least— and then he visits them at their 'Farm' on Sundays. and their are flights of charming little notes always coming to create a pleasing titillation of the philosophic Spirit!— M*rs* Buller in her graceful quizzical way insisted I should 'see a little into the thing with my own eyes,' and promised to give me notice the first time she knew beforehand of the Intellectual Circe's coming to her house— And accordingly M*r* Buller came last Monday to ask me to meet her that evening at tea at seven o'clock— She is in *delicate health* you may remember and not up to parties or late hours— I said at once yes—and appointed him to bring the carriage for me at half after six— He was not long gone—when it flashed thro' my mind that a whole bevy of Americans male and female were coming *here* to tea by invitation at seven....What to do?—I posted off to Chester Place to explain the necessity of my giving up the Lady Harriet for that time. But the Bullers would not hear of it—'it was my husband not *me* all these Americans were coming to stare at— I would simply pour out the tea for them—and if I spilled it or committed any awkwardness they would go home and *put it in a book'!* —there was truth in these suggestions and finally it was agreed that M*r* Buller should still bring the carriage for me, and unless Carlyle made violent resistance, should snatch me away like Proserpine out of the American environment! C was at first quite furious at the project—but I got the better of him by saying 'Well then there will be nothing for it but to let M*r*

Buller when he comes *stay here'*—the idea of *that*—the
deafness & the trumpet was worse than anything—so he told
me 'in Heaven's name to do anything rather than introduce
such an element into the concern'—

Happily M*r* B came first—and off I went in cold blood—
leaving C to pour out the tea himself and make what excuses
for me he pleased!— I do not remember when I did such a
spirited thing or one which I so little repent of doing— *I* have
no reason to study politeness with the Americans.— But Lady
Harriet!— I liked her on the whole—she is immensely *large*—
might easily have been one of the *ugliest* women living—but
is almost beautiful—simply thro the intelligence and cordiality
of her expression— I saw nothing of the impertinence and
hauteur which people impute to her—only a certain
brusquerie of manner which seemed to me to proceed from
exuberant spirits and absence of all affectation— She is
unquestionably very clever—just the *wittiest* woman I have
seen—but with many aristocratic prejudices—which I wonder
Carlyle should have got over so completely as he seems to
have done—in a word I take her to be a very loveable spoilt
Child of Fortune—that a little *whipping*, judiciously
administered would have made into a first rate woman—we
staid till eleven and as there were no other strangers, I had
ample opportunity of estimating the amount of her
seductions— — What *she* thought of *me* I should rather like to
know—she took prodigious looks at me from time to time—
In the *last* note to Carlyle inviting him to Addiscombe for next
Sunday she says—'I meditate paying my respects to Mrs
Carlyle—so soon as I am again making visits— She is *a reality*
whom you have hitherto quite *suppressed.'* ...

*With Carlyle on holiday, Jane supervised decorators at home. A
friend, John Robertson, sub-editor of Mill's* **Westminster Review**,
*accompanied her to a meeting in Whitechapel held by the Irish Catholic
temperance preacher Father Mathew. In August she went with old
Edward Sterling to the Isle of Wight, where she encountered bedbugs,
and more bedbugs on returning home. A young journalist, the future
Edinburgh professor David Masson, called at Cheyne Row. In his*
Memories of London *(1908) he recollected her brilliant talk,'full of
light esprit.... Her most characteristic vein was the satirical' (37). News
of Italian uprisings excited Mazzini and aroused Jane's fears for him
and his apparently naïve political schemes.*

JOHN WELSH   NLS 602.116
Maryland St, Liverpool

[18 July 1843]

Dearest, dear, only Uncle of me!

I would give a crown that you could see me at this
moment, thro a powerful telescope! you would laugh for the
next twelve hours—I am *doing the rural* after a fashion so
entirely my own! To escape from the abominable paint-smell
and the infernal noise within doors; I have erected *with my
own hands* a gipsey-tent in the garden, constructed with
clothes-lines—long poles and an old brown floor-cloth!—under
which remarkable shade I sit in an arm-chair, at a small round
table—with a hearth rug for carpet under my feet—writing
materials sewing materials—and a mind superior to Fate!— The
only drawback to this retreat, is its being exposed to 'the envy of
surrounding nations'—so many heads peer out on me from all
the windows of *the Row*—eager to penetrate my meaning!— ...

—Not to represent my contrivance as too perfect, I must
also tell you that a strong puff of wind is apt to blow down
the poles and then the whole tent falls down on my head!—
this has happened once already since I began to write—but
an instant puts it all to rights again— Indeed without
counteracting the indoors-influences by all lawful means I
could not stay here at present without injury to my health
which is at no time of the strongest—our house has for a
fortnight back been a house possessed with seven devils!— A
painter, two carpenters a paper-hanger, two non-descript
apprentice-lads and *'a spy'*—all playing the devil to the
utmost of their powers—hurrying and scurrying 'up stairs
down stairs and in my Lady's chamber'! affording the liveliest
image of a sacked City! When they rush in at six of the
morning and spread themselves over the premises, I instantly
jump out of bed and 'in wera desperation' take a shower-bath.
Then such a long day to be virtuous in! I make a chair and
sofa covers—write letters to my friends—scold the work
people, and suggest improved methods of doing things—and
when I go to bed at night I have to leave both windows of my
room wide open—(and plenty of ladders lying quite handy
underneath) that I may not as old Sterling predicted 'awake
dead' of the paint— The first night that I lay down in this
open state of things, I recollected Jeannies house-breaker-

adventure last year, and not wishing that all the thieves who *might* walk in at my open windows should take me quite unprepared, I laid my policeman's-rattle and my dagger on the spare pillow—and then I went to sleep quite secure— But it is to be confidently expected that in a week more things will begin to subside into their normal state—and meanwhile it were absurd to expect that any sort of *Revolution* can be accomplished with *rose-water*. . . .

My husband has now left his Welchman and is gone for a little while to visit the Bishop of St Davids Then he purposes crossing over somehow to Liverpool—and after a brief benediction to Jeannie— passing into Annandale— He has suffered unutterable things in Wales from the want of any adequate supply—of tea! the *Spooney!* For the rest his visit appears to have been pretty successful—plenty of seabathing— plenty of riding on horseback—and of *lying under trees!*— I wonder it never enters his head to lie under the walnut tree here at home—*it is a tree!*—leaves as green as any leaves can be even in South Wales!—but it were too *easy* to repose under that— —if one had to travel a long journey by railway to it— then indeed it might be worth while!

But I have no more time for scribbling just now—besides my pen is positively declining to act— So God bless you Dear and all of them— Ever your affectionate / Jane Carlyle

TC   NLS 602.120, 124, 134
Maryland St, Liverpool
                                     [24 July 1843]

Dearest / . . . Robertson brought here last night to tea a youth from Aberdeen of the name of Mason [Masson]— a news-paper Editor poor thing, and only twenty!—he is one of your most ardent admirers and *immitators*— Robertson said 'he had come up to town to see the *lions* and so he had brought him to *me*'— ('my Brother plays the German flute' &c)— He is a better 'speciment' of Aberdeen than I ever saw before—an innocent intelligent modest affectionate-looking creature— I quite took to him— When he went away, which he seemed to do very unwillingly, I said that he must come and see us when he returned to London and I hoped to make up then for his present disappointment by introducing him to you—to which he answered with a cordial grasp of my hand 'Eh! What a real

shame in ye to say *that*'! He told me 'if I would come to
Aberdeen they would get up a mob for me in the fish-market
Place, and give me a grand hurrah—and a paragraph of *course!* I
must tell you before I forget When Helen was handing me over
some of the books she said—'take care—that ane's the Maister's
sartor RESART—and a capital thing it is—just *noble* in *my*
opinion'!!— She told me the other day—that 'Bishop Terrot was
really a wee *noughty* [insignificant] body as ever she set een
upon' I like that word '*noughty*' much—

I have got for reading Fielding's *Amelia*! and *the Vicar of
Wakefield*—which I am carrying on simultaneously—I find the
first a dreadful bore—one prays to Heaven that the poor
woman would but once for all get herself *seduced*, and so let us
have done with her alarms and precautions; on any terms!
'Upon *my* honour' I do not see the slightest sense in spending
one's whole existence thro out three volumes in taking care of
one's *virtue*!—do you?— Love to them all—without kisses
since you are not *up* to these— I shall send the Examiner to
you today— How happy the Choreleys will be and M*rs*
Paulet—Oh bliss! Ever your / J Carlyle

*

Scotsbrig

Ryde / Pier Hotel [Isle of Wight]
Wednesday [9 Aug. 1843]

...And now let me tell you ... a little piece of *Hero-Worship*
that I have been after— 'My youthful enthusiasm' as John
Sterling calls it is not extinct then, as I had supposed—but must
certainly be *immortal*! Only think of its blazing up for—*Father
Mathew*!— You know I have always had the greatest reverence
for that Priest—and when I heard he was in London— —
attainable to me, I felt that I *must* see him—shake him by the
hand—and tell him I loved him considerably!— I was
expressing my wish to see him to Robertson the night he
brought the Ballad-collector—and he told me it could be
gratified—quite easily— ...

I fixed next evening— He (Robertson) called for me at
five—and we rumbled off in Omnibus all the way to *Mile
end*—that hitherto for me unimaginable goal!—then there
was still a good way to walk—the Place was a large piece of
waste ground [*JWC adds above the line:* The new lodging]

boarded off from the Commercial Road for a Catholic cemetery— I found 'my youthful enthusiasm' rising higher and higher as I got on the ground and saw the thousands of people all hushed into awful silence; with *not a single exception* that I saw—the only *religious* meeting I ever saw in Cokney-land which had not plenty of scoffers hanging on its outskirts.— The Crowd was all in front of a narrow scaffolding from which an American Capt was then haranguing it—and Father Mathew stood beside him so good and simple looking!— Of course we could not push our way to the front of the scafold where steps led up to it—so we went to one end—where there was no steps or other visible means of access—and handed up our letter of introduction to a Policeman—he took it and returned presently—saying that Father Mathew was coming.— And he came—and reached down his hand to me—and I grasped it—but the boards were higher than my head—and it seemed that our communication must stop there— But I have told you—I was in a moment of enthusiasm— I felt the need of getting closer to that good man— I saw a bit of rope hanging in the form of a festoon from the end of the boards— I put my foot on it—held still by Father Mathews hand—seized the end of the boards with the other—and in some to myself, up to this moment, incomprehensible way—flung myself *horizontally* onto the scafolding at Father Mathew's feet!!— He uttered a scream!—for he thought (I suppose) I must fall back—but not at all—I jumped to my feet—shook hands with him and said what?— 'God only knows'— He made me sit down on the only chair a moment, then took me *by the hand* as if I had been a little girl and led me to the front of the scafold to see him administer the pledge—from a hundred to two hundred took it—and all the Tragedies and theatrical representations I ever saw melted into one could not have given me such emotion as that scene did— There were faces both of men and of women that will haunt me while I live—faces exhibiting such concentrated wretchedness—making, you would have said, its last deadly struggle with the powers of darkness—there was one man in particular with a baby in his arms—and a young girl that seemed of the 'unfortunate' sort—that gave me an insight into the lot of humanity that I still wanted—and in the face of Father Mathew when one looked from them to him, the mercy of heaven seemed to be laid bare— Of course I *cried*—

but I longed to have laid my head down on the good mans shoulder and taken a hearty cry *there* before the whole assembled multitude!! He said to me one such nice thing— 'I dare not be absent for an hour'—he said 'I think always if some dreadful drunkard were to come! and me away; he might never muster determination perhaps to come again in all his life, and *there* would be a man *lost*'!

I was turning sick and needed to get out of the thing— but in the act of leaving him—never to see him again thro all time most probably—*feeling* him to be the very best man of modern times (*you* excepted)—I had another movement of youthful enthusiasm—which you will hold up your hands and eyes at— Did I take the pledge then?— No—I *would* tho', if I had not feared it would have been put in the newspapers!— No—not *that*—but I drew him aside—having considered if I had any *ring* on—any *handkerchief*—any anything that I could leave with him in remembrance of me—and having bethought me of a pretty memorandum book in my reticule— I drew him aside and put it into his hand—and bade him keep it for my sake, and asked him to give me one of his medals to keep for his!—and all this in tears and the utmost agitation!!— Had you any idea that your wife was still such a fool! I am sure *I* had not— The Father got thro the thing admirably—he seemed to understand what it all meant quite well— inarticulate tho I was— —he would not give me a common medal but took a little silver one from the neck of a young man who had just taken the pledge for example's sake, telling him he would get him another presently and then laid the medal into my hand—with a solemn blessing— I could not speak for excitement all the way home,—when I went to bed I could not sleep—the pale faces I had seen haunted me—and Father Mathew's smile—and even next morning I could not any how subside into my normal state until I had sat down and—written Father Mathew a long letter—accompanying it with your *Past and Present*!!! Now my dear if you are ready to beat me for a distracted Gomeril [fool]—I cannot help it—all *that* it was *put into my heart to do— Ich könnte nichts anders* [I could do no other] . . . . / Bless you always—love to them all / Your J C. . .

*

Scotsbrig

Sunday night [27 Aug.1843]

...Well! the Italian 'movement' has begun—and also I suppose
ended— Mazzini has been in a state of violent excitement all
these weeks—really forcibly reminding one of Frank
Dickson's goose with the one addle egg!—nothing hindered
him from going off to head the movement—except that—
unexpectedly enough—the *movement* did not *invite*
him—nay took pains to 'keep him in a certain ignorance'—
and his favorite conspirator abroad the movement sent into
Sicily 'to act there *alone*'!— 'Plainly indicating that it
meditated *some arrangement of Italy* such as they two
would not approve—something, what shall I say—*consti-
tutional*'— He came one day and told me quite seriously that
a week more would determine him whether to go singly and
try to enter the country in secret, or—to persuade a frigate
now here, which he deemed persuadable, *'to revolt openly
and take him there by force'*— 'And with one frigate said I
you *mean* to overthrow the Austrian empire—amidst the
general peace of Europe?'— 'Why not? the *beginning* only is
wanted'— I could not help telling him that 'a Harrow or Eton
schoolboy who uttered such nonsense and proceeded to give
it a practical shape would be *whipt* and expelled the
community as a mischevous blockhead!' He was made very
angry of course—but it was impossible to see anybody
behaving so like *'a mad'* without telling him ones mind— HE a
conspirator *chief*!— I should make an infinitely better one
myself— What for instance can be more out of the *role* of
Conspirator than his telling *me* all his secret operations ...
and the names of people who are organizing it?—*me* who do
not even ever ask him a question on such matters—who on
the contrary evade them as much as possible?— A man has a
right to put *his own* life and safety at the mercy of whom he
will—but no amount of confidence in his friend can justify
him for making such dangerous disclosures concerning
others— ... Bologna was the place where they were *first* to
raise there fool'scap-standard— The Examiner mentions
carelessly some young men having collected in the streets and
'raised seditious crys and even *fired some shots at the
Police*'— Cannon were planted &c— 'Austrians ready to
do march.' not a doubt of it—and seditious cries will make a
poor battle against cannon! Mazzini is confident however

that the thing will not stop—here—and if it goes on is
resolute also in getting into the thick of it— 'What do you say
of my head?—What are the results?—is there not things more
important than ones head?' 'Certainly—but I should say that
the man who has not *sense enough* to keep his head on his
shoulders till *something is to be gained by parting with it*
has not sense enough to manage or dream of managing any
important matter whatever'—! Our dialogues become
'warm'!—

But see how much I have written about this which you
will think six words too many for — .../ Good night I must go
and sleep—

*Carlyle returned from Scotland early in October troubled by sickness
and insomnia. Tormented by cock-crowing and a neighbouring pianist,
he rashly demanded more alterations to the house. Jane wrote to the
feminist novelist Martha Lamont about their problems, thanking her
for her latest book. She enjoyed a rousing Christmas party at the
Macreadys', and gained a new admirer, the writer Arthur Helps. She
found ripe targets for satire in the visit of some Americans, including
the elder Henry James, and in the affectation of the Unitarian educator
Elizabeth Jesser Reid.*

SUSAN STIRLING   NLS Adv. MS 20.5.25.29
Cottage, Dundee

[14 Nov. 1843]

...Your letter found me just in the thick of *un*packing and
putting by my husband—the *unpacking* was got
accomplished within a reasonable time, but the *putting by*—
Oh *Dio!*—*that* has proved a work of some difficulty—and
has kept my hands full—up to the present hour!! The whole
period of his absence I was as busy as a *Slave of the
Lamp* in making this old house bloom up into new
conveniences and comelinesses to charm his soul and senses
at his return—the quantity of needlework alone which I
accomplished in the shape of chaircovers sofa-covers all sorts
of covers was enough to put Penelope for ever out of peoples
heads as the model of industry and to set up M*rs* Thomas
Carlyle in her place.— And to be sure for three days the man
was in '*a certain*' admiration over the improved state of
things especially over his new-papered newcarpeted new-

everythinged Library—but on the fourth day the young Lady of next house took one of her fits of *practising*—whereupon he started up and declared in a peremptory manner to the Universe that 'he neither would nor could write, or think, or *live* any longer, alongside of *that accursed thing'!*— In pursuance of which resolution the Carpenter (the last man on earth I was wishing to see in a hurry again) was summoned to hold deep consultation on all the possibilities and impossibilities of the case—and the practical result thereof was a new household earthquake, little inferior in awfulness to that which I had just got so thankfully to the end of! up went all the carpets which my own hands had nailed down for twelve months at least—in rushed the troop of incarnate demons—bricklayers, joiners, whitewashers &c whose noise and dirt and dawdling had so lately driven me to despair—down went a partition in one room up went a new chimney in another—Helen instead of exerting herself to stem the torrent of confusion seemed to be struck (no wonder) with a temporary idiocy—and my husband himself at sight of the uproar he had raised was all but wringing his hands and tearing his hair—like the German Wizards servant who had learnt magic enough to make the broomstick carry water for him but had not the counter-spell to stop it!— Myself could have sat *down* and cried—so little strength or spirit I had left to front the pressure of my circumstances— —but crying makes no way,—so I went about *sweeping* and *dusting* as an example to Helen—and *held my peace* as an example to my husband—who verily as Mazzini says of him 'loves silence somewhat *platonically'*— It was got thro in the end—this new hubbub—but when my husband proceeded to occupy his new study he found that Devil a bit he could write in *it* any more than beside the piano—'it was all so strange to him'! The fact is the thing he has got to write—his long projected life of Cromwell—is no joke—and no sort of *room* can make it easy— And so he has been ever since shifting about in the saddest way from one room to another like a sort of domestic wandering Jew!—

    ... Alas! one can make fun of all this on paper but in practice it is anything but fun I can assure you—there is no help for it however— A man cannot hold his genius as a sinecure. . . . God bless you dear Susan— I love you always. . . .

MARTHA LAMONT   Strouse
Liverpool

...Friday [29 Dec. 1843]

...Thanks also for having said a word in season to my husband
on the heterodox state of his opinions respecting us women.
That he thinks us an inferior order of beings—that is, an order
of beings born *to obey*; I am afraid there is not the shadow of a
doubt!—not that he is in the habit of promulgating such
opinion with any offensive clearness. He never almost speaks
about *women in the abstract*, and for this and the other
concrete woman I have heard him express a very passable
admiration: but this reticence—I should say from his practice—
proceeds not from any misgivings on the question of our
inferiority, nor yet from any delicacy towards *our* feelings; but
simply and solely from that self-complacency of full conviction
which finds its natural expression *in silence*; just as nobody
thinks it worth while to call peoples attention at midday to the
fact of its being daylight!— Never mind!— As Napoleon said at
St Helena when they *would* make him into *General Buonapart*
'They may *call* me what they like they cannot hinder me *being*
what I *am*!'— So these arrogant *men* may please themselves in
their ideas of our *inferiority* to their hearts content; they cannot
hinder us in *being* what we *will* and *can* be. Oh we can afford
very well to laugh at their *ideas*, so long as we feel in ourselves
the power to make slaves, and even fools of the wisest of
them!— .../ with sincere esteem / Jane Carlyle

JEANNIE WELSH   NLS 1892.133
Maryland St, Liverpool

[9 Jan. 1844]

...Last Sunday I had thought to write you *such* a letter—as long
as my arm—and as interesting 'as—as—*anything*'! But 'the
Countess' came and made me go out with her 'against my
sensations,' and I came in so chilled that I had to warm myself
with *brandy* and nestle on the sofa under the big shawl; that I
might be resucitated for a party of *Americans* that was to take
effect the same evening— and the wretches all came—and
there was such a drawling and *Sir*-ing!— I would have given a
crown that you had been there for 'it was *strange* upon *my*
honour'! There was a Mr James with a wife and wifes-sister. 'Not
a *bad* man' (as C would say) 'nor altogether a fool,'—but he

has only one leg—that is to say only one real available leg—the other, tho the fellow of it to appearance consisting entirely of cork— Now a man may be as agreeable with one leg or three legs as with *two* but he needs to take certain precautions— The onelegged man, is bound in mercy to all people with merely ordinary nerves to use some sort of *stick* instead of trusting to Providence as this Mr James does. So that every time he moves in the room it is as if 'a blind destiny' had been set a-going, and one awaits in horror to see him rush down amongst the tea-cups, or walk out thro the window-glass, or pitch himself head-foremost into the grate! from which and the like imminent dangers he is only preserved by a continual miracle! For *me* with *my* nerves you may fancy the *awfulness* of such a visitor!— Of his two women what could anybody say?—unless that they giggled incessantly, and wore *black* stockings with lightcoloured dresses. Then there was an American '*General*'!— *General Baird*—the very image of Mr Pecksniff, without the slyness. His ample breast was covered with a white waistcoat—open very far down to shew the *broach* in his shirt—hair set round with pearls—the whole thing about the size of a five-shilling piece! He seemed there as a living confirmation of Dickens's satires on the American *great men*—and several times I burst out laughing in his face— *The General* was brought by a Mr Coleman who was sent us last summer by John Greig—an exceptional yankee!—so full of life and glee, tho turned of sixty!—a sort of man one feels tempted to *kiss*. so benevolent and *good* without any cant about it—and with such affectionate eyes— I daresay I SHALL kiss him someday—the other night I found to my surprise that I had got the length of standing with one of my arms round his neck!! Which must have been a cruel sight for *Creek* who was also of the party—*brought* by Arthur Helps and his beautiful little atom of a wife in their carriage— He had been dining with *them* the promoted Creek!—and *they* had asked my leave to come and SEE the Americans and 'took the liberty of bringing Mr Craik along with them.' He behaves very well now the 'poor fellow'!—does not come above once in the two months—and still his *devotion* survives even this self-inflicted absence—if I fling him one civil word he looks as if he would fall down and kiss my great toe! and answers in the plaintive tone of a lovelorn Shepherd in the Poetry of the Middle Ages— I begin to be *wae* for 'poor Creek'! Such unrequited devotion I have not found in all Israel! . . .

Remember me to Gambardella since he has emerged again into the sphere of visibility. you may tell him I met his M*rs* Reid at that Birthday party—and had the honour of being regarded by her with a marked terror and dislike—happily she went away soon— You would have laughed to have heard her as I did trying to *indoctrinate* one of Dickens's small children with *Socinian benevolence*—the child about the size of a quartern loaf was sitting on a low chair gazing in awestruck delight at the reeking plum-pudding which its Father had just produced out of 'a gentleman's hat'— M*rs* Reid leaning *tenderly* over her (as benevolent gentlewomen understand how to lean over youth) said in a soft voice—*professedly* for *its ear* but loud enough for mine and everybody elses within three yards distance—'*Would* not you like that there was such a nice pudding as that in every house in London tonight? I am sure *I* would'!— The shrinking uncomprehending look which the little blowzy face cast up to her was inimitable—a whole page of protest against *twaddle!* if she could but have read it!

Mazzini was here yesterday so *bright* as I hardly ever remember to have seen him. I saw one sunny flash in his eyes which might have been the first waking to life of Pygmalions Statue! his face is all but well now— But besides *that*, some 'change has come over the spirit of his dream'— I know not what it is— I know only that he looked almost dazzlingly beautiful yesterday and that this beauty was plainly the expression of some inward newfound joy! Elizabeth [Pepoli] came in—'the white face with which I had left her on Sunday had haunted her all the afternoon and she could not be easy till she knew how I was'— 'but I see' said she 'with a peculiar look and tone that you are QUITE *well* now'— The fact was, Mazzini and I had just been regaling ourselves with wine *figs* and gingerbread, and when the rap came to the door I bade him put away the glasses and he put them into—*my writing desk*! so that when she opened the room door we both presented an unusual appearance of discomposure—which Elizabeth whose head is always running on 'what shall I say—strange things upon my honour'— interpreted doubtless into a 'delicate embarrassment'— Elizabeth to have been always *virtuous*, as I am sure she has been has really a curious incapacity of comprehending the simplest *liason* between man and woman. She would not *sit down*—but having quite *looked us thro and thro* (as she thought) went home 'to write letters'—

I have got back Geraldine's MS. very much altered and amplified I cannot give an opinion of it as yet having read only two Chapters—

Mrs Paulet *said* true in *saying* that I *said* that I felt *tempted* to run away to Liverpool but the end of the sentence, which she suppressed, undid the beginning—

I do feel so *tempted* almost every day of my life at present for to be here in the present state of Cromwell is almost more than flesh and blood can bear— However there is no use in Jeremiahds over what cannot be helped— Cromwell *must* come to an end or *he* and I will come to an end—and in either case where will be—an end!— . . . .

Determined to advance Geraldine's career as a novelist, Jane persuaded Carlyle's publishers to look at Zoe, *calling on Edward Sterling and George Lillie Craik to write in its favour. She and Carlyle were moved by the plight of Mrs William Fraser, an abandoned wife who was accused of adultery and compelled to appear in court. Jane was then off to Liverpool to see her uncle John, Elizabeth Paulet nearby and Geraldine Jewsbury. It was a time when her bankrupt but favourite cousin, Captain James Baillie, a former notorious 'dandy', was sent to the debtors' prison. In September, the Carlyles were devastated by John Sterling's death. Yet, only a few weeks later, when the 'lovably improper' Elizabeth Paulet was in London, old Edward Sterling pondered how anyone could not 'fall in love with her'?— the answer lying, Jane fancied, in '"one's" seventy four years of age!—with the additional fact of having just lost by death the noblest of sons . . . . O the thrice-grained Goose!' (CL 18:232). Jane and Carlyle generously helped to remove Richard Plattnauer, an aristocratic German exile, from a lunatic asylum. At which point Edward Sterling's son Anthony began to express what Jane called 'family' feelings towards her. His wife Charlotte was convinced that they were lovers, and a similar accusation was levelled by Bessie Helps. However unwise Captain Sterling may have been, nothing came of it; and whatever affection they shared was later changed to resentment when some years later he objected to Jane's influence on John Sterling's daughters, to whom he was guardian.*

GERALDINE JEWSBURY   NLS 3823.91
Manchester

[29 Feb. 1844]

. . .The very day I last wrote to you, finding *after I was in it* that I might take Sterlings carriage to the Strand, I drove to Chapman

& Halls and presented myself to these Dignitaries, without either M.S. or *Credentials* but on what M*rs* Mudie would call 'the broad basis' of my own feminine merits! You may think that it was taking my hens to market in a rainy day, going with my *feminine merits* to an old dingy bookshop in the Strand— But trust me for always knowing where and when I can turn my *womanhood* to account—*that* I believe is an instinct which every woman beyond the rank of an idiot brings into the world with her— M*r* Chapman had been several times to this house on business with my husband—and in my husbands invisible hours had been shown in to *me* as a substitute—and on these occasions he had—*blushed* as if he were going to break a blood-vessel! and I having a great feeling for blushing men (when they are not sheepish withal) treated him with 'a certain' marked politeness— So I said to myself thou hast thrown thy bread on the waters and shallt find it after many days. Accordingly I asked not for Messrs Chapman and Hall—but for M*r* Chapman and was told—that his Sister was just dead and he could not be seen—but that M*r* Hall was forthcoming— I had chosen precisely the wrong moment— However to come away with nothing whatever accomplished was contrary to my nature so I requested to see this Hall—and a poor little insignificant spectacle it was! ... I requested to be taken into a private room and the small Hall with a look of considerable perplexity bowed me into his dark *Sanctum* where stood to my consternation poor Chapman leaning on the mantlepiece and all bewept! the large face of him absolutely swollen with weeping—however such is the ennobling power of a deep grief that he received me this time without any embarrassment but with the air of the most perfect Gentleman, and it was to him that I addressed myself after all— I told him my own impression of your book, the impression which it had made on two men of cultivated minds, and my husbands idea of your general tallents 'tho he had not had time to spare from Cromwell to inspect this particular manifestation of them.' And moreover I told him you were a sister of Miss [Maria] Jewsbury—but very unlike her—and to my thinking a person much more likely to suit our *existing* public taste—on which Chapman surprised me by saying 'Oh he remembered you perfectly he had seen you one day in my house' —tant mieux— The result of this first visit was a promise from both Partners to 'give the *M S* their *most serious consideration*' — I did not however send it to them immediately—judging that it would be better to wait a little till Chapman should have got thro' the sad cares of his Sister's funeral and be a little more in a condition for giving 'serious consideration' to any earthly thing— Meanwhile I got a note of *general recommendation* from Carlyle—which I am sorry I did not keep a copy of for your *amusement*— He had not read this M.S. himself, he said but 'a friend of *mature years* (that's me!) quick insight and *sufficiently impatient tempe*r had read it all thro even in its Manuscript state and without a single expression of weariness—but with apparent interest and pleasures, a fact which of itself said much he considered to its credit.' To this note I added a repetition of my own favourite opinion, backed with that of the Thunder of the Times and the Author of the Pictorial history of England—and having tied up all this along with a kind message to Mr Chapman not as a Publisher but a *Man* and the *Corpus delecti* itself of course. I left it at the shop on Saturday last—and am now waiting with my 'sufficiently impatient temper' for their answer.

I wish *something* would really prosper in my hands—just to show me that I am not like Mazzini under a *fatality*.

Oh Geraldine have you been reading the daily papers last week? If so you could not miss a *crim con* process which filled many columns of them for four successive days. But little would you think of the downright *agony* of suspense in which *I* was watching its progress— I neither a *principal* nor even a witness! I was not when this infernal prosecution was first started a friend of Mrs Fraser's— She called on me at my first coming to London with her 'handsome husband' but they were just newly married then and she looked so happy so *triumphant* over her bad bargain that I did not take to her— never returned her call—refused their invitation to dinner—and there our intercourse terminated— John afterwards became intimate with her at Munich where her husbands extravagance compelled them to reside for several years—and from him I had heard much of her virtues as a Mother and *housewife*—and Carlyle who dined with them after their return to this country had also a good opinion of her—and was very sorry for her when after a horrid course of dissipation and extravagance her husband finally deserted her some two years ago—about a month before the birth of her last child! When this Process came to light Carlyle and John were both *certain* of its atrocity and that the poor woman had *done nothing*—for me after such

treatment I should have stood up for her whether I believed
that she had *done anything* or no—in fact I have quite made
the case *my own*— '*Esprit de Corps* my Dear'? says Carlyle—
Before her acquittal I sent her a message by John that I begged
permission to come and be of some comfort to her—and on
Saturday I went to see her—perfectly indifferent in the warmth
of my indigation how many people might *cut* my acquaintance
in consequence. Had you found her as I did—streching out her
arms to me from her bed, with a burst of hysterical weeping—
so pale and wasted and nearly out of her wits you could hardly
have resisted the temptation to go off and assassinate the
wretch of a husband on the spot— I fear she will never be
herself again in this world—tho the verdict was in her favour it
appeared to be due to the Jurys detestation of her husbands
conduct rather than to their conviction of *her* innocence and
this is the public feeling about it—for *me* I solemnly believe her
innocent—but *that* as I have said would hardly have increased
my sympathy with her . . . . I will do all I can to console her—but
it is so little! for I fear after all his diabolical usage and this
infernal climax to it, she is still *in love* with her own husband!
several things she said to me the other day left that impression
on my mind—and that sort of feeling makes a woman eternally
irrevocably a *victim*—

   I have been very ill again myself—but I have no more time
for writing— God bless you Your affectionate / JC

TC   NLS 602.152
Cheyne Row
                                [Liverpool, 1 July 1844]

Dearest— I was in considerable perplexity how I should
manage on Sunday— For you cannot displease my uncle more
than by declining to go to church—as early as Saturday
morning he was questioning me as to which church I meant to
go to— By way of compromise, I timidly murmured something
about James Martineau— Providence however kindly took the
matter into its own hand—and arranged it so that I stayed at
home and yet gave no offence—for when the Sunday morning
came, I was sufficiently ill of headach to convince all beholders
that I really could not get up—and if I could not get up it
followed that I could not go to church— I rose before dinner in
time to address your newspaper, and today I am quite well

again—that is to say as well as one CAN be, living as I feel to be doing just now, in a sort of exhausted receiver!— The manner of being in this house is really—'what shall I say?—strange— upon MY honour'! the preparation, and deliberation and unwearying earnestness with which they all dress themselves *three times a day* is a continual miracle for me combined as it is with total want of earnestness about every thing else in Heaven or earth!— I declare I am heartily sorry for these girls so good naturally, so gentle and even intelligent—and all in this absurd way 'sailing down the stream of time into the ocean of eternity for Christ's sake—amen'— As for Babbie she is sunk into the merest *young Lady* of them all!—her Indolence is absolutely transcendental! and I cannot flatter myself that it is the *reaction* of any secret grief—the only confession which with all my *Schupingsing* [*clairvoyant*] quality I have been able to draw from her is that 'one ought really to have A LITTLE EXCITEMENT in one's life and there is none to be got here'!— How grateful I ought to be to you Dear for having rescued ME out of the young-Lady-sphere! It is a thing that I cannot contemplate with the proper toleration—

I wonder how you are to day—and if you made out your visit yesterday? I am sure you are working too hard without the interruptions of your necessary Evil— ...

HELEN WELSH   NLS 1893.67
Maryland St, Liverpool
                                    Tuesday [12 Nov. 1844]

... If I had not been very busy in these weeks, I really think I should have been tempted to send for sixpenny-worth of Arsnece [arsenic]—and put myself out of pain— Everlasting rain—the air a solution of soot—the universe one abominable 'Clart [Mud]'—no possibility of taking outdoors exercise, and no faculty of *sleeping* without it— And every body that comes in, sworn (one might think) in a general conspiracy, to tell one something tragical or disagreeable— I really do think sometimes that a sort of things occur to ME which occur to noone else, at least they occur with a *frequency* which has no parallel *There* is another of my intimate acquaintance gone mad!—madder than twenty March hares—and as if *I* must needs be mixed up with all the madness that occurs in my sphere—*the idea* of her *Monomania* is, that her husband is *my Lover*!!— The poor creature (Mrs Anthony Sterling) has done nothing—absolutely nothing—these many years but read *novels*—and now I suppose we are witnessing the *consummation* of her futile existence!— It is more than a fortnight ago, that hearing accidentally she was *ill*, I put on my things like a good Samaritan and went off in the rain, to see whether I could be of any help— The servants looked *strange* at me—the Master looked *strange*—the whole house had an atmosphere of *strangeness*, which puzzled my unsuspecting mind— Anthony shut the door of the Library cautiously on himself and me—and then told me his wife was 'out of her wits simply and shortly'—'Good gracious! I asked do you seriously mean that she is gone mad'?— Yes said he—she is at present in a decided state of Monomania—which the Drs say the slightest contradiction may drive into '*Hysterical phrenzy*'— 'Monomania? said I and what is her particular *idea*?'— Her 'particular idea' said Anthony with all the *military* composure in the world, 'is, that I have fallen in love with *you*—that *you* are a dreadful person—and that I ruin myself in making you presents'!—Actually the poor wretch was raving one day about his (Anthony's) having *given me my new dining room carpet and new piano*—'She was sure it was *he*'!!! and all these base visions growing out of the one poor little fact of her husband's having once given me a *crockery jug*!! You may fancy if I sat very comfortable in my chair after this *revelation* He offered me wine, which I declined tho really *needing* it—as I also declined his offer to send the carriage home with me; tho' I should have been the better of that too—in short I conducted myself like an angel of *discretion*, and *came away* with all despatch—but MY *discretion* never succeeds. The unhappy woman was told by one of John's children that I had been there, and forthwith fell into the *Phrenzy* which the Drs apprehended— For several days the poor Husband's state was truly pitiable—he could not leave her room a moment without her shrieking out that he was 'going to walk with Mrs Carlyle'—and flinging *the poker* all about— At last she suddenly took a violent *dislike to him* and would not suffer his presence, which was so far good— He still keeps her in his own house—but shut up with *three* experienced attendants in a part of the house which is *boarded* off from the rest with improvised planks—lined with *flock* to prevent her noise being heard. It is very horrible—she is sometimes like to lay all waste and has to be put in a straight waistcoat— I wish she had chosen one of her maids or some other of her *friends* than *myself* to be jealous of—almost *anybody* would have been more feasable— Nevertheless Anthony tells me this jealousy has been an affair of some standing—tho' neither of us can recall a single circumstance that could have given a rational or even irrational ground for it— Meanwhile it is slightly annoying to have ones name uttered in *shrieks*, before assembled Drs and servants—and coupled with the most ignominious epithets. Happily I never liked her much, so that I can bear her misfortune *like a christian*—and her madness is of such a very repulsive sort that one cannot feel any *tender* sympathy with it—fancy the meanness of the creature— On the night after my visit—Carlyle went up 'to speak a word of comfort to poor Anthony' and she being not yet *boarded off*—nor contradicted in any of her caprices—sent her own maid *to listen all the while at the Library door to hear what Carlyle and her husband were saying of her!!*

Curiously enough—another married Lady of my acquaintance [Bessy Helps]—*not* mad—has just at this moment—misfortunes never coming single—taken up a rabid jealousy of poor innocent *me!* Has done such absurd things . . . that *even Carlyle* 'has no longer a doubt of it' He Carlyle is making himself very merry at what he calls '*the judgement come upon me*' and calls me oftener than 'Jane' or 'my Dear' '*Destroyer of the peace of families*'! This morning as I was sitting only half-awake over my coffee, he suddenly exclaimed—'just to look at you there, looking as if butter would not melt in your mouth, and think of the profligate life you lead'! As John Carlyle would say 'it is is *very* absurd'!— He John Carlyle is expected to arrive here this evening. . . . And now with kisses world without end to all and several—I bid you adieu / Your affectionate cousin / Jane Carlyle . . .

To amuse her uncle, Jane wrote to him about the topical question of mesmerism. Harriet Martineau, 'sunk to the lips in animal magnetism' (CL 18:256) and fervently believing that it had cured her of a fatal illness, had just published her 'Letters on Mesmerism' in the weekly **Athenaeum***. Amalie Bölte was a German governess who had begun calling on the Carlyles in 1841 and for whom they had just found a post with the Bullers. She was radical, spirited, independent and a devoted correspondent of Carlyle's friend the Prussian ex-diplomat Varnhagen von Ense, who had an insatiable wish to know about the*

Carlyles' private life. Bölte pandered to it in a long correspondence feeding Varnhagen von Ense's almost prurient curiosity with gossipy accounts of her regular visits, which no biographer has yet fully explored. Jane could be impatient with her; Carlyle sometimes comes off badly in her accounts; but she revered them both, declaring that in their company 'the hours flew like minutes'(CL 25:x).

JOHN WELSH   NLS 603.256
Maryland St, Liverpool

13th December [1844]

My dearest Uncle
    I write to you *de profundis*—that is to say from the *depths* of my tub-chair, into which I have migrated within the last two hours out of the still lower depths of my gigantic red bed, which has held me all this week—a victim to 'the inclemency of the season'! ...
    Nevertheless I am sure 'I have now got the turn' for I feel what Carlyle would call *'a wholesome desire'*—to smoke! which cannot be gratified—as C is dining with Darwin—but the tendency indicates a return to my normal state of health. The next best thing I can think of is to write to *thee;*—beside one's bedroom-fire, in a tub-chair, the family-affections bloom up so strong in one!— Moreover I have just been reading for the first time Harriet Martineau's outpourings in the Athenaeum and *'that* minds me' as my Helen says that you wished to know if *I* too had gone into this devilish thing— Catch me! what I think about it were not easy to say, but one thing I am very sure of, that the less one has to do with it the better—and that it is all of one family with witch craft—demonaical possession—is in fact the selfsame principle presenting itself under new scientific forms and under a polite name. To deny that there is such a thing as animal magnetism, and that it actually *does* produce many of the phenomena here recorded is idle—nor do I find much of this, which seems wonderful because we think of it for the first time, a whit more wonderful than those Common instances of it which have never struck us with surprise, merely because we have been used to see them all our lives—every body for instance has seen children thrown almost into convulsions by some one *going thro the motions* of tickling them! Nay one has known a sensitive Uncle shrink his head between his shoulders at the first *pointing of a finger towards*

his neck!—does not a man *physically tremble* under the mere *look* of a wild beast or fellow man that is stronger than himself—does not a woman *redden all over* when she feels her lovers eyes on her—how then should one doubt the mysterious power of one individual over another!—or what is there more surprising in being made *rigid* than in being made *red*? in falling into sleep than in falling into convulsions? In following somebody across a room—than in *trembling* before him from head to foot?— I perfectly believe then in the power of magnetism to throw people into all sorts of unnatural states of *body*—could have believed so far *without* the evidence of my senses, and *have* the evidence of my senses for it also— I saw Miss Bölte magnetized one evening at Mrs Buller's by a distinguished Magnetiser who could not sound his *h* s, and who maintained nevertheless that mesmerism 'consisted in moral and intellectual superiority'— in a quarter of an hour by gazing with his dark animal-eyes into hers, and simply holding one of her hands, while his other rested on her head he had made her into the image of death—no *marble* was ever colder, paler, or more motionless, and her face had that peculiarly beautiful expression which Miss Martineau speaks of—never seen but in a dead face or a mesmerized one— Then he played cantrups [tricks] with her arm and leg and left them stretched out for an hour in an attitude which no awake person could have preserved for three minutes. I touched them and they felt horrid—stiff as iron—I could not bend them down with all my force—they pricked her hand with the point of a penknife she felt nothing—and now comes the strangest part of my story— The man who regard[ed] Carlyle and me as Philistines said, '*now* are you convinced?' 'Yes said Carlyle there is no possibility of doubting that you have stiffened all poor little Miss Bölte there into something very awful'— 'Yes said I pertly but then she *wished* to be magnetized what I doubt is whether anyone could be reduced to that state without *the consent of their own volition* I should like for instance to see anyone magnetize ME!' 'You think I could not'? said the man with a look of ineffable disdain—'Yes said I—I defy you'!— 'Will you give me your hand MISS'? 'Oh by all means' and I gave him my hand with the most perfect confidence in my force of volition and a smile of contempt—he held it in one of his and with the other made what H Martineau calls some '*passes*' over it—as if he were darting something from his finger ends— I looked him defiantly in the face as much as to say, you must learn to sound your Hs Sir before you can produce any effect on a woman like *me*! and whilst this or some similar thought was passing thro' my head— flash—there went over me from head to foot something precisely like what I once experienced from taking hold of a galvanic ball—only *not nearly* so violent— I had presence of mind to keep looking him in the face as if I had felt nothing and presently he flung away my hand with a provoked look, saying 'I believe you would be a very difficult subject, but nevertheless if I had *time* given me I am sure I could mesmerize you at least I never failed with anyone yet.' Now if this destroyed for me my theory of *the need of a consenting will*—it as signally destroyed *his* of *moral and intellectual superiority*—for *that* man was superior to *me* in nothing but animal strength as I am a living woman! I could even hinder him from *perceiving* that he had mesmerized me by *my* moral and intellectual superiority! . . . Of course a vast deal of what one hears is humbug—this girl of Harriets seems half diseased—half make believing— I think it a horrible blasphemy they are there perpetrating in *exploiting* that poor girl for their idle purposes of curiosity! In fact I quite agree with the girl that had this Mrs Winyard lived in an earlier age of the world she would have been burnt for a witch—and deserved it better than many that were—since her *poking* into these mysteries of nature is not the result of superstitious ignorance but of *educated* self-conceit. In fact with all this amount of belief in the results of Animal magnetism I regard it as a damnable sort of tempting of Providence which I 'as one solitary individual' will henceforth stand entirely aloof from— And now having given you my views at great length I will return to my bed and compose my mind.

Love to all—thanks to Helen—with tremendous kisses / Your devoted Niece / Jane Carlyle

that wretched little Babbie does not write because I owe her a letter—a letter from her would have been some comfort in these dreary days of sickness but since she has not bestowed it I owe her the less thanks—

Harriet Martineau, in fact, was profoundly attracted by her 'dearest Jenny'. Jane also always welcomed the 'handsome', 'charming' and 'noble' Tennyson, unlike Browning, whom she never liked. Carlyle had been working to obtain Tennyson a Civil List Pension.

HELEN WELSH   NLS 1892.294
Maryland St, Liverpool
                                                  [31 Jan. 1845]

... Carlyle went to dine at Mr Chadwicks the other day, and I
not being yet equal to a dinner altho I was asked to 'come in a
blanket and stay all night!' had made up my mind for a nice
long quiet evening of *looking into the fire*, when I heard a
carriage drive up, and mens voices asking questions, and then
the carriage was *sent away*! And the men proved to be Alfred
Tennyson of all people and his friend M*r* Moxon— Alfred lives
in the country and only comes to London rarely and for a few
days so that I was overwhelmed with the sense of Carlyles
misfortune in having missed the man he likes best, for stupid
Chadwicks especially as he had gone against his will at *my*
earnest persuasion. Alfred is dreadfully embarrassed with
women alone—for he entertains at one and the same moment
a feeling of almost adoration for them and an ineffable
contempt! Adoration, I suppose for what they *might be*—
contempt for what they *are!* The only chance of my getting
any right good of him was to make him forget my
womanness—so I did just as Carlyle would have done had he
been there; got out *pipes* and TOBACCO—and *brandy and
water*—with a deluge of *tea* over and above,— The effect of
these accessories was miraculous—he *professed* to be
ashamed of polluting my room 'felt' he said 'as if he were
stealing cups and sacred vessels in the Temple' but he smoked
on all the same—for *three* mortal hours!—talking like an
angel—only exactly as if he were talking with a clever *man*—
which—being a thing I am not used to—men always *adapting*
their conversation to what they *take* to be a womans taste—
strained me to a terrible pitch of intellectuality— When
Carlyle came home at Twelve and found me all *alone* in an
atmosphere of tobacco so thick that you might have cut it
with a knife his astonishment was considerable!—twenty
kisses for your long amusing letter—the books came perfectly
safe—love to all Your own affectionately / Jane Carlyle

Chapter Five

Finding a Mission, 1845-47

Irritated by visits from Amalie Bölte and a young Scottish cousin, Jane
was also at first annoyed with Geraldine Jewsbury for not coming to
see her often enough while she was in London. Then, after an
emotional visit to the Welshes at Liverpool, Jane went on to Jewsbury
and the Paulets. She realized Carlyle was spending more of his spare
time with Lady Harriet, and resented his ingratiating remarks about
her 'charming bits of letters'. Jane met more Liverpudlian Unitarians,
but with the exception of James Martineau, found them a 'spoonful of
dishwashings' (CL 19:149).

JEANNIE WELSH   NLS 1892.340
Maryland St, Liverpool

                                                          [15 June 1845]

...Here has been no Row but plenty of Bother— I was *obliged*
to take in Miss Bölte for a few days in the first place, and she is,
with her many talents and good qualities, a most teazing
inmate—in as much as she never ceases *staring* at you from
morning to night— But of course I know her ways by this time
and merely took her as a disagreeable piece of *virtue* calling on
me to do it—and so it is done— She is now gone to a very
good situation where she has a hundred a year and it is
devoutly to be hoped she may remain there for a time and half
a time.At all events I have determined if she cannot stick there;
to wash *my* hands of her future— Then the very day she went
arrived my Uncle Roberts eldest son from Edin*r*— He wrote me
a letter a good number of weeks ago—taking me on my weak
side—exploiting our relationship and saying very pretty things
in the tone of regret that he should know me only by name—
He might perhaps 'run up to London for a few days in June,'
when he had undergone his law-trials and 'wished to know if
he would find us then here'— You know I had not seen him
since he was in petticoats—and I detest his Mother—but my
own Fathers nephew—I *must* be kind to him at all *risks*— So I
asked Carlyle in fear and trembling if it would bother him
much should the Boy come here to stay during 'the few days'

they talked of— 'Oh I suppose you will sedulously keep him out of *my* road' said C 'and in that case he can do me no particular harm'— And so I asked him to come here at once instead of going to a lodging—an invitation seized on with avidity—and which was of course the *aim* of his sudden development of 'natural affection' for me his unseen Cousin—

It is now near *a fortnight* that he has been here, turning the house at least all ones regularity and quietness upside down—and then he is not one of those loveable people for whom one can resign oneself to be put about— He is a long sprawling ill-put together youth—with a low brow a long nose and hanging jaw a sort of cross betwixt a man and a greyhound!— He never *sits*—and his boots always creek as if they had a Devil. He is argumentative and self-complacent beyond anything that one can conceive out of Edinr—not a bad fellow absolutely—with a certain *shrewdness* and a certain *honesty* and even *naiveté*—but *so* disagreeable! And then *of course* he is out every night at some theatre or other devilry—and I never gate to bed till far on in the morning—and then he cannot be got wakened in time for *our* breakfast but after repeated assaults on 'the wooden guardian of his privacy' which he carefully *locks* every night as if he were a delicate virgin—he comes sprawling down at ten or eleven o'clock and needs a second breakfast made for him—and in the same manner he runs after *Sights* at our dinner time and needs a second *dinner* made for him—and all this fuss in such hot weather drives me to despair— I sincerely hope he will be got home to Edinr next week—where he had better remain for the future— Carlyle could almost *kill* him I see—but there is no help for it now— If you heard him spouting off his Edinr Logic on Carlyle!—with no more respect for his superior years and wisdom than if himself were the Archangel Michael! or if you had seen him the other night dashing in with the rudest questionings and contradictions into the talk of Lady Harriet who unluckly had come to tea—you would wonder we have let him continue to breathe so long! One comfort is that he is in the fair way of going home with what he calls his *Principles* entirely subverted—for the first few days I was bored to death with the *free kirk*—and the *respectabilities* and 'the three thousand punctualities'—and now—today for example— *Sunday* (the better day the better deed) he is stretched out *on the green* (thank God) reading—*Zoe!*—with intense

enthusiasm—feeling he says as if it were 'to constitute a new
era in his spiritual existence'— He saw Geraldine on her way
thro' and *she* gave by her *profane talk* the first shock to his
principles but *the Book* is still more effectual— I told him a
few minutes ago that 'having ascertained the slight tenure by
which he held these respectabilities of his; it was to be hoped
he would henceforth cease from *twaddling* about them,' and
he took the advice quite gaily— Geraldine was two days in
London and spent most of her time here while the Brother and
Sister in law went after Sights— I received her very coldly but
there is no quarrelling with that creature! before she had been
in five minutes she sat down on the floor at my feet and untied
my shoestrings— What are you doing I asked?— 'Why my dear I
am merely going to rub your feet— You look starved—I am
sure your feet have not got well rubbed since I did it myself last
year'!! and all the two days she did not leave off rubbing my
feet whether I would or no for a quarter of an hour together—
I never saw her look so well—she actually looked like a
woman—not as formerly like a little boy in petticoats—
Whether it be her love affair that has developed some new
thing in her I cannot say; but their was now and then a gleam
on her face that was *attractive*— I could now fancy a *man*
marrying her! She had not left this house two minutes on the
Sunday night when Robertson came! I was so glad they had not
met *here*—and an hour after Robertson Gambardella rushed in
like a madman 'had a cab at the door to take us off instantly to
see a comet thro his Telescope'—we went and saw the Comet
and various stars— He comes ocasionally—not too often—and
is always *good* for *me* as ever—which is a miracle—and really
his attentions to Carlyle are most goodnatured he came the day
before yesterday 'to take Carlyle to bathe him and give him a
swim'—but C had fortunately gone to ride. He has a horse now
and rides every day— Ah how well I should like to run alone
down upon you for a week—even without that sugar plum of
having my *costs cleared!!*—but C looked *grim* and utterly held
his peace when I put out a feeler on the question— Tell my
Uncle that I think a still more judicious application of his
windfal were to pay his own expences up here— It is a perfect
shame for him never to have seen the metropolis of his own
kingdom I have breakfasted at Rogers's this morning where
was Thomas Moore— I have many things more to tell you but
enough for one Ever your own J C

TC   NLS 603.187
Cheyne Row

Seaforth—/ Sunday / before post time
[10 Aug. 1845]

'*Monsieur le President!* I begin to be weary of the
treatments I experience here'!— Always my 'bits of letters' and
'bits of letters' as if I were some nice little Child writing in
half-text on ruled paper to its Godpapa!— Since Jeffrey was
pleased to compliment me on my 'bits of convictions'; I have
not had my '*rights of* WOMAN' so trifled with! *He* payed the
penalty of his assurance in losing from that time forward my
valuable correspondence; with *you* I cannot so easily cease to
correspond, 'for reasons which it may be interesting not to
state'; but a woman of my invention can always find legitimate
means of revenging herself on those who do not 'treat her with
the respect due to Genius'—who put her off with a pat on the
head or a chuck under the chin, when she addresses them in all
the full-grown gravity of five feet-five-inches-and-three-
quarters—without her shoes! So let us hear no more of my *bits
of letters*, unless you are prepared to front a nameless
retribution! ...

On wednesday we called for the Martineaus in their new
house in the Prince's Park—the extreme *West End* of
Liverpool— A pie-crust sort of house, with all the 'curiosities
and niceties' that a Unitarian Minister could wish, including a
magnificent Broadwood Grand Pianoforte—'presented' as M*rs*
M. made haste to tell us 'by the congregation.' The People
themselves were 'as I had known them—methinks
better—certainly not worse'— M*rs* Martineaus *beard*, all over
the chin, had grown indeed some half inch longer since last
year, but that is quite an extraneous circumstance. James
appeared to be still fighting it out with his conscience, 'abating
no jot of heart or hope'! I never saw a man whom I felt such an
inclination to lead into some sort of wickedness—it would do
him 'so much good'!— If he were beside *you* I am persuaded he
would soon become the sincerest disciple that ever you
had—he seems so very near kicking his foot thro the whole
Unitarian Concern already!— He was arguing with Geraldine
that day about 'the softening tendencies of our age' 'the
sympathy for knaves and criminals' 'the impossibility of great
mind being disjoined from great morality' 'the stupidity of

expecting to be happy thro doing good'— Nothing *could* be
more *orthodox*! But what would have *ingrushed* him with *you*
more than anything—was in talking of Cromwells doings in
Irland,'after all' he said 'people make a great deal more outcry
over massacres than there is any occasion for—one does not
understand all that exorbitant respect for *human life*, in
overlooking or violating every thing that makes it of any value'!
He is coming here to dine at *two* on Wednesday, with his wife
and his 'little ones'— ...

Here is my letter from the post office at last— The Seaforth
Minister does not allow the postbag to be opened till after
Church time—'that peoples thoughts may not wander to their
letters during service'—I should fancy ones thoughts likely to
wander much more after a letter *in the bag* than *out of it*. Now
I must send this off, without further chatterment.... Ever your /
Affectionate / Jane ...

*Jane was beginning to fear that she was losing her role as companion
to 'genius'—yet she took pride in corresponding with Carlyle's new
followers, including the Irish nationalist Charles Gavan Duffy, who
edited the weekly* **Nation**. *He was to be tried for treason in 1848, when
Carlyle supported him, and he escaped conviction. He was later premier
of New South Wales. After looking forward to a six-week stay at the
Ashburtons' over Christmas, 1845, Jane was soon bored with idleness
and luxury, humiliated by Carlyle's flirting with Lady Harriet, and
resentful at his liking to be away from home. Though Lady Harriet tried
to gain Jane's trust, Jane saw her as a rival.'She said of her to me', said
Thomas, 'Something in her like a Heathen Goddess!'* **(Reminiscences**
99). *She was not the only woman whose jealousy was aroused: on
marriage to Mill, Harriet Taylor had refused to let her husband accept
the Ashburtons' invitations.*

*Plagued by feeling neglected, headaches, drugs and insomnia, Jane
confronted Thomas and seems to have demanded that he restrain himself
and stop seeing Lady Harriet. Carlyle only partly understood but asked Lady
Ashburton to stop writing to him. Jane felt betrayed and unwanted, but
nothing could distract Carlyle while he was revising for the second edition
of his* **Cromwell**. *Stopping only to appeal to Mazzini, she shot off to stay
with the Paulets at Seaforth. Some of her letters for this time are missing.
She wrote to Mary Russell that the 'Great heat of London' had made her
'quite ill again ... when, I made up my own mind ... independently of
him, and started off hither'* (**CL** 20:228). *To Carlyle she declared, 'I shall
do quite well here for a while .... For you, you must feel as if a millstone*

had been taken off your breast' (CL 20:222). Mazzini wrote to her: 'It is only you who can, by a calm dispassionate fair re-examination of the past send back to nothingness the ghosts and phantoms you have been conjuring up. . . . Let the rest to Providence'. Yet her dramatic account of the scene at the post-office shows her immense relief at receiving her husband's birthday letter to his 'poor little Jeannie—no heart ever wished another truly "many happy returns" . . . thou art dearer to me than any earthly creature'. Even so, her situation was far from settled.

CHARLES GAVAN DUFFY   Strouse: a copy
Dublin
                                               [14 Sept. 1845]

. . . Thank you—*emphatically*—for the beautiful little volume you have sent me [his *Ballad Poetry of Ireland*], 'all to myself' (as the children say). Besides the prospective pleasure of reading it; it is no small immediate pleasure to me as a token of your remembrance; for when one has 'sworn an everlasting friendship' at first sight, one desires, very naturally, that it should not have been on your Irish principle, '*with the reciprocity all on one side*'!

The book only reached me—or rather I reached it—last night—on my return home after an absence of two months, in search of—what shall I say—*a religion*? Sure enough if I were a good Catholic, or good Protestant, or good anything; I should not be visited with those nervous illnesses which send me from time to time out into space to get myself rehabilitated after a sort by 'change of air.'

When are you purposing, thro the strength of Heaven, to break into open Rebellion? I have sometimes thought that in a Civil War I should possibly find my 'mission' *moi*! But in these merely *talking* times a poor woman knows not how to turn herself; especially if, like myself, she 'have a Devil'—always calling to her— 'march! march!' and bursting into infernal laughter when requested to be so good as specify; *whither!*

If you have not set a time for taking up arms; *when* at least are you coming again to '*eat terms*' (whatever *that* may mean)? I feel what my Husband would call 'a real, genuine, healthy desire' to pour out more tea for you! My said Husband finished his Cromwell two weeks ago—then joined me at a place near Liverpool—where he remained a week in a highly *reactionary* state—and then *he* went North and *I* South; to meet again here when he has had enough of peat-bog and his *platonically* beloved 'Silence'—perhaps in three weeks or a month hence. Meanwhile I intend a great Household Earthquake! thro the help of Chimney Sweeps, Carpet beaters and other the like products of the Fall of our first Parents....

Success to all your wishes except for the destruction of us Saxons and believe me always very cordially yours / Jane W. Carlyle

From the time of Jane's mother's death at Templand, Mary Russell (the wife of Dr John Russell) shines out as Jane's special friend.

MARY RUSSELL   NLS 603.216
Thornhill

...30*th* December [1845]

...We are just returned from our Hampshire visit—and I can answer for one of us being so worn out with '*strenuous idleness*' as I do not remember ever to have been before! Six weeks have I been doing absolutely nothing but playing at battledoor-and-shuttlecock—chess—talking nonsense—and getting rid of a certain fraction of this mortal life as *cleverly* and uselessly as possible—nothing could exceed the sumptuosity and elegance of the whole thing—nor its *uselessness*!— Oh dear me! I wonder why so many people wish for high position and great wealth when it is such an 'open secret' what all *that* amounts to in these days—merely to emancipating people from all those practical difficulties which might teach them the *fact* of things, and sympathy with their fellowcreatures. This Lady Harriet Baring whom we have just been staying with is the very cleverest woman—out of sight—that I ever saw in my life—(and I have seen all our 'distinguished Authoresses') moreover she is full of energy and sincerity—and has I am quite sure an excellent heart—yet so perverted has she been by the training and life long humouring incident to her high position that I question if in her *whole life* she have done as much for her fellow creatures as *my mother* in *one year*—or whether she will ever break thro' the cobwebs she is entangled in so as to be any thing other than the *most amusing* and most *graceful* woman of her time The sight of such a woman should make one very content with one's own trials even when they feel to be rather hard! ...

I have never yet thanked you for your welcome letter—but not the less have I thanked you in my heart— I was just expecting my husband's return when it came, and was busy making all sorts of preparations for him—then; after he came, I was kept in a sort of worry till we got away to Bay House— ... God Bless you dear M*rs* Russel and your Father and husband. ...

HELEN WELSH   NLS 1893.31
Maryland St, Liverpool

Friday [24 April 1846]

... I would have answered your letter in the *enthusiasm of the moment* if the moment had not been needed for more practical purposes. There was much to be put straight on my return *morally* as well as *materially*, and I had not even my *normal* amount of force either moral or material to bring to the work: for the excitement of a houseful of the most exciting and excited people during the last ten days had been a prodigious overbalance to the '*pure* air' and other advantages of Addiscombe. The more I see of aristocratic life, the more I wonder how people with the same system of nerves as oneself, and with the same human needs, can keep themselves alive in it—and *sane*! Lady Harriet especially, who is the woman of largest intellect I have ever seen—how *she* can reconcile herself to a life which is after all a mere dramatic representation, however successful, fills me with astonishment and a *certain* sorrow. But like the pigs they 'are used to it.' and nobody, I fancy knows till he try how difficult it is to tear himself loose from the network of Lilliputan packthreads in which our nobility grow up from their earliest days. a *poor* woman has enough of serious occupation cut out for her by the nature of things—sometimes *more* than is good for her—and therein lies *her* grievance—we in *our* sphere have also something given us to *do*—how far it may suit our taste is another question and a secondary one—we see at least how our activity may be turned to account better or worse. but a great Lady—should *she* take a notion to wrap herself in a blanket and go to sleep like *Beauty* for a hundred years; what would stand still that needs to go forward?—only herself!—and should she take the better notion to put away Great-Lady-things and lead a rational useful life how is she to set about it? how extricate herself from the imposed *donothingism* of her *position*?— As Lady Harriet herself once said to me 'one would have to begin by quarrelling with all one's husbands relations and one's own'—a beginning that one may be excused for finding rather questionable!— No! it is not *easy* for a Great Lady in these days to be anything but 'an ornament to Society in every direction,' and *that* her Ladyship succeeds in being—to perfection! The old illustration of the camel passing thro' the eye of a needle still holds good— Let those who are not in the camels shoes, among whom are you and I, be thankful— ...

The Cromwell-turmoil is again subsiding and the second edition will be out in a few weeks.'*Thanks* God'! And now I hope we shall really be done with that man! if he had been my Husband's Own Father he could not have gone thro' more hardship for him! We have lived 'in the valley of the shadow' of Cromwell now, as of Death, for some three years— But every thing comes to an end if one have patience— What is to come next Heaven knows— We have been enquiring all about for houses in the country—without, it seems to me, much chance or even *much intention* of a practical result— Sometimes—in desperately bilious days Carlyle speaks of returning to Scotland and living *there* 'in seclusion for his few remaining years'— I do not look for much practical result to *that* idea either— Still this perpetual talk of moving takes away all ones pleasure (such as it was) in Chelsea— I feel myself no longer in a *home* but in a *tent* to be struck any day that the commanding officer is sufficiently bilious. When the warm weather comes and it is coming fast—the present restlessness will mount into a crisis of some sort—a journey somewhere— But as yet I do not see a fortnight before my nose....

I wish you would go oftener to Seaforth— Mrs Paulet is a *real* woman full of kindness and a sort of dreamy intellect— whom you would get to like—and she is much disposed to like *you*. She is full of *bashfulness* little as she *looks* it, and does not know how to accommodate herself to *young Ladies* but such a young lady as you might find it easy enough to accommodate yourself to *her*. When I hear the talk of the women that come about you in Liverpool I have often thought what a godsend for you a *friendship* with a woman of Mrs Paulets *natural* character and speculative turn of mind might be— You would soon find, if you took to studying her, that her disorderly housekeeping and all that first shows itself make a very small fraction of the whole woman— Kisses without number to my uncle....

TC   NLS 603.219
Cheyne Row

[Seaforth Hall, near Liverpool]
Tuesday [14 July 1846]

Oh my dear Husband Fortune has played me such a cruel trick
this day!—but it is all right now! and I do not even feel any
resentment against fortune for the suffocating misery of the last
two hours. I know always, even when I seem to you most
exacting, that whatever happens to me is nothing like so bad as
I deserve— But you shall here all how it was—

Yesterday in coming back from the Post office where I had
gone myself with the letter to you, my head took to aching and
ached ached on all day in a bearable sort of fashion till the
evening when Geraldine came over from Manchester—and the
sudden bounce my heart gave at sight of her finished me off on
the spot— I had to get myself put to bed and made a bad
wakeful night of it—so that this morning I was nervous as you
may figure—and despairing of all things—even of the letter
from you that I expected so confidently yesterday.

*Encourage*ment came however from a quarter I was little
dreaming of—*before* the post time—before I was dressed in
fact—heaven knows how she had managed it—there was
delivered to me a packet from—Bolte! at Cambridge!—a pretty
little collar and cuffs of the poor things own work with the
kindest letter—after all my cruelties to her!— Well I thought if
she can be so loving and forgiving for me—I need not be
tormenting myself with the fear that *he* will not write today
either— And I put on the *collar* there and then, and went
down to breakfast in a little better heart— At ten—the post
hour I slipt away myself to the post office but was 'detected'
by Betsy and Geraldine who insisted on putting on their
bonnets and accompanying me— I could well have dispensed
with the attention—however I trusted there would be a letter
and their presence would only hinder me reading it for a
little— And *two* were handed out which *I* stretched *my* hand
to receive—both for Betsy!— *None* for *me* the postmistress
averred!—not a line from you on my Birthday—on the fifth
day! I did not burst out crying—did not faint—did not *do*
anything absurd so far as I know—but I walked back again
without speaking a word, and with such a tumult of
wretchedness in my heart as you who know me can

conceive— And then I shut myself in my own room to fancy
everything that was most tormenting— Were you finally so out
of patience with me that you had resolved to write to me no
more at all?—had you gone to Addiscombe and found no
leisure *there* to remember my existence?— Were you taken ill
so ill that you *could* not write? that last idea made me mad to
get off to the railway and back to London— Oh mercy what a
two hours I had of it!— And just when I was at my wits end, I
heard Julia crying out thro' the house— 'Mrs Carlyle Mrs
Carlyle! Are you there! here is a letter for you!' And so there
was after all!—the Postmistress had overlooked it—and given
it to Robert when he went afterwards not knowing that we
had been. I wonder what *love-letter* was ever received with
such thankfulness!— Oh my dear I am not fit for living in the
World with this organisation— I am as much broken to pieces
by that little accident as if I had come thro an attack of Colera
or Typhus fever— I cannot even steady my hand to *write*
decently— But I felt an irresistible need of thanking you by
return of post— Yes I have kissed the dear little cardcase—and
now I will lie down a while and try to get some sleep—at least
to quieten myself will try to believe—oh why can I not believe
it once for all—that with all my faults and follies I *am* 'dearer
to you than any earthly creature'— I will be better for
Geraldine here she is very quite and nice become—and as
affectionate for me as ever / Your own / JC

*Geraldine Jewsbury wisely realized that Jane was happiest when
busy. Visiting Manchester Jane enjoyed meeting the inventor and
industrialist Joseph Whitworth, and a Greek merchant Stauros
Dilberoglue. She was impressed by the northerners' directness, but bored
by her family in Liverpool, and upset by their slovenly housekeeping
and 'mania about dress' (CL 21:34).*

TC   NLS 603.223
Scotsbrig

Carlton Terrace [Manchester] /
Sunday morning [23–24 Aug. 1846]

My Dear—I came here meaning to stay two days—and behold I
have stayed two weeks! *four* several times I have engaged to be
in Liverpool and broken my word—a thing unprecedented in
my annals of visiting! But really Maryland Street is no pleasant

outlook—only to be undertaken in fact from a sense of
duty—and then Chelsea after!— I cannot profess to feel any
impatience for *that* either as the case stands—so that finding
myself well here for the time being I have needed only *pressing*
enough to keep me. I am to go tomorrow however at last, and if
I should never see Manchester again the recollection of the
kindness I have experienced in it and the good it has done me
will make it dear to me as long as I live. I long to tell you all I
have seen and done—but it would fill a volume and must lie
over till we meet—the amount of exercise of body and mind I
have gone thro has astonished myself and proves I think clearly
enough that I have no 'liver-complaint' whatever other devilries
I may have— Geraldine no sooner perceived that I took interest
in the practical activity of this place than she applied herself to
getting me admission into all sorts of factories, and day after day
has passed for me in going up and down in '*hoists*' and thro
forests of machinery for every conceivable purpose— I have
seen more of the condition of my fellow-creatures in these two
weeks than in any dozen years of my previous existence—and
shall return to London quite as well qualified to write *little
books* on the 'manufacturing districts' as either Camilla Toulman
or Arthur Helps— Only *one* day we let ourselves be kept at
home by rain of which there has been plenty and two days were
spent out of Manchester—one with Bamford in his 'Cloughs'
[Hills]—and the other with a very interesting *Lady* at
Bolton—there is no lack of interesting people here—and they
have a great superiority over the London people in as much as
they do not answer 'God knows!' to any question whatever—but
every man knows what he is about and is able and willing to
give a straightforward account of it— Whitworth the inventor of
the besom-cart and many other more wonderful machines has a
face not unlike a baboon speaks the broadest Lancashire could
not invent an *epigram* to save his life but has nevertheless 'a
talent that might drive the Genii to despair' and when one talks
with him one feels to be talking with a *real live man*—to my
taste worth any number of Wits 'that go about'— We spent
yesterday at his house in the country (for I am now in Monday
morning) which is the reason of your being a day longer
without letter. his cab which was to fetch us arrived in the
midst of my writing—quite promiscuously—at half after eleven!
and we did not like to keep it standing in the rain till I should
finish— A young Greek merchant whom I very much like—an

admirer of yours, but still more I am afraid of Emerson's, came
home with us and staid till twelve—and even at that late hour I
started writing after I had gone up to bed—not knowing what
might come in the way this morning to hinder me—but the
fates had decided once for all that I should not sign and seal a
letter for you yesterday— While I was sitting scribbling with all
my clothes still on, even to the broaches and bracelets, down
plumped my candle into the socket and left me in total
darkness—to scramble into my nightclothes as I could—

I start at twelve from this house—but shall only go from
Manchester by the five oclock train—having several *offices* to
take leave at—besides being to dine at Mr Whitworth's office at
two—along with the town-Clerk!! Geraldine has kept to her
purpose of not leaving me a single vacant hour up to the last
minute—and her treatment I believe has been the most
judicious that was possible—it has brought back something like
colour into my face and something like calm into my heart—but
how long I shall be able to keep either the one or the other
when left to my own management God knows best—or perhaps
another than God knows best— Nor is it to Geraldine alone that
I feel grateful—no words can express the kindness of her
Brothers—tonight I shall be with all of my family that remains
but that thought cannot keep the tears out of my eyes in
quitting these strangers who have treated me like the dearest of
Sisters— You will write to Maryland Street—I shall not stay
there beyond a week I think—I will write to Lady Harriet at my
first leisure tho' her note did not seem to want any answer

My kind regards to your Mother and the rest Ever yours / JC

HELEN WELSH   NLS 1893.78
Maryland St, Liverpool

Hon*ble* W. B Baring / Bay House
Alverstoke / Hants / Wednesday
[20 Jan. 1847]

... Lady H received me most kindly with a certain recognition of
my *weak* state—hardly to have been hoped from her— She
actually ordered me some hot soup—*before* dinner—and had
assigned *me* the largest bedroom this time and C my old little
one— There is no soul here but herself— Lady Anne Charteris is
in the neighbouring house and comes in *during* the HEAT of the
day—but she is a prisoner after sunset— — Mr Baring and Mr

Charteris went up to London yesterday morning—not to return till the end of the week— C Buller will come every Saturday and stay till Monday—

—I do not go out here either—it feels quite as cold as in London and I have got some cold *in my head* but that is nothing to cold in my *left lung*. Nothing can exceed Lady H's TACT so far—and I feel very grateful to her—as I am not *up* to much *agitation* just now— Many thanks dear for your punctual discharge of my commissions—satisfactory in all but the *drawing out of the bill* which cannot stand as it is—the beautiful blue and white ribband I will take as a present and be thankful but that is all I can take on *that* principle— Never mind the *auricolas*—I *shall get thro the thing* without *them*— I do not know how long we shall stay Lady H does not mean to go to Town till the 1st of March—and 'really *does* hope that now I *am* here, I will stay—and *let Mr C go back by himself if he wishes it—he might surely spare me a while for my good.'* She will read no german with him— 'Now that her health is so improved she has no longer any pretence for giving up society—and she cannot carry on *that* and find time for studying languages'— Moreover she has got a green parrot—to which she pays the most marked attentions even in spite of his calling it a *green chimera*— And the *Parrot* does not mind interrupting *him* when he is speaking—does not fear to *speak thro him* (as that phrase is) and her Ladyship *listens to the parrot*—even when C is saying the most sensible things!— By Heaven she is *the very cleverest* woman I ever saw or heard of—*she can* do what she wills with her own— I am perfectly certain there is not a created being alive whom she could not gain within twenty four hours after she set her mind to it— Just witness myself— how she plies *me* round her little finger whenever she sees I am taking a reactionary turn—

Lady Anne is a dear little Soul—*true* to the back bone—and so beautiful! How ridiculous my life is as a whole! such shifting scenes—such incongruities,—material splendour alternating with material squalour—one time unable to get a cup of tea without two or three men-servants mixing themselves with the concern—another day advertising in the Times for a Maid of All-Work—and thankful to get one who can boil a kettle! Ach Gott! I like more 'even tenor' in ones life—it requires a versatility of genius to adapt oneself to these abrupt changes—which *if I have it*—I should prefer not being

required to use it.— My *mind* at all events keeps on the even
tenor of its way—always with more *weight* on it than it can
well bear always envelloped in London fog (figuratively
speaking) burn this letter of course— ....

MARGARET WELSH   Huxley, *IJWC* 623
Maryland St, Liverpool

Bay House, Hants
22nd January [1847]

...I had a great domestic calamity some two months ago which
was indeed the immediate occasion of my illness—a maid
[Helen Mitchell] who had been with me eleven years and took
entire charge of my house and self was invited to Dublin by a
prosperous brother to keep house for him— He is making very
rich as a manufacturer of coach-fringe and had suddenly
bethought him of having this sister to be his servant—I
fancy—not his 'Mistress' as she flattered herself. And it was too
much to expect that her human nature could resist such
tempting offer. So off she went not without tears to leave
me—and I entered into possession of a young woman selected
for me in Edinr by our old Haddington Betty. Betty has taken
into the Free Church and I fear has lost her once excellent
judgment in it for the creature she sent me turned out to have
nothing earthly but 'free grace' plenty of *that*—but no '*works*'
nor disposition to acquire any. She informed me to my horror
that she had been partly educated at religious meetings held by
my Aunt Anne!! Had I known *that* at first she should never have
sailed to London at *my* expense. In trying to get her to do her
work—and doing it for her when she could not or would not; I
caught the dreadful cold which confined me nearly a month to
bed and from which I am only now emerging— Just a fortnight
after her arrival—whilst I was lying at death's door—a doctor
seeing me every day—she sent me word by my cousin one night
that if I did not let her go away she 'would *take fits*—and *keep
her bed for a year* as she had done once before in a place she
did not like'!! *One* in bed was enough at a time and so next
morning a *Sunday morning* (Oh my Aunt Anne!) she went her
ways dressed out like a street walker—in the finest
spirits—leaving me as I have said in bed—no servant in the
house—a visitor who had to turn herself into a servant—and so
full was she of free grace that it never once seemed to cross her

mind that there was no reason in justice that I should have paid two guineas—to afford *her* an opportunity of paying a visit to some cousins she had in London!— Defend me from servants educated by religious Ladies they are all alike— ...

Chapter Six

Looking out into the Vague, 1847-49

On 13 April 1845 Jane had begun a notebook of rather desultory anecdotes. After her death Thomas noted on it 'Piece of the destroyed **Autobiog***[hy] (for most part)'. Among her tales, some of which are already known, are two about Jane's Temperance 'cousin'.*

MS and *CL* 30

...Of all the people who come about our house nobody tells me more 'interesting particulars' than my five times-removed Cousin John Dunlop, the Father Mathew of Scotland and England. Pity that with so many genuine things to articulate, he should have so defective a gift of articulation! Pity too that he should give that weary *'chick'* with one corner of his mouth in every pause of his sentences! Surely his Wife was very neglectful of her duty that she did not drive that *'chick'* out of him in the first years of their wedlock—she might, by making a row every time he committed it— I have driven more than one such tendency out of *my* husband, of which his future Biographers will never know to thank me. Among the things which he (John Dunlop) told me on his last visit were two adventures which had befallen little Balfour, his Agent in the Temperance business, or as he calls him his *'Lieutenant'*— Lovers of adventures, seem to me the only class of Mortals on this world who verily find always what they seek This little Balfour has a great love of adventures and his luck for them is quite wonderful. He has been *'working'* of late months in the Seven Dials ... and strange to think of, considering what off-scourings of Creation are there huddled together, he is listened to for most part without insult, and a considerable number sign his pledge! Being in a house one night in this tabooed quarter with many persons about to crown his wishes by *signing*; he asked; 'but *can* you? you are rather a *rum-looking* set for being able to write'! 'Oh yes' said they 'we can all read and write—and more than that, there is one up stairs who knows Greek and Hebrew!' Balfour of course did not come away without mounting up stairs to investigate into this Seven Dials Phenomenon of Scholarship and there on a wretched garret he found a Middle-aged Man, horrid-looking with sickness and want—his clothes in rags, and his shoes *tied on his feet in seperate pieces*. When Balfour had spoken with him a little, the other, seeing he had to do with a Temperance-Man, enquired whether he knew Mr Dunlop? Balfour was only too happy to answer in the affirmative, and then it came out that this Unfortunate with his Shoes in several pieces, starving in a garret of the Seven Dials, had been some ten years ago an acquaintance of Mr Dunlop's and a prosperous Physician in Glasgow. He had in the most sudden incomprehensible manner, fallen into drink,—lost his practice, been cut by his friends, tried what beating his Wife could do for him; until she also took to drinking in sheer despair: and *there* were the Couple cast on the wide world, with no prospect when little Balfour found them but that of Death by Starvation and *delirium Tremens* in a garret of *Seven Dials*! ...

Can *I* do nothing? How helpless in Gods Universe do I sit here, compared with little Balfour *ci-devant Marine Stores-Dealer*—and himself a reformed drunkard! ...

————————

The second adventure of the little Temperance Lieutenant was of a still more romantic character.

In leaving a house in Seven Dials one day he saw two men at the end of the street who seemed to be watching and waiting for him, and these men he knew by heaven knows what mysterious signs to be pick-pockets or '*Crack-Men.*' Being a brave little Balfour however, he would not turn out of his natural direction, but walked on keeping all his eyes about him until he had come up to the men who accosted him with the question; whether he was not in the habit of *praying* with the people thereabouts? He told them that he did not meddle with anything so sacred as *that* and that they might easily find themselves a seemlier joke. But the men insisted that he *could pray*, and they were not joking at all; but really wanted his prayers for a sick friend of theirs who had sent them there to look for him. Since that was the case said Balfour he would attend them to their sick friend and do his best—and they led him away into Drury Lane the most questionable looking stairs

and closes and up into a little room—very poor but very clean
and comfortable—where he found a young woman whose face
he had seen often enough—on '*the streets*'—a street walker in
fact who led him to a bed where was lying a young man of
twenty two or so in the last stage of consumption.The sick man
thanked him for coming and begged him to read to him the 5th
chapt of James.While Balfour was reading he heard a noise of
persons running up the stairs; and then the two men who had
fetched him and who had stationed themselves like sentinels at
the open door, exclaimed *hush* hush! And gently closed the
door, themselves remaining outside.After a little more fuss on
the stair a voice called thro' the keyhole '*Joe's acquitted*'! the
sick man made a gesture of satisfaction, and a gleam of
satisfaction lighted up his face—for a moment—but he took no
further notice. He told Balfour that his only comfort was in
thinking of *the Thief on the Cross*. Balfour visited him twice
afterwards, but when he went again the poor young man was
dead— From a Scotch Baker close by, and other persons in the
neighbourhood, he learned that this sick Thief had been thro
the whole of his long illness—that is to say for eight or nine
months supported in [e]very possible comfort by two *thieves*
who fetched Balfour to pray with him, and tenderly nursed and
cared for by the young woman whom Balfour saw there—a
Common Prostitu[t]e! When Balfour spoke to these about the
wickedness of their lives; they told him 'they knew all that as
well as he did, but *what could they do*? their characters were
gone—nobody would give them honest work'—'What could
they do?' repeated Carlyle at this point in the story—'They
could do *this* at least—*die*—rather than go on in such a coil of
infamy'—But dear Carlyle, is not life sweet even to 'the scum of
Creation'? Is it not very hard to make up ones mind to *die* rather
than crib [steal] a gentlemans silk handkerchief? . . .

*Cheyne Row was enlivened by a visit from the heir apparent of the
Grand Duke of Saxe-Weimar, drawn by Carlyle's connection with Goethe.*

HELEN WELSH   NLS 1893.125
Maryland St, Liverpool
                                                  Monday [5 July 1847]

. . . I have been worse than usual all last week and do not seem
tending to betterness this week— Perhaps the *iodine* of which

I had been taking daily (by Johns order) for a fortnight *ninety* drops (!) at three takings, had got to disagree with me— Anyhow I gave it up on my own judgement—leaving the dumpling to its fate for the present— John approved my doing so—when I told him—but *all* Johns prescribings are on the pattern of that one recorded by his Sister Mary when her children had the measles 'You had better give them some *senna—or perhaps you had better not*'— The lump has got no larger—neither is it perceptibly diminished and as it gives me no pain and no inconvenience the least in the world beyond that of having to wear something round my throat it may stick there till it grow more formidable and then I will consult some *regular* Dr—

If it had not been for my plenty of headaches; I would have sent you sooner, for the benefit of my Uncle chiefly, a penny-a-line account of the Grand-Duke's visit to Cheyne Row—and now it looks an old story, and I cannot get up even penny-a-line steam about it— Here however is *the* fact of the business— Saturday gone a week the Secretary announced in *official* style, that 'his Royal Highness Reigning Duke of Saxe Weimar' would call for Mr Carlyle next day at twelve *if convenient*—and received of course an affirmative reply— On Sunday morning I *dusted all my little things* very accurately—put clean water to some flowers I already had—saw that Anne bloomed out into her best gown—(for Anne unless expressly ordered would not dress herself *out of the usual time* for Queen Victoria, never to speak of a foreign Highness—) and then—I walked off into space!

Had I staid at home I was going to have felt myself 'in a *false position*'—either I must have been put *au secret* in my own house—or invited down to my own sitting room, as an ineffable condescension—and I did not feel any *besoin* of the *condescension* of anybody— With Carlyle it was all right—the Prince had to do with *him*—and the visit was honourable to both parties—but I should only have embarrassed his Highness and he me—and so I went up to Mrs Buller's— She insisted on my staying till her driving hour, when she would take me home— I came in half an hour after the dinner hour expecting to be reproved—but C's first words were 'you have just missed these people by ten minutes'!— 'From twelve till twenty minutes after five'? What a frightful royal visit I thought; but it had not been so bad as that— At twelve the little Secretary had arrived 'all in a sweat' to say the Queen Dowager (*our visitors* Aunt) had insisted on his going to Church with her!! So it was hoped an hour or two later would make no difference— About four they came that is to say the Prince his Chamberlain and Secretary in a handsome open carriage with two servants behind, who excited Ann's admiration by their 'genteel dress—plain black coats, blue breeches, and white silk stockings— Nothing the least fine about them except their—*gold garters*!' Another thing seemed to have stuck her rather forcibly—'So soon as the carriage stopt the Prince took off *his hat* and then all the rest did the same—and at going away they all remained bear headed till the Prince put on his hat after he had sat down in the carriage' And all this uncovering of heads I really believe Ann considered honour paid to— —her Master!— In which blessed illusion I allowed her to remain, as a new reason for cooking his chops to the best of her power!— C liked the Prince very well—but who would not like a Prince that came to pay one a morning visit,—he is only some four or five and twenty—very handsome C said, 'with beautiful blue eyes' 'extremely aristocratic looking'—(who is to look aristocratic if not Kings and Queens?)—'the most dignified German' C had ever seen '*More* dignified, than Plattnauer,' I asked— 'Why—no—the indistructable dignity of Plattnauer in *all sorts of coats* is what one *never* sees the like of.' When they arrived C was doing *a Yankee* of all things—introduced by Emerson, but he had him up stairs and dismissed him summarily—with apologies—the Yankee loitered, and seemed to think it strange that *he* should not be invited to assist at the interview—

When C came down to the low room he found his Highness *standing* with the other two men. He apologised for *intruding on his retired habits* &c &c then said looking about that he could fancy himself at home in Weimar here; so many reminiscences of Goethe and of Germany:—then he went about looking at the various portraits of Goethe and finally seated himself on the sofa and *invited* C to be seated— *That* was one of the prospective etiquettes that scared me *out*—having to *stand* till I was permitted to sit down on my own chair!— He staid some hour and quarter talking 'intelligently enough' and being talked to I imagine *emphatically* enough— He invited C to Weimar—promised to show him various things—promised to send him a scarce book

they had talked of—begged that 'he would not forget
him'—(how touching! and I should think *superfluous*) and
then went in peace—

I have heard nothing of Geraldine for many days She is
very busy finishing her book down there— By the way I had
to write to M*rs* Paulet the other day that I must have back my
miniature— When she got it I told her it was C's
property—but a chance of he would remember any thing
about it till after my death when she was to be sure and
restore it— *You* had one picture of me already and if she *liked*
to have the keeping of it I thought it better there than here in
a dark box— But C happened to ask where it was and much
displeased at its being at Seaforth 'where it would be either
lost or spoilt like every thing else' and desired I should
immediately write for it so I have written and desired her to
take it to Maryland Street—that *you* may send it by the first
person you know of coming to London— ...

*The Carlyles went to Derbyshire in July as 'declared Tourists', when
the holiday was rescued by the Quaker businessman W.E. Forster, who
stirred Carlyle's interest in Ireland and attracted Jane by his youth
and affluent good looks. She once spoke of William Forster as 'the sort
of person who would have suited me very well' as a husband
(Caroline Fox, ed. H.N. Pym,* **Memories of Old Friends***, 1882, 245).
He found her one of the 'few women to whom a man could talk ... or
listen all day, with pleasure' (Wemyss Reid,* **Forster** *1:205). In
November, John Forster asked her to read the proofs of Jewsbury's
new novel,* **The Half Sisters***. Influenced by* **Corinne***, it tells the story
of the illegitimate Bianca, an Italian-English actress-'Genius', who
overcomes poverty and prejudice to achieve social eminence. Unlike
Corinne, she refuses to sacrifice her career for a useless lover, Conrad
Percy. She is contrasted with her legitimate half-sister Alice Bryant,
who has married a domineering industrialist who loves but ignores
her. Alice starts an adulterous relationship with Percy, but before they
run away she suddenly dies of fever. Jewsbury embarrassed Jane by
dedicating the novel to her and Mrs Paulet. She may also have based
the Bryant marriage on the Carlyles', and Bianca on the American
actress, Charlotte Cushman. In September Jane's admirer the old
Edward Sterling died, making way for his son Anthony. October
brought R.W. Emerson, whom they had last seen at Craigenputtoch
in 1833.*

LADY HARRIET BARING   NLS Acc. 11388.28
The Grange

Thursday [28 Oct. 1847]

... So far, all has gone better than you predicted; they do not
hate one another *yet*; C still calls Emerson 'a most polite and
gentle creature! a man of a really quite Seraphic nature! tho' on
certain sides of him overlaid with mad rubbish'—And Emerson
still (in confidence, to me) calls C 'a good *Child* (!) in spite of
all his deification of *the Positive, the Practical*—most
astonishing for those who had first made acquaintance with
him in his *Books*'!

Polite and *Gentle*, this Eme[r]son certainly *is*; he avoids
with a laudable tact, all occasions of dispute, and when
dragged into it, by the hair of his head, (morally speaking) he
gives, under the most provoking contradictions, with the
softness of a feather-bed.

For the rest; I hardly know what to think of him, or
whether I like him or not. The man has *two* faces to begin with
which are continually changing into one another like
'*dissolving views*,' the one young, refined, almost beautiful,
radiant with—what shall I say?— '*virtue its own reward*'! the
other decidedly old, hatchet-like, crotchety, inconclusive—like
an incarnation of one of his own *poems*! In his speech he is not
dogmatical the least in the world, nor anything like so
fantastical as his letters give one to suppose; in fact; except for
a few phrases consisting chiefly of odd applications, of the
words '*beauty*' and '*child*'; he speaks simply and clearly, but
without any eloquence or warmth— What I should say he
failed in is what the Yorkshire wool-cleaner called 'natur'— He
is *genial*, but it seems to be with his *head* rather than his
heart—a sort of theoretic geniality that (as Mazzini would say)
'leaves me *cold*.' He is perhaps the most *elevated* man I ever
saw—but it is the elevation of a *reed*—run all to hight without
taking breadth along with it. You will not I think dislike him as
you expected, but neither will you like him— He is to breakfast
with Rogers tomorrow morning under the escort of M*rs*
Bancroft, and goes to Liverpool I believe tomorrow night, to
lecture '*all about*.' When he returns to London, as a Lecturer, I
fancy he will go into Lodgings—

I am sure C. is *disappointed*, thinks him, if he would 'tell
the truth, and shame the Devil' a man of no sort of

significance—but he is still under the restraining grace of
Hospitality, and of *a certain* regard to consistency: besides he
has had no opportunity of unbosoming himself to me on the
subject, as we have literally not been *five minutes* alone
together since Emerson arrived: he (Emerson) sits up after me
at nights and is down before me in the mornings. till I begin to
feel as if I had got the measles or some such thing. . . . Ever most
truly / Yours / Jane Carlyle . . . / Please burn the letter

JOHN FORSTER　　　　　　　　　　　　　NLS 604.267, 266
Lincoln's Inn Fields

Saturday [15 Jan. 1848]

'*Great God*'! (as *you* say) Is not our young friend 'coming it
rather strong'? More *actresses*! more 'hysterical seizures'! more
of 'all that sort of thing' which played the deuce with her last
book! But what can you or I help it; since, as herself said of
herself long ago, she 'has absolutely no *sense* of decency' What
I regret more than the questionability of these chapters is the
total want of common sense— But perhaps my illness makes
me see things worse than they are— At all events I feel it idle
for *me* to protest any more— . . . / Ever affectionately yours /
Jane Carlyle

*

Friday night [21 Jan. 1848]

. . .Thanks for your note. *She* desired me to send the Chapter on
to *you* and so I send it—tho' it will just have to travel back to
her— This is worse than anything in Zoe, to my judgement; in
fact perfectly disgusting for a young English woman to
write—and from Chapman's point of view quite 'unfit for
circulation in families.' I would not have such stuff *dedicated to
me*, as she proposed, for any number of guineas. But I am done
with counselling her, her tendency towards the unmentionable
is too strong for *me* to stay it.

　　I am not going tomorrow after all—nor any other day for
the present. Tho' suffering from the change of temperature to
an extent that made such an enterprise a considerable risk, I
would still have forced myself to go had not a letter from Mr C
this morning indicated a sudden wish that I would give it
up—and so leave *him* free to come home immediately if he

did not get rid of a cold which *he* has caught there— 'An
interesting family' aint we? And my maid barks like a
house-puppie—and my kitten when I saw her last was running
at the eyes— . . .

*In March Mazzini left via Paris for Milan where an uprising had
broken out against the Austrians. Jane pretended to shock her cousins
with the news that she and Thomas had been the guests of Mrs Norton,
notoriously accused in a court case in 1836 of an adulterous affair
with the prime minister, Lord Melbourne. Though cleared, polite society
was wary of her. The great granddaughter of Richard Brinsley Sheridan,
she was living separately from her husband who had violently ill-
treated her. She persistently stood up for the rights of women, and her
efforts led to new legislation. To the Carlyles' great distress, Charles
Buller died later in the year, followed by his mother in March 1849.
These were also the days when Carlyle would tease their friend Amalie
Bölte, who asked him what a woman should do if her husband grew
'tired of her?' 'That is her own fault', he said, 'why cannot she make
herself agreeable? . . . She must . . . wait till he comes back to her and
then behave better'. At this, Jane seems to have stayed quietly
'thoughtful'. Yet a visit from a little god-daughter was a painful
reminder of her childlessness. But she also knew that through Carlyle
she had met such men as Godefroy Cavaignac, who died in 1845, and
whose brother General Louis Eugène had just brutally suppressed the
June 1848 rising after the deposition of Louis Philippe.*

HELEN WELSH   NLS 1893.142, 166
Maryland St, Liverpool

[16 July 1848]

. . . We dined at Mrs Nortons one day! We grow very *compatible*
dont you think?— Well she is a beautiful witty graceful
woman—whatever else. Then a dinner at the Macreadys where
was Count D'Orsay! and old Lady Morgan 'naked as robins
halfway down'—age seventy-five!—and Lady Duff Gordon and
an american M*rs* Jay (I must tell you something of *her*—a friend
of Lady Harriets had her at dinner—and after they had gone up
to the drawing room, invited her *selon les regles* to go to a
bedroom—'no indeed' said Mrs Jay with a Lady's maid air and
tone which I can give you no notion of—'no indeed—in *our*
country we never think of such a thing!— *We consider such
practices extremely injurious*! Just twice a-day we retire for

that purpose and never oftener, unless when we are in the family-way'—!! You may figure how the *English* Lady of Rank stared! Tell my uncle this tho '*decency forbids*'

Then we had another dinner at the Procters—where were Adelaide Kemble and her husband—and a morning music party at Lady Eddisburys—'the beautiful Mrs. Stanley'—that was—Darwins '*Moonface*'— Young girls—*very* young and pretty—sang with the self-possession of Grisis to an immense concourse of Ladies and (more to the purpose) of *young marriageable Lords* one of whom (Lord Dufferin) said to me—'a charming way of passing a morning this!—and such a capital thing—don't you think for *curing them* of all sort of shyness'? Decidedly!— There was one girl a real beauty—the daughter of Sir James Graham—about seventeen—with the most innocent modest face in the world and there she stood with her face to the company—trilling and quavering with *the smile* of a consumate Opera singer! It seemed to me really *bad* all this!

But I went to hear Chopin too—once in private and once at a morning concert and Chopin has been *here*!! I never heard the piano played before—could not have believed the capabilities that lie in it— Quantities of more things of the same nature I have *done*—I was going to say *in my sleep*—but *in a bad dream* were nearer the truth.

The one earthly thing that I have been getting any real satisfaction out of has been something very far away from all that—the wise and valourous conduct of General Cavaignac —and the admiration he has won from all parties— If I had been his Sister I could not have watched his progress with more interest—

Anne has had no more 'accidents'—and I suppose may hold out a while longer—but it is an inconvenient item in a servant having a prospective Husband to fall back upon in all emergencies. . . .

*

Saturday [20 Jan. 1849]

. . . I have been interrupted dreadfully these two weeks, but the wonderfulest '*go*' of all has been a *child*! Yes indeed! I have had a child—to keep,—to sit at meat with, and *sleep* with (good God!) and dress dolls for, and wash and comb and all that sort of

thing—and also (—most fatiguing of all—) to *protect* it from Mr
C who gave manifest indications of a tendency to wring its
neck! Where did I pick the creature up?— Ah my Dear! the
creature picked up me—'quite promiscuously'— I went some
six weeks ago to call at the Macreadys—and dined at the
childrens dinner and was reminded that I had a Godchild, *by
seeing it*. Not one godmotherly thing had I ever done towards
that child! and really it was a Godchild to be proud of. So now I
took it on my knee and kissed it and, like a fool, asked 'will you
go with *me*?' I should like it very much said the Child.'*That she
would*' said the Mother;'and you need not be afraid of her
misconducting herself for she is a good child'— I saw the thing
had been taken on the serious so I backed out of it as well as I
could,'Some time we shall see!—when I come again *with a
carriage*.'Well! ten days ago I went there again with Anthony
Sterling—and was asked gravely by the eldest daughter if I
'meant to take Jane Lydia back with me'? 'She had never ceased
talking about *her visit* since I had been there.' I was in for it! so I
said 'not today'; (it was necessary to prepare C's mind as well as
my own) 'but if her Mother would bring her any day she like to
name I should do my best with her'— So Saturday was
named—and the little creature delivered over to me in a
transport of joy, (hardly mutual) to stay as 'long as I could be
troubled to keep her'— I modestly suggested that three days
and three nights—just the time that Jonah was in the whale's
belly—would probably be enough of it for *her* as well as for
me—and the Mother went and I remained alone—with a child
of six years—very *stirring* and very small and delicate! during
the first day I 'ran horses' at her bidding, and performed my new
functions with a determined energy— —but the night came, I
durst not put her to sleep in the spare room—for fear of her
crying in the night—and awaking Mr C, and being herself very
miserable so after infinite perplexity in getting off her clothes
(all *sewed* together) I laid her in my own bed, where she soon
commenced—singing!—after an hour's waiting upon her I left
her still awake—when I went up again she was asleep but lying
accross the bed—at twelve I placed her properly, and went into
bed myself; but of course not to sleep: all night long she pitched
into my breast with her active little heels—and when she awoke
at seven and threw her arms about my neck calling out 'Oh I am
so glad to be here!' I had not once closed my eyes and in this
state to have to wash and dress her and play at horses again! it

was a strange and severe penalty for being a Godmother—next
night I put her in the spare bed at all risks—with a good fire and
trusted in Providence—and she did very well there—but I had
got some cold by the job and the idea of being *laid up* in such a
cause after having got so far thro' the winter on foot was very
vexatious so I kept the house a few days and when the childs
time came Anthony Sterling took her home for me!! I have a
great quantity more to tell you about this '*go*' and other
things—but Mr C has been bothering ever since I began to
write about helping him to pack a boxful of old clothes and
things for Scotsbrig—and in an hour I have to be off to Mrs
Buller so I will finish this letter to Babbie— God bless you all
your affectionate / Jane Welsh

JEANNIE WELSH   NLS 1893.169
Maryland St, Liverpool
                                                Monday [29 Jan.1849]

... Really the business of *society* gets to be quite business
enough for me without aiming at any other so long at least as I
have no *carriage* to help me thro' it.— I never go out in the
evening, indeed there have been no evening invitations for *me*
yet. ... But the forenoon irruptions of people are endless—the
other day I had poor Tom Jewsbury Geraldines *rough* brother,
who was so very kind to me in Manchester and had never been
in London since— I was quite glad over *him*, he seemed so
enchanted to see me: but William Forster (Mrs Paulets Forster)
came in and drove him away— My chief social occupations
however have been Mrs Buller and Lady Sandwich— The former
I go to from a sense of duty the latter because I like it—for Lady
S. amuses me more than any woman I ever heard speak more
than even her daughter— *She* is going off to Paris again
however presently and there will be an end of *that*. The
Ashburtons have been in town for a week, returned today to the
Grange for another week and then back to London for *the
Season*— Lady A came to see me on her arrival with an *armful
of shawl* which she laid into *my* arms, saying 'there, dear Mrs
Carlyle—there is my *late* newyear to you—at newyears day we
had so much to think of else!' and she kissed me— It was well
and graciously done— Still, *valuable* presents, for which I can
make no return, distress me always from that quarter—there are
people from whom I can take things without any *spoiling* sense

of obligation, but then I feel that I can repay them with
love—now Lady A. can do perfectly well *without* love of
mine—love from me beyond a certain point would *bore* her
rather than otherwise— She looked quite herself again—all her
wild grief over C Buller crushed down out of sight into the
bottom of her heart, or perhaps *out of it* altogether— She spoke
of him with *supreme* composure—and was in a racket of
company all the time of her stay— Poor Mr C will never
succeed in making her 'more *earnest,*' dear, gay hearted, high
spirited woman that she is! God bless her for her seeming
determination *not* to be '*earnest*' for *his* pleasure, or anyone
else's, but to be just what God has made her, the enemy of *cant*
and lover of all mirthful things— It is a great faculty that of
being able to throw off grief— I would not somehow care to
have it, and yet I see well enough how much better people, who
have it, both enjoy their life and contribute to the enjoyment of
'others'— The Anthony Sterlings are living at the Knightsbridge
house at present—he intends that Mrs S—should henceforth
remain there, and the children and Governess at Headly where
he will spend most of his days, out of the tear and wear of his
Wife's *incompatibility*—it is a great pity she will not separate
from him—it would be better for herself as well as for him—for
he cannot conceal the worse than indifference which all that is
past between them has left in his mind towards her, One cannot
blame him—he was the most devoted husband for sixteen
years—and even her madness did not estrange him from
her—until she got into that horrid state in Rome and *exposed
her person* before the male servants—no man's *love* could stand
that—his died of it, and cannot be brought to life again and he
is not a man to make-believe what he does not feel. and she
hates him (naturally) because having loved her so long and
passionately he now shies away from her— You may fancy the
little domestic *hell* of all this!—a little of 'the new ideas' might
really be introduced into English married life with benefit— ...

Robertson who has again appeared on our horizon—is to
bring Louis Blanc to tea here on Friday night— He (Robertson)
was trying to make me get up an interest about it, and when all
else failed, he said— 'I am sure you will like him—he was
talking to me today many things that would have interested
even *you*— It was in *his* arms, he tells me that Godefroid
Cavaignac died'!— I started as if he had shot me—the thing
took me so by surprise. and I could not answer one word—this

man was coming on Friday night! I felt as he would transmit me
even thus late Godefroid Cavaignac last breath! And Robertson
was watching the effect of his words!—I cared not—why
should I?— I had my boa gloves reticule &c in my lap, I flung
them all violently on the floor—why. I don't know—I could not
help it! Robertson went on to say that he Louis Blanc talked of
Godefroid as of a Divinity that General Cavaignac was very
inferior to *him* in Blanc's opinion—and then, seeing that I was
not even going to make an effort to converse on the topic he
stooped and gathered up my things saying with a significant
look—'*that*, I *suppose*, is not the place where these articles are
meant to remain, Mrs Carlyle'— I took them out of hands and
left the room— I could have killed him— I cried a little up stairs
then dressed myself, and returning to the parlour where C had
by this time joined Robertson, I said to the latter with proud
defiance enough; '*now*, Mr Robertson I have *thrown off* my
spattered gown and *everything* that made me unfit for enjoying
your agreeable company'— He looked hard at me with his
diabolic look, and said 'the metamorphosis is really astonishing!
I never saw you so magnificent before' 'Yes,' said Mr C, '*it is a
smart gown*'! I believe Robertson said that about Godefroid, in
the devilish intention of seeing its effect on me— I *know* he
had been heard to speculate on my intimacy with him— Well!
let him draw his inferences—it is no disgrace to any woman to
be accused of having loved Godefroid Cavaignac. The only
reproach to be made me is that I did not love him as well as he
deserved!— But now he is dead I will not *deny him* before all
the Robertsons alive!— . . .

*Samuel Rogers' malicious cross-questioning suggests how far Carlyle's
friendship for Lady Harriet was a matter for popular gossip. In spite of
her outward coolness, Jane was wounded and worried that her own
public sarcasms at Carlyle's infatuation were misinterpreted.*

JEANNIE WELSH   NLS 1893.219
Auchtertool Manse, near Kirkcaldy
                                    Holy Thursday [17 May 1849]

. . . I have had no more headachs since that dreadful one I told
Helen about—now that the weather is warmer I can stand a
pitcher of cold water on the back of my neck every morning

and that always agrees with me— I have been to several
parties—a dinner at Dickens's last Saturday where I never went
before—'A Great Fact!'—Forster might have called it. Such
getting up of the steam is unbecoming to a literary man who
ought to have his basis elsewhere than on what the old
Annandale woman called 'Ornament and Grander'— The dinner
was served up in the new fashion—not placed on the table at
all—but handed round—only the desert on the table and
quantities of *artificial* flowers but such an overloaded
desert!—pyramids of figs rasins oranges—ach!— At the
Ashburton dinner served on that principle there were just *four
cowslips* in china-pots—four silver shells containing sweets,
and a silver filigree temple in the middle! but here the very
candles rose each out of an artificial rose! Good God!— Mrs
Gaskell the Authoress of *Mary Barton* was there—I had already
seen her at my own house a natural unassuming woman, whom
they have been doing their best to spoil by making a lioness of
her— Before dinner, old Rogers, who ought to have been
buried long ago, so old and illnatured he is grown, said to me
pointing to a chair beside him, 'sit down my Dear—I want to
ask you; is your Husband as much infatuated as ever with Lady
Ashburton?'— 'Oh of course'—I said *laughing*, 'why shouldn't
he?'— — 'Now—do *you* like her—tell me honestly is she kind
to *you*—as kind as she is to your husband?'—'Why you know it
is impossible for *me* to know *how* kind she is to my
husband—but I can say she is extremely kind to *me* and I
should be stupid and ungrateful if I did *not* like her'— 'Humph!
(disappointedly) Well! it is very good of you to like her when
she takes away all your husbands company from you—he is
always there isn't he?'— 'Oh good gracious no! (still laughing
admirably) he writes and reads a great deal in his own
study'— 'But he spends all his evenings with her I am told?'—
'No—not at all—for example you see he is *here* this evening.'—
'Yes he said in a tone of vexation I see he is here this
evening—and *hear* him too—for he has done nothing but talk
across the room since he came in'— Very devilish old man! but
he got no satisfaction to his devilishness out of *me*— ...

Poor dear Mazzini—all my affection for him has waked up
since I knew him in jeopardy and so gallantly fulfilling his
destiny—and not mine only—the public sympathy is fast going
over to his side—under the atrocious injustice of the
French—who one year ago loudly invited all nations to form

republics and now proceed to shoot lead into the only one that
has obeyed the call— It will be the ruin of Napoleon's
government this work in Italy— I have had an *Italia del populo*
sent me daily since Mazzini started it in Rome—and you may
fancy how anxiously I expect it every morning—not sure
whether its discontinuance will not indicate that the French
have overcome— I sometimes feel myself up to wishing that
the Romans and Mazzini included may let themselves be all
blown to atoms and their city made into a heap of ruins—it
would be perhaps *that* the best thing that could be done to
rouse Italy into a right fervour of patriotism— ...

*In the summer Carlyle made a momentous tour of Ireland with
Gavan Duffy, while Jane visited the Ashburtons at Addiscombe, Joseph
Neuberg in Nottingham, W.E. Forster at Bradford and her cousins at
Auchtertool in Fife. She was moved by meetings in Edinburgh with her
old servant Betty Braid and her father's three sisters, followed by an
encounter with her once teenage-'lover' John Stodart, and the
remarkable 'Much ado' of her return to Haddington.*

TC   NLS 604.296
Galway

Benrydden / Friday 20*th* [July 1849]

... I suppose [W. E.] Forster has sent you a Bradford paper
containing the report of our meeting for 'Roman Liberty'—It
went off very successfully *as a meeting*, but did not bring in
to Forster all the 'virtue's own reward' he anticipated—and he
was out of humour for twentyfour hours after— His speech
was long-winded, not good, and his delivery the worst in
nature— The *people* (*il populo*) often cried '*Time—time*'! to
him—and once they cried 'sweet soap'!—the yorkshire for
'soft sawder'— In fact the Bradford *Gentlemen* on the
platform were like Bess Stodart's legs 'no great things'—but
the Bradford *men*, filling the Hall to suffocation, were a sight
to see!—to cry over 'if one liked'!— such ardent, earnest half
intelligent, half-bewildered countenances! as made me, for the
time being, almost into a *friend of the species* and advocate for
fusion de biens. And I must tell you— 'I aye thocht meikle
[much] o' you': but that night I 'thocht mair o' you than ever'—
A man of the people mounted the platform and spoke—a
youngish, intelligent looking man, who alone of all the

Speakers seemed to *understand* the question, and to have *feelings* as well as *notions* about it—he spoke with a heart eloquence that '*left me* WARM'—I never was more affected by public speaking— When he ceased I did *not* throw myself on his neck and swear everlasting friendship, but I assure you, it was in *putting constraint* on myself, that I *merely* started to my feet and shook hands with him—all the *Gentlemen* immitated my example and shook hands with him—then 'a sudden thought' struck me; *this* man would like to know *you*—I would give him my address in London— I borrowed a pencil and piece of paper, and handed him my address when he looked at it he started as if I had sent a bullet into him—caught my hand again, almost squeezed it to 'immortal smash,' and said; 'Oh! *it is* your Husband!—Mr Carlyle has been my teacher and Master— I have owed everything to him for years and years'!— I *felt* it a credit to you really to have had a hand in *turning out* this man—was prouder of that heart-tribute to your genius than of any amount of Reviewer-praises or of aristocratic invitations to dinner— Forster had him to breakfast next morning—...

Mrs Paulet is asleep on a sofa beside me—so young and pretty and happy looking—I wonder at her—

God bless you Dear—.../Your affectionate / Jane W C

MARTHA LAMONT   NLS 8992.188
Belfast

Auchtertool Manse 1*st* August [1849]

...Your letter has reached me within these five minutes—here in the heart of Scotland! While my Husband has been *toiling thro* Ireland, I also have been on my travels, taking it more easy— At this moment I really dont know where a letter could catch him— He *may* sail to Scotland from Belfast; his *programme* took in that possibility—and if so it is likely he may be in Belfast sooner than this letter, so I recommend you to try and '*lay salt on his tail*' yourself— I will forward your invitation to the next address he gives me—but *that* I rather expect will be Scotsbrig Ecclefechan *Scotland*—

I had just read this morning the announcement of your book—and wondered whose it was— Good luck to you and it. I hope it wont be to write up what they call 'The rights of Women' at all rates— I am so weary of hearing about these

rights of ours— and always to the tune of 'don't you wish you
may get them'?

Your '*life*' looks useful and satisfactory—I wish I could
say the same of mine—which has been for long standing still,
and looking out into the Vague. I have had ideas about
breaking out into *insurrection*, for the sake of the excitement
of the thing, and joining Garabaldi and Mazzini, or latterly the
more successful Hungarians!—but have carried them no
further into practice than by showing myself on the platform
at a meeting for 'Roman Liberty' which came off the other day
at Bradford. . . .

*An account of her visit to Haddington at the end of July, was written
only on 7 August, after reaching her cousin Walter's manse at
Auchtertool. It seems to have been meant as a record for herself rather
than a letter, though she speaks elsewhere of an account written for
Carlyle which she tore up.*

JWC'S 'MUCH ADO'   Bodleian Library, MS. Don d. 53/1

Much ado about Nothing

On Tuesday 24*th* July 1849, I left Rawdon after breakfast, and at
five of the afternoon reached Morpeth; where I had decided to
pass the night. William Forster escorted me thus far, and stayed
to start me by the 2 o'clock train next day;—out of pure
charity, having adopted Donovan's theory of me, that I am
wholly without *observing Faculty*, with large *Reflectiveness*
turned inward;—a sort of woman, *that*, ill adapted for travelling
by railway, alone, with two boxes, a writing-case, and carpet-bag.
Anyhow, I was much the better of such a cheerful companion;
to stave off the nervousness about Haddington; not to speak of
the *material* comforts,—a rousing fire, brandy-negus &c,—
which he ordered for me at the Inn, and which I should not
have had the audacity to order on my own basis.

. . . From Morpeth to Haddington is a journey of only four
hours; again 'the wished for come too late'! rapidest travelling to
Scotland now, and no *home* there any more!

The first locality I recognised was *the Peas Bridge*: I had
been there *once* before, a little child, in a postchaise with my
Father; he had held his arm round me while I looked down the
ravine; it was my first sight of the Picturesque, *that*, I

recognised the place even in passing it at railway speed, after
all these long years. . . .

A few minutes more and I was at the H. Station; where I
looked out timidly, then more boldly, as my senses took in the
utter *strangeness* of the scene; and luckily I had '*the cares of*
LUGGAGE' to keep down *sentiment* for the moment. No vehicle
was in waiting but a dusty little Omnibus licenced to carry—
any number, it seemed! for on remarking there was no seat for
me I was told by all the Insides in a breath; 'never heed! come
in! *that* makes no difference!'— And so I was trundled to *The
George Inn*, where a Landlord and Waiter, both strangers to me,
and looking half-asleep showed me to the best room on the first
floor—a large old-fashioned, three windowed room, looking on
on *The Fore Street*—and, without having spoken one word, shut
the door on me, and there I was at the end of it!—actually in the
George Inn, Haddington, alone, amidst the silence of death!

I sat down quite composedly at a window, and looked up
the Street,—towards our old House; it was the same old street,
the same houses; but so silent,—dead,—*petrified*! it looked, the
old place, just as I had seen it at Chelsea in my dreams—only
more dreamlike!— Having exhausted that outlook, I rung my
bell, and told the silent Landlord to bring tea, and took order
about my bedroom. The tea swallowed down; I notified my wish
to view 'the old church there,' and the keeper of the keys was
immediately fetched me. In my part of stranger-in-search-of-the-
Picturesque, I let myself be shown the way which I knew every
inch of,—shown the 'the school houses,' where myself had been
Dux [head pupil],—'the play-ground, the *Booli*ng [g]reen,'—and
so on to the church-gate, which so soon as my guide had
unlocked for me, I told him he might wait—that I needed him
no further.

The Church-yard had become very full of graves. Within
the Ruin were two *smartly got up* tombs; *His* looked old, old;
was surrounded by nettles; the inscription all over moss; except
two lines which had been quite recently cleared.—by *whom*?
who had been there, before *me*, still caring for *his* tomb after 29
years? The old *Ruin* knew, and could not tell me! that place *felt*
the very centre of eternal silence—silence and sadness world
without end! When I returned to the sexton, or whatever he
was, he asked would I not walk thro the church; I said yes, and
he led the way, but without playing the Cicerone any more; he
had become pretty sure there was no need. *Our* pew looked to

have never been new-lined since *we* occupied it; the *green*
cloth was become all but *white* from age! I looked at it in the
dim twilight till I almost fancied I saw my beautiful Mother in
her old corner, and myself a bright-looking girl in the other! it
was time to 'come out of *that*'! Meaning to return to the
Churchyard next morning, to clear the moss from the
inscription; I asked my conductor where he lived—with his key.
'next door to the house that was Dr. Welsh's'; he answered, with
a sharp glance at my face; then added *gently*; 'excuse me mem
for mentioning *that*, but the minute I set eyes on ye at the
George, I *jaloosed* [deduced] it was *her* we all looked at after
whenever she went up or down.' 'You won't tell of me?' I said
crying, like a child caught stealing apples; and gave him half a
crown to keep my secret, and open the gate for me at eight next
morning. Then turning, up the waterside by myself, I made the
circuit of *The Haugh, Dodd's Gardens* and *Babbies Butts*—the
customary evening walk in my teens; and except that it was
perfectly *solitary* . . . the whole thing looked exactly as I left it
22 years back! the very puddles made by the last rain I *felt* to
have stepped over before.— But where were all the living
beings one used to meet? What could have come to the place to
strike it so dead? I have been since answered; the railway had
come to it, and ruined it. . . . Leaving the lanes I now went boldly
thro' the streets, the thick black veil, put on for the occasion,
thrown back; I was getting confident that I might have ridden
like *the Lady Godiva* thro Haddington, with impunity,—so far
as recognition went,— I looked thro' the sparred [fastened]
door of our old coachhouse, which seemed to be vacant; the
House itself I left over till morning, when its occupants should
be asleep. Passing a Cooper's shop which I had once had *the
run of*, I stept in and bought two little *quaichs* [drinking cups];
then, in the character of the travelling Englishwoman, I
questioned the Cooper as to the *Past and Present* of his town.
He was the very man for me, being ready to talk the tongue
small in his head about his town's-folks, men, women, and
children of them. He told me amongst other interesting things,
that 'Doctor Welsh's death was the sorest loss ever cam to the
Place';—that myself 'went away to into England and—died
there!' adding a handsome enough tribute to my memory—'Yes!
Miss Welsh! he remembered her famously,—used to think her
the *tastiest* young Lady in the whole Place—but she was very—
not just to call *proud*,—very *reserved in her company*.'— In

leaving this man, I felt more than ever like my own gohst; if I had really been *walking* after my death and burial, there could not I think have been any material difference in my sensations.

My next visit was to the front gate of the Sunny Bank, where I stood some minutes, looking up at the beautifully quiet House.... How would my old godmother and the others have looked, I wondered, had they known who was there, so near them? I longed to go in and kiss them once more, but positively *dared* not; I felt that their demonstrations of affection would break me down into a torrent of tears, which there was no time for; so I contented myself with kissing—the gate (!) and returned to my Inn, it being now Dark....The rest of that night I spent betwixt sleeping and waking, in night-mare efforts to 'sort up my thoughts.' At half after five I put my clothes on, and began the business of the day destroying, in a moment of enthusiasm—for *silence*—the long letter 'all about feelings' which I had written the night before. Soon after six I was *haunting* our old house, while the present occupants still slept.—I found the garden door *locked*, and *iron staunchions*,—my Heavens!—on the porch and cellar windows, 'significative of much!' for the rest, there was a general need of paint and white wash: in fact the whole premises had a bedimmed melancholy look as of having '*seen better days*.' It was difficult for me to realise to myself that the people inside were only *asleep*—and not *dead—dead since many years*. Ah! one breathed freer in the church-yard, with the bright morning sunshine streaming down on it than near that (so-called) habitation of the Living! I went straight from one to the other. The gate was still locked; for I was an hour before my time; so I made a dash at the wall, some seven feet high I should think, and dropt safe on the inside—a feat I should never have imagined to *try* in my actual phase, not even with a mad bull at my heels, if I had not trained myself to it at a more elastic age....

When I had scraped the moss out of the inscription, as well as I could with the only thing in my dressing case at all suited to the purpose, namely *his own* button hook with the mother-of-pearl handle, I made a deliberate survey of the whole church-yard, and most of the names I had missed out of the *signboards* turned up for me on the *tomb-stones*. It was strange the feeling of almost *glad* recognition that came over me, in finding so many familiar figures out of my childhood and youth all gathered together in one place. . . . When the sexton came at eight to let me in, he found me ready to be *let out*. 'How in the world had I got in?'—'over the wall.'—'No! surely I couldn't mean *that?*'— 'Why not?' —'Lordsake then, cried the man in real admiration, there is *no* END to you!'—

He told me at parting, 'there is *one* man in this Town, Mem, you might like to see—James Robertson. Your Father's old servant.' Our old Jamie! he was waiter at *The Star* good gracious! had returned to Haddington within the last year. 'Yes indeed'—I said, 'he must be sent to see me at the George an hour hence, and told only that *a Lady* wanted him.'. . .

My friend the Cooper, espying me from his doorway, on the road back, planted himself *firmly* in my path: 'if I would just comple*mennt* him with my name, he would be *terribly* obliged; we had been *uncommon comfortable* together, and he *must* know what they called me!'— I told him, and he neither died on the spot nor went mad; he looked pleased and asked how many children I had had. *None*, I told him. 'None!' (in a tone of astonishment, verging on horror) 'None at all! then what on the Earth had I been *doing* all this time?' 'Amusing myself,' I told him. . . .

Breakfast stood ready for me at the Inn and was discussed in five minutes. Then I wrote a note to Mr C, a compromise betwixt '*all about feelings*' and '*the new silent system*'—of the *Prisons*. Then I went to my bed room to pack up. The Chambermaid came to say a gentleman was asking for me. 'For *me?*' 'Yes! he asked for THE *Lady stopping* here.' (no influx of company at the George it seemed) 'Did you see him' I asked, divining Jamie to the Life! and I threw my arms round his neck, that did I— He stood quite passive and quite pale with *great* tears rolling down; it was minutes before he spoke, and then he said only, low under his breath; 'Mrs—Carlyle!' So nice he looked, and hardly a day older, and really as like 'a Gentleman' as some Lords; he had dressed himself in his Sunday Clothes for the occasion, and they were capital good ones. 'And you knew me, Jamie, at first sight,' I asked?—'*Toot! We* knew ye *afore* we seed ye.'— 'Then you were told it was me?'— 'No! they told us just we was to speak to a Lady at the George, and I knew it was Mrs Carlyle,'—'But how *could* you tell, dear Jamie?' 'Hoots! *who else could it be?*' (!) Dear funniest of created Jamies!— . . .

And now there only remained to pay my bill and await the Omnibus. I have that bill of 6/6 in my writing case; and shall

keep it all my days; not only as an eloquent memorial of human
change—like grass from graves and all that sort of thing; but as
the first Inn bill I ever in my life contracted and paid *on my
own basis*. . . .

At Edin*r* Jeanie's sweet little face looked wildly into the
carriage for me, and next minute we were *chirping* and
twittering together on the platform whilst the eternal two
boxes writing case and carpet-bag were being once more
brought into one focus. . . . I was back into the Present! and it is
only in connection with the Past that I can get up a sentiment
for myself. The Present *Mrs* Carlyle is what shall I say?—
detestable—upon *my* honour! . . .

JOHN R. STODART   NLS Acc. 7012
Edinburgh

Sunday [30 Sept. 1849]

Well to be sure!—After all!— But I have not been so much
surprised by that letter as you would naturally suppose—your
frigid reception the other day did not *quite* take in *me*: it only
satisfied my Aunt Anne that I 'had wasted a good half hour of my
one day on a person who to all appearance did not care three
straws for me;—*had no more feeling than a stone*'! 'Yes,' I told
her '*to all appearance*, it was even so: but I had a mild trust that
appearances might be, in this instance as in so many other—
deceitful.' For old affection spoke up for you in my heart, that *a
quarter of a century* even, however it might 'mak a great odds'
on a man as well as 'on a girl,'—could not have *changed his
nature*—nothing but death is *up* to doing that—the 'dear John'
of 1816 was *loyal, constant, deeply affectionate, that* was *his
nature* and *all that* he must be still, must be always *at heart*;
however years and sorrows, of which doubtless he had had his
share as well as I, as well as all who live long, might have frozen
and deadened him outwardly.— And how reconcile *such*
abstract notions about you with my Aunt's notion of your 'not
caring three straws' for myself?— Indeed I did not so much as
try to reconcile them, it would amaze you to know how surely I
relied on your affection for me; how surely I have relied on it
thro' all these years: tho' no sign of it was discoverable thro' the
minutest microscope! never a visit, nor a message, nor anything
to show you recollected my existence! and when at last you
were *obliged* to see me 'quite promiscuously,' looking at me as if

I had been my own cousin twenty times removed. But in all that I saw *only* 'force of circumstances.' Not that I have a vanity equal to anything—equal to fancying myself so very loveable, that wherever I have 'been *known and appreciated*' (as your cousin Mrs.Aitken is always saying of '*David*') my image must have been, henceforth and for ever, preserved in lavender!— Oh dear no! Whatever I may have been as a girl, as a woman I am not vain the least in the world! I should like to see *the individual vanity* that could hold its own in the position of worser half to a 'celebrated author'! Decidedly it has been from no egregious sense of my own loveableness, past or present, that I have believed myself always dear to you, but simply from my immense faith, taken up long ago, in your affectionate and constant nature.

So you see how it is that your letter did not at all astonish me.

You tell me you have lost your fortune, and are obliged to *work* for your bread. Well! to speak truly, I feel no sorrow over this. If your heart ach; *work*, above all, obligatory work is the only remedy worth trying. Oh don't I know *what* a privelege is that of sitting, with folded hands, thinking over a past that *is* past, because in the present, and future, all is too dark—ailment and sorrow overclouding the present, and the future without hope or object! Oh depend on it, dear John, the loss of fortune or whatever it be that curtails one of *that* privelege is a thing to thank God for, is perhaps the one interposition that has saved me out of madness!— But your health, the loss of that is indeed a thing to grieve over, ill health is the misery of all miseries, complicates life for me to a degree that none can understand who have not tried it. It seems to me always that if one were quite well, it would be so easy to be *good*!—that every sort of amiable quality would bloom up in one like the bean tree in the fairy tale so soon as that physical pressure was lifted off! and one must go on, good God! getting always more hardened more embittered, to live and more difficulter to be lived with! Is it not very sad?—but is not life *all* very sad? I have found it so— A person who tells me he is '*happy*' looks to me either the greatest of Impostors or the greatest of miracles!— So changed I am since the days when we danced quadrilles and divined nothing of all that!

I do not know whether you meant me to answer your letter, but have followed the monition of *nature* in the

matter—and have written with my accustomed indiscretion I
suppose— But you will burn this, and it will be all the same as
if I had written to the dictation of Mrs Ellis' *à la Women of
England*. Come next time and see if I be still here—meanwhile
I wish you 'for a reason which it may be interesting *not* to
state' to write *no* other letter to me till I have seen you or
written to you again. / Ever affectionately / Your J.W.C

I got home a week ago—very ill and have continued ill
ever since— As in your case the D*rs* and I interpret in a different
sense

Chapter Seven

Unease in Zion, 1850-56

The early 1850s were often sombre for Jane and Thomas, with occasional cheerful developments, such as the arrival of a companionable white terrier, Nero. They began with the publication of Carlyle's **Latter-Day Pamphlets***, his 'Nigger Question', the outwardly conventional biography of John Sterling and reluctant preparations to write about Frederick the Great. Old Mrs Carlyle died at last (1853) and more suddenly John Carlyle's new wife (1854), while Thomas felt himself hardening into old age. As he recalled, 'No daughter or son ... had been appointed to us' and his books 'were our only "Children" ... in a true sense ... verily ours.' Yet they were to turn into the 'Friedrich affair . . . "hugging unclean creatures" (Prussian Blockheadisms)'* (**Reminiscences** *155). He insisted on working continuously being, as Jane once wrote to John Forster, 'too much occupied with the Dead ... now to bestow a moment on the living'.*

JEANNIE WELSH Huxley, *JWCLF* 341
Auchtertool

Saturday [13 April 1850]

. . .This is the only sheet of paper I have in the world, and I dare not interrupt Mr. C at his *pamphlet*, to borrow some, so I must write close and to the purpose. When I wrote last I was in the thick of a cold caught at Addiscombe. . . . Lady A. was *well* this time and in '*tearing* spirits' very kind and somehow I felt more *comfortable* than usual in most respects, but there was one grand drawback quite fatal to my enjoyment . . . there commenced the very day I left home an outrageous pimple on the very top of my nose, making me really 'too ugly for anything' and so painful that I *could* not get it forgotten if I had had philosophy enough to forget it for a moment. Could there be a more unsuitable position for transacting such a thing? it only reached its 'culminating point' the day I came away—and has since been gradually subsiding, but there is still a *redness* very distressing to my own sense of the beautiful as well as to other people's. The only person who put me at ease about it was Anthony S. [Sterling] who when I told him how it had annoyed me at Addiscombe exclaimed cordially—'Damn your nose! for a

1 Miniature of Jane Carlyle, 1826, by
   Kenneth Macleay

2 Jane Carlyle, 1843, by Spiridione
   Gambardella

3 Dr John Welsh and Grace Welsh, Jane's father and mother

4   *Notre Dame de Chelsea*, by Elizabeth Paulet

5   Anthony Sterling

6   Jane and Geraldine, 1855

7   Lady Harriet Ashburton, sketch by
    Francis Holl

8   Jane Carlyle, 1850, sketch by Carl
    Hartmann

9   Giuseppe Mazzini

10   Charles Gavan Duffy

11 Thomas Carlyle, about 1854

12 Jane's cousin, Jeannie Welsh, by
    Spiridione Gambardella

13 *A Chelsea Interior*, 1858, by Robert Tait

14   Erasmus Darwin

15   Ellen Twisleton

16   Jane Carlyle, about 1853

17   W.E. Forster, photographed by
      M. Bowness, Ambleside

18   Robert Tait

19   Jane Carlyle, 28 July 1854

20   Jane and Nero, 31 July 1854

21   Thomas and Lord Ashburton,
     photographed by Vernon Heath, 1862

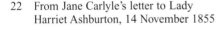

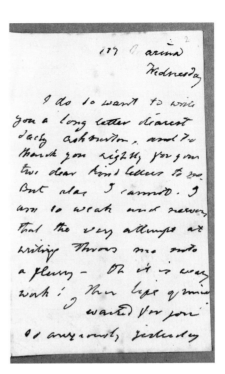

22 From Jane Carlyle's letter to Lady
    Harriet Ashburton, 14 November 1855

23 From Jane Carlyle's letter to Louisa
    Lady Ashburton, 25 May 1864

24 The Grange, drawing by J.F. Neale, engraved T. Matthews

25   Charlotte Cushman, photographed by Gutekunsi

26   *Punch*, 14 April 1866, showing Carlyle as Rector of Edinburgh University

27   Jane and Louisa Lady Ashburton in the 1860s

28   Jane Carlyle, 1862, by William Jeffray

sensible woman you have really the *oddest* ideas! as if anybody
really attached to you could love you an atom less if you were
all covered over with small-pox!!!' I should not like however to
try human love with permanent small-pox. . . .

JOHN CARLYLE   NLS 604.318
Scotsbrig
                                                [28 April 1850]

. . .A woman came to me the other morning from *Helen*
[Mitchell]—a *decent* enough looking person *respectably*
dressed and the only suspicious looking feature in whose
appearance was the *character* she *gave herself* for sobriety,
charity, piety and all the virtues. Her business was to ask me to
give the said Helen a *character* that she might seek another
place. Otherwise she (Helen) 'spoke of atempting her Life'—
'She has been long speaking of that' I said— 'Yes—and you are
aware maam of her having *walked* into the Thames, after she
left the last place you found her? Oh yes she got three months
of Horsemonger Lane jail for *the* attempt—and if a waterman
had not been looking on and *taken the first opportunity of
saving her* she would have *probably* been drowned.' I said it
was well if she had not been in jail for anything worse— Ever
since coming out she has lodged with this woman—her
Brothers in Dublin sending her money—'but very little'—from
time to time—but they seem tiring of that, and so Helen thinks
she will try service again— I recommended that she should as
a more feasable speculation go into the Chelsea Work House
where they would take care to keep drink from her, and *force*
her to work— As for recommending her to a decent service I
scouted the notion— And the woman herself said she 'seemed
to have no faculties left,'—and was always wanting 'sixpence
worth of opium to put an end to herself'— . . . But the sun is
shining brightly outside. . . . Jane Carlyle

HELEN WELSH   NLS 1893.231
Maryland St, Liverpool
                                                Thursday [4 July 1850]

. . .The Bath House Ball threw me into a perfect fever for one
week—as I had got no dress for it; not understanding that I was
to go—but Mr C was 'quite determined for once in his life to see
an aristocratic Ball and if I chose to be so peevish and

ungracious as to stay away there was no help for me'— I
pleaded the want of a dress—he 'would pay for any dress I
chose to get'; and then I fell back on the horror of *stripping*
myself, of 'being bare'—at my age after being muffled up so
many years! and that if I didn't I should be like no one else—to
which he told me angrily—'true propriety consisted in
conforming to other peoples fashions!!! and that Eve he
supposed had as much sense of decency as I had and *she* wore
no clothes at all'!!! So I got a white silk dress—which first was
made high and longsleeved—and then on the very day of the
ball was sent back to be cut down to the due pitch of
indecency!— I could have gone into *fits* of crying when I began
to put it on—but I looked so astonishingly well in it by *candle
light*, and when I got into the fine rooms amongst the
universally *bare* people I felt so much in *keeping*, that I forgot
my neck and arms almost immediately— I was glad *after* that I
went—not for any pleasure I had at the time being past
dancing, and knowing but few people—but it is an additional
idea for life, to have seen such a party—all the Duchesses one
ever heard tell of blazing in diamonds, all the young beauties of
the season, all the distinguished Statesmen &c &c were to be
seen among the six or seven hundred people present—and the
rooms all hung with artificial roses looked like an Arabian
Nights entertainment — What pleased me best was the good
look I got *into the eyes* of the old Duke of Wellington—one has
no notion, seeing him on the streets what a dear kind face he
has— Lady Ashburton receiving all these people with her grand-
Lady airs was also a sight worth seeing— On Saturday I went to
Addiscombe with a party of *boys* and *girls* and returned on
Monday night. . . . I cant imagine why Lady A always asks me to
help her with these flirting young ladies and gentlemen I feel
more disposed to wring their necks than take part in their
riotous nonsense.

Now; all is changed in *that* quarter by the death of Peel—
Lady A was deeply attached to him—she is off into the country
again to escape parties; came here on her way, all in tears, and
asked Mr C to come by himself *this* week—as one asks the
Clergyman when one is in affliction!—indeed this death has
produced a greater dismay than any public event of my time.
Not only among his own set but crowds of working people
pressed round his house all the time of his illness demanding
news which a Constable lifted above their heads tried to make

heard in vain—and written paper bulletins were finally hoisted up to be read by the crowd from hour to hour— Mr C is mourning over him as I never saw him mourn before—went today to look at the house where he lies dead!

But no impression lasts long in London society—in a few weeks they will all be visiting and 'making wits' again as if nothing had happened—

I have seen little of Geraldine—she comes pretty often but has always engagements to hurry her away— She has sworn friendship with Fanny Lewald the German Authoress [a German 'George Sand'] who is also lionizing in London at present—and gives me much of her semi-articulate company— I also met Jane Eyre (Miss Bronte) one night at Thackeays a less figure than Geraldine and extremely unimpressive to *look at*— ...

TC   NLS 604.330
Scotsbrig

Friday night [6–7 Sept.1850]

Here is a letter from Lady Ashburton, the first I have had during your absence; neither had *I* written to *her* (till I answered this today by return of post—) partly because, she had said at our last meeting that *she* would write to *me* first; and partly because, in the puddle I have been in, I felt little *up to* addressing Serene Higher Powers,—before whom one is bound to present oneself in 'Sunday clothes'—whereas I have been feeling all this while like a little sweep on a Saturday night!— But the letter you forwarded to me had prepared me for an invitation to the Grange about the end of this month, and I was hoping that, before it came, you might have told me something of *your* purposes, whether you meant to go there after Scotland, whether you meant to go to them in Paris that you might have given me in short some skeleton of a programme by which I might frame my answer. In my uncertainty as to all that, I have written a stupid neither-yes-nor-no sort of a letter—'leaving the thing open' (as your phrase is) But I said decidedly enough that I could not be ready to go so soon as the 23*d*— What chiefly bothers me is the understanding that I 'promised' to go alone— The last day I saw Lady A she told me that she could not get *you* to say whether you were coming to them in September or not; that you 'talked so darkly and mysteriously on the subject, that she did not know what to make of it'—that you refered her as usual to *me*, and then she said 'I want you both to come Mrs Carlyle—will you come'? I said 'Oh, if he go I should be very glad'— 'But if *he* never comes back as he seems to meditate, couldn't *you* come by yourself?' I answered to that, laughing as well as I could; 'Oh he will be back by then, and I dare say we shall go together. And should he leave me too long I must learn to go about on my own basis'— Went to bed— Saturday—I dont think *that* was a *promise* to go to the Grange alone on 'the 23*d* of this month.'— Do you think it was? most likely you will decline giving an opinion. Well! in this as in every uncertainty one has always one's '*do the duty nearest hand &c*' to fall back upon.... Once more 'all straight' here, I shall see what time remains before the journey to Paris, and which looks easiest to do, whether to go for a week at the cost of some unsettling, or to stay away at the risk of seeming ungrateful for kindness....

Yet Jane went and even stayed on amicably after the houseparty as Lady Harriet was ill and her husband abroad. Jane was not exasperated with her, but with Thomas. On return she fell, accidentally bruised herself, and thought him heartlessly unconcerned. She received more sympathy from her nieces.

HELEN WELSH   NLS 1893.307
Maryland St, Liverpool

6*th* December [1850]

...'The Immortal Gods' are not favourable to writing this day. Firstly, we have 'a London Fog' coming on, and if it advance at the same rate in half an hour more I should need candles to write by; secondly my morning hours have been unavoidably taken up in rehabilitating my chief winter-gown, and now I am in momently expectation of Miss Williams Wynn who is in town for two days and has written that she will come today betwixt 2 and 4—and then, today I *must* write to John Carlyle who asked last night in a letter to his brother that 'Jane would write to him *herself* about that accident'—with all this bearing me away from you, however I feel as if it would be a sort of sin not to tell you at once how grateful I feel for your and Jeanies letters containing such kind and also—oh how rare in this world! such *judicious* sympathy—and to relieve you also from any painful speculating about my accident *more than the occasion requires*— The day before yesterday I was sensible,

for the first time, of a considerable diminution of the pain, it
has been growing less and less ever since; I really *think* it is
going away altogether; I *hope* there will be no return of it; and
from the first minute I could assure myself it was *beginning* to
feel better I begun to cheer up my heart— Oh God forbid that I
should die a *lingering* death, trying the patience of those about
me; beside a Husband who *could* not avoid letting me see how
little patience his own ailments have left him for any body
else's—should *such a thing* come upon me in reality, I should
go away from here, I think, and ask *one of you* to tend me and
care for me in some little place of my own—even my low
spirits about the thing which in the first days I *could* not
conceal from him—nor in fact did I think there was any
obligation on me to *keep up appearances* with *him* brought
down on me *such* a tempest of *scornful* and wrathful words,
such charges of 'impatience' 'cowardliness,' '*impiety*,'
'contemptibility,' that I shut myself up altogether and nothing
should ever wring from me another expression of suffering—to
HIM— ...I wonder after all how I come to be grown such a
coward, for I was certainly one of the bravest little children
alive—used to bear pain like an Indian—take *hissing Ganders*
by the neck—and show myself up to every emergence— I
suppose my bravery active and passive must have been like
most of my other good qualities 'for the occasion got up'—
assumed to gain my Fathers approbation, to be *praised* by him,
and kissed, and 'loved very much indeed'— that was the right
handle to take me up by—not 'shoving me out of creation' for
my faults and weaknesses, not trying to make me heroic by
abusing me as 'contemptible and impious'!—
    How much in these two weeks past I have thought of my
Aunt Jeanie and of my 'aunt Mary'—your Mother—the latter I
never saw in her illness but I heard often of her Roman
fortitude,—and my aunt Jeanie Oh! *her* I was with in her last
weeks, and was the first who found out about her breast—and
Oh if ever a woman behaved like an Angel it was that one
When I think of her sitting whole days altering at *my* ill-made
marriage clothes, with her sad but ever gentle loving face, and
trying to keep up every body's spirits, while she was already
suffering agonies day and night—when I think of my Mother
finding fault with her for always 'using her left hand' of myself
laughing at her because when I galloped my pony and hers
followed, she *screamed* (with *pain* she told me long after) Oh

God when I look back over that whole time I feel such love and veneration for that woman! I think if I had her again for one day one hour that I might fall at her feet and ask her pardon for never having enough recognized the angel in her, till I came to *realize* thro selfish fears all she had to suffer and triumph over! Do you know what she said when I had by a sort of inspiration discovered her state and insisted on telling my Mother that she might be brought immediately to Edin*r* 'Oh no dear Jeanie! for Gods sake not yet—not yet—just wait till Mary and the children are gone back to Liverpool—*dont spoil the poor childrens visit for them*—it does them so much good to be here'! And the night before that on which she died—when I had gone to her bedside when she was in a paroxysm of pain, as soon as she could speak again—she looked to me and said 'Oh Jeanie *do* go to your bed—you are sure to have such a *headach* to morrow'! But I am writing myself into a fit of crying—and Miss Wynn on the way

God bless you all—this letter is half for Babbie / Your affectionate / Jane Welsh

You may tell Babbie for her comfort as I know she never liked him that I have had a *row* with Anthony Sterling which I intend shall be *final*— If you would like to know the *outside quarell* I will tell you another time

We do not know what the cause of the disagreement was, though it may have arisen from Anthony Sterling's dislike of Jane's influence on his late brother John's daughters. But about this time, he was the subject of a note by Jane on an odd scrap of paper (private MS) which Thomas dated '1850 or so'. She clearly took the trouble to keep it. It told how he had casually encountered in Hyde Park a respectably-dressed but unemployed beggar with his family. To test a new law against begging Sterling had given him in charge to a policeman and brought to trial. The magistrate tried to persuade Sterling to give up, but Anthony answered, 'I am not such a fool as to have brought the man here for the purpose of interceding for him—I have given myself all this trouble to see what the Law does to its beggars, and I expect you to show me that'. The man was sentenced to two weeks' hard labour, and, as Jane notes, at the cost of £1.2.6 donated to the man's wife, Sterling went off satisfied. It has been suggested that Sterling was the man for whom (as Jewsbury said) Jane was ready to leave Carlyle, but it seems extremely unlikely.

Both Thomas and Jane showed remarkable consideration for the violently estranged wife of Sir Edward Bulwer Lytton; she had written to Thomas about Sir Edward's meanness and cruelty, asking him for help in placing her new novel, which was blocked by her husband's influence with publishers.

LADY BULWER LYTTON   S.M. Ellis 25-26
Sloane Sq., London
                                                                [Early Jan. 1851]

After all you have told me, and with all my ardent *esprit de corps*, what excited in me the *realest*, the most *human* sympathy for you, is this brave eagerness to do *anything* in *honesty* for the discharge of your involuntary debts. Surely if we fail to give you any furtherance in this good purpose of yours, it shall not be for want of earnest wishing and trying.

When you describe that man and his treatment of you, I feel *amazed* before the whole thing, as in the presence of the Infinite; it is all so diabolical—so out of the course of nature, that I, who have mercifully had to do with only imperfect *human* beings at *worst*, *never* with an incarnate devil, cannot *realise* it to myself, and cannot get any more intelligent impression from it than from a bad dream, or a Balzac novel.

The very *inhumanness* of your wrongs makes it impossible for me to pity them after a right genuine human fashion; but when, not only superior but defiant of fine Ladyism and 'all that sort of thing,' you speak resolutely of *helping* yourself, and set forth your *qualifications* for a *Housekeeper*, a Companion,—you brought up to be waited upon, and one of the *cleverest authoresses* in England!—then my whole practical Scotch nature applauds you, and cries 'God speed you!' . . .

JOHN WELSH   NLS 604.343
Maryland St, Liverpool
                                                5 Cheyne Row / 7*th* January [1851]

. . . I am sure . . . you would be amused with an account of our visit, the other day, to Pentonville Prison—if I had left myself time and breath to tell it— 'Oh my!' (as old Helen used to say) 'How *expensive*'! Prisoners costing 50£ a year each!—you may fancy their accommodations are somewhat remarkable—

In each cell I saw a pretty little corner cupboar[d]—on one
shelf of which was *the dressing apparatus* a comb and brush
and *small tooth comb*! laid on a neatly folded-up towel—a
shaving jug *with mettle top* on one side, an artistic soap box
on the other!— In one cell I remarked a blue tassell with a bit
of steel chain attached to it hung from a brass rail— 'What *is*
the use of that tassell' I asked the Inspector— 'That tassell
Mam—why—that tassell is—a *fancy* of the Prisoner's own!—
we allow them to have their little fancies!'— They all wear
masks when in each others presence—that should they
afterwards meet in society their feelings may be spared—they
have such charming *bath rooms*(!)—each man has a good
sized court all to himself to run about in for an hour at a
time—and while we were there they all 'went to school' with
books and slates under their arm—*masked*!!— If any man
wants to have the comforts of life, and be taught—and 'have
his fancies' let him rush out and commit a felony!— We went
to hear their religious teaching in the Chapel— An under
Chaplain stood on the Altar with a bible in one hand and a red
book (like a butchers) in the other he read a passage from the
bible then looked in the red-book for the *numbers* (they have
no *names*) whose turn it was to be examined—for instance
he read about the young man who came to Jesus and asked
what he should do to be saved—then after consulting the red
book he called out 'Numbers *32* and *78*, what shall I do to
enter into eternal life'?— 32 & 78 answered, the one in a
growl the other in a squeal, 'sell all that thou hast and give to
the poor'—Now, my blessed Uncle did you ever hear such
damned nonsense? If a grain of logic was in the heads of 32
and 78, mustnt they have thought; 'Well what the devil are *we*
taken up, and imprisoned and called criminals for; but just,
because *we* take this injunction seriously, and *help you* to
carry it out, by relieving you of your watches 'and other
sundries'—

I should tell you too that each prisoner has a bell in his
cell!—one man said to some visitor 'and if I ring my bell a fool
answers it'!

Uncle dear, good night— If you and I were the
Government wouldn't we sweep such confounded humbug out
of creation....

The Great Exhibition, or Crystal Palace, opened 1 May.

JEANNIE WELSH   NLS 1893.245
Auchtertool Manse
                                        Sunday [11 May 1851]

...If you have heard from Liverpool in these days they would
perhaps tell you that I am scheming to have Helen up for a week
or two to see this eternal 'Exhibition' If Mr C had only carried
out his project of going off to Copenhagen the beginning of May,
great things might have come off—in which *you* might have
taken some part—but instead of what I had set my heart on I
find myself more tied up even than usual— Mr C *here,
correcting proofs* with no more tendency towards Denmark for
the present—and oh horror! the old story of a change of
servants to be gone over again the week after next! (...I have an
elderly *widow* coming this time—whom I took to at first sight
from a sort of look she has of our old Betty— I must wait till I
see whether *she* can keep the house over our heads before I fix
about bringing Helen, tolerant as I found her on a former
memorable occasion, into it—) I was not purposing to go near
the Exhibition myself till I took *her* or someone to see it—I had
not so much as gone to view the outside since it was roofed in—
But the other day Forster offered us his Examiner-ticket which
admitted both Mr C and *a Lady*—so we went and oh how—tired
I was!—Not that it is not really a very beautiful sight—especially
at the entrance; the three large trees, *built in, because the people
objected to their being cut down*, a crystal fountain, and a large
blue canopy give one a momentary impression of a Bazaar in the
Arabian Nights Entertainments—and such a lot of things of
different kinds and of well dressed people—for the tickets were
still 5/—was rather imposing for a few minutes—but when you
come to look at the wares in detail—there was nothing really
worth looking at—at least that one could not have seen *samples*
of in the shops. The big diamond indeed—worth a *million! that*
one could not have seen at any jewellers—but oh Babbie what a
disappointment! for the big diamond—unset—looked precisely
like a bit of chrystal the size and shape of the first joint of your
thumb! And the fatigue of even the most cursory survey was
indiscribable and to tell you the Gods truth I would not have
given the pleasure of reading a good Fairy Tale for all the
pleasure to be got from that 'Fairy Scene'! I have surely a great
many things to tell you *not* about the *Exhibition*— but I have
only a horrid steel pen and my paper appears to be scarce....

The Carlyles stayed four weeks at Dr James Gully's fashionable water-cure establishment at Malvern.

HELEN WELSH   NLS 1893.253
Auchtertool Manse

Wednesday [27 Aug. 1851]

...We leave Malvern on Saturday which completes the
appointed month—and on the whole I think it has been as fair
'*a go*' as discontented people like us could have found for
themselves—The *Place* has continued to please me beyond any
other 'beautiful Nature' I ever sojourned in—such endless
variety of quiet walks and drives—most soothing after
Piccadilly and the eternal *Kings-road!* Two days ago they took
me a three hours drive in the whole course of which, after
clearing the village, we met just *one* living being!—a boy
wheeling a barrow—and then if you want gaiety—there are the
hills all swarming, like bee-hives, with Ladies and gentlemen—
in astonishing wide-awakes—and embroidered *baréges*!—
clambering over the furz with Alpine poles in their hands!
Several of our acquaintances from London turned up—Mr
Twisleton—A large family of Seniors— The Miss Scott I made
such a brutal stand out against in London, who to my shame be
it spoken, turns out to be an excellent, rather agreeable old
woman, with whom I have got quite friendly—&c and the Drs
two sisters have turned out quite as nice as their first
appearance indicated— Throughout they have shown the most
perfect *tact* and politeness, as well as kindness in their
treatment of us, and *old* and *cold* as I am grown, and little
addicted any longer to 'swearing ever-lasting friendships,' I
think it was quite worth while coming to Malvern to make
their acquaintance— The Dr himself impresses me as a
decidedly clever man, with a great deal of *character*, but there
is something anti-pathetic between him and me that keeps me
as reserved with him as I felt the first day—which is probably
as well as he is dreadfully persecuted with the devotion of
LADIES— All his female patients seeming to feel it their duty to
fall in love with him—he has whole drawer-fuls of purses,
greekcaps, braces and other Ladies works—besides all the
chairs sofas and tables in the house being covered with
worsted work!— If the poor Ladies only saw the fun that is
made of their presents they would send them to any bazaar

rather!—As for the water cure I remain *open to light* about *it*—
I see people here on whom it has worked miracles, by all
accounts—to M*r* C I should say it has done simply—*nothing*—
neither ill nor good— He has been much better since he has
been here—but, no better than I have seen him invariably in
other country places, where he had the same benefits of good
air, immense exercise, early and regular hours, and wholesome
diet— All the packing and sitz-baths seem to have been a mere
exercise of his patience, which I am glad to find he has such a
stock of,—on emergency. . . .

At the end of September, Thomas was off to Paris with the Brownings,
on whom he 'left a deep impression' of a 'loving' and 'interesting human
*soul' (**CL** 26:201). He had joined the Ashburtons there, but returned*
before them as Lady Harriet was unwell. Jane went to the Grange early
in December and Thomas came later.

JEANNIE WELSH   NLS 1893.257
Maryland St, Liverpool
                                    Wednesday [15 Oct.1851]

. . . M*r* C has been sleeping like a top and eating vigourously
since his return from Paris— The Ashburtons were only two
days behind him—a fact which threw some light on his return
sooner than was expected— They (the Ashburtons) are now in
town— She brought me a woolen scarf of *her own knitting*
during their stay in Swizerland and a cornelian bracelet and—a
similar scarf only smaller for M*r* C—in fact I believe the dear
woman would never have done all that knitting for *me* unless
as a handsome preparation for doing the comforter for M*r* C—
She is really 'What shall I say?—*strange* upon *my* honour'— On
her first arrival in London she staid only two hours and drove
down here with these things— I was gone out so she left
them—with M*r* C whom she saw—and then wrote me a note
of invitation to the Grange—which I answered negatively—
'being so wearied of visiting for the present'—but begged she
would let me see her on her coming to town this week—I
would go up to her at any hour morning or evening—after
knitting me a scarf one might have supposed she would have
cared to see me for ten minutes in six months and after having
M*r* C away in Paris she might have felt it *decent* to constrain
herself to receive his wife whether she liked it or no— But not

at all! When *Mr* C who of course was there so soon as she
arrived and before *I* knew she was to arrive that day asked 'if
she would be disengaged at any time so that I might see her'
she made no answer,—he said, and in the following morning
comes a note which I will enclose— *Because* she must go to
the Exhibition with Lady Sandwich one day she could not have
me come to see her any of the three days she was to be in
town!— And the very day this note came—and after reading it
Mr C walked off and sat an hour with her and is off now again
thro a pouring rain to sit till dinner time— And he 'could not
see what the devil business I had to find anything strange in
that or to suppose that any slight was put on *me*—' on the
contrary she 'had spoken of the *impossibility* of receiving me
in the most goodnatured manner'!!— I suppose I ought to
feel by this time quite resigned to such annoyances—or rather I
ought to feel and to have always felt quite superior to them—
but I am angry and sorrowful all the same— It is not of course
any caprice *she* can show to me that annoys me— I have long
given up the generous attempt at loving her— But it is to see
him always starting up to defend everything she does and says
and no matter whether it be capricious behaviour towards his
wife—so long as she flatters himself with delicate attentions—
This did not get finished in time for the post—thro the Sterling
girls coming to call—and while they were here your letter
came— Thanks for it dear Babbie—it is very kind of you to
write at such length besides so often—when you must have
your hands and head and heart all so busily employed— With
your letter came a note from Lady A to *Mr* C which turned out
be be an invitation to *him* for this evening at 9 and after that
another note came begging he would come at 8—and he is
now off there again— I will not write any more tonight being
in rather a bitter mood and the best in such moments is if
possible to consume one's own smoke—since one cannot help
smoking—God bless you all / Your affectionate / J Carlyle

KATE STERLING   NLS Acc. 9086.8
London

The Grange / Thursday [11 Dec. 1851]

. . .The cold I caught so suddenly *that night* became much
worse on my arrival here—and has kept me so thoroughly
wretched, that I really think I should have gone home ere now,

to my own red bed, but for the fact that both Lady Ashburton and Lady Sandwich have fallen ill also—and even *as I am* I am *up to* more than either of *them*, and can do them some good by staying— I don't *go* much *on doing good*, in a general way, all that unitarian twaddle about 'thinking only of *others*''studying the welfare of *others*' &c &c I leave to Miss Rankin and the like of her—but Lady Ashburton has been extremely kind to me for many years—and our relative positions afford so few opportunities for my showing her any *practical* gratitude that when one *does* offer itself I am naturally very glad to seize it— Lord A has been from home for a week and if I were not here to sit with her in her bedroom, her situation amidst all her grandeur would be rather desolate— And as for Lady Sandwich with her french manners it requires all the good sense I can bring to bear on her to keep her *quiet*— There being about a quarter of a mile of corridors and staircases between the bedrooms of the two; I get plenty of *indoors* exercise, at least, in travelling, from the one to the other!—but in this way I have hardly any time to myself—to write my own letters or think my own thoughts—besides that when I do get to my own room for a little while I need to lie on my sofa with my eyes shut—to rest my wearied spirit— I look forward to Saturday with perfect terror—the House is to be filled with people on that day—and if Lady A cannot appear I shall have to *do* them all myself—with *this cold*! While Lady A was coughing and blowing her nose this morning *I* was taken with a violent fit of *sneezing*— 'Gracious!' she exclaimed when she could speak 'what *do* you suppose Mrs Carlyle is the meaning of all this?'— 'I could do without knowing the *meaning* of it I said, if I could only predict the *end* of it—*what* is going to become of us on Saturday'!— 'Oh the end—, said she—of the end there can be *no* doubt—Mr Salmon will have to come and read the funeral service over us all—and I shall send him a note today to prepare him!'—

Poor Saffi has written me two charming letters one in English one in Italian and has received no answer to either— the english letter I will send you but don't lose it—keep it for me—I was very frightened at first that they would all rush off into that row—strange that nobody should have as yet shot the President—but there is a good time coming please God!— Did you see the account of General Cavaignacs arrest—that man *does* every thing and *suffers* everything like a man out of

Plutarch's Lives— If the young Lady to whom he is affianced dont have the spirit and wit to effect his escape—someone else must— Why not I?— Ledru seems to have miscalculated strangely— Lady Sandwich who is a violent Aristocrat was scolding me the other night about my faith in Ledru—adopted from Mazzini entirely—at last she exclaimed 'M*rs* Carlyle Ledru must either be or have been *your Lover!*—only *that*—only a passion could have so blinded and perverted your judgement' —Lady A looked up from her work—(a dolls shift)—and asked gravely '*was* he ever your Lover M*rs* Carlyle?'— 'Never,'! I said laughing—'the very reverse of that'! *'The very reverse'!* repeated Lady A. What *does* that mean I wonder! Oh I have it— you mean to say that *he had prevented somebody else from being your lover*!!! ...

HELEN WELSH   NLS 1893.266
Maryland St, Liverpool

The Grange [27 Dec. 1851]

... Our Christmas Tree came off with great success on Wednesday evening— It stood in the middle of the servants Hall which was profusely decorated with evergreens, and inscriptions written in red berries '*God* Save the Queen'— 'Long live Lord and Lady Ashburton &c &c'— the tree was a fir tree six feet high—stuck quite full of apples and walnuts gilded with dutch leaf—lighted coloured wax tapers—and little bundles of comfits—the presents, of which the seven dolls were much the finest, lay on a table erected all round the tree and covered with white cloths— the forty eight children with their school mistress and Mothers and most of the servants, were ranged round while Lady A, attended by his Lordship, the Clergyman and his wife and two daughters M*r* C and myself, distributed the presents calling up each child by name and saying something graceful and witty along with the doll, top, or whatever it might be— M*r* C had begged to have a map of the world in pieces given to *him*, which was done very cleverly— 'Thomas Carlyle—The *Scholar,*' shouted her Ladyship and the *Scholar* humbly advanced—'*there* is a map of the world for *you*—see that you put it all together and make the pieces fit'— *The scholar* made his bow, and looked as enchanted as any little boy or girl among them—there was afterwards some MUMMING executed before us by country lads in paper dresses—

and then we came away leaving the children and their mothers
to enjoy the mugs of tea with large junks of currant loaf spread
for them on a long table— The whole thing had a very *fine
effect*—and might have given occasion for a laudatory
newspaper paragraph but one reflection that I could not help
making spoiled it for *me*—viz: that the whole *forty-eight*
presents had cost just 2 pounds twelve and sixpence! having
been bought in the Lowther Arcade the most rubbishy place in
London—with a *regard of expence* that would have been
meritorious in the like of us but which seemed to me—what
shall I say?—*incomprehensible*—in a person with an income of
40,000£ thousands a year—and who gives balls at the cost of
700£ each, or will spend 100£ on a china jar!— I should have
liked each child to have got at least a *frock* given it—when one
was going to look munificent— But everyone has his own
notions on spending money....

*Carlyle left, on 31 August, for a five- or six-week German tour to
prepare for writing* **Frederick the Great,** *while Jane stayed to see to
repairs and decorating the house. She was greatly cheered by hearing
from John Stodart again.*

JOHN R. STODART   NLS Acc. 7012
Edinburgh
                                                      [10 Sept. 1852]

...I suppose it is in the highest degree unconventional to tell
another man than ones lawful husband, that one cares about
his love and is grateful to him for it— But what matter? I never
followed the 'three thousand punctualities' when I was a girl,
and yet got through with *character*, enough for practical
purposes; why on earth then should I take the conventional
Law on me *now*, when I can point to the ciphers in your letter
'40' years— Ah! about a love of 'near 40 years' standing one may
speak with freedom enough!— Especially backed out by
several hundred miles of intervening space! For until I can
bring myself to wear a *cap* like other *Women of England*, to
conceal my hair which *wont* turn grey, I cant precisely turn my
age alone to all the credit one might suppose.
    I am sitting here in what might be called fitly '*the belly of
Chaos*'!— For ten unblessed weeks has this house been
undergoing 'a *thorough repair*' and I staying in it!— I shall

know for the rest of my life what '*a thorough repair*' means, and
never be so mad as *constitute* myself again the presiding Genius
of such complicated *night mare*. . . .

At all events I must cut *short* (!) my writing—and go off to
the City—and try my Genius in a wholly different line—viz. in
persuading a bookseller to publish a female MS—not my *own*—
if it were I would give more for its chances of getting
published—

My little dog sends you his kind regards and hopes to
make your acquaintance some time and I remain—what I have
always been for you—yours affectionately / Jane W C

I was out of town for a couple of days when your letter
came and yesterday I was ill with headach and *couldnt* write

*Mazzini also stirred her love and anxiety, as when he returned to
London in 1850 after the defeat of the Roman Republic and she
grasped his hands in 'almost an embrace' and caressed his grey beard
(CL 25:92).*

KATE STERLING   NLS Acc. 9086.8
London

Wednesday night [16 Feb. 1853]

. . . M*rs* Hawks had a very little note from *him* [Mazzini] this
morning, from which I *understand* the whole miserable
business. In f*orty eight hours* more, the Insurrection was to
have broken out in a great many towns at once. But a
discovery had been made at Milan of the *Milan* part of it—
and a search for Arms was the consequence— They failed in
discovering the *depot* of arms, indeed the whole of what is
called the *Material of War* remains intact—but these poor
men, some *seventy* in all knew that they were doomed and
said 'better to die fighting than on the scaffold'—and rushed
out with their poinards not in hope of overturning the
Government but of obtaining themselves a handsome
death— A great number of Mazzinis and Kossuth's
proclamations were in readiness to be circulated at the
commencement of the general insurrection and these
unfortunates had obtained *two* copies; that was all that were
'pasted up' but enough to give the stamp of Mazzini's
authority to the madness in the eyes of all Europe. When
Mazzini heard what had been discovered, he sent an express

to every town except Bologna where the conspiracy was on foot to order them to keep quiet—to Milan also he sent but the answer was from these few poor fellows 'We will die fighting not like sheep be butchered' Mazzini is still safe so far as a man can be safe in a country where every means of travelling is cut off—and not a soul allowed to pass out of it—he speaks nevertheless of returning to England in *two months*— He says he knows nothing of Saffi and Pestrucci except that they are *not* taken—what a fright Madame Pepoli would have been in had she known of the volcano under her feet at Bologna. I trust nothing has happened there Mazzini dreaded it might compromise itself not having time to warn it.— Your loving JC

There was anxiety about the health of Carlyle's mother, and Jane was anxious for a holiday to see her new sister-in-law Phoebe at Moffat. She and John Carlyle had married in 1852. Jane reported more-or-less favourably on all three.

TC   NLS 605.371, 382
Cheyne Row
                                    Moffat House Friday [8 July 1853]

...The most important thing I have to tell you is that you could not know me here as I sit from a red Indian! that I was kept awake the first night after my arrival by a—*Hyaena!* (yes upon my honour! and *you* complain of a simple COCK!) and that yesterday I was as near as possible for giving occasion for the most romantic paragraph of the 'melancholy accident' nature that has appeared in any newspaper for some years! ... I felt very bothered all Wednesday, and gladly accepted Johns offer to tell you of my safe arrival, meaning to write myself yesterday—but it was settled that we should go yesterday to see St Mary's Loch and the Grey-Mares Tail—we started at nine of the morning in an open carriage.... It was the loveliest of days and beautifuler scenery I never beheld; besides that it was full of tender interest for me, as the birth place of my mother .... We went on together to the customary point of view and then I scrambled on by myself (that is with Nero) from my habitual tendency to go a little further always than the rest— Nero grew quite frightened and pressed against my legs and when we came close in front of the Waterfall he stretched his neck out at it from under my petticoats and then barked furiously— Just then I saw John waving his hat to me from the top of the hill—and *excited* by the grandeur of the scene I quite forgot how old I was how out of the practice of 'speeling [climbing] rocks,' and quite forgot too that John had made me take the night before a double doze of morphia which was still in my head making it very light—and I began to climb up the precipice!!—for a little way I got on well enough but when I discovered that I was climbing *up a ridge* (!)—that the precipice was not only behind but on *both sides* of me—I grew, for the first time in my life that I remember of, *frightened—physically* frightened— I was not only afraid of *falling* down—but of losing my head to the extent of *throwing* myself down—to go back on my hands and knees as I had come up was impossible—my only chance was to look at the grass under my face and toil on till John should see me— I tried to call to him but my tongue stuck fast and dry to the roof of my mouth—Nero barking with terror and keeping close to my head still further confused me— John had meanwhile been descending the hill; and holding by the grass. We reached one another. he said hold on—dont give way to panic I will stand between you and everything short of death— We had now got off the ridge onto the slope of the Hill but *it* was so steep that in the *panic* I had taken my danger was extreme for the next quarter of an hour—the bed of a torrent had been for a long time the object of my desire— I thought I should stick faster there than on the glassy slope with the precipice at the bottom of it but John called to me that 'if I got among those stones I should roll to perdition' He was very kind, encouraging me all he could—but no other assistance was possible— In my life I was never so thankful as when I found myself at the bottom of that hill with a glass of water to drink— None of them knew the horrors I had suffered—for I made no screaming or crying—but my face was *purple* all over with a large black spot under each eye—and today I still retain something of the same complexion and I am all of a tremble, as if I had been on the rack. . . .

*

Maryland Street, Sunday
[31 July 1853]

... I have been this morning to James Martineaus Church—
close by here—and heard *not* James Martineau but a perfect
blockhead whom I could hardly help ordering to sit down and
hold his peace.—all about 'virtue' being its 'own reward'—
'with the same relish!'—'not only God' he said but (what he
seemed to consider infinitely more important) 'all people were
merciful towards the merciful man!' As if it were not plain to
me and to everybody of common sense that the *merciful man*
gets himself made into mince-meat by 'all people'—and serve
him right, for being such a spooney as to expect any good to
himself or 'others' out of following the profession of *mercy* at
this time of day! ...

*In desperation Carlyle had decided to build a 'soundproof' attic study.
Plattnauer was an aristocratic radical German exile whom the Carlyles
had rescued from an insane asylum in the 1840s.*

JOHN CARLYLE   NLS 1763.267
Moffat
[7 Sept.1853]

... Here we are again in a crisis of discomfort, as you know. for
the last week however Irish labourers have ceased to tumble
down thro the up-stairs ceilings, bringing cartloads of dust and
broken laths and plaster along with them— *five* times this
accident occurred!!—the last time within a yard of my head as I
was stooping over a drawer—had he dislocated my neck as
might so easily have happened one of us would have been
provided with 'a silent appartment' enough, without further
botheration. It is a fine time for John Chorley who has
constituted himself the overruling Providence of the whole
thing and is to be seen running up and down the long ladder in
front of the house the first thing of a morning when one looks
abroad— How with *his* head he dare—surprises me.
Meanwhile neither Mr C nor I have set eyes on the silent
appartment which is progressing so noisily over head. for the
rest the Cocks are kept in the house by the Washerman till
about nine in the morning and our sufferings thro them are
rather of an imaginative sort— London is as empty as I ever
saw it—one was thankful almost for the return of Plattnauer—

He made the most particular inquiries after you and the Lady—
is less mad considerably than last year—in fact shows no mad
symptoms at present but spending money with a rashness! ...
    Mazzini is in hopes of kicking up another shine almost
immedialy He told me when I last saw him he might go off
again within ten days— I am out of all patience at his reckless
folly—if one did not hear every day of new arrests and
executions one might let him scheme and talk hoping it might
all end in smoke—but it ends in blood—and that is horrible—
1300 arrests in the Papal states within a week! . . . .

*Jane's beloved uncle John of Liverpool, who so reminded her of her
mother, had retired to Auchtertool to live with his son Walter, who was
the minister. He died suddenly, and his daughter Helen died soon after.*

HELEN WELSH   NLS 605.385
Auchtertool
                                                [12 Oct. 1853]

. . . I know not what I am going to say. I am quite stupified. I had
somehow never taken alarm at my Uncles last illness. I had fixed
my apprehensions on *the journey home* and was kept from
present anxiety by that far off one. My beloved Uncle. All that
remained to me of my Mother. A braver, more upright, more
generous-hearted man never lived. When I took leave of him in
Liverpool, and he said 'God bless you *Dear*' (He had never called
me Dear before) I felt it was the last time we should be
together—felt *that* distinctly for a few hours—and then the
impression wore off, and I thought I 'would go back soon—
would go by the *cheapest train*' (God help me) since it gave
him pleasure to see me— That we have him no longer is all the
grief! it was well he should die thus—gently and beautifully—
with all his loving kindness, fresh as a young man's—his
enjoyment of life not wearied out all our love as warm for him
as ever—and well he should die in his own dear Scotland amid
quiet kindly things— We cannot ought not to wish it had been
otherwise—to wish he had lived on till his loss should have
been less felt— But what a sad change for you all. and for me
too; little as I saw of him, to know that kind good Uncle was in
the world for me—to care about me however long absent—as
nobody but one of ones own blood can—was a sweetness in my
lonely life which can be ill spared. . . .

CHARLES REDWOOD   NLS Acc. 9294
Bovington, South Wales

25*th* Decemb / 53

... Mr Carlyle and I were on a visit at Lord Ashburtons which commenced on the 4*th* of December and was to have lasted till about new-years day. But last Monday I was despatched to London about certain—*Cocks!* and a *Macaw!* which you have perhaps heard of—'the great first Cause least understood' of that 'Silent apartment' which M*r* C built this summer at an outlay of some 200£ The Silent Apartment having proved a complete failure having proved in fact *the* apartment most accessible to sound in the whole house (no wonder! having 14 air-holes in frank and free communication with the before and behind!) it became imperative, that unless we were both to be landed in Bedlam *he* thro' these Demon-birds and I thro their effects on *him*—some thing else should be done of real efficacy— *Poisoning* them was his fixed idea; but *that* I held him back from all I could—especially at this time of the year when the newspapers have no *debates* to fill their pages,— such a recourse would have been questionable. It was finally settled we should try to *take* the house No. 6 ourselves for three years and eject the present occupants——*if we could*—and to achieve *this* I was sent to Chelsea 'quite promiscuously'— To be in time for the Xmas term, the utmost despatch was needed— The fine people at the Grange, were greatly *amused* as well as astonished to see a Wife sent off from the midst of Xmas festivities to consult with house agents and house owners— But M*r* C was quite right in insisting 'She can do it better than I'— Decidedly he had neither the temper nor the dexterity (!) to bring this romantic undertaking to the happy issue I have brought it to— For I not only *got* the house but got rid of it when gotten, and by the potency of a notice to quit got rid of the whole lot of birds in consideration of a present of 5£—and have my neighbour *legally* bound at this moment 'not to keep or allow to be kept on these premises any birds or *other nuisance* under penalty of 10£ and a notice to quit'— I will *tell* you someday how I managed it— Meanwhile I am here still, alone—with painters (of the Silent Apartment) in the house creating an atmosphere! M*r* C receiving from Scotland daily letters about his Mother's increasing weakness, felt when left

behind at the Grange that it would be much more suitable he
should go to Scotland and see her once more than stay on
amidst these festivities and so he came to town last
Wednesday and started for Scotsbrig on Thursday night. I was
very urgent to hurry him off, since he WAS going; for fear of his
finding his Mother no more— I know what *that* is!—dashing
along a railway in agonies of impatience and uncertainty to be
told at the end 'your Mother is dead'— . . .

Carlyle's mother died on 25 December.

TC   NLS 605.389
Scotsbrig

5 Cheyne Row / Tuesday
[27 Dec. 1853]

. . . Oh my Dear! Never does one feel oneself so utterly
helpless as in trying to speak comfort for a great
bereavement. I will not try it. Time is the only Comforter for
the loss of a Mother. One does not believe in Time while the
grief is quite new. One feels as if it could never be less. And
yet all griefs, when there is no *bitterness* in them, are soothed
down by Time. And *your* grief for your Mother must be
altogether sweet and soft. For you must feel that you have
always been a good son to her, that you have always
appreciated her as she deserved, and that she knew this, and
loved you to the last moment. How thankful we may be that
you went when you did, in time to have the assurance of her
love surviving all bodily weakness, made doubly sure to you
by her last look and words. Oh what *I* would have given for
last words; to keep in my innermost heart all the rest of my
Life—but the words that awaited *me* were; 'your Mother is
DEAD'! And I deserved it should so end—I was not the dutiful
child to my Mother that you have been to yours. . . . / Ever
yours. / JWC

*William Allingham was to become the Carlyles' regular friend,
recording his visits in his diary. Anna Montagu, Basil Montagu's
widow, was living with her daughter Mrs Procter when Jane went to
see her, and they remembered how they once wrote to each other about
Jane's love for Irving. The Ruskins' marriage was dissolved in 1855.*

WILLIAM ALLINGHAM   NLS 3823.165 and *CL* 29:35-6
Southampton Row, London

5 Cheyne Row / Wednesday
[1 March 1854]

...You are not taking it ill of me that I did not thank you for
your poems *before reading them?* at least were I in your case
and knowing what I know, it would be far from me to take it
ill!

I have now read every line of these poems—a great
praise in itself—considering the anti-poetic atmosphere I live
in, and how impatient I am become, at second-hand, of the
general run of Poems; and to speak quite sincerely I find all of
them good reading, and some of them really beautiful and
worth getting by heart. 'The Dream' in particular pleases me,
and one verse of it brought a gush of tears from my eyes, and if
you knew what remarkably dry eyes I read with generally—
nay, live with generally—you would attach some importance to
this manifestation of feeling!

Even *Mr.* C. read 'The Dream' without a word of objection
and a good many of approbation. I wish you great success in
your enterprise. It must be a hard fight in the beginning for
anybody unless born with 'a popular novel' in his mouth, to
live by literature in London. But I do believe always to a
certain imaginable extent, that 'our wishes are presentiments
of our powers.'

Come and tell me all about it the first Sunday morning you
have leisure. . . .

JOHN CARLYLE   NLS 605.394A
Moffat

Tuesday [9 May 1854]

...I have got the Influenza again—caught cold returning from a
dinner-party at the Procters on Saturday night, and am at
present in the third stage of the thing— the coughing and
sneezing stage—

I saw '*the Noble Lady*' that night— and a strange tragic
sight she was sitting all alone in a low-ceilinged confined room
at the top of Proctors house— a french bed in a corner— some
relics of the Grand Bedford Square Drawingroom—(small
pictures and the like) scattered about— Herself stately, artistic
as ever—not a line of her figure, not a fold of her dress changed

since we knew her first, 20 years ago and more. She made me sit
on a low chair opposite her—(she had sent for me to come up)
and began to speak of Edward Irving and long ago as if it were
last year—last month! There was something quite overpowering
in the whole thing— The *pagan* grandeur of the old woman—
retired from the world, *awaiting death*, as erect and unyielding
as ever, contrasted so strangely with the mean bedroom at the
top of the house—the uproar of *company* going on below—and
the past which she seemed to live and move in felt to gather
round me too, till I fairly laid my head on her lap and burst into
tears. She stroked my hair very gently and said 'I think, Jane, your
manner never changes, any more than your *hair* which is still
black I see.' 'But you too are not changed' I said— 'You know she
said when I was still a young woman, I dressed and felt like an
old one and so age has not told so much on me as on most
others.' When I had staid with her an hour or so she insisted on
my going back to the company—and embraced me as she never
did before

Her embrace used to be so freezing always to my 'youthful
enthusiasm' but this time she held me strongly to her heart and
kissed my cheek many times heartily—like a mother—I was
near going off into crying again. I felt that she was taking eternal
farewell of me in her own mind. But I dont mean it to be so—I
will go again to see her very soon. The great gentleness was
indeed the chief change in her—not a hard word did she say
about anyone—and her voice tho' clear and strong as of old had
a *human* modulation in it. You may fancy the humour in which I
went back to the *party* which was then at a white heat of
excitement—about nothing!

...There is a great deal of talking about the Ruskins here at
present. Mrs Ruskin has been taken to Scotland by *her* parents—
and Ruskin is gone to Swizerland with *his*—and the separation is
understood to be permanent—there is even a rumour that Mrs
Ruskin is to sue for a divorce— I know nothing about it—except
that I have always pitied Mrs Ruskin while people generally
blamed her—for love of dress and company and flirtation— She
was too young and pretty to be so left to her own devices as she
was by her husband who seemed to wish nothing more of her
but the credit of having a pretty well dressed wife....

*Neuberg was a retired German-Jewish businessman who, from
admiration for Carlyle, volunteered to help him with historical research.*

JOSEPH NEUBERG   NLS 554.51
Willesden House, Willesden

Wednesday [14 June 1854]

...I kept *it* in my hands some five minutes unopened, and
pinched it, and guessed about it, and finally decided it was
worsted stockings!!— Upon my honour I never *can* understand
why you are so good to me!?— Do you understand it yourself?
Sometimes I think it is because I am 'Mr Carlyles wife'—and
then I feel tempted to gather together all the things you have
given me and fling them at your head. I am so dreadfully tired of
being *'made of'* on *that* principle! Sometimes I explain it on the
ground of your immense abstract benevolence! and that
solution don't please me either— Never mind— You will
consider the question at your leisure and tell me at our next tete
a tete as now we have no longer the lottery ticket (thank God)
to discuss in secret What a pen!—besides my fingers are
shaking—there has just been 'a solution of continuity' in the Life
of Nero,—three boys picked him up when he was out with Mr
C before breakfast—and the Postman has been seeking him all
the while he should have been delivering his letters! He is
found however and has cost me only 'a pot of beer' to two
different 'parties' on this occasion

Oh dont speak of dinner!— Let us do something in the
forenoon—in the open air—not dine hotly in a party— John
and his Wife would also like the forenoon best—and *curds
and cream* or some such refection / Yours affectionately /
Jane Carlyle

*The Ashburton connection continued at the same time as growing
concern for Lady Harriet's health. Carlyle retired deeper into* **Frederick**.
*Old friends, such as Geraldine Jewsbury, came closer and new ones
appeared. Among these were Edward Twisleton and his young wife Ellen
from Boston. Though their contact was interrupted by the Twisletons'
visits abroad, Ellen and Jane were immediately attracted.*

MARY RUSSELL   NLS 605.394B
Thornhill

[13 July 1854]

...We are still in London with no present thought of leaving
it. The Ashburtons have again offered us Addiscombe to
rusticate at while they are in the Highlands But in spite of

the beauty and magnificence of that place and all its belongings I hate being there in the family's absence—am always afraid of my dog making footmarks on the sofas or carpet of asking the *fine* housemaid to do something 'not in her work' &c &c and so would for my part much rather stay in *my own* house all the year round. When Mr C gets ill with the heat however, if this year, there is to be any—he may choose to go there for a few weeks—and will need *me* to order his dinners.

I am hoping for a considerable acquisition before long. Miss Jewsbury the Authoress of *The Half-Sisters* &c, the most *intimate* friend I have in the world—and who has lived generally at Manchester since we first knew each other, has decided to come and live near me for good. Her Brother married eighteen months ago—and has realized a Baby, and a Wife's Mother in the house besides— So Geraldine felt it getting too hot for her there. It will be a real gain to have a woman I like so near as the street in which I have decided on an apartment for her— All my acquaintance lie so far off, that it is mechanically impossible to be intimate with them.

. . . From my Cousins I hear very little now. Jeanie in Glasgow, never was a good correspondent, I mean always wrote *remarkably bad* letters considering her faculty in some other directions, *now* there is a little tone of *married-woman*—and *much-made-of married woman* added to the dullness and longwindedness that irritate me into—*silence*. As for the others, they all seem to think I have nothing to do AT MY AGE but send *them* two or three letters for one!— When my dear Uncle was alive—my anxiety to hear of *him* overcame all other considerations and I humoured this negligence more than was reasonable— Besides Helen wrote pretty often poor Dear—and *good* letters, telling one something. *Now* as they are all healthy, and 'at ease in Zion,' I mean to bear in mind more than heretofore—that *I* am *not* healthy, and have many demands on my time and thought, and am besides sufficiently their elder to have my letters answered. . . .

Dr John Carlyle's wife Phoebe died after giving birth to a stillborn child, leaving three teenage stepsons to his care.

ISABELLA CARLYLE   NLS Acc. 7988
Scotsbrig

5 Cheyne Row / Monday
[28 Aug. 1854]

... Oh my dear Isabella what a horrible thing! I do not know if
he have written to you himself. I write in case he has not, to tell
you that M*rs* John died on Saturday night at nine o'clock— After
finishing my letter to you, I was on my way to some warm baths
in this neighbourhood, to take one, feeling very unwell, and my
friend Geraldine who was with me, having insisted a warm bath
would do me good, when D*r* Carlyle jumped out of a cab that
met us, to say he had been going to our house to say that
Phoebe had just been delivered of a dead child—the whole
thing had passed over in ten minutes— D*r* Rigby was leaving
the house when the nurse ran after him to say she was sure M*rs*
C was in labour—he returned and the child was already half
born— She was 'doing well' Jhon said and leapt into his cab
again and drove home. I came home to tell M*r* Carlyle then I
went and had the bath and then I went to bed to keep quite
still—between 8 and 9 Marianne M*rs* John maid was shown up
to my bedroom— She had come to see if I could give them 'a
quantity of napkins'—they had not any of the necessary linen at
all—a boxful all ready packed had been left at Moffat!! and here
were they as ill off as the poorest people!— She said her
mistress had had a dreadful flooding which if D*r* Hunter had not
been at hand to stop would have carried her off. but now she
was all right— I sent for Geraldine Jewsbury to take Marianne to
a shop where everything needed could be got ready made—for
among us all we could not raise as many things as would be
needed— They had been gone about a quarter of an hour when
M*r* Carlyle came into my room crying out 'Oh my Dear! my
Dear! what a thing!'— I said 'She is dead!'— 'Yes she is dead'!—
Just in the brief time of her maid's absence who had never left
her all the week the poor woman had expired— She was lying
quite quiet when something came over her like a return of the
fits with which her illness began—it never came to a fit exactly
but her breathing became weaker and weaker till it ceased—a
woman who had gone up from here with some sheets she had
been washing in a hurry for them, had brought the news—M*r*
Carlyle went up immediately and did not return till about 12
when he brought John to sleep here. He continues to sleep

here but is at his own lodging during the day— The funeral is to
be on Wednesday. the poor baby who was to have been put
under ground the night of its birth to be buried now with its
mother— It was a large fine Baby Marianne told me—a boy. and
'so like the Doctor'— All this horrible tragedy resulting Dr
Rigby is perfectly sure from the fright she got on the railway,
three days before the fits began— Oh if they had only been
poor people, with no time or money for racketting about, she
might have born him a living son and they might have been
very happy over it. He is in a strange stupified state—indeed we
are all quite stunned. . . . / God keep you both / Affectionately
yours / Jane Carlyle

    Nothing can be more kind and gentle than Mr Carlyle is
with John

*Mary Mills had been Grace Welsh's servant at Templand. She was part
of the memories with which Jane often indulged herself.*

MARY RUSSELL   NLS 605.395
Thornhill

                                                         [4 Oct.? 1854]

. . . On getting your first letter dear Mrs Russell—before
reading a word of it—I *knew* it was about poor Mary; that it
was to tell me she was dying or dead. for, you see; glad as I
should be to hear from you oftener, you never write to me '*all
from yourself—out of your own head*' (as the children say)
and of poor old Mary at her age, any *news* could be hardly
good news. . . . It is well the poor old kindhearted creature has
had so gentle an end—at her age *life* could scarcely be a
blessing and yet she seemed content to hold to it such as it
was, and so one wished her to live—Besides I have always felt
her a sort of living legacy from my darling Mother, and now
even that poor little tie is broken! and there is one heart fewer
in the world of those *who loved* my mother and gratefully
revered her memory. . . .

    We have staid quietly here this whole year, in spite of the
Cholera— But indeed what use is there in flying from Cholera
in a town, when it finds it way into such fresh open places as
about Ecclefechan— It was very sad to walk out here for many
weeks—in a single half mile of street I often met as many as
six funerals. I think I have not written to you, have I, since Mrs

John Carlyle's death—That was a horrid business— It looked such a *waste* of a Woman and Child. Of course she was to die— Yet humanly viewed one could not help believing if she had staid at home and taken the ordinary cares of herself that her situation required, she might have born a living child and done well. But her constant excursions on railways and sightseeings and house huntings seemed to us often even *before* the *accident* which brought on her mortal illness, a sheer tempting of providence.

I heard from my Aunt Elizabeth the other day, and she sent with her letter a small book on '*Grace*' They are indefatigable in their efforts at conversion— Except to '*Convert Me*' they seem to take no interest in me whatever. . . .

JESSIE DONALDSON   NLS 1797.217
Haddington

19*th* January [1855]

. . . I am so glad my godmother and you like the Portrait! It is a perfect likeness,—*now*; Mr Carlyle has got a *beard* like the greater number of people here, which makes him look rather more ferocious than *that*. Your description of my god mother bending over the print to see it unrolled, went into the very heart of my heart—and I longed to catch her in my arms and give her such a hug! While I am on the subject of pictures; I must ask you have you any friend that *sketches*? I dont say beautifully but truthfully— I want so much to have a little sketch of *Sunny Bank* to hang up beside *Templand*, and *the house* at Haddington, and *Craigenputtoch*, and the *Haddington Church*, and dear Helen Donaldson's little miniatures, and *Madame Recamier* (that used to hang over the drawing mantlepiece at home—so like my Mother;) and a few other very dear pictures—all in one little room—especially *my own*— I am sure that sharp pretty Mrs Foreman (for instance) must be *up* to sketching!— Will you ask her, when the weather has turned warm enough for out-of-doors-work? I should be so much obliged to any body that would do it for me! . . .

Jane's patience broke at last with problems about the 'budget' or housekeeping, which she would not bring herself to speak about to Carlyle. She left him a statement, to which he cheerfully responded. But in a real sense, it was about her own money as, since her mother's

*death, the rent for Craigenputtoch had been paid to Carlyle. She writes
to him as if addressing the Chancellor of the Exchequer. She was now
reaching a breaking point in health, general resentment, a sense of
purposelessness and jealousy of Lady Ashburton.*

TC   Bodleian Library, MS. Don. c. 50
Cheyne Row
                                                    [7 Feb. 1855]

BUDGET of a *Femme* incomprise
I dont choose to *speak* again on the *Money question!*
The 'replies' from the Noble Lord are unfair, and unkind, and
little to the purpose. When you tell me 'I pester your life out
about money'—that 'your soul is sick with hearing about it,'
that I 'had better make the money I *have* serve, at all rates—
hang it!—let *you* alone of it'; *all that* I call perfectly unfair,
the reverse of kind, and tending to nothing—but
disagreement—
        If I were greedy, or extravagant, or a bad manager; you
would be justified in 'staving me off' with loud words: but you
cannot say *that* of me (whatever else) cannot *think* it of me! At
least I am sure I never 'asked for more' to myself from you or
anyone—not even from my own Mother in all my life; and that,
thro' six and twenty years, I have kept house for you, at more or
less cost according to given circumstances, but always on *less*
than it costs the generality of People, living in the same style.—
What I should have expected you to say, rather, would have
been; 'My Dear, you *must* be dreadfully hampered in your
finances, and dreadfully anxious and unhappy about it, and quite
desperate of *making it do*; since *you* are 'asking for more'!
Make me *understand* the case then. I can and will help you out
of that *sordid* suffering at least. Either by giving you 'more,' if
that be found prudent to do; or by reducing our wants to within
'the present means.' *That* is the sort of thing you would have
said, had you been a perfect man. So I suppose you are not a
perfect man. Then; instead of crying in my bed half the night
after, I would have explained my *Budget* to you in peace and
confidence. But *now*; I am driven to explain it on paper, 'in a
state of mind'! *driven*; for I *cannot*, it is not in my nature, to live
'entangled in the details.' And I *will not!* I would sooner hang
myself—tho' 'pestering you about money' is also more
repugnant to me than you dream of.

You 'dont understand why the allowance which sufficed in former years no longer suffices'?

That is what I would explain to the Noble Lord if he would but—what shall I say?—*keep his temper.*

The Beginning of my Embarrassments, it will not surprise the Noble Lord to learn—since it has also been 'the beginning of' almost every human ill to himself—was *The Repairing of the House.* There was a *destruction*, an *irregularity, an incessant recurrence of small incidental expenses*, during all that period, or *two* periods; thro which I found myself, in September gone a year, *ten* pounds behind, instead of having some pounds saved up toward the Winter Coals.— I could have worked 'out of that' however in the course of time; if habits of *unpinched* house-keeping had not been long taken by *you* as well as myself; and if new unavoidable, or not to be avoided; *current* expenses had not followed close on those incidental ones.— I will show the Noble Lord, with his permission, what the new current expenses are and to what they *amount, per annum. ('Hear'! 'Hear!'* and cries of *'be brief').*

...Do you finally understand why the allowance which sufficed formerly no longer suffices? and pity my difficulties instead of being angry at them? ...Yes! I have the *strongest* idea what amount of money would 'satisfy' me. I have computed it often enough as I lay awake at night; and 'didn't I wish I might get it?'—indeed, when I can't sleep now, it is my 'difficulties' I think about, more than my sins; till they become 'a real mental agony in my own inside!'— The above-named sum 29£, divided into quarterly payments would *satisfy* me (With *a certain* parsimony about *little* things somewhat less might do.) I engaging my word of Gentlewoman to *give back* at the year's end, whatever portion thereof any diminution of the Demand on me might enable me to save.

...There only remains to disclose the actual state of the Exchequer. It is empty *as a drum! ('sensation'!)* If I consider 29 more pounds indispensable (things remaining as they are) for the coming year, beginning from the 22*d* of March;—it is just because I have found it so in the year that is gone. And I commenced *that*, as already stated, with *ten pounds* of arrears. Now, you 'assisted' me with 15 pounds, and I have 'assisted' *myself* with *ten* pounds—*five* last August which I took from the *Savings Bank*, and the *five* you gave me at newyear, which I threw into the coal account. (Don't suppose, 'if thou's i' the

habit o' *supposing*' that I tell you this in the *un*devout
imagination of being *repaid*; by all that's *sacred* for me—*the
memory of my Father and Mother*—(what else can an
'irreligious creature' like me *swear* by?) I would *not* take back
that money, if you *offered it*, with the best grace, and had
picked it up in the street! I tell it you simply, that you may see I
am not so dreadfully *greedy* as you have appeared to think
me—latterly.— Setting *my ten pounds*, then, against the
original arrears, with *fifteen pounds* in 'assistance' from you; it
would follow from my own computation, that I should need
fourteen pounds 'more' to clear off arrears on the weekly bills,
and carry me on, paying my way, till the 22*d* of March (next
quarter-day). (cries of *'shame'!* and *'Turn her out'!*) . . . Mercy!
to think there are women, your friend Lady Ashburton for
example (*'rumeur'* and *'sensation'*) I say, *for example*; who
spend not merely the 'additimental' pounds, I must make such
pother about; but four times my whole income *in the Ball* of
one night! and none the worse for it; nor anyone the better!—It
is—'what shall I say?'—*curious* 'upon *my* honour!'

*Both Carlyles were withdrawing more and more into themselves. Yet
Jane at least had the resource of such friends as Geraldine Jewsbury
and Ellen Twisleton. Jane and Ellen would call on each other, and
Ellen's sister Elisabeth Dwight, from Boston, reported her conversation
(29 April) as 'fun beyond any, though it is sometimes rather bitter, and
if you could hear the stories about London life . . . you would think
"Vanity Fair" and Becky Sharp were mild under-statements of the truth'*
(**CL** 29:299; *MS, Houghton, b45M-98*).

KATE STERLING NLS Acc. 9086.8
Monday [2 April 1855]

'Och pretty Kate! my darling Kate' . . . The eternal east
wind has got into every corner of my heart and brain, shrivelling
up my faith, hope and charity, as it had already shrivelled up the
outer skin of me! I think seriously of retiring to bed, and
abjuring my fellowcreatures—all but Nero—till it turns into the
West: I have such difficulty in keeping myself from *flying out* at
every body, and telling them considerable portions of my mind!
Poor Geraldine is worst off with me—for having unbounded
confidence in her devotion, I don't bother to *keep up
appearances* with *her*, but scold at her whenever we are

together which is twice a day *at least!* Her new novel is much
praised in the newspapers and among my acquaintance—but
she has some half dozen other peoples novels passing thro her
hands every week *to be reviewed*; and knows how soon the
'most successful novel of the season' is superseded by another
with 'others yet behind'—and is not the least '*carried*' by this
lyrical recognition of her own one— 'My Dear,' she said
yesterday, 'if they will *buy* it as well as praise it, so that it may go
to a second edition; I shall get 50£ more you know!'. . . I
chaperoned her to a party at Milnes's one night where she was
solemnly introduced (by Milnes) to Miss Wynn's Sister. . . .

I never chaperoned a young Lady in my life before, and I
found it distracting work! I was constantly losing her, and
'feeling it my duty' to recover her, and every time she opened
her mouth I dreaded an outrage to the 'three thousand
punctualities.' *That* was my only SOIREE for months. I have been
twice out at dinner since Xmas,—my *Gaities* are not killing. In
fact we live here up to the eyes in Frederick the Great—and he
is become such a horrid bore to me that I *dream* about him in
my bad nights! Under these circumstances it is clear I cannot
write an *amusing* letter—and to be *edifying* is not my line. . . .

*To Jane's distress, Carlyle often talked of acquiring a Scottish country
cottage. Now she countered with a plan to take a seaside one, perhaps
with their friend the artist Robert Tait. Thomas was then visiting Edward
FitzGerald.*

TC   NLS 605.400
Farlingay Hall, Suffolk
                                                  [14 Aug. 1855]

. . . No Dear; I dont take to *your* sea-bathing place, because I
have a place of my own in view! Positively I fancy I have found
the Coming Cottage! I am just off to consult Tait about it. And at
all events you must go and look at it with me next Monday,
before we incur any lodging-expenses—which would be best
laid out on a place 'all to oneself.'

I took such an amount of air and exercise yesterday as
would have DONE FOR most nine-teenth century *females*!
Started at eight, by the boat, with a good tide and was at the
station a quarter before nine. Was quite well situated in my
open carriage and reached Brighton without the least fatigue.

Bathed the first thing; and then walked along the shore to a
little Inn I had been told of by Neuberg and Ballantyne; as a
charming quiet place 'for *even* Mr Carlyle' to stop at; found it,
of course, noisy, dirty, not to be even *dined* at by Mrs Carlyle—
and walked on, still further along the cliffs, to a village I had
SEEN ON THE MAP, and was sure must be very retired. The name of
it is Rottingdean. It is 4 miles *at least* from the Brighton
Station. I *walked* there and back again!! and in the last two
miles along the cliffs I met just ONE man! in a white smock!
Thus you perceive the traveller expences to one of the
quietest sea villages in England is just per boat & third class
train 3/10d!, a convenient locality for one's cottage at all rates.
The place itself is an *old sleepy* looking little village close on
the sea, with simple poor inhabitants, not a trace of a Lady or
gentleman bather to be seen!— In fact except at the Inn there
were no lodgings visible. I asked the maid at the Inn, 'was it
always as quiet as this?' '*always*,' she said, in a half whisper,
with a half sigh,—'a-most *too* quiet!'— Near the Inn, and so
near the sea you could throw a stone into it, are three houses
in a row—the center one old—quaint, and empty—small
rooms but enough of them—and capable of being made very
livable in at small cost—and there are *two 'decent women'* I
saw, who might either of them be trusted to keep it— But I
should fill sheets with details without giving you a right
impression—you must just go and *look*. I returned to Brighton
again—after having dined at the Rottingdean Inn on two fresh
eggs a plateful of homebaked bread and butter, and a pint
bottle of *Guiness* (*chaarge* 1/6d)— I walked miles up and
down Brighton to find the Agent, for that cottage—did finally
get him by miracle—name and street being both different from
what I set out to seek—and almost committed myself to take
the cottage for a year at 12£ (no taxes or rates whatever) or to
take it for 3 months at six pounds— However I took fright
about *your* not liking it,—and the expences of furnishing &c
&c—on the road up—and wrote him a note from Alsops shop
that he might not refuse any other offer and hold me engaged
till you had seen and approved of it. If Tait shared *this* cottage
and went halves in the furnishings it would cost very little
indeed— My only objection to it this morning, is that one
might not be able to get it *another year* and then what be
done with the furniture? But oh what a beautiful sea! blue as
the Firth of Forth it was last night!— I lay on the cliffs in the

stillness, and looked at the 'beautiful Nature' for an hour and more, which was such a *doing* of the picturesque as I have not been up to for years. The most curious thing is the sudden solitude beggining *without gradation* just where Kemptown ends— It is as if the Brighton people were all *enchanted* not to pass beyond their peir. . . .

The scheme came to nothing. Instead came Lady Harriet's invitation for another Christmas at the Grange, which was to be the last.

LADY HARRIET ASHBURTON   NLS Acc. 11388.28
The Grange

Wednesday [14 Nov. 1855]

Indeed, indeed, dear Lady, it never entered into 'the imaginating of the thoughts of my heart,' that at such time of year and on so short a stay, *you* might, could, would, or should, have driven down to Chelsea! Far from that, I did not even find it permissible to seek to see you at Bath House on that 'one day'; tho' I had already walked to the end of Bolton Street in the course of making up my mind, whether I might ask to see you or had best *not*.

'There is no chance of our coming to the Grange?'— 'Isn't there?'! I was fearing something quite different; that there was no chance of our being invited. I donot think Mr C's staying sulking at home last winter, turned out so well for him, body or soul, that he should ever again 'take that line' (*your* phrase) as long as he lives. Even if there weren't a *book* in the House, he would go this year, I am sure, if *only* you were so goodnatured as to invite him— As for me, it was no illusion on the *advantages* of giving up the only bit of cheerful life that the year brought round for us, and 'sticking to one's work' in grim silence at home— I did not need to *miss* our visit for the next twelve months, to make me know what I had gone and done!— I knew it perfectly well at the time— But it was all but *impossible* for me to go last year, *under the circumstances*. . . .

Poor little Mrs Twistleton has been suffering agonies from acute rheumatism—caught at sea on their return from America. She is now out of bed on a couch in her bedroom. *He* was so upset by the sight of her sufferings that he actually *blasphemed* a little, in my own hearing!

Mrs Wedgwood took me last night to hear Lord John

[Russell] lecture in Exeter Hall—and a horrid headach is what I
have gained by it. . . . It was more of a sermon than a lecture—
but what I found most curious; every time his Lordship named
'*Christ*,' which was very often, the House thundered applause
so loud and long and obstreperous that I expected it always to
end in '*hip hip hurrah*'!— Was it surprise and admiration that a
Lord should have heard of Christ? or what was it that set their
hands a clapping and feet thumping at that name? One time
Lord John had said something very complimentary to Christ,
and the applause began—but I heard one man cry 'order'—
'order'—and another 'no! no'— . . .

*The Carlyles were getting to know and like Ruskin better now that his
marriage was annulled.*

WILLIAM ALLINGHAM   NLS 3823.123
Ballyshannon, Ireland
                                                    Feby 23*d* [1856]

. . .What you say of Ruskins book is excellent. 'Claret and
buttermilk' till one don't know which is which! But what
could be expected from a man who goes to sleep with, every
night, a different Turner's picture on a chair opposite his bed
'that he may have something beautiful to look at on first
opening his eyes of a morning' (so his mother told me) Mrs
Ruskin I suppose was not beautiful *enough* to open one's
eyes on the first thing; and, *hinc illae lachrymae* [hence
these tears]! You see Millais (I dont know how to spell him)
and she *have* married—you wouldn't believe me. I have heard
of her several times since her marriage, from people who had
seen her in Scotland—one said she looked 'sad'; another that
she looked '*cross*'; another that she kept Millais in order; and
another that she was 'in an interesting situation.' As for
Ruskin; I never saw a man so improved by the loss of his wife!
He is amiable and gay, and full of hope and faith in—one
doesn't know exactly *what*—but of course *he* does. Twice last
summer he drove Mr C and me and *Nero* out to his place at
Denmark Hill, and gave us a dinner like what one reads of in
the *Arabian Nights*, and strawberries and cream on the lawn;
and was indulgent and considerate for even *Nero!* and I
returned each time more satisfied, that Mrs Ruskin must have
been hard to please. One feels always, one could manage

other women's husbands so much better than they do—and
so much better than one manages one's own husband!

We lived in the same house with Alfred Tennyson lately—
at Lord Ashburton's in Hampshire—and he read *Maud* and
'other poems' aloud to us—and was much made of by all the
large party assembled there. He seemed strangely excited
about *Maud*—as sensitive to criticisms on it as if they were
imputations on his honour—and all his friends are excited
about *Maud* for him! and an unknown Cambridge gentleman
wrote to Mr Carlyle to ask him to be so good as inform him
what was *his* opinion of *Maud!!!* You may imagine how Mr C
would toss that letter into the fire, sending a savage growl
after it! . . .

*On 18 January Ellen Twisleton wrote to a sister that 'Mrs Carlyle is a
little alarming, she is fearfully against everybody,—and the back-biting
that one hears, all round, from people, who actually and when
convenient, are on the most intimate terms, is enough to reduce me to
Edward's silence, & reminds me of nothing but the School for Scandal'
(MS, Houghton, b45M-98, box 2). She wrote again, 8 February, that
Ruskin had 'asked the Carlyles to dinner on the day that Mrs Ruskin
married Mr Millais. He is what the Germans would call an "Unmensch,"
I think! He professes himself so happy without her, so thankful for his
release, that no minor considerations can touch him' (MS, Houghton,
b45M-98). Ellen's sister Elisabeth Dwight also reported 'Tea at the
Carlyles, where Jane appeared in a crimson velvet gown; Carlyle kept up
a low chaunt of lamentation', and Geraldine Jewsbury 'sat in the
background, & collected materials for her next novel, and wasn't
pleasant' (7 March 1856; MS, Houghton, b45M-98).*

ELLEN TWISLETON   Houghton MS b45M-98 (90)
London
                                                  . . . [13 June 1856]

Darling! That last was the most provoking *miss* of all! We
had just returned from Addiscombe, where we had been since
the previous Saturday, and when you came I was close at hand;
at Geraldine Jewsbury's in the next street! I had run over to give
her some commissions before retiring myself from public life,
into my fourposted red bed! I had come home with such a
faceache and such a sorethroat! instead of those charming
results always promised from 'change of air.'

All yesterday I was too ill to write you even a bit of a
note— While at Addiscombe I dreamed about you one night—a
wretched dream—that you were sitting as white as a sheet,
slowly weeping, and refusing to be comforted; because Mr
Twistleton and you were to be *'separated'! for political reasons*;
I partly believed; but I could not make it out, and knew only that
you were miserable and *he* was misereable, and Miss Dwight
and I were crying over you! On waking I determined I should
go and see you the day after my return. . . .

MARY RUSSELL   NLS 605.406
Thornhill

Auchertool Manse / Kircaldy
Wednesday [30 July 1856]

. . . I am quite sure of being in Scotland *now*—for lo and behold!
I am here—at Auchtertool! And if ever a poor woman was
thankful to see her own land and her own people again, after
long and weary exile it is *me!*
    We left London as I predicted we should *'quite
promiscuously'* at the last. Lady Ashburton was going to her
Highland shooting quarters and engaged the great big railway
carriage called *'the Queen's Saloon'* to take her to Edinr. So
having lots of room to spare she offered one day to carry both
Mr C and me along with her free of all trouble and expense. And
the offer was both too kind and convenient to be refused. . . .
    We staid over night at a Hotel with the Ashburtons and then
they went north, and I came over the water to Auchtertool—Mr C
accompanying me; for a twenty four hours stay.
    Oh mercy into what *freshness* and *cleanness* and
kindness I have plumped, here!—out of the smoulder and din
and artificiality of London! It has been like plumping down
into a bed of rose-leaves with the dew on them! My Cousins
are so kind! and the only thought that comes to spoil my
enjoyment is that I must go back to London some time! cannot
get staid here *for ever!* . . .

TC   NLS 605.420
Kinloch Luichart

[19 Sept. 1856]

. . . Your letter this morning is a *degree* more *legible* than the
first one! but dear me! what galloping and spluttering over the

paper, as if you were writing in a house on fire! and bent on making a *little* look *as much as possible!* I have measured the distance between your lines in the letter just come, and it is precisely *one inch!* In the first letter it must have been an inch and half! I call that a foolish waste of writing-paper! If you have an excellent bedroom could you not retire into it, for, say one hour, in the course of the whole week, and write composedly and leisurely—*why* write in the midst of four people?

For the rest—in spite of all objections 'for the occasion got up'; I dare say you are pretty comfortable. Why not?— When *you* go to any house, one knows it is because you *choose* to go, and when you stay it is because you *choose* to stay— You don't, as weakly amiable people do, *sacrifice* yourself for the pleasure of '*others*' So pray do not think it necessary to be *wishing yourself at home* and 'all that sort of thing' on paper. 'I don't believe thee'! If I were inclined *to*; I should only have to call to mind the beautiful letters you wrote to me during your former visit to the Ashburtons in the Highlands, and which you afterwards *disavowed* and *trampled into the fire!!*

...Whether I return to Scotsbrig or not will depend on *your* arrangements— Lady Ashburton is very kind to offer to take me back pray make her my thanks for the offer— But tho' a very little *Herring* I have a born liking to '*hang by* my own head.' And when it is a question simply of paying my own way or having it paid for me—I prefer 'lashing down' my four or five sovereigns *on the table all at once!* If there were any *companionship* in the matter it would be different—and if *you* go back with the Ashburtons it would be different, as then I should be going merely as part of your luggage—without self responsibility— Settle it as you like; it will be all one to me— meeting you at Scotsbrig, or in Edin*r*—or going home by myself from Thornhill

This is the 19*th* of September—the day of my Father's death—Jamie is going to take me a little drive at one o'clock....

MARY RUSSELL NLS 605.427, 425, 429
Thornhill

Chelsea [10 Oct. 1856]

...Geraldine says 'why on earth, when I was beside a Doctor I had confidence in, didn't I consult him about my health?' Why? because when I was beside Dr Russell and indeed (except for a common cold) all the time I was in Scotland—nothing ailed my health! . . . I arrived here with a furious face ach; Mr C having insisted on my sitting in a violent draught all the journey. *That* kept me perfectly sleepless all night in spite of my extreme fatigue—and so I began to be ill *at once* and have gone on *crescendo*—in the same ratio that my worries have increased— Figure *this!*— Scene—a room where everything is enveloped in dark yellow London *fog!*—for air to breathe a sort of *liquid* soot!—breakfast on the table—'adulterated coffee' 'adulterated bread' 'adulterated cream' and adulterated—*water!* Mr C at one end of the table, looking remarkably bilious—Mrs C at the other looking half-dead!

. . . Oh my Darling—I wish you were here—to give me a kiss and cheer me up a bit with your soft voice— In cases of this sort Geraldine with the best intentions is no help She is impractical—like all women of genius!— My Dear she said to me 'how is it that women who dont write *books* write always so much nicer *letters* than those who do?'— I told her— It was, I supposed, because they did not write in the valley of the shadow of their possible future *biographer*—but wrote what they had to say frankly and naturally. . . .

*

[Oct. 1856]

. . . Just this day week gone a week, I took what Lady Ashburton is always taking '*a chill*' which developed itself into a violent cold 'with tetanic complications' (I havent read Palmers Trial for nothing!) For *five* nights I couldn't get a wink of sleep— only one night of the five I passed in as near an approach to the blessed state of *Nirwana* as any one not a worshipper of *Buddha* need aspire to—that was from a doze of Morphia —I had given myself—and to which I ascribe the 'tetanic complications' (served me right for being so cowardly as to take it.) I didn't mean to take any more Morphia after what Dr Russell said about it. . . . And I can assure Dr Russell I *am* 'very ill' when I *scream*—not to say scream without intermission for half an hour together!! Dont let him fancy I make a practice of taking Morphia whenever I cant sleep I hadn't taken any for four months. . . . / I kiss you twenty times / your affectionate / Jane Welsh Carlyle

Relief had to come from writing to her friends. On 11 December Ellen Twisleton found Jane pale after 'a horrid attack' so that 'it almost kills her to write'. Lady Harriet had left for Nice because of her worsening ill health, and there were to be no Christmas festivities at the Grange.

5 Cheyne Row Chelsea [28 Nov. 1856]

My Darling
  You cant think what difficulty I have had to keep Geraldine from firing off letters at you every two or three days, with the most alarming accounts of my bodily state! It is her besetting weakness by nature,—and her trade of Novelist has aggravated it,—the *desire of feeling and producing violent emotions*.When I am well I can laugh down this sort of thing in her; but when I am ill it fatigues me dreadfully, and irritates my moral sense as well as my nerves. . . .
  The book Geraldine told you we were about sending 'all to yourself' is her *'Half Sisters'*—the one of all her novels which I like the best.And it has bonafide arguments in it, betwixt her and me, written down almost word for word as we spoke them in our walks together. . . .

Yet Geraldine could be out of favour. On 3 December, Ellen Twisleton writes of calling on Jane, when the 'everlasting Jewsbury was there, & after sitting and looking gloomy about ten minutes, got up & went away.' Ellen apologized for intruding but, to her surprise, this brought 'a burst of feeling' from Jane, 'to the tune that she was very glad when she did go, & that it would be very hard if she couldn't see me alone when I came, etc. Evidently, the "best friend" has no sort of self-control, & knows nothing about illness, cries over Mrs Carlyle, spills her jellies, knocks over the coal-pail, kisses her, & writes a letter of fourteen pages sent in before breakfast, to complain of "coldness" . . . & altogether there was a considerable glare of light thrown on the subject of their relations, calculated to relieve my scruples' (MS, Houghton, b45M–98, box 2).

ISABELLA CARLYLE   NLS Acc. 7988
Scotsbrig

[ca. 10 Dec. 1856]

. . . I had despaired of getting out of doors at all till the winter was over; but who could have anticipated such warm weather as this? The canaries, who were constantly quarrelling and pecking one another during the frost like any human married pair, now chirl and twitter so lovingly all day long, that I am in terror they carry things the length of *laying eggs*! ... Mr Carlyle *stands* them better than one would have expected. He even assisted in fixing a pulley in the Drawingroom ceiling, by which I swing them up into a region of safety at nights, and when I am out for my drive....

Both *the Secretary* and the Horse are valuable acquisitions the Horse especially! A countryman of the Secretarys wrote to me the other day that he hoped the said secretary was going to prove of great use to *me*— 'as a *lightening-conductor!!'* There is really some truth in the idea—especially while I dont get up to breakfast; so that Mr Marten [Martin] is the *first to catch it!* Mr C came down from him the other day much excited—and black as thunder—I durstn't ask what was wrong; but after vigourous puffing of tobacco smoke over my fire, he turned on me fiercly and said;'My Dear, will you tell me what on earth I am to do with that fellow upstairs?''Marten?' I asked in surprise— 'Why I thought you were satisfied with his work'!— 'His work!—Oh his *work* is well enough! but how the devil am I to put a stop to his *sniffing thro' his nose!!'* And then he made a frightful immitation of the obnoxious habit, which I then heard of for the first time! ..

On leaving for home, Elisabeth Dwight arranged for Jane to be presented with a chair, on which an outrageous Thomas is said to have promptly rested his feet. Jane replied to Elisabeth, grateful for her gift at a time of increasing strain, of which she successfully made light.

ELISABETH DWIGHT   Houghton b52M-179 (16)
Boston

5 Cheyne Row, Chelsea
19*th* December / 1856

You dear best Girl in all America, I embrace you with all my heart, (as you left it) and all my strength (considerably impaired); and thank you warmly for having given me a surprise, and a pleasure, and a consolation all in one!

Had your sister consulted the stars for the favorablest moment, to present that chair, she could have done no better. The moment when she hit upon one, when my soul (if I could any longer be said to *have* a soul) was crying aloud to Mr *Carlyle's* friends *'The Destinies,' 'The Immortal Gods,' 'The*

Supreme Powers' to bid something happen; and if possible *pleasant.* My very physical life was feeling to depend on something '*out of the Blue*' (as your friend Miss Sedgwick quoted us)— God forgive her! For, my Dear, I was in a crisis of disordered *nerves* complicated with the 'contradictions of sinners,' and for the rest was it not 'the gloomy month of November in which,' as the Frenchman began his novel, 'the people of England hang and drown themselves'? ... Geraldine Jewsbury told me that every morning she *knew* I was lying dying there, '*all for want of tonics?!*' ... Meanwhile your Sister sat on a low chair beside my sofa cheering me like '*The Singing Tree, the Talking Bird* and *the Golden Water*' all in one! and when she went away leaving me alone with my chair I found myself *saved*—for that time ...! Upon my honour I dont quite believe that woman is a *woman* at all! ... Oh I do love her dearly! And always the more the longer....

I did intend to write a long letter; and to tell you about everybody and everything; but I am already *tired*—being about as *effective* as an eel trying to stand on its tail! However I get out now most days for a drive—and expect before long to be able to do a little walking ... Your affectionate friend ...

Chapter Eight

Two Interludes

(i) The Cry from Craigenputtoch

Ellen Twisleton had written to her sister Mary Parkman on 23 November 1855 about a 'long and interesting talk' with Jane 'the other day, all about their life just after they were married— . . . a more miserable story I never heard,—but never say so'. *Soon after Ellen evidently wrote down the story in a tiny notebook made of her folded letter-paper, and checked it with Jane. It is curious why they should do so, writing it as an interview, then discreetly setting it aside; and it was an accident that it survived among the remains of Ellen's papers, unnoticed by biographers, after their removal to the United States on Edward Twisleton's death. Was the interview part of the two women's wish to record Jane's point of view without expecting it to be known— written, as she says in her* **Journal** *(21 Oct. 1855), 'for posthumous admiration and sympathy'? Both she and Ellen were married to older, excessively studious and withdrawn husbands, and may have had a special fellow-feeling.*

I asked Mrs Carlyle if the description of Craigenputtoch in this Memoir was like;—she said,'Yes, for it was the dreariest place on the face of the earth—I lived there five years, & the only wonder is I didn't go mad; the only women that had been there before me were four farmer's wives,—& of that *kind* of woman, with all their own rough work about them which they were used to occupy themselves with doing, three went mad and the fourth took to drinking!'

'But what made you go there, or what made you stay there,' I said;'did you like the idea of it *before* you went?'

'Oh no, I *never* liked the idea of it— oh, there's no way of making ye understand what kind of a wretched place it was,—I had seen it only once in my life, when my *grandfather* [John Welsh of Penfillan] took me, there, when I was quite a little child, & had always remembered it as the most dreadful, lonesome barren of places,—and all thro' my childhood I used

to be *frightened* with it,—it used to be the *threat*, if ye
understand, 'if ye behave so badly, ye shall go to
Craigenputtoch';—& I remember once, when I must have been
fourteen years old, & was self-willed about something, my
Mother telling me that I 'deserved to be sent to Craigenputtoch
to live on a hundred a year';—and to think that I *did* live there
five years, with not much more than a hundred a year. It was
that sort of *hopeless* place, that as long as my grandfather lived,
there was never anything attempted to be done with it,—but
when my father began to manage the property,—(who was the
sort of man that never can have anything that belongs to him
out of order,)—he drained it, & manured it, & planted it where
it was possible— And did all else that could be done about it;—
but there was very little of it that ever, could be made into
anything but a black peat moss;—have ye ever seen one—if ye
have, ye know what an ugly, dreary thing that is,— & of course,
they were only the hardiest trees would grow—& so all the
plantation there was of Scotch firs, which make a wood fit to
hang oneself in. But Carlisle took a strong fancy to it, & offered
to me that we should be married & live there,—it was a time
when he was very much out of health, & very desponding
about himself, & didn't see at all what he should do in life, & he
took it in his head that if he could go & live there, & have a
horse to ride, he was sure he should get well & get on— So I
wrote him back word that I wouldn't live at Craigenputtoch
with an *angel.*—& how I'd been always *scared* with it, as a
child &c.; & that was given up. And then my Mother took a little
jewel of a house for us in Edinboro', & furnished it—all for us,
so that it was the neatest, prettiest thing—as *pretty* as any
picture, & we went into that. But we hadn't been there two
months, before Carlyle grew perfectly frantic with it all, &
couldn't support it any way, couldn't endure his life at all nor
get on with the people that were about us,— but had it all this
time fixed in his head that if he were only at Craigenputtoch he
should be well, & everything that was wrong would grow
right;— I might refuse before, but then, you know, it was a
different matter, & there was no use refusing. Be ye may
imagine my ——————— situation, & how I felt it, for we'd
no money, & I had to go for it to my Mother—which I was
excessively loth to do,—for she was no longer so well off
herself as she had been used to being—had done a great deal
for us already,—and we had to take a thousand pounds from

her which was *sunk*, literally *sunk* in all that was to be done to
this place before we could get there as I knew it wld. be—in
buying out the farmer who was there & persuading him to give
up the rest of his lease, & then in taking down that house &
building another for us, which would never be fit either for a
farmer afterwards,—such a house as no farmer cares to have
the expense of to keep up. However it was all done, & we
went; & then Mr Carlyle's brother [Alexander] came, & he was
to manage the farm, & to pay rent to my Mother. But nothing
cld. turn out worse than that for he was a man of the most
outrageous, coarse, violent temper— (he's gone to Canada,
since, and done very well there, I believe,) & nobody can
imagine what I went through with that man,—and it had to be
all alone,—for I could never say a word to Carlyle, that would
be to drive him perfectly crazy, & 'my dear, what *can* I possibly
know, or do, about all this!' So his brother was always getting
into difficulties with his workmen, & everybody on the place, &
all were brought to me to 'the Mistress' as they called me, to
settle;— (they called him 'the Master,' & me 'the Mistress,' &
Carlyle 'the Laird'—) and one day I'd have the people in
declaring they'd all *leave*, at once,—and then we'd perpetual
trouble about *keeping* them,—he wanted they should have had
food so as to eat less—and I, of course, tho't only to make them
comfortable. In those days no bargain was ever concluded in
Scotland without the parties *drinking* together, they always
must sit down together over their whisky, or gin, or whatever it
was,—so, of course, every time he went into Dumfries on our
business, he came back as drunk as a man could be—and at
that time he did all the errands of the household, and got me all
the things I needed from Dumfries—so ye may imagine the
state they used to come in, the keg of gin broken into the bag
of flour—& the powdered sugar mixed up with the *sugar-of-
lead* I was goin' to say, & so forth. I had to learn to do & undo
everything, & down to doctoring horses. Carlyle & his brother
both lost their horses, & then mine fell sick of the same thing,
& I would not let any of them touch him— I sent a boy to a
sensible physician there was in Dumfries, & asked him what he
would do to a *person* who had a severe inflammation—& then
I applied the blisters & doses to my horse, only increasing the
quantity according to my own ideas,—& I carried him thro' so
that he got well again. But I used to get up & go out to the
stable to him three times in the night, while he was so sick.'

'How old were you then,' I asked.

'About 22 then [meaning 27],' she said.'And that man lived with us for four years [or rather less]; after he was gone, I could manage to live better. But one of my miseries was about the rent for he seemed to think because he was Carlyle's brother, it was no matter to be accurate about that, when he paid it or almost whether he paid it at all,—& there was my Mother, I knew, wanting her money & waiting for it—& she that had had every luxury all her life, not knowing where to turn for ten pounds,—as I knew, tho' she never told me so— and I not able to get her rent paid her! I remember one time, it had not been paid for four months beyond the time, & Carlyle got some money from London for something he'd written, in a cheque upon the Dumfries bank; I seized the cheque, got on my pony, & rode all alone no servant with me, into the town, to the bank, got my money, & off another sixteen miles to my Mother's (for it was in a kind of *triangle* were, 16 miles one way from her, & the other way from the town,—) and gave her the money, & then another 16 miles home again'.'Three times 16 miles in one day, I said, & alone,— did you not make yourself ill?'

No, I wasn't ill—I was so thankful to get the money for her;—of course I had one of my dreadful headaches the next day.— One thing about it was that it was a place you couldn't get servants to come to, except the roughest & wildest sort of creatures, such as I had never been used to, & didn't know how to manage,—but nobody that could help one, or be friendly with one. I've often thought since, that the only thing that *kept* me from going crazy, was just what I tho't then eno' to *make* me so, that I had so much of the r'el har'rd work to do the family,—for often I couldn't read; I had to get a Dodds's Cookery-Book & learn how to cook every single thing that was eaten, & how to mix & bake the bread,— for I never had a servant the whole time we were there, who could make bread,—and Carlyle thought all the bread we could get at Dumfries made him ill. Finally I had a sister of Carlyle's come, & she was with me 18 months, & those were the worst of the whole— she was a coarse, rude, girl and had such a temper, & such a tre-MENDOUS will as I never met with in any other woman but herself;—a will just like Carlyle's, with anything besides to induce ye to put up with it.— She assumed authority over the servants, & made constant quarrels with them *in* the house, as his brother did out,—& I had no authority over her, for if I found fault with her she went to Carlyle, & 'Jane' was doing this & that to her, & that couldn't be done you know. So she would come to breakfast with her hair in curl-papers, which I never could put up with, & other things of the sort. I used to go out & sit down in the middle of the moor, on a stone, & *wonder* if this were I, & how the same persons could live such a life, that had lived the one I had been used to before,— so petted generally, (though I got a whipping enough, to be sure, at times;) but, being an only child, even if I was *punished*, I always felt myself an object of importance, at any rate.

Living at Craigenputtoch, it wasn't as if I saw anything of Carlyle;—he went to his own room directly after breakfast, & worked there till 2 hours before dinner, & always rode those two hours. And he rode *alone*, because he only galloped or walked, and it fretted him to have my horse cantering along by the of his side; so he rode alone, & I rode alone; then he came to dinner very much *worked-up*, as bilious people always are by a ride, & he was 'dangerous,' you know, & there was no freedom of communication during dinner; then he went to walk for an hour, which wasn't very wholesome, I always tho't, right after eating, & to his room till tea; & afterward to his room, until about ten o'clock, & then he'd come in, quite tired out with his work, & say, 'Jane, will ye play me a few of those Scotch tunes'—& I would sit down & play Scotch tunes till he went to bed,—oftenest with the tears running down my face, the while I played.—'

'And was there nobody you cared for in the *town*,— had you no friends that ever came to see you from Dumfries?' 'No, nobody:— sometimes, when I couldn't bear it any longer, I'd go over to my Mother, spend the night with her;— but I had to be back in the morning, for it couldn't go on without me,— we'd no servants that could be trusted.' 'And did you really live five years,' I groaned out, 'that fearful life?'

'Yes,' she said, 'except at the end of the fourth [i.e. third], we came for a few months to London. Carlyle came down to see about publishing Teufulsdröck's [*Sartor*], & then afterwards wrote for me to come' [1831; followed by a stay in Edinburgh, 1833]

'And then from Craigenputtoch where did you go?'

Then we came to London [1834], & have been here ever since; in this same house we are now.

I asked who was *kind* to her—what friends she found—

'She said Mrs Austin [Sarah Austin] was kind to her, whom she had known before, when she was in London for a short time —but that didn't last.'

'What was the matter?'

'Why, she was the sort of person I *couldn't* be friends with—everybody's friend—with superficial kindness enough & to spare, but no real comprehension. No, it couldn't possibly have lasted long, tho' I've got her letters, now, beginning 'Dearest of friends' & all that sort of thing. Then there was Mrs Basil Montague, whom I had known a long time; i.e. I hadn't *seen* her till then but I'd corresponded with her— Edward Irving talked to me about her, & made her write to me, & I tho't so much of her letters! He admired her so much, & used to call her the 'Mother of the Gracchi,'—nice kind of *Gracchi*, Carlyle said one ended in prison, & another in a drunken fit, or something of that kind. But all those sort of people fell off. About the first people that *really* were kind were the Stirlings [Edward and Hester Sterling]— I don't think I knew anybody that was, till I knew them:— they used to live in the old red house that stands just below yours, here. The first winter after we came to live in London, I got a dreadful illness, & nothing could be so kind as old Mrs Stirling—she was in my room every morning & by ten o'clock, though it was winter & the snow on the ground. But finally they had to send for my mother, & I didn't get better till she came. [She came in a hot August 1835].

She travelled night & day, & came quicker than anybody thought was possible, before, but she came into my room as quietly as if she'd had neither hurry nor fear. She was such a gentle, beautiful woman, & everything she did, she did so well! & when she came I grew better.

Oh, I used to be so fond of her—though I didn't see her much— once or twice I went to Scotland, & once she made me a visit— but I was always thinking about her,— thinking what would please her, and looking about for some little cheap thing I could send her—or if I met anyone she would like to hear about—so that it has never seemed the same since she died, & at first I seemed to have no object any more, & nothing to live for.—

Unlike Jane's letters of 1828-34, written from Craigenputtoch, her outburst in Ellen's account was considered. It shows her as frustrated, sick, and despairing at Carlyle's apparent indifference. For Carlyle was 'sunk in Frederick' (**Reminiscences** 157). *Yet if the memoir was meant to justify her, it failed. Ellen died in 1862, aged thirty-two, when Jane noted,* 5 June: *'Dear little Mrs. Twisleton, so young, and beautiful and clever, so admired in society and adored at home.... The strong affection she testified for me has made her death a keener grief than I thought it would be'* (**LM** 3:99). *Carlyle always remembered attending her 'affecting funeral' at Broughton Castle, to which he rode from Oxford with Browning, and where her grave shared with Edward can still be seen.*

Edward sent Jane a silhouette or profile of Ellen. She replied: 'I like to have this, and like to have it from you! ... but I have a photograph of her [begged from a Bond St photographer] ... to keep her image clear in my heart—I loved her—love her so much! And she was not a sort of woman to be ever replaced in one's affections' (MS, Houghton, bMS Am 1408(61)).

We gain further insights into the Carlyle circle from some letters of Ellen's sister Elisabeth. After the Twisletons had returned from Boston with her in 1855, Elisabeth wrote that Ellen had to spend a few days in bed. They were enlivened by 'a delightful visit' from Jane: 'She seemed to be the most entertaining person I ever heard talk, in her style, which is story-telling. She could write a modern Arabian nights.—Her talk was almost entirely about people ... & if she had sketched them on the wall they could not have been more graphically represented there in her broad Scotch accent' (8 Nov.). Her next call 'was as entertaining as one of Thackerays novels & in much the same style' (16 Nov., MS, Houghton, b45M-98).

Elisabeth continued to record impressions of their friends, and left a vivid description of their Christmas visit to the Grange, where she admired the 'perfectly enchanting' Lady Harriet, whose expression was 'almost wholly intellectual, & her manner not haughty, but exceedingly reserved & dignified'. She liked her too: 'she is wonderfully clever, not in the least petty ... and if a person is to be judged by works, not words, I must call her kind' (14 Dec.). Ellen wrote that, on departing, Carlyle was left 'scolding, Lady Ashburton entertaining, Mrs Brookfield smiling & laughing, Mrs Carlyle neither smiling nor laughing ....Certainly no one could pass a more amusing week.' If 'there is rather too perpetual a demand for ready conversation, there is also a wonderful supply.... Lady Ashburton deserves admiration for more than her wit', and is 'free from petty ways of thinking of & dealing with other people.— To see her with Carlyle is better than any play I ever saw; for she bears his howls with the serenest of laughs, & evidently refreshes him, as much as she does the rest of the company. You will see that I am considerably in love with her' (26 Dec., MS, Houghton, b45M-98).

(ii) Jane's *Journal* and the Swine's Foot

Alongside the letters Jane at times kept a more personal **Journal***; but she received a blow, as diarists do, when an old friend was caught reading it when it was left in the sitting-room. Neither she nor Carlyle ever quite forgave George Lillie Craik for stepping into it with his 'swine's foot'* (**Reminiscences** 72–3). *She had promptly burnt the diary and almost everything of the kind she could lay her hands on, showing by her reaction how much it meant to her, the shock of intrusion, and a sense of her folly at leaving it out. Yet she still felt a need to record her thoughts when there seemed no point in going on. As Froude explains, she began a new diary near 'the end of 1855'* (**Life** 4:180). *It was from this that her husband 'first learnt' after her death 'how miserable' she had been as a result of his friendship with Lady Harriet. Froude had already selected parts of the* **Journal** *for his* **Letters and Memorials***. He explained that after believing her husband 'destined for something extraordinary', she had worked for him 'like a servant'; but 'when she found he had leisure for Bath House, she became jealous and irritable. ... She had a fiery temper. ... The shadow slanted backwards over their whole lives together; and ... she came to think with bitterness' about their past* (**LM** 2:256–7). *Hence, on reading the* **Journal***, came Carlyle's remorse. To some extent, Carlyle would have agreed. Yet, in writing his* **Reminiscences***, he does not mention the situation with Lady Harriet, but blames Jane's unhappiness and her 'deeper breakdown in health' on his absorption in writing. He adds that she was 'sore' and 'harshly distressed', but that her diary was not to 'be destroyed, however tragical and sternly sad'* (**Reminiscences** 157). *Here it is given selectively.*

21*st* October, 1855

Neither my birthday nor newyear's-day this; anniversaries on which I 'feel it my duty,' usually, to bloom out into the best intentions, beginning and ending always with the intention to resume my old Journal! But if 'carried out' to the extent of a few pages, it has 'gone', even that smallest of good intentions, 'to the greater number,' before a week was out! Decidedly I am no longer the little girl who used to say over her most difficult tasks, 'I'll *gar* [make] myself do it'! *The mother of Invention* has *garred* me do so much against the grain, that I am too fatigued now to gar *myself* do anything I can get let alone—

And after all; one may keep a journal very minutely and
regularly and still be a great fool,— all the greater perhaps for
this very labour of selfconsciousness which is so apt to
degenerate into a dishonest striving 'to make a silk purse out of
a sows ear'—for posthumous admiration or sympathy— from
one's Executors; or even for present self-complacent
mistification of *oneself!*— I remember Charles Buller saying of
the Duchess de Praslin's murder;'what *could* a poor fellow do
with a wife who kept a journal, *but* murder her?'There was a
certain truth hidden in this light remark.Your Journal 'all about
feelings' aggravates whatever is factitious and morbid in you;
that I have made experience of; and now the only sort of
journal I would keep should have to do with what Mr. Carlyle
calls 'the fact of things'— It is very bleak and barren this 'fact of
things' as I now see it—very! And what good is to result from
writing of it in a paper-book is more than I can tell. But I have a
notion TO; and perhaps I shall blacken more paper this time,
when I begin 'quite promiscuously,' without any moral end in
view but just, as the Scotch Professor drank whiskey,'because I
like it, and because it's cheap.'

    22d— I was cut short in my *Introduction* last night by Mr
C's return from Bath House.That eternal Bath House. I wonder
how many thousand miles Mr C has walked between there and
here, put it all together? Setting up always another milestone,
and another, between himself and me! Oh, good grasious! When
I first noticed that heavy yellow House without knowing or
caring to know who it belonged to, how far I was from
dreaming that thro' years and years I should carry every stone's
weight of it on my heart! ...

    23rd— A stormy day, within doors; so I rushed out early
and walked, walked, walked! If peace and quietness be not in
one's own power, one can always give oneself, at least, bodily
fatigue—no such bad succedaneum after all!— Life gets to
look for me like a sort of kaleidiscope: a few things of different
colours (black predominating) which Fate shakes into new
and ever new combinations, but always the *same* things over
again! ...

    24th— Rehabilitated two old bonnets having failed to find
a new one large enough Went to thank the Countess but did
not find her.— Called at the Farrars; ...The American, Mr James,
with the cork leg, who used to be so often here ten years ago,
turned up again tonight, and welcome,—American tho he

be. He was very amusing about the Spirits. On *their* side of the water, he said the 'Spirits' had outbreaks of devilishness, which made them less tiresome than our Spirits 'on this side.' An acquaintance of his, having been answered gravely by a Spirit for some time, was going on with 'but there is the other thing I wish to'— 'Go to Hell you infernal idiot'! said the Spirit—and the words came with the more startling effect that they were *spoken*: the *Medium* being a little sickly innocent child! . . .

25*th* / Oh good gracious *alive*! what a whirlwind—or rather whirl-pool of a day!— Breakfast had 'passed off' better or worse, and I was at work on a picture-frame,— my own invention and pretending to be a little 'work of art,'— when Mr C's bell rang like mad, and was followed by cries of, 'Come! Come! *are* you coming?— Arrived at the second landing, three steps at a time, I saw Mr C and Ann in the spare bedroom, hazily, thro a *waterfall*! The great cistern had overflowed; and it was 'raining and pouring down' thro' the *new* ceiling, and plashing up on the *new* carpet! All the baths and basins in the house and even 'vessels of dishonour' were quickly assembled on the floor, and I on my knees mopping up with towels and sponges. When the water ceased to pour thro' the ceiling, it began to pour thro' the roof of the bed! If the water had only been clean! but it was black as soot, and the ground of the carpet white! At last it faired in the spare room, and I retired to change my shoes and stockings, which were soaked, as if I had been *fishing*. . . . What *am* I to do with all these spoiled ceilings and carpets? . . .

26*th* / My morphia a dead failure last night,—gave me neither sleep nor rest; but only nausea— So much the better perhaps. If morphia had *always*, instead of only at long intervals, its *good* effect on me—making me all *whole*, for the time being, like a cracked dish boiled in sweet milk, I don't know what the *principle* would be strong enough to keep me from slowly poisoning myself with it. Today then I have been *up* to nothing, naturally. . . .

30*th* / Ruskin has sent an answer to my answer; and in this instance the *man's* Letter is ten times as long as the *woman's* was.—How charmingly amiable Ruskin shows himself since his wife divorced him! Is it 'out of *vengeance*'? . . . More likely it is satisfaction at having got out of his *complication* on any terms that gives Ruskin this ineffable air of 'peace and goodwill towards men', —and women—ay, and *dogs* too my little Nero, as *you* know! . . .

31st — ...Today's post brought the kindest of letters from
Geraldine, including a note from the Lady de Capel Broke she is
staying with, inviting me to Oakley Hall. This Lady's 'faith in
things unseen' excited similar faith on my part, and I would go
had I nothing to consider but how I should like it when there. I
had to write a refusal however, Mr C. is 'neither to hold nor to
bind' when I make new visiting acquaintances on *my own*
basis, however exceptionable the person may be. And there
were other reasons 'which it may be interesting not to state.' ...
The evening devoted to mending; — Mr C's trousers, among
other things! 'Being an only child' I never '*wished*' to sew men's
trousers—no never!—

    1st November ... From Chapel Street, I walked on to Queen
Anne Street— Found Darwin, and *Mrs* Wedgwood into the
bargain. She drove me to the London Library in search of a book,
and put me down after at Fortnum & Mason's, whence I *walked*
the whole way home. Pretty fair for a woman! considering that
'we women' (as Mrs Austin told Carlyle!) 'are not intended by
nature to *walk* like men, being less favourably constructed about
the *hips*'!— Did you ever?—No, I never!— ...

    2d / Not having slept one wink all last night, I came
down today in a mood!— No use trying to work at anything. To
live under the circumstances was the most England could
expect of one! Nevertheless I went by appointment to see
dear little *Mrs* Twislton in her sick room. They gave me
luncheon, and *warmed* me with their kindness. Mr Twislton
then accompanied me to Lady Sandwichs; and from South
Street home to my own door. Lady S speaking of Lord Elgin
today told us that on his Father's death her (Lady S's) relative
Lady Olivia Sparrow fell to work to console the widow, on
christian principles; hoping her grief might be made the
means of her *conversion*. 'Oh don't trouble me with all that',
said Lady Elgin one day, impatiently, 'there is no,—no
consolation for me but in *Euclid*!' Mr *Fairie* this evening,
when I was already *so* spent. The Fates are never above
'pouring water on a drowned mouse.'

    5th ...Alone this evening. Lady A. in town again, and Mr C
of course at Bath House.

> 'When I think on what I is,
> And what I use to was;
> I 'gin to think I've sold myself
> For very little *cas*.'

6th Mended Mr C's dressinggown and washed some 'finery'...Then off to Geraldine who gave me a nice little 'early dinner.'...'Peacefully sated with revenge and food,' we streamed off to Pimlico and bought clogs; as usual staying out till twilight. I am very idle just now, and cause of idleness in others—at least *one* other (Geraldine). But it is not wilful idleness exactly. Much movement under the free sky is needful for me to keep my heart from throbbing up into my *head* and maddening it. They must be comfortable people those who have leisure to think about *going to Heaven!* My most constant and pressing anxiety is to *keep out of Bedlam*—that's all! Ach!— If there were no *feelings*, what steady sailing craft we should be....

7th More family-needlework...I saw today for the first time in my life blood-red blanketts! A shop-window in Leicester Square was full of them. Horrid!—they looked to me made expressly to be murdered in! Nevertheless Geraldine and I are going to have scarlet Petticoats! Dear! Dear! What a *sick* day this has been with me! Oh my Mother! Nobody *sees* when I am suffering now; and I have learnt to suffer 'all to myself.' From *only-childness* to THAT is a far and a rough road to travel!

> 'Oh little did my mother think,
> The day she cradl'd me,
> The Lands I was to travel in,
> The Death I was to dee!'

11th /...It is not *always*...that unjust treatment, harshness and disdain in her Husband drives a woman *jusqu'au désordre*; but infallibly it drives her to *something*, and something not to *his* advantage any more than to hers.

Today has been like other days outwardly. I have done this and that and people have come and gone—but all as in a *bad dream*....

15 / November.— ...Two little children [William and Arthur Allen], one 12 months, the other 5 years old, have been fished out of the River tonight at the bottom of this Street, and brought to life by 'the Doctor,'— Three caps have been found, by which it would seem a *third* child has *perished*. The present story is that a man and woman were seen to leave Battersea Pier in a boat with three children. Did the man and woman take the children to drown them? Are *they* drowned themselves? The only thing certain is, two small children have

been picked out of the Thames, restored to life and taken to
the Workhouse.— Where I should like excessively to follow
them and bring them home. But '*Man* does what he *will*
woman but what she *may*.'

16*th* There was neither 'boat' nor 'man' in the case; but a
woman did take her three children to drown them— and no
doubt but the eldest is drowned,— the two babies were saved
by a miracle. They *floated*, poor little things; one all the way
from Cadogan Pier to opposite the bottom of this Street, the
bigger of the two about half that distance and *never ceased
screaming* so that the waterman were guided thro' the fog to
first one and the other little terrified thing. . . . While the
Doctor was busy with them, *their Father* turned into the
Magpie, in passing, to *see what it was all about* — and it was
about his own drowned and half-drowned children,— and
their Mother his own wife the murderess! . . . This morning she
underwent her examination before the Magistrate or rather
appeared before the Magistrate. For the Magistrate, being a
man of singular sensibility, it would seem, declared he 'would
not have asked her a question for the whole world'!! . . . It is
generally believed she was led to murder her children by
jealousy! Jealousy of a pretty apple-woman, who has a stall on
the Cadogan Pier! And what astonishes me is, that these
tradespeople, my informants, in lyrically recognising the
'dreadful thing' she has gone and done, don't seem to find it
unnatural but speak pityingly of her, as if the drowning of
one's children were an unavoidable tho' 'dreadful'
consequence of one's husband's infidelity; expressed or
understood. Decidedly, what *Mr C* calls *George Sandism* must
be spreading *downward*. . . .

18*th* (Sunday) / . . . Mr Whitworth of Manchester dropt in
to tea, as from the moon. An *interesting man*, for *once*; thank
God for all his mercies! Whitworth is still the *mechanic* in
appearance and bearing; all the perfumes of—the Bank of
England cannot wash *that* out of him. And besides he looks
cousin once removed to a Baboon; but then he *knows* what he
says, that man; and *says* what he *knows*; and is lucid as spring-
water, and natural as a *gowan* [daisy]. He has been employed by
Government to make a model rifle, and has made one that will
send a ball about *two miles!* . . .

20*th* Half the day spent in *redding up* [tidying] boxes and
drawers. Sat an hour with Geraldine who tho better, is still in

bed. I have been fretting inwardly all this day at the prospect of
having to go and *'appeal'* before the Tax Commissioners at
Kensington tomorrow morning. Still it must be done. If Mr C
should go himself he would run his head against *some* post in
his impatience, and besides, for me, when it is over it will be
over, whereas he would not get the better of it for twelve
months, — if ever at all!...

    21*st O me miseram* [O wretched me]!... Set down at 30
Horton Street, I found a dirty private like house, only with *Tax
Office* painted on the door. A dirty woman-servant opened the
door and told me the Commissioners would not be there for
half an hour, but I might walk up.... There was an instant of
darkness while the one door was shut behind and the other
opened in front; and then I stood in a dim room where three
men sat round a large table spread with papers, One held a
pen ready over an open ledger, another was taking snuff ....
The third who was plainly the cock of that Dungheap, was
sitting for Rhadamanthus.... 'What is this? Why is Mr Carlyle
not come himself? Didn't he get a letter, *ordering* him to
appear?—Mr Carlyle wrote *some nonsense* about being
exempted from coming and I desired an answer to be sent;
that he *must* come—*must* do as other people.'— 'Then sir,' I
said, 'your desire has been neglected, it would seem— My
Husband having received no such letter— and I was told by
one of your fellow-commissioners that his (Mr Carlyle's)
personal appearance was not indispensable.' — '*Huffh! Huffh!*
What does Mr Carlyle mean by saying he has no income from
his writings. When he himself fixed it in the beginning at a
hundred & fifty?'— 'It means, sir, that in ceasing to *write* one
ceases to be paid for writing—and Mr Carlyle has published
nothing for several years.'... 'Take off—fifty pounds—say—a
hundred—take off a hundred pounds', said Radamanthus to
the horned owl.— 'If we write Mr Carlyle down at a hundred
and fifty he has no reason to complain, I think! There you may
go! — no, no! Mr Carlyle has no reason to complain!'... In
stepping out into the open air, my first thought was what a
mercy Carlyle didn't come himself....

    24*th* But for the persuasion I have that the unrest in my
nerves would go to my *brain*, if I did not work it off outwardly;
I should hate myself for the life I am leading, —all the available
hours of the day spent in walking, in making *calls* and things
that leave no trace except on the soles of my shoes.... Why has

everybody such horror at the idea of going mad? Insanity is not necessarily a state of suffering. . . . No, it is not the *sufferings* of insanity that are so full of terror for me; it is the unconscious *disgrace*— To be *kept, treated, hidden away!* To be a thing of horror for one's friends—if one have any—of disgust for the world at large! It is *that* I would *walk* myself to death to stave off! . . .

26*th* / Last night there was a lump on my brow, as big as a plover's egg, and I felt *all heels over head* — like 'a *Drunk*.' But a spoonful of henbane did wonders in composing me to sleep; and this morning the lump is nearly gone, and I feel no bad effects from my blow. I am getting '*accomplished*' in knock[ing] my head against mantle-pieces, as William Forster pronounced me in falling out of gigs 'as if I had been brought up to it.' . . . I went and sat for an hour with Mrs Twisleton—(able to be in the Drawing room now)— Meant to sit as long with Geraldine, but she met me with a little cankered look that it set me off in a huff. 'Boppery Bopp!' . . .

27 . . . Paid a long visit to Miss Wilson. . . . Miss Wilson dislikes me, I was told last year, by a credible authority, and speaks ill of me behind my back. And yet she looks glad to see me always, and presses me to stay. And the best is that I dont like *her* a whit the less for that superfluous *warning*, —but rather strive to please her more than I used. I need to love people terribly well, that I should hate them for not loving *me*. . . .

28*th* / . . . Took the black silk, Lady A[shburton] presented me with last Christmas to Catchpool; that it might be made up *for The Grange*. 'Did you buy *this* yourself Mam?' said Catchpool, rubbing it between her finger and thumb. 'No, it was a present—but why do you ask?' 'Because, Mam, I was thinking, if you bought it yourself, you had been *taken in*. It is so poor! Very trashy, indeed! I don't think I ever saw so trashy a MOIRE'! . . .

4*th* [Dec.] / I hardly ever begin to write here, that I am not tempted to break out into *Job*isms about my bad nights— How I keep on my legs and *in* my senses with such little snatches of sleep, is a wonder to myself. Oh! to cure any one of a terror of annihilation, just put him on *my* allowance of sleep! and see if he don't get to long for sleep—sleep—unfathomable and everlasting sleep, as the only conceivable Heaven!. . .

That woman who threw her three children in the water *is* mad, poor creature! She has been 'out of her mind' for more than a year (a person who knows her told me) 'Her Mother was

mad before her.' 'Up to a year ago she was the tenderest of
Mothers and a good Wife.' Then she took a fixed idea that her
three sound beautiful children were 'all eaten up with scurvy';
that they would grow up hideous to look at, and in frightful
sufferings—To save them from which, it was her duty as a
Mother, she said, to make away with them. . . . What a dense mass
of lies one must hustle thro' to get at the truth of any smallest
transaction here! My informant (our Baker's wife), a sensible,
little, old woman, scouted the idea of '*jealousy*' in the
business—'Nonsense—downright, nonsensical nonsense! Mam.
They were as loving a couple as you could find—never a *word*
between them!'. . .

11*th* / In a great hurry scurry all morning—letter about
the Toys ('God particularly damn them!') to be written to *my
Lady*. . . . Oh dear I wish this Grange business were well over. It
occupies me (the mere preparation for it) to the exclusion of
all quiet thoughts and placid occupation (reading novels for
instance). To have to care for my dress at this time of the day,
more than I ever did when young and pretty and happy (God
bless me! to think that I was once all that!) on penalty of being
regarded as a blot on the Grange *gold and azure*, is really too
bad. *Ach gott!* If we had been left in the sphere of life we
belong to how much better it would have been for us—in
many ways.

12*th* Off early to shop. What a lot of trumpery things it
takes to make me into a 'Woman of England'— *for a month*!
Met Miss Farrer coming here, and lunched at *her* house on my
way to M*r* Tait's where I had appointed Lady A's *Ex Lady's
Maid* to meet me and help about the *Toys*. Waited in vain for
her an hour and quarter! Walked home in a rage, *re infecta*
[nothing done], but got my fan (!) from the Mender, and
bought a warm petticoat. . . .

A month at the Grange where I DRANK a gargle! On my return
home sprained MY SIDE. Recovered from that I took cold.

24th of *March, 1856!*

Heavens!—My poor dear Journal! I have used you
shamefully! I took you to comfort me in a time of need,—

something to hold on to in the darkness and loneliness; and the
first will o'wisp (of *distraction*) that crossed my path, away I
went after it, full drive towards the bottomless quagmire,
without even a good-by to you my poor Journal! as if you had
been merely so much waste paper that might be taken to light
the fire with; for any further use that was in you, or for anything
I cared! Pardon, dear Journal! I return to you penitent and
punished. What more can I say? Ah! and *you* are so good! so
discreet! ... Look straight before you then Jane Carlyle, and, if
possible, not over the heads of things either; away into the
distant vague! Look, above all, at 'the duty nearest hand,' and
what's more, *do* it! Ah! the spirit is willing, but the flesh is weak.
And four weeks of illness have made mine weak as water. No
galloping over London as in 'seven league boots' for me at
present! Today I walked with effort one little mile and thought it
a great feat! But if the strength has gone out of me, so also has
the unrest; I can sit, and *lie* even, very patiently doing nothing. ...
In fact *Sleep* has come to look to me the highest *virtue*, and the
greatest *happiness*, — that is, *good* sleep, untroubled, beautiful,
like a child's— Ah me!

    25th March. / ... Four or five years ago John Robertson
brought here a Man of whom, it seems, I said (aside) to
Robertson, 'that is a born-*natural*; where did you pick him up?'
Four or five days ago Kate Sterling brought here the same man
to introduce to me as her *fiancé*!!— '*What a waste*!' ... That
brave, passionate-hearted girl the wife of such a nauseous
creature!— Nauseous is the word for him! Oh dear! Oh dear!
What misery awaits her, when she shall awake from her
bewitchment,—bedevilment! I never saw a case of love that
made more in favour of Dr Carlyle's opinion: 'love is merely a
disease of the nerves— a mild delirium!'! Really one should pray
for the gift not only 'to see ourselves as others see us,' but also
to see our Lovers as others see them.

    26th / Today it has blown knives and files! A cold rasping,
savage day; excruciating for sick nerves. Dear Geraldine, as if she
would contend with the very elements on my behalf, brought
me a bunch of *violets*, and a bouquet of the loveliest most
fragrant *flowers*!

    Talking with *her* all I have done or *could* do. ...

    'Have mercy upon me O Lord; for I am weak: O Lord heal
me; for my bones are vexed. But thou, O Lord, how long? Return
O Lord deliver my soul; oh save me for thy mercies sake.'

27*th* / . . . Mr C took Nero out with him to night, and half
an hour after he opened the door with his latch key, and called
in, 'is *that vermin* come back?' Having received my horrified
'No!' he hurried off again, and for twenty minutes I was in the
agonies of *one's dog lost*—my heart beating up into my ears. At
last I heard Mr C's feet in the street and (Oh joy!) heard him
gollaring [shouting] at something, and one knew what the little
bad something was! Ach! 'we could have better spared a better
dog'! . . .

29*th* / I insert a letter received this morning from my
'handsome Cousin,' Captain Baillie—a remarkable document for
those who knew him in his days of London Celebrity; when he
was a *chief Dandy*, spending his Capital at the rate of fifteen
thousand a year, on fine clothes, horse carriages, and King
Charles Spaniels. I wish I had preserved . . . his Taylors *bill* as it
figured in the newspapers some 25 years ago; and an *Article*
upon him in Fraser's Magazine a few year's later, in which he
was described as 'a mixture of Mars and Adonis,' 'perfuming the
air of Rotten Row with his embroidered handkerchief, as he
rode along on his splendid black horse.' —

And now it has come to borrowing *half sovereigns*, with
him. Alas! and he had *talents* as well as good looks; and a heart
'not bad,' by any means. . . . I found him in a poor but decent-
looking house in a mean street. Having sent my name by his
Landlord, I was shown up; and the *mixture of Mars and
Adonis* received me at the door with as stately a grace as he
had ever displayed on his famous Black Horse. He is still very
handsome, and his dress tho' threadbare was clean and
peculiar as of old. . . . The room he was in, very small, served
evidently for parlour, bed room and kitchen— In one corner
was a fourposted bed,—the posts rising desolately to the
ceiling without a morsel of curtain. The floor was well-
scowered, with a bit of darned carpet in the middle. . . . Ah
Heaven! There was not even a toilet, on which to have laid out
his beautiful gold & silver dressing-case, had it been to the fore!
A very thrifty poor-person's fire, with a brass nail knocked into
the mantle-shelf—to serve the purpose of roasting. All *that* I
noticed—and I don't think there was much besides. And on this
ruins of his Carthage sat 'the elegant Jim Baillie' doing the
Marius of Dandyism as well as it *could* be done. Not a word of
apology for his environment—not an allusion to it—not even
recognition of it by look. A more perfectly unembarrassed,

courteous reception I never met in my life! I asked where was his—'*wife*'? He answered, 'Why, here to be sure'! *Then* I understood that air of comfort in the midst of exigence! Only a *woman* could have compassed it; and even a woman could have compassed it only thro *love*! . . .

Poor woman indeed! Ruined by him in fortune and reputation fallen and still holding on in her unselfish love. And the *virtuous* would frown on her—She is not his wife. I wish I had seen her to shake hands with her, and express my *admiration*! . . .

11*th* [April] / I really couldn't help it! There was no time for you, my Journal—poor passive friend! . . . I took my little Cousin [Maggie] to the Liverpool train the day before yesterday and her sweet, good face smiling on me thro' tears as she shot away, went to my heart like a remorse. But could I help being so weak and nervous that the continual presence of a fellow-creature especially a young, light-hearted fellow-creature irritated and fagged me beyond measure? all the more that in common kindness I had to repress any outward expression of my feelings! . . .

14*th* Lay on the sofa most of the day feeling 'too ill for anything'— Nevertheless, took myself upstairs towards seven o'clock and dressed myself very fine, and was driven to Bath House to a dinner party. The Twisletons, Milnes, 'The Bear,' Goldwin Smith, and Delane. Came home with virtue's own reward in the shape of a sore throat. My throat fairly made sore by telling Lord A French Criminal Trials, all the evening, out of a book he hadn't seen. He was so unwell! and since he *was* there; instead of where he should have been viz: in his bed, I 'felt it my duty' to amuse him without letting him talk. . . .

15*th* April 1856 / I am really very feeble and ailing at present. And my ailment is of a sort that I understand neither the ways nor outlooks of; so that the positive suffering is complicated with dark apprehensions. Also, alas and there is nobody I care to tell about it! not *one*! poor *ex-spoilt-Child* that I am!

To keep up the appearance of being alive is quite as much as I can manage. Every day I get up with the *wish to* do ever so many things; but my wishes are no longer 'presentiment of my powers', if they ever were so! At the day's end I find I have merely *got thro' it*, better or worse; not employed it; all strength for *work* of any sort being used up in bearing the bodily pressure without crying out. . . .

20*th* April (Sunday) / Plattnauer in the morning. I was too poorly for walking with him, so we talked *intimately* over the fire. Except Geraldine, not other callers. I fell asleep while Geraldine was here, and again after she had gone! This weakness is incomprehensible—if I had any person, or any thing to take hold of, and lean my weight on! . . .

21*st* I feel weaklier everyday; and my 'my soul is also sore vexed.' 'Oh how long?'

I put myself in an omnibus, being unable to walk, and was carried to Islington and back again. What a good shilling's worth of exercise! The Angel at Islington! It was *there* I was set down on my first arrival in London; and Mr C with Edward Irving was waiting to receive me. —! 'The past is past; and gone is gone!' . . .

25 While talking philosophy with Mr. Barlow today, there drove up a carriage, and I heard a voice inquiring if I were home, which I knew, tho' I had not heard it for ten years!— Mr Barlow I can see is trying to '*make Mrs. Carlyle out*'! (don't he wish he may get it?) What he witnessed today must have thrown all his previous observations into the wildest confusion. 'The fact of her being descended from John Knox had explained much in Mrs Carlyle which I hadn't' (he, Mr Barlow, said to Geraldine) 'been able to *make out*.' Did it explain for him my sudden change today, when flinging my accustomed indifference and 'three thousand punctualities' to the winds, I sprang into the arms of George Rennie and kissed him a great many times! Oh, what a happy meeting! for he was as glad to see me as I to see him. Oh it has done me so much good this meeting! My bright, whole-hearted, impulsive youth seemed conjured back by *his* hearty embrace. for certain; my late deadly weakness was conjured away! *A spell on my nerves* it had been; which dissolved in the unwonted feeling of *gladness!* I am a different woman this evening! I am WELL! I am in an atmosphere of *home* and *long ago!* George spoke to me of *Shandy* while he caressed *Nero!* It was only when I looked at his tall Son he brought with him, who *takes after his Mother*, that I *could realize* the life time that lay between our talks in the drawing room at Haddington, and our talk here in Cheyne Row Chelsea.—

Dear me! I shouldnt wonder if I were too excited to sleep, however. . . .

28*th* / Mrs George Rennie came to *insist* on our dining

with them on the 7*th* May. Would send the Brougham for us; and it should take us after to our *Soirée* at Bath House. In short it was *dining made easy*; and Mr C said finally, with inward curses, that 'there was no refusing her'. She looks very well, and was kind in her cold, formal way. I had been fretting over the need of a *new dress* for the Bath House affair; but now I went after it with alacrity. George should see that the smart Girl of his Provence wasn't become a *dowdy* among *London* women of a 'certain age.'— . . .

30*th* . . . Dined at the Wedgwoods. Such a large party: 'distinguished females, not a few'! M*rs* Gaskell said; 'M*rs* Carlyle! I am astonished to meet you here; Miss Jewsbury told me last week she thought you dying;' 'She was right,' I said, and there our discourse ended. . . . What is that quality in the skins of some women, both in pictures and in real life, which always suggests nakedness.—Striptness. M*rs* G for instance always reminds me of a servant girl who has pulled off her gown to *scrub her neck at the pump*! . . .

———————

15*th* May — Alack! *hiatus* of a whole fortnight! for no particular reason, only a general indisposition to do anything today that could possibly be put off till tomorrow. Perhaps it is a symptom of returning health, this almighty indolence; or is it a premonitory symptom of apoplexy? Im sure I don't know; and sometimes don't care.

Our dinner at the Rennies' was, *like everything looked forward to with pleasure* an entire failure! The *Past* stood aloof; looking mournfully down on me while the clatter of knives and forks, the babble of the guests, and the tramping of waiters, confused my soul and senses. It was a London dinner-party! *voilà tout*! And the recollection, which I could not rid myself of, that the gentlemanly 'iron-grey' man who as Landlord offered me 'roast duck' and other 'delicacies of the season' *had been* my lover, —my *fiancé*—once on a time—served only to make me *shy*, and in consequence *stupid*. And it was a relief when Ruskin called for us, to go to a great *Soirée* at Bath House. *There* I found my tongue—and used it 'not wisely, but too well.' *There* too I felt myself remarkably well dressed. At the Rennies' I was always pulling my scarf up to my throat, with a painful consciousness of being over smart— . . .

16th / . . . *The Messiah at Exeter House*, tho' perfectly
got up— *'given'* they call it—left me—calm and critical on my
rather hard bench . . . . Geraldine said her Sister (the 'religious
Miss Jewsbury'—in contradistinction from Geraldine)
wouldn't let her go to the Messiah when a girl because
'people she thought, who really believed in their Saviour
would not go to hear *singing* about him.' I am quite of the
religious Miss Jewsbury's mind. *Singing about him* with
shakes and white gloves and all that sort of thing, quite
shocked my religious feelings; tho' I *have* no religion.
Geraldine *did* a good deal of *emotional weeping*, at my side;
and it was all I could do to keep myself from shaking her and
saying 'come out of *that!*' . . .

18th [June]— Another break!— On the 7*th*, went to
Addiscombe and stayed till the 11*th*.The place in full bloom, and
her Ladyship *affable*! Why? What is in the wind now? As usual at
that beautiful place I couldn't sleep. . . .

20*th* [June] A thunder-showery day. . . . A short walk with
Geraldine— A call from Darwin. —Oh— I had nearly forgotten
the one bit of amiability I have done for weeks. I wrote a little
complimentary letter to Miss Kelly or Kelty, the unseen old
Governess who sends me from time to time a little book 'all out
of her own head', Poor lonely old soul! this time she has burst
out into *Poems*! '*Waters of Comfort*' so-called! For the
'*Comfort*' it may be *strongly doubted*: tho' nobody can deny
'*the water*,' but the fact of a lonely old ex-Governess pouring
herself out in *Waters* (even only meant to be) 'of Comfort,' at an
age when most of us harden into flint, or crumble into dry
dust, is of itself beautiful and touching! And I wrote to tell her
this, as I know she is very sensitive to sympathy. . . .

22*d* (Sunday) . . . Today is the first time I have felt natural
with George Rennie The presence of Geraldine helped to give
me possession of my present self. He looked at me once as if he
were thinking I *talked* rather well. In the old times we never
thought about how one another talked nor about how oneself
talked! One had things to say and said them, just! . . .

24*th*— . . . At night Mr C and I went to a small very family
party at Lady Charlotte Portal's I like that Lady better than any
aristocratic young Lady I have yet seen. . . . She said, 'I cant speak
to Lady Ashburton; it isn't that I am afraid of her cleverness: I
have known cleverer people that did not produce that
impression on me; but if I were merely wishing to say to her "I

have enjoyed my visit," or "thank you for your kindness," it would stick in my throat.' . . .

26 June. The chief interest of today expressed in blue marks on my wrists!

This was the day about which Froude was to consult Geraldine Jewsbury, who declared that she recalled it 'only too well' because of the 'blue marks'. She told him, so Froude says (and repeated the tale in her last illness) that Jane said that they came from Carlyle's 'personal violence'. Carlyle had purposely left the 'incriminating passages' (26 June) in the Journal, but they were removed by his niece Mary and Alexander Carlyle; Jane certainly made the entry; there is only doubt about Froude's account of what Jewsbury told him and their interpretation. Were the marks accidentally made? Was Carlyle trying to restrain Jane? Was she acting in self-defence? There are uncertainties, but this is what Jane wrote. Geraldine's own testimony is contradictory. She says that Carlyle was 'the nobler of the two', and that Jane was 'extremely provoking' (Froude, My Relations 22-3). The entry for the 26th is from a photograph of MS, W.A. Dunn, Froude and Carlyle (1930), opp. 93.

27*th* Went with Geraldine to Hampstead; preferred to be boiled on a heath to being broiled in Cheyne Row. Dined at the *Spaniard*, and came home to tea—dead weary, and a good many shillings out of pocket. . . .

4*th* [July] Called for Mrs Montagu who is 'breaking up' they say. But her figure is erect and her bearing indomitable as ever. 'The *Noble Lady*' to the last! Browning came while I was there and dropt on one knee and kissed her hand, with a fervour! And I have heard Browning speak slightingly of Mrs Montague. To my mind Browning is a considerable of 'a fluff of feathers' in spite of his cleverness which is undeniable. He kissed *my* hand too, with a fervour, and I wouldnt give sixpence for his regard for me. Heigho, what a world of vain show one walks in! . . .

5*th* spent the forenoon reading in Battersea Fields. In the evening alone as usual, a very sick and sad day with me; like many that have gone before and many that will come after if I live to the age that the Prophetess foretold for me 72.

The Journal closes, not to be resumed. Carlyle added to the MS: 'A very sad record. We went to Scotland after; she to Auchtertool (Cousin Walter's) I to the Gill (sister Mary's)'.

Chapter Nine
Past Mending, 1857–60

A period of relative serenity began, as Jane's health slightly improved and she accepted Mazzini's advice to help herself by helping others. She had already responded to Mary Smith, who ran a successful school in Carlisle, and was a radical journalist, speaker, and supporter of women's rights, but who longed for a larger life. Jane became friends with her when she returned from visiting Scotland. Drawing from her own experience, she now realized how many much less fortunate women there were. They were to meet, and Mary says that Jane 'divined your tastes, and talked about what you wanted to hear, namely the great Thomas himself' (**Autobiography** 243). *She was impressed by Jane's sincerity.*

MARY SMITH Smith, *Autobiography* 308-12
Carlisle

11th January, 1857

. . . *This* time you come to me as an old acquaintance, whom I am glad to shake hands with again. The mere fact of your being still in the same position after so long an interval, and with such passionate inward protest as that first letter indicated, is a more authentic testimony to your worth, than if you had sent me a *certificate of character* signed by all the clergy and householders of Carlisle! . . .

I can't think how people, who have any natural ambition, and any sense of power in them, escape going *mad* in a world like this, without the recognition of that! I know I was very near *mad* when I found it out for myself (as one has to find out for one-self *everything* that is to be of any real practical use to one). Shall I tell you how it came into my head? Perhaps it may be of comfort to you in similar moments of fatigue and disgust.

I had gone with my husband to live on a little estate of *peat bog*, that had descended to me, all the way down from John Welsh, the Covenanter, who married a daughter of John Knox. That didn't I am ashamed to say, make me feel Craigenputtock a whit less of a peat bog, and most dreary, untoward place to live at! In fact, it was sixteen miles distant on every side from all the conveniences of life—shops and even post office!

Further, we were very poor; and further and worst, being an only child, and brought up to 'great prospects,' I was sublimely ignorant of every branch of useful knowledge, though a capital Latin scholar and a very fair mathematician!! It behoved me in these astonishing circumstances to learn—to *sew*! Husbands, I was shocked to find, wore their stockings into holes! and were always losing buttons! and I was expected to 'look to all that!' Also, it behoved me to learn to *cook!* . . .

So I sent for Cobbett's 'Cottage Economy,' and fell to work at a loaf of bread. But knowing nothing about the process of fermentation or the heat of ovens, it came to pass that my loaf got put into the oven at the time *myself* ought to have put into bed, and I remained the only person not asleep, in a house in the middle of a desert! *One* o'clock struck, and then *two*, and then *three*; and still I was sitting there in an intense solitude, my whole body aching with weariness, my heart aching with a sense of forlornness and degradation. 'That I who had been so petted at home, whose comfort had been studied by everybody in the house, who had never been required to do anything but *cultivate my mind*, should have to pass all those hours of the night in watching *a loaf of bread!* which mightn't turn out bread after all!'

Such thoughts maddened me, till I laid down my head on the table, and sobbed aloud. It was then that somehow the idea of Benvenuto Cellini, sitting up all night watching his Pericles in the oven, came into my head; and suddenly I asked myself, 'After all; in the sight of the upper powers, what is the mighty difference between a statue of Pericles and a loaf of bread, so that each be the thing one's hand found to do? The man's determined will, his energy, his patience, his resource, were the really admirable things, of which the statue of Pericles was the mere chance expression. If he had been a woman, living at Craigenputtock, with a dyspeptic husband, sixteen miles from a baker, and *he a bad one*—all these same qualities would have come out most fitly in a *good* loaf of bread!' . . .

But here I am beginning on a third little sheet and you are waiting for my opinion of the verses! If you knew how completely I have lost all taste for poetry (so called), you would not have appealed to *my* judgment of all peoples! . . .

I have read these verses very carefully several times over,
and what I feel about them is that they are full of *thought* and
sense, and deficient in *music*. They give me the impression of
thought put into verse by *force of will*, rather than from a
natural *taste for singing itself*. . . .

I should hardly have trusted my own judgment in such a
matter, if Mr. Carlyle had not confirmed it. I read the verses to
him, having first given him my notions about them, and he said
'Well, they are just what you said. The young lady has something
in her to write, but she should resolve on sticking to prose.'
That from him was rather high praise, I assure you. . . .

MARY RUSSELL   NLS 606.473
Thornhill
                                                  [20 April 1857]

. . . Anne said this morning while lighting my bed-room fire,
'Upon my word, those three warm days were given us *for a
complete deception*!' I could not help saying aloud 'Gracious! if
my Aunt Anne heard you'! My cough is almost gone however,
and I get generally about five hours sleep— I am wearying to
know how *you* go on in that particular. . . . Thackerays
daughter's were here yesterday, and speaking of their
grandmother's sleeplessness—she had just come from Paris to
try what change of air would do. 'We told her about *you*' said
the eldest Miss Thackeray, 'we thought it would be *such a
comfort* to her to hear of somebody in the same way as
herself—and you can't think how pleased she was!!'— *Naïve* at
least! I do think a young Human-being who has never known a
day's sickness or sorrow, whatever *good humour* may lie on
the surface, is as cruel as a young Tiger! For after all one cannot
bring intelligent sympathy into the world with one; as one
brings one's hair or teeth! It has to be *learnt*, painfully, by
experience— It takes fellow-feeling to 'make us wond'rous
kind.' I should have *loved* you, dear Woman, in whatever
circumstances I had had the opportunity to know your good,
pure heart, and winning ways; but I could not have entered into
your present grief as I do, if I had never lost my own parents;
and if I had slept soundly all my life, I should not have
shuddered as I do, in hearing of your bad nights. And so, I felt
no temptation to box poor Annie Thackeray's ears when she
made that *hard* speech, looking the while ready to burst with

health and happiness! I merely thought; 'poor girl! you will
understand better about all that by and by!'

The german project rests in abeyance. Indeed I am sure
Mr C will not have the two volumes of his book off his hands
in time to go any such road for a good many months to come.
And a *winter* at Berlin (which he seemed to contemplate) I
would positively not agree to. The cold there is dreadful in
winter; and I am not so suicidally disposed as to subject my
delicate lungs to its action I would do a great deal that is
disagreeable to meet his wishes and *keep him quiet*; but I
would *not* carry my complisance so far as to go and *die and
be buried* among strangers.

However I escape a great deal of angry discussion by
letting all his ideas take their course till the moment of carrying
them into *action*. So few of them ever reach that point! and
they efface themselves all the sooner for not being stimulated
by contradiction! ...

*Mrs Gaskell always annoyed Jane, whether because of her success as
a woman writer, her airs of virtue or her meddling with other peoples'
concerns. In her biography of Charlotte Brontë, she made charges of
adultery against Lady Scott (formerly Mrs Robinson) that in fact could
not be proved. After the* **Life** *was published, she was reluctantly
compelled to make a complete public retraction in* **The Times**, *30 May,
before returning from Italy to face further controversy. Jane's views were
shared by many of her friends such as Ellen Twisleton, who found
Gaskell 'artificial and unlikeable'.*

GEORGE LILLIE CRAIK   Strouse
Holywood, Belfast

[4 May 1857]

...*Et tu Brute* [you also Brutus]*!* Oh how *could* you fill so
much of your paper with the *Life of Miss Bronte*. A topic I
have got to almost scream at the first word of! I am so sick of
Mrs Gaskell, Miss Bronte poor thing, and all that 'day of
(literary) small things'! I dont think I am malevolent the least
in the world, I cant usually *be at the trouble* to hate people
enough to wish them ill; but upon *my* honour it was with a
sensation wonderfully like pleasure, that I heard from dear old
John Richardson two days since, a prosecution is commenced
against Mrs Gaskell by '*that woman*' whom she has so

needlessly, indelicately and cruelly gibbeted. Who the Devil
wanted to know the amours of a low scamp like young
[Branwell] Bronte? And who constituted Mrs Gaskell the
avenging Deity of Public morals? Is no woman to be obscure
enough for escaping the prying eyes of bookmakers and
penny a liners? I am so glad Lady Scott has had the courage to
step forward and say; 'you mean *me*, and you *lie*.' And I hope
Mrs Gaskell will be made to know that 'A Nemesis' may 'follow'
a woman in Paternoster Row as well as in Mayfair Sir George
Stephen who has undertaken the prosecution has telegraphed
to Rome, where Mrs Gaskell, having thrown her poisoned shaft
into 'that woman's' heart and life (she thought) had gone to
disport herself with her two daughters, leaving *her* Husband
(this Rhadamantha of conjugal life) to nurse the younger
children and keep the house, as he has to do one half the year!
And desired Mrs Gaskell to come home and defend herself
against the charge of defamation— Lady Scott denies the
whole accusation and declares Mr Bronte to have been *mad*
and a great liar Her Husbands will, she says, contained no
mention of Bronte whatever—and he left his fortune to her
without a single condition. I am the readier to believe the poor
woman innocent or at least nothing like so bad as Mrs G has
painted her; because I have had the evidence of my own
senses that Mrs G speaks too fast, and nothing she narrates is
to be wholly relied on The novel writer tendency to dramatise
everything, the desire to *ingratiate* herself as a popular
Lioness, and (I think) a natural deficiency of *precision* both in
her thoughts and feelings make her *I have found* a person
rather dangerous to associate with. . . .

*Lady Ashburton died, 4 May, in Paris. 'Poor woman!' Jane had written
to Mary Russell (16 April), 'this sick life must be a sorer trial to her than
to any of us'. Mary Russell might have read* **The Times** *obituary (8
May), mentioning her 'private virtues' as well as the Ashburtons'
hospitality, 'open to all excellence'. Her death must have brought Jane
some relief, but, as the Twisletons passed a smiling Mrs Brookfield on
the day of the funeral, Ellen remembered just having left 'Mrs Carlyle—
so pale & so wretched, hardly able to speak without crying . . . the true
and the false as Edward said curtly' (27 May). Ellen herself grieved
deeply and admitted, 'I did not know till now how much I cared for
her'. She had been 'considerate' to Edward, and 'I am so deeply sorry for
Carlyle . . . he must be sitting in such blackness of darkness, now'. Lady*

Ashburton was 'a star that shone so bright in our firmament, and it has shot from its zenith ... I do not think anyone will take her place for many years' (8 May, MS, Houghton b45M-98, box 2).

MARY RUSSELL   NLS 606.439
Thornhill

[18 May 1857]

...I have been long in answering your dear letters; If you saw Lady Ashburton's death in the newspapers you would partly guess why; that I was shocked, and disspirited, and feeling *silence* best. *But* you could *not* guess the *outward* disturbance consequent on this event! The letters and calls of inquiry and condolence that have been eating up my days for the last two weeks! distressingly and irritatingly— For it does not require any particular accuteness to detect, in this fussy display of feeling, more impertinent curiosity than genuine sympathy. *Some* Ladies (of her circle) & who never were here before, have come, out of *good* motives, taking to us as *her* friends, out of regard for her memory— But the greater number of these *condolers* have come to ask particulars of her death (which we were likely to know) and to see how we, especially *Mr Carlyle*, were taking her loss! ...

Last Tuesday *Mr* C went to the Grange to be present at her funeral— It was conducted with a sort of royal state, and all the men, who used to compose a sort of *Court* for her, were there; *in tears*! I never heard of a gloomier funeral. ...

I have not made a single call *yet*; but when I have finished this letter I am going off in a cab to call for the old Countess of Sandwich (Lady A's Mother). (She said yesterday she would like to see me) and I tremble at the prospect! Her daughter and she could never live together without misunderstandings and disagreeableness; but now the poor old woman thinks of her and talks of her as 'such a kind daughter as never lived'! 'Would have given HER anything she had had in the world'!— Dear! Dear! When I think of the dreadful hard things I have heard Lady Ashburton say of her Mother, at all times and always; how am I to join in, about her kindness to that Mother! in a way to please the beautiful mystification of the Mother-heart! ...

Carlyle grieved but kept busy with his proofs for the first two volumes of **Frederick**, *to appear in December 1858, while Jane escaped to Fife, Edinburgh and Haddington, where she read aloud from them to her old aunts.*

LADY AIRLIE   NLS 20767.24
Cortachy Castle

Auchtertool, Kircaldy
31*st* July [1857]

... I had a charming letter from poor Lady Sandwich the other
day, in which she tells me M*r* Carlyle is going with her, to
Addiscombe, for a week— I hope it is true; for he writes as if he
were growing into a sort of savage, under his ten-shillings worth
of calico, out in that wretched little garden! I trust in god, I
shan't find him *tatooed* when I go back, and that he has eaten
Nero raw! The said dear little Nero writes to me occasionally—
Geraldine Jewsbury *holding his paw!*

I suppose to go to Addiscombe will be better than going
nowhere; still a sadder place to go to *now*, for either of these
two, I can hardly figure.

And what must Loch Luichart look like to Lord Ashburton?

He (Lord Ashburton) came down to Chelsea, the evening I
left it, and gave me a gold chain and bracelets of *hers*. I had
seen them on her when we went *together* to Edin*r* the year
before! Oh they made me so sick, these things! .../ God bless
you ....

TC   NLS 606.459
Cheyne Row

Craigenvilla [Edinburgh]–Monday
[24 Aug. 1857]

Oh my Dear! What a magnificent Book *this* is going to
be! The best of all your Books! *I* say so who *never flatter*, as
you are too well aware; and who am 'the only person I know
that is always in the right'! So far as it is here before me; I
find it forcible, and vivid, and sparkling as *The French
Revolution*, with the geniality, and composure, and finish of
Cromwell—a wonderful combination of merits! And how you
have contrived to fit together all those different sorts of
pictures, belonging to different Times, as compactly and
smoothly as a bit of the finest mosaic! Really one may say of
these two first Books at least, what Helen said of the letters
of her sister who died—you remember? 'So *splendidly* put
together; one would have thought that *HAND* couldn't have
written them!'...

Robert Tait had already made a large competent portrait of Carlyle.
Now he had the idea for his ultimately successful **A Chelsea Interior**,
shown at the Royal Academy in 1858.

MARY RUSSELL   NLS 606.469
Thornhill

[20 Nov. 1857]

... My chief impediment has been that weary Artist who took
the bright idea last spring that he would make a picture of our
sitting room—to be 'amazingly interesting to Posterity a
hundred years hence'— I little knew what I was committing
myself to when I let him begin— For the three months before I
went to Scotland he came and painted twice a week—while I
was in Scotland he came four times a week; and for the last six
weeks he has been overshadowing me like a night-mare *every
day*!! Except when, please God, the fog is so black that he can't
see! These lower rooms are where I have been always used to
live *at this season*; and to keep up fire there, and in the
drawing-room as well—besides in Mr C's study at the top of the
house—is a great expence, where coals are seven and twenty
shillings a cart load—and is also a great *trouble to one* servant
So I have kept my ground hitherto; always hoping he would get
done—but my Heavens! he will make his great 'Work of Art' last
him into 1860, I begin to think!— A whole day painting at my
portfolio! another whole day over my work box and so on! not
the minutest object in these three rooms, opening into one
another, but what is getting itself represented with Vandyke
fidelity! And all the while the floor *wont* be *flat* for the life of
him! I suspect he aims at more than posthumous fame from
this picture—hopes perhaps—some admirer of Mr C's with
more money than wit to guide it, may give him a thousand
pounds for Mr Cs 'Interior' the portraits of Mr C himself, and
Mr C's wife, and Mr C's dog inclusive!— The dog is the only
member of the family who has reason to be pleased with his
likeness as yet!— ...

*But Tait was out of favour as 'the man who always does the flatsoled
underbred thing', and who irritated Jane. He was to show her an article
in the* **Illustrated London News** *(23 and 30 October and 6 November
1858) that committed the crime of speaking of her father as a former
veterinary surgeon, not relieved by praise of herself as 'most highly*

talented and cultivated'. It was one that everyone else had been careful to avoid calling her attention to. Geraldine was also in disgrace for having or wanting an affair with Walter Mantell, a New Zealand geologist. He was soon to return home, after which the old friendship with Jane was resumed, though neither she nor Ellen Twisleton showed much sympathy for Geraldine.

MARY RUSSELL   NLS 606.471
Thornhill

[16 Jan. 1858]

... I think I told you in my last, that both of us (I mean Mr C and I) were going to the Grange for a short time. And very little pleasure was I taking in the prospect. The same houseful of visitors! the same elaborate apparatus for living—and *the life* of the whole thing gone out of it!— *Acting* a sort of *Play of the Past* with the principal Part suppressed—obliterated by the Stern hand of Death! I didn't see at all how I was going to get thro' with the visit! when lo! my Husband's friends *'The Destinies'* cut me out of all *that* difficulty, by laying me down in Influenza. . . .

Geraldine is all but as good as gone out of my life!!! . . . Latterly she has quite ceased to write to me!!!— She has been making 'a considerable of a fool' of herself; to speak plainly. And has got estranged from me utterly *for the time being*; partly because her head has been pack-full of nonsense, and partly because I made no secret of that opinion. You have several times asked about her, and I always forgot to tell you— *or* it was too unpleasant to tell. Geraldine has one besetting weakness. She is never happy unless she has a *grand passion* on hand—and as unmarried men take fright at her impulsive demonstrative ways; her *grand passions* for these *thirty years* have been all expended on *married* men—who *felt themselves safe*— And she too always went quite safe thro these romantic affairs, meaning really nothing but whirl winds of *sentiment*, and the men too somehow meaning as little—or less! But when I was in Scotland—with *you*—she made an intimacy with a Mr Mantle who had been ten years in Australia, unhappily *not* married, only *engaged* or *'as good as engaged'* to a young cousin of his own— For a long time it was an intimacy 'with the reciprocity all on one side.' . . .

I could not see her committing herself as she did, and hear all her acquaintance chattering about her 'assiduites' for Mr

Mantle, without testifying my displeasure, and in proportion as she attached herself to *him* she drew away from *me* got pettish, suspicious, and mysterious. . . .

But all that makes me so angry, and what is worse disgusts me! It is making herself so small! openly making the craziest love to a man, who having eight hundred a year may *marry* her at any moment—(unless he is going to marry another which dont make the case better!) and doesn't give any sign of intending to marry her! Gracious what a luck I had no daughters to guide! . . .

Marian Evans knew Jane only through George Henry Lewes, who may have told her how much **Scenes of Clerical Life** *(1858; published in* **Blackwood's Magazine,** *1857) and* **Adam Bede** *(1858) attracted Mrs Carlyle. Jane rightly guessed that she vainly hoped that Carlyle himself might read the novels. George Eliot's anonymity was kept until the middle of 1859.*

GEORGE ELIOT   Yale
London
                    5 Cheyne Row Chelsea / 21st January / 58

Dear Sir

I have to thank you for a surprise, a pleasure, and *a— consolation* (!) all in one Book! and I do thank you most sincerely. I cannot divine what inspired the good thought to send *me* your Book; since (if the name on the Title Page be your real name) it could not have been personal regard; there has never been a *George Eliot* among my friends or acquaintances. But neither I am sure could *you* divine the circumstance under which I should read the Book, and the particular benefit it should confer on me!— I read it—at least the first volume— during one of the most (physically) wretched nights of my life; sitting up in bed, unable to get a wink of sleep for fever and sore throat; and it helped me thro that dreary night, as well— better than the most sympathetic helpful friend watching by my bedside could have done!

You will believe that the book needed to be something more than a 'new novel' for me; that I *could*, at my years, and after so much reading, read it in positive torment, and be beguiled by it of the torment! that it needed to be the one sort of Book, however named, that still takes hold me, and that grows rarer every year—a *human* book—written out of the heart of a live man, not merely out of the brain of an author—full of tenderness and pathos without a scrap of sentimentality, of sense without dogmatism, of earnestness without twaddle—a book that makes one *feel friends*, at once and for always, with the man or woman who wrote it!

In guessing at why you gave me this good gift; I have thought amongst other things; 'Oh, perhaps it was a delicate way of presenting the *novel* to my Husband, he being over head and ears in *History*.'— If that was it; I compliment you on your *tact!* for my Husband is much liklier to read the *Scenes* on *my* responsibility than on a venture of his own—Tho', as a general rule, never opening a novel, he has engaged me to read this one, when ever he has some leisure from his present Task . . . .

I hope to know someday if the person I am addressing bears any resemblance, in external things to the Idea I have conceived of him in my mind—a man of middle age—with a wife from whom he has got those beautiful *feminine* touches in his book—a good many children—and a dog—that he has as much fondness for as I have for my little Nero! for the rest—not just a Clergyman; but Brother or first cousin to a Clergyman!— How ridiculous all this *may* read, beside the reality!

Anyhow; I honestly confess I am very curious about you—and look forward with what Mr Carlyle would call 'a good, healthy, genuine desire' to shaking hands with you some day—In the meanwhile I remain your obliged / Jane W. Carlyle

ISABELLA CARLYLE   NLS Acc. 7988
Scotsbrig
                                               [Feb. 1858]

. . . Mrs Gilchrist, our next door neighbour had a 'thoroughly respectable' nurse-maid, to whom she 'forgave an unpleasant temper, for the sake of her good moral character and the example to the children;' and one morning before breakfast, the exemplary young woman bore a child, and strangled it, and locked it away in her trunk! and there had to be a coroners inquest and the Devil to pay! Such things happen in well regulated families. . . .

BETTY BRAID   NLS 606.438
Edinburgh

Addiscombe—Croydon /
Saturday [8 May 1858]

...I have been here a week on a visit at Lord Ashburtons, to try
and pick up a little strength after my four months confinement.
It is the first visit I have made at any of Lord A's Places since
Lady Ashburton's death, and the first coming was very
miserable—every thing exactly as she had left it; and yet such a
difference! But I am getting accustomed to missing her; and her
Mother, who is here, and Lord A himself do all they can to make
one comfortable in the house....

MARY RUSSELL   NLS 606.478
Thornhill
[June 1858]

...I have had plenty of excuse for all my sins of ommission of
late weeks. First, my Dear, the *heat* has really been nearer
killing me than the cold—London heat!—Nobody knows
what *that* is till having tried it! ...Then Mr Carlyle, in the
collapse from the strain of his book, and the biliousness
developed by the heat, has been so wild to 'get away' and so
incapable of determining where to go and when to go, that
living beside him has been like living the life of a
weathercock in a high wind, blowing from all points at once,
sensibility superadded! ...The imaginary houses in different
parts of the Kingdom, in which I have had to look round me
on bare walls, and apply my fancy to *furnishing; with the
strength I have* (!)—(about equal to my Canary's, which,
every now and then, drops off the perch on its back and has
to be lifted up!)—would have driven me crazy I think, if one
day I hadn't got desperate and burst out *crying!!* Until a
woman *cries*, Men never think she can be suffering! Bless
their blockheadism! However when I *cried*, and declared I
was not strong enough for all that any more; Mr C opened his
eyes to the fact so far, as to decide that for the present he
would go to his Sister's (the Gill) and let me choose my own
course after— And to the Gill he went last Wednesday night
and since then I have been *resting*—and already feel better
for the rest, even *without* 'change of air.' ...

Cheyne Row continued to be a magnet for exiles. Vassily Petrovich Botkin (1811–69), was an influential aesthete, travel writer, translator and friend of Belinsky, Herzen, Tolstoy and Turgenev, all of whom valued Carlyle's ideas and regarded him as a European rather than a British thinker. Turgenev, who had met Carlyle a year earlier in a lively encounter, provided Botkin with a letter of recommendation: 'I have the pleasure in introducing ... a distinguished literary thinker who is the first to introduce the Russian public to your writings, portions of which he has translated recently with great talent and distinction. ... Please give my compliments to Mrs Carlyle and my warmest best wishes to you, from one who continues to admire and respect you' (12 March 1858; **Collected Works and Letters of Ivan Turgenev**, second edn, 30 vols. [Moscow, 1987] 3:303–4).

TC   NLS 606.484
The Gill

Sunday / night / [11 July 1858]

NOTES OF A SITTER-STILL

Botkin (what a name!), your Russian Translator, has called. Luckily Charlotte had been forwarned to admit him if he came again— He is quite a different type from Tourguénéff tho' a tall man, this one too. I should say that he must be a Cossack, not that I ever saw a Cossack or heard one described!—*instinct* is all I have for it!! He has flattened, high-boned cheeks—a nose flattened towards the point—small very black deep-set eyes, with thin semi-circular eyebrows—a wide thin mouth—a complexion whity-grey, and the skin of his face looked thick enough to make a saddle of! He does not possess himself like Tourgueneff, but bends and gesticulates like a Frenchman. He burst into the room with wild expressions of his 'admiration for Mr Carlyle'— I begged him to be seated and he declared 'Mr Carlyle was the man for Russia' I tried again and again to 'enchain' a rational conversation but nothing could I get out of him but rhapsodies about *you* in the frightfulest *English* that I ever heard out of a human head! It is to be hoped that (as he told me) he *reads* English much better than he *speaks* it—else he must have produced an inconceivable Translation of *Hero-Worship*. Such as it is, anyhow, 'a large deputation of the Students of St Petersburg waited on him (Botkin) to *thank* him in the strongest terms for having translated for them Hero Worship and made known to them Carlyle—*and* even the

young Russian Ladies now read *Hero Worship* and
'unnerstants—it—thor—lie'— He was all in a perspiration
when he went away—and so was I! I should like to have asked
him some questions; for example how HE came to know of
your works (he had told me he had had to send to England for
them 'at exteem cost') but it would have been like asking a
cascade! The best that I could do for him I did—I gave him a
photograph of you, and put him up to carrying it in the top of
his hat! . . .

*Meanwhile, Jane explains, Lady Lytton had challenged her husband,
Sir Edward (Secretary for the Colonies), in his election campaign, to
which he promptly replied by putting her in a lunatic asylum. She was
soon released. John Forster was entangled in the dispute as Lytton's
friend and his son Robert's godfather.*

TC   NLS 606.486
The Gill
                                     Monday night [12 July 1858]

NOTES OF A STILL-SITTER

I have sent for a penny *Telegraph* (Today's) in which there is a
long account of Lady Bulwer's incarceration. Meanwhile here is
what I already know of this scandal.
    Lady B, true to her oath that she 'would oppose Sir Liar
Coward' at every step 'of his career'—*rendered* herself, escorted
by her Taunton Landlady at Hertford, the evening before his
Election. For that night she kept her self *incognita*. But the
Town was astonished in the morning, at seeing itself placarded
all over with insults to Bulwer.
    In *his* absence (for he did not arrive till the business of the
day commenced) his son, Robert Lytton, never dreaming who
had done this thing, employed people to rush about and tear
the placards down. Meanwhile Lady B presented herself at the
house of the Mayor, and demanded as a British subject to hire
the Town Hall—therein to deliver a Lecture on her Husband!
The Mayor horribly perplexed refused to see her; sent his wife
to her to—offer her a glass of wine! which her Ladyship politely
declined, saying that if anything but water passed her lips that
day, her Husband would call her drunk. She then made her
way—to the Hustings. Sir Liar had meantime arrived and seated
himself on the platform. Mercifully for *him*, his wife was

under the impression that it was at the Town Hall he would show himself. If she had known he was so near her, and got her eye on him, I don't doubt but she would have taken up and shaken him; as the Taylors-dog did to Nero. . . .

I have only heard two quotations from her address to the crowd—and neither of them indicates *insanity*, I should say—the very reverse! *'Colonies!'* she said—'Yes—*that* is the thing for him. He would have been *sent to the Colonies* years ago if people got their rights'! And this was her description of Sir Liar's personal appearance 'The head of a ram on the body of a monkey'—There is a report that he inveigled her up to London by the offer of 'an amicable arrangement' and increased income—and then handed her over to a *mad doctor*—instead of a *solicitor!*— Forster (who was here again with wife today) contradicts this—to the whole extent at least. But even as *he* had it, the case looked very bad against Bulwer. . . .

A pleasant holiday brought unusual gossip:'Skittles' was Catherine Walters (1839-1920), later Mrs Bailey or 'Anonyma', a notorious prostitute, well-known as an equestrian, and well-connected in high society. See Cyril Pearl, **The Girl with the Swansdown Seat** *(1955), and K. Atkinson, Courtesans (2003).*

TC   NLS 606.502
The Gill

Bay House, Alverstoke
Thursday [12 Aug. 1858]

. . . I am glad the meeting with Lord A[shburton] came off, and so successfully. But what of 'man with a yacht?' such a lot of yachts are doing nothing in Portsmouth harbour!— I have been on board a man of war and shown every corner of it by the Captain. *Mrs* Mildmay hearing me say I had never seen one, immediately recollected that the Captain of The *Renown* had been her husbands Lieutenant and took me on board it.

Another day, she stopt the carriage on meeting a certain Cap*t* Hamilton, and made him come in—and I found it was that he might accompany us there and then to the *Camp*, which I had expressed a wish to see, and could not go to without a male escort. I never saw a more goodnatured woman, or a more lively. She never lets Emily and me stagnate. She was telling us a deal about the Duke of Malakoff our present Russian Ambassador—a great Bear, and a great Profligate. He was dining in company with Lady Jersey who happened to assert, in her affected way, that *she* for *her part regretted nothing*— 'Pas vrai,' said Malakoff,'Pas vrai Madame! vous regrettez bien de choses! vous regrettez d'être *veille femme!!* vous regrettez beaucoup beaucoup votre *beauté fletri*'!!!

There is a most improper female whose name very properly is *Skittles* (!) she road alone in the Park every day this summer, and was I dare swear one of those 'perfectly respectable Ladies' whom you remarked riding without escort. On her way to the Park she passed before the Windows of Malakoff— 'Ah! Said he, voila Mademoiselle Skittles! Je voudrais bien la regardez pres!' (I am not sure of my French but you see what I would say) and thereupon he ordered his aiddecamp to go and bring Mademoiselle Skittles to him! A nice commission for a Gentleman! which however the aid de Camp felt bound to execute. But Miss Skittles being politely stopt and told the Duke's wish, answered scornfully;'say to the old Brute if he wants to see me he may come here!' and set off at a gallop! . . .

DAVID DAVIDSON   Davidson, *Memories* 311; Private MS

Bay House,Alverstoke, Hants.
[17*th* Aug. 1858]

. . . Since I came here three weeks ago I have been no longer recognisable for the same woman, who in London was described by a 'fast' Lady of my friends, as 'the very *seediest* looking Party she had ever set eyes on.'

I have recovered the highly useful faculties of sleeping and eating, and quite ceased to cough; and life is no longer a horrid nightmare I had been feeling it for many months. So excellently has my 'change of air and scene' succeeded that I mean to go on with it a while longer. I return to London on the 21st or 23rd, but shall only stay there till I have replaced—the ribbons on my bonnet! and made a few other necessary feminine arrangements —and then start off again—to Dumfriesshire next! Mr. Carlyle will sail in two days from Newcastle for Hamburg to make a grand looking up of *Battlefields*. He will be gone for some four or five weeks—so why should I stay 'like an owl in Desert' at 5 Cheyne Row, which has got to look to me, I regret to say, something compounded of a Hospital a Prison and a Madhouse! such long

confinements and miserable illnesses, and horrors of
sleeplessness I have transacted there of late years!
    I shall not see *you* tho' I go to Scotland....

Carlyle returned before her. Jane wrote to her young servant.

CHARLOTTE SOUTHAM   EUL Gen. 1730 (Carlyle 19)
Cheyne Row

                                   Thornhill Dumfries / Thursday
                                              [16 Sept. 1858]

...I should like that he had stayed away a week or two longer that
I might have been home to receive him; but not expecting him so
soon, I have staid all my time at one place and have several friends
and relations to visit still before I leave this country. And it would
be a pity to have incurred so much of travelling expence for less
than a month's stay. Besides *hurry-scurrying* back in time for *him*
would probably undo any good I have got by coming.

    So I must just trust to your making him comfortable for a
week or so; and the week after next I will return; and relieve
you of your *responsibility* at least.

    You know his ways and what he needs pretty well by this
time. Trouble him with as few questions as possible— You can
ask him whether he will take tea or coffee to breakfast?—and
whether he would like broth, or a pudding to dinner? you must
always give him one or other with his meat and either an egg to
breakfast or a slice of bacon. I think you can now cook most of
the things he likes oftenest boiled fowl, mutton broth, chops
and bread and ground rice puddings— If you take pains to
please him I have no doubt you will. And if he look fussed and
cross, never mind, so long as you are doing your best; travelling
always puts him in a fever....

*Feeling, as she said, 'fractious' and ready to 'box somebody's ears', Jane
wrote to impart the startling news of Lord Ashburton's engagement to
Louisa Stewart Mackenzie.*

MARY RUSSELL   NLS 606.515
Thornhill

                                              [30 Oct. 1858]

...I have come to *understand* and enter into the late Lady
Ashburtons terror and horror of what she called '*all about*

feelings.' — Speaking of *her*; a piece of news came to us the other day that I have not recovered the shock of *yet*! Lady Sandwich came to call, and handing me an open letter said, 'Read that. I thought you would like to hear it from *me*.' The letter was in Lord Ashburton's handwriting — and the first words that caught my eye were 'I have proposed to Miss Stewart McKenzie and she has accepted me!' — No doubt of *that* if she had the chance! Louisa McKenzie has been on the look out for a great match these ten years. She was notoriously 'setting her cap' at Lord A six weeks after his wife's death. *He* is very *trusting* and has been very lonely — like a child that had lost its mother — in a wood! Carlyle said from the first, 'I don't think Lord Ashburton will every marry again; but I wont answer for his not *letting himself be married!*' In whatever way the thing have come about there it is! a fact! and the marriage will take place as soon as the *Trousseau* and *Settlements* can be got ready. I shall never like the new Lady Ashburton — that I am sure of! She is full of affectation, and pretension if not pretence! Lady Sandwich looks at this speedy replacing of her daughter from a quite practical point of view, and is 'prepared to adopt Miss Mc as a daughter' 'If she (the new wife) make Ashburton happier *that* is all *she* (Lady S) must think of!' — Louisa McKenzie who never saw Lady S has written asking for 'her love' and blessing and so forth! And it is all going on in a paradisiacal fashion *for the present*!

Tomorrow we dine at Lady S's, with Lord A, just arrived from the place in the north where he has perpetrated this piece of rashness. It makes me sick to see how soon the most admired and adored woman gets her place filled up! He (Lord A) says, poor man, in the letter he wrote to tell Mr C of the marriage, that 'lonely as he felt, he would not have married again if he had not found another of the same high nature'! *That* aggravated me more than anything! — ...

GEORGE ELIOT   Yale
Wandsworth, London

                                     ... 20*th* February / 59

Dear Sir

I must again offer you my heartiest thanks. Since I received your *Scenes of Clerical Life* nothing has fallen from the skies to me so welcome as *Adam Bede, all to myself*, 'from the Author.'

My Husband had just read an advertisement of it aloud to
me, adding; *Scenes of Clerical Life? That* was *your* Book
wasn't it?' (The '*your*' being in the sense not of possession but
of predilection) 'Yes,' I had said, 'and I am so glad that he has
written another! *Will* he send me this one, I wonder?' —
thereby bringing on myself an utterly disregarded admonition
about 'the tendency of the Female Mind to run into
unreasonable expectations'; when up rattled the Parcel
Delivery cart, and a startling double-rap having transacted
itself, a Book-parcel was brought me. 'There it is!' I said, with a
little air of injured innocence triumphant!— 'There is what, my
Dear'?—'Why, *Adam Bede* to be sure'!—'How do you know?'
(I had not yet opened the parcel) 'By *divination.*'— 'Oh!—
Well!— I hope you also *divine* that *Adam Bede* will justify
your enthusiasm now you have got it'!— 'As to that'
(snappishly) 'I needn't have recourse to divination, only to
natural logic!'— Now; if it had turned out *not Adam Bede*
after all; where was my 'diminished head' going to have hidden
itself?— But Fortune favours the Brave! I had foretold aright,
on both points! The Book was actually *Adam Bede*, and *Adam
Bede* 'justified my enthusiasm;' to say the least!

Oh yes! It was as good as *going into the country for one's
health*, the reading of that Book was!— Like a visit to Scotland
minus the fatigues of the long journey, and the grief of seeing
friends grown old, and Places that knew me knowing me no
more! I could fancy, in reading it, to be seeing and hearing, once
again a crystal-clear, musical, Scotch stream, such as I long to lie
down beside and—cry at (!) for gladness and sadness; after long
stifling sojourn in the South; where there [is] no *water* but what
is stagnant or muddy!

In truth, it is a beautiful most *human* Book! Every *Dog* in
it, not to say every man woman and Child in it, is brought home
to one's 'business and bosom,' an individual fellow-creature! I
found myself in charity with the whole human race when I laid
it down—the *canine* race I had *always* appreciated—'not
wisely but too well!'—the *human*, however,—Ach!—*that* has
troubled me—as badly at times as 'twenty gallons of milk on
one's mind'! For the rest; why are you so good to *me* is still a
mystery, with every appearance of remaining so! Yet have I
lavished more childish conjecture on it than on anything since I
was a child, and got mistified about—a *door* (!) in our diningroom. What *did* that door open into? Why had I never seen it

opened? ... I never *told* how that door had taken hold of me, for
I '*thought shame*'; it was a curiosity too sacred for speech! ... It
was a door *into—nothing!* Make-believe! *There* for uniformity!
Behind it was bare lath and plaster; behind *that* the Drawing-
room with its familiar tables and chairs! Dispelled illusion no. 1!
and epitome 'of *much*!' (as Mr Carlyle might say) ...

The Newspaper Critics have decided you are a
Clergyman, but I don't believe it the least in the world. You
understand the duties and uses of a Clergyman too well, for
being one! An old Lord, who did not know my Husband, came
up to him once at a Public meeting where he had been
summoned to give his 'views' (not *having any*) on the
'Distressed Needle women,' and asked; 'pray Sir, may I inquire,
are *you* a Stock-Broker?'— 'A Stock-Broker'! certainly not!'—
'Humph! Well I thought you *must* be a Stock-Broker! because,
Sir, you go to the root of the matter.'— If that be the signal of a
Stock-Broker I should say you must certainly be a *Stock Broker*,
and must certainly *not* be a *Clergyman*! ...

*George Eliot replied through her publisher to say that she was
delighted with Jane's letter, 'one of her best triumphs', but that she
wanted Carlyle to read the novel, because his 'pre-philosophic period—
the childhood and poetry of his life lay among the furrowed fields and
pious peasantry', and she wanted to give him 'the same sort of
pleasure he has given me in the early chapters of* **Sartor**, *where he
describes little Diogenes eating his porridge on the wall in the light of
the sunset and gaining deep wisdom from the contemplation of pigs
and other "higher animals"'.*

BETTY BRAID   NLS 606.521
Edinburgh

Friday [early April 1859]

... It's no good trying to '*gar* [force] myself' do things *now*. If I
overdo my strength one hour, I have to pay for it the next with
utter impossibility to do *anything*! ... Indeed I should rather be
thankful that I am got so far in the road to wellness, that I am
now *capable* of *resting* and leaving the rest to shift for itself. ...

Last Tuesday I spent two or three hours at George
Rennie's! Oh you can't fancy what an old worn-looking man he
is grown. He has a grand house, and his cousin Jane whom he
married (instead of *me*) seems to make him a devoted Wife; but

his life is not a happy one I think. Great ambition and small
perseverance have brought him a succession of
disappointments and mortifications which have embittered a
temper naturally none of the best! And his children (three
Sons) must have disappointed him worst of all; for they are all a
long, straggling, foolish sort of creatures; indeed the eldest, who
had a stroke of the Sun in India, is become a quite helpless
idiot! In spite of all this, I am always glad to meet George, for
the sake of dear old long ago; and if *he* is not glad to meet *me*,
he is at least still very fond of me, I am sure. I saw at his house
the other day for the first time Marion Manderson (Margaret
Rennie's only daughter) She is the image of what Margaret was
when she went with me to the Ballincrief Ball—my *last* Ball in
Eastlothian! I have been to Balls *here*—very grand ones too; but
never with the *same* heart I carried to that one—before any
shadow of death had fallen on my young life! . . .

Have you any snowdrops or crocuses blown? My Cousin
Walter sent me a dozen snowdrops from Auchtertool in a letter.
They arrived as *flat* as could be, but when I put them in water, I
could positively *see* them drinking and their little bellies
rounding themselves out—till they looked as fresh as if they had
been just brought in from the Garden. . . .

The Carlyles took summer holiday lodgings near Auchtertool.

GERALDINE JEWSBURY   Turnbull Library, Wellington
London

Humbie Farm / Aberdour/ Fife / N B
Tuesday [5 July 1859]

. . . In a day or two please God I shall be in possession of a —
'cuddy' (donkey) 'all to myself'—on which I may get about in a
more placid state of mind— As for *walking!* I cannot so much
as get up and down stairs without holding on to the
bannisters!! And so I have only been *once* down since I came
here—when I went on the horse yesterday! Our rooms are all
on one floor happily. Such nice rooms! well sized well
furnished—and so *clean!* And by a little invention we have
managed to have *two* sitting rooms as well two bedrooms. As
for the *view* it is beautiful beyond all description! Charlotte is
the happiest of girls, no end of 'young men' making up to her
Nero the happiest of dogs, curing his mange by sea bathing—

and the Horse as I have said in 'perfect ecstasy'! Mr C and
myself are the least benefited! Mr C bathes every morning and
overdoes the milk diet—and I think the *betterness* he professes
to feel is nothing but biliousness— As for me I am past
mending— / Yours ever / JWC

*Lord Ashburton and Louisa Mackenzie had married in November
1858, and had returned from a honeymoon in Egypt in July.*

LADY STANLEY   Duke
Alderley
.... Haddington / 18*th* Sepr [1859]

.... I should feel obliged to you if you will insinuate to Mr C's
mind when you see him, that *taking health by the throat*, as it
were, never comes to a good end! that dividing one's time in
the country betwixt galloping like the wild Huntsman, and
walking in seven league boots, make the country no healthier
than the Town for one! that is, when one happens to be turned
sixty and not sixteen! Anything like the follies that wise man
committed at Humbie (the '*horrid hole*' as *you* well called it,
in the spirit of prophecy) Any thing like his excesses in
bathing, and riding and walking, and what he called 'soft food,'
I never *assisted* at, even in a bad dream!
     As for me; I passed my time much like a picketted sheep!
pottering about within a circle of one mile, on the most
despicable of donkies! which finally flopped over on its side
one day, as if its legs had been shot off; plashing [forcibly
striking] me on the highway, and itself accross me; thereby
bruising three of my toes, and disgusting me with that 'species
of quadruped for the rest of my Life'! But in spite of the mortal
ennui of such an existence, complicated with what Mazzini
calls '*cares of bread*' (housekeeping) 'under difficulties'—every
thing to be brought such a distance, and nobody to bring it!—
and the worries incident on genius, dieting itself on 'soft food,'
and bathing and walking and galloping itself into bilious
fever!—in spite of all that I am stronger a little, in body and
much less nervous than when I took leave of you in London
     It is reported that Miss Stewart Mackenzie (I never *can* call
her *Lady Ashburton*) is in a touching situation! What bliss for my
Lord! and what horror for the '*pauvre enfans*' [her in-laws]! ...

JAMES CARLYLE   NLS Acc. 7988
Scotsbrig

5 Cheyne Row / Chelsea
[late Oct. 1859]

...The worst symptom I observe in him at the present time or
for a long time back is his excessive irritability. But I scarcely
believe *that* to be now a symptom of illness so much as a bad
habit which he has *let himself go to*— Please to send what I am
here writing *no further*— Indeed burn my letter— It is one of
the disadvantages of being connected with a distinguished man,
that ones own little obscure letters and speeches must be
written and spoken always under a chilling sense of future
Biographers! to say nothing of present Gossipers!—

Meanwhile my Cat has been confined of four kittens! and
only *two* of them being bespoke, I told Charlotte to drown the
other two, which was done before they had come to
consciousness of being alive. A deep hole was then dug for them
in the garden, and they were put in it and covered up. In spite of
Mr C's assertion that 'Cats have no arithmetic,—are quite
insensible to whether you leave them *one* kitten or four' my Cat
showed much perturbation of mind when her two kittens were
removed—and left the two living ones, to see what Charlotte
was doing with the dead ones—running between the two in the
kitchen and the two getting buried with a great deal of
perplexed mewing. She certainly had a dim notion of arithmetic
for the next few hours—it was night before her mewings
ceased—that was eight days ago. Yesterday I was standing at the
back door, and I saw the Cat tearing laboriously at the place
where the kittens had disappeared, and uttering sharp wailing
cries rather than mews....

SUSAN STIRLING   NLS Adv. MS. 20.5.25
Dundee

21*st* October [1859]

...I assure you I have often gone into my own room in the
Devil's own humour—ready to swear at—'things in general'—
and some things in particular; and my eyes resting by chance
on one of my photographs—of long ago *places* or people—a
crowd of sad gentle thoughts has rushed in my heart and
driven the Devil out, as clean as ever so much holy water and
priestly exorcisms could have done! I have a photograph of

Haddington Church-Tower and my Father's tombstone in it—of
every place I ever lived at as a *home*—photographs of old
lovers! old friends, old servants, old *dogs!*— In a day or two,
you, Dear, will be framed, and hung up among the 'friends.' And
that bright, kind, indomitable face of yours will not be the least
efficacious face there, for exorcising my Devil; when I have
him!— Thank you a thousand times for keeping your word! Of
course you would! that is just the beauty of you that you never
deceive nor disappoint! . . .

My Dear! I haven't time—nor inclination for much
letterwriting— Nor have you, I should suppose;—but do let us
exchange letters *now and then*—a friendship that has lived on
air, for so many years together, is worth the trouble of giving it a
little human sustenance. . . .

LADY AIRLIE   NLS 20767.33
Cortachy Castle
                                                 [28 Nov. or 5 Dec. 1859]

. . .The present Lady Ashburton . . . has indeed—(so Lord A wrote
to his Brother Frederick Baring, who had not had a scrape of a
pen from him since the marriage)—has indeed 'passed the
critical point at which *the dear* GIRL had miscarried hitherto.'
Twice she had miscarried; Lord A told my Husband, 'with the
simple ingenuousness of a young Boy' (these were M*r* C's
words). Also M*r* C said, that Lord A, to do him justice, seemed
'extremely anxious that THE THING *should get itself born this
time*; much more out of anxiety about his wife's health, than
from any selfish notions about an heir!' In fact Lord A and M*r* C
talking together on this subject, with their mutual 'simple
ingenuousness' must be something grand to hear! . . .

My poor little dog—*my* substitute for a little bundle of
flannel,—being in a musing and trustful state of mind on his
return from Fife, got run over by a Butchers Cart— Ach! Yes!
The wheel passed over his poor little neck! and he was
brought home to me in the arms of the sobbing Charlotte, all
huddled up like a crushed spider, and the eyes all but started
out of his head! For a week he was despaired of; but my
loving cares prevailed to restore him to what an old Lady of
my acquaintance would call his 'frail usual' (she is always
writing to me— I am THANKFUL to say I am in my frail usual!).
Since then however his incipient Asthma has developed itself

at a fearful rate—The dog doctor has now ordered him to keep the house all winter if he wouldn't die— So the choice is to die of Asthma or Indigestion. Meanwhile I have made him a little warm coat, which gives him the looking of an inchanted human being! and I devote myself to soothing his sufferings! ...

Hearing from Isabella McTurk, her pleasant friend from the time before marriage and the early period of Craigenputtoch, Jane replied with affectionate memories of happier days.

ISABELLA McTURK   NLS Acc. 12039
Dumfriesshire

6th December [1859]

... I was so much the better for seeing you all again. I mean by 'you all' the few friends dating from 'dear old Long Ago,' who still remain for me in Nithsdale. Upon my honour I begin to think, that the people who go away *remember* more deeply and tenderly than those who stay still—which is not what might be expected beforehand. . . . I drove to *Strathmilligan* one day with 'Robert MacTurk'!! — God preserve us!— One doesn't need to have died, and been buried and 'walked' to know the feelings of a *ghost*, in all their strange dreariness and pathos! ...

I brought some woodroof, pulled up with the roots, from dear old Glenshimmel, and planted it in my (so called) '*garden*' here—beside some little things from Templand. . . . Both you and I are past the age when the unknown and unseen can excite any lively interest. What is common between *us* is . . . not our *present* pains and *pleasures* (if any)—but some bright, glad memories of our youth! ...

God bless you, I have a photograph of *Thornhill high-street* . . . and I stand before it often enough in raptures; as if it were a Correggio's Holy Family!— . . . / Yours affectionately / Jane Carlyle

Early in the new year the Carlyles stayed once more at the Grange where Jane dramatically swore eternal friendship again in response to Louisa Ashburton's warmly generous affection. 'A really amiable and lovely woman', Jane told Mary Austin.

LOUISA LADY ASHBURTON   NLS Acc. 11388.28
The Grange

5 Cheyne Row Chelsea /
16*th* Jan. [1860]

Dear Lady Ashburton

The worst of that Arabian-Nights-Entertainment sort of thing is that, coming back to one's ordinary Life, one finds it has gained immeasureably in dinginess and dulness!

Our ordinary Life recommenced at Waterloo station; where I had to leave off thinking about The Grange, and its *goings on*, and about *you* and your adorable kindness; that I might seek and identify our various luggage, which Mr C insisted was 'hopelessly engulphed in the Belly of Chaos'!— where it might have remained, for any step that he would stir in the matter!—

Then followed the drive in a rickety bad-smelling street-cab, thro' fog and mud; justifying Mr C's exclamation: '*Ough!* my Dear! this is a *terribly clarty* [dirty] City we are come back to!'...

For the rest; having come back to a 'clarty City' is nothing like so bad as having come back to *Frederick the Great*! You can't imagine what it is to have to pass one's days in the Valley of the Shadow of that dead man! I am sure he is taking many years of life out of me, as well as out of his Historian! Better be an 'owl in Desert' at once and cry to-hoo! to-hoo! than have an articulate speaking tongue in ones head and next to no opportunities of using it! ...

I have brought back with me . . . loving and trusting feelings towards *you*, my Lady, which are a pleasant wonder to myself! so set had I been on never caring for you the least bit! having got it in my head that it would be a sort of infidelity, a sort of disloyalty to ever care for another Lady Ashburton than Her who had shown me so much kindness and exercised so much influence over me, during some fourteen years! ...

This is a delicate topic to engage in with *you* but you encouraged me by saying the first word; with a noble frankness which touched me more than I can express!

—And so—at parting— I made you that proposal, meaning every syllable of it; and hoping that, by its *audacity* if nothing else, you might be surprised into bearing it practically in mind....

Mr C was again, at breakfast this morning, lyrically recognising your 'recklessness,' and wondering how you were!— If he were your monthly Nurse he couldn't be more interested than he is in your 'getting successfully thro' the thing'!!

God bless you—sincerely yours / Jane W Carlyle

Though they knew Darwin, neither of the Carlyles took to his **Origin of Species** *(1859), and Jane was even less impressed with Isabella Duncan's* **Pre-Adamite Man** *(1860). Mary Russell sent it to her because Mrs Duncan was the daughter of the Dumfriesshire Dr Henry Duncan, whom Carlyle had known well as a young man. Her earnest book is a geological and Biblical mish-mash, with references to local prehistoric footprints found by her father.*

MARY RUSSELL   NLS 607.539A
Thornhill
                                                        [28 Jan. 1860]

. . . Oh my Dear! I am very much afraid, the reading of that Book will be an even more uncongenial job of work for me than the jacket! and won't have as much to show for itself when done!

If there be one thing I dislike more than *Theology* it is *Geology!* And here we have *both!* beaten up in the same mortar, and incapable, by any amount of beating to coalesce! What *could* induce any live woman to fall awriting that sort of Book? And a decidedly clever woman!— I can see that much from the bits I have already read of it, here and there. She expresses her meaning very clearly and elegantly, too.

If it were only on any subject I could get up an interest in, I should read her writing with pleasure. But even when Darwin, in a Book that all the scientific world is in ecstasy over, *proved* the other day, that we all come from shell-fish! it didn't move me to the slightest curiosity whether we are or not! I did not feel that the slightest light would be thrown on my practical life for me by having it ever so logically made out, that my first ancestor millions of millions of ages back had been or even had *not* been an oyster!— It remained a plain fact that *I* was no oyster!—nor had no grandfather as oyster within my knowledge and for the rest, there was nothing to be gained for this world or the next by going into the oyster-question till all more pressing questions were exhausted! So—if I cant read Darwin—it may be feared I shall break down in Mrs Duncan!— Thanks to *you* however for the Book. which will be welcome to several of my acquaintances— There is quite a mania for Geology at present in the female mind! My next-door neighbour would prefer a Book like Mrs Duncan's to Homer's *Iliad* or Milton's *Paradise Lost*— 'There is no accounting for Tastes'!

I have *done* my visit to the Grange, and got no hurt by it....

The Lady was Kindness's self—and gave general satisfaction. Even I who had set my mind against liking her, could not resist the pains she took to make me.— By the way— I don't wonder you thought Lord A not too happy when you took that sentimental letter I sent you for his! The letter was from *Lady* A—and he merely broke into it near the end, and then signed HIS name.— Oh no! He shows no sign of *regret!* His devotion to the new Lady is perfect....

Nero had been painlessly put down by Jane's doctor; but he had been photographed by Tait and a professional photographer for **A Chelsea Interior**. *The brooches were supplied, and Charlotte's survives in the groundfloor china cupboard at Cheyne Row, with a photograph of Jane which Tait had used for his portrait.*

LOUISA LADY ASHBURTON   Wilson, *Carlyle* 5:378-81
The Grange
                                        [12 Feb. 1860]

...Oh it was too horrible, could not be ended too soon. So I called him (the Dr.) back, and said *now* was no worse than any other time would be, and bade Charlotte take my little dog away. I *could* not lift him to put him into her arms, but I kissed his poor little head. And *He licked my cheek*....

My Dr. kept his promise, the little creature died in *one moment* (Charlotte said) without struggle. Fortunately Mr. Carlyle was himself entirely upset by little Nero's death; so that he could not *lecture me* on my 'excessive grief,' his 'own heart being' (as he expressed it) 'quite *unexpectedly* and *distractedly* torn to pieces by the misery of the thing.'— His lyrical recognition of 'the poor little creature's docility, and loyalty, and sense of duty, and *manifold undeniable* merits,' interrupted

more than once by downright human *tears*, might have seemed
to some people a fall from his (Mr. C's) philosophical heights.
But for me, I liked him for it more than for all the philosophy
that ever came out of his head. . . .

ROBERT S. TAIT   NLS 1808.104
12 Queen Anne St, London
                                                [Feb. 1860]

. . . My little Nero is dead Mr Tait. You know how fond I was
of the creature, but my sorrow over him is my own affair—
incomprehensible, of course, to anyone besides myself—and
perhaps good little Charlotte who has gone about with red
eyes ever since. Charlotte has all along been extremely good
to the dog, grudging no trouble with him and I want to
make her a little gift, to remember him by: and it has
occurred to me that a little portrait of him mounted in a
brooch would be a keepsake that she would dearly value.
Now the dog in even the smallest of Caldesi's negatives is
too large for my purpose— There were some of *yours*
which made me think at the time 'what a nice brooch that
would make!'— He was alive and well then, and it was only
a passing fancy—now he is dead—and I want it carried into
effect—and the Interiors of *your own* doing which you
gave me are all parted with, *one* for Charlotte—but I have
said two?— Well Mr Tait—to confess the truth I want the
second—to be put in a brooch for *myself!* If you choose to
laugh at me you may— It is no laughing matter to me
however—but the very most *crying* matter that has come
across me for many a day! . . .

*Jane was comforted by sharing the news of George Rennie's death
with his aunt, not seen for forty years.*

GRACE DINNING   Ireland, *JWC* 260-2; copy at EUL Dc.4.94
Belford, Northumberland
                                    32 York Terrace / Regents Park
                                        Friday 23*rd* [March 1860]

. . . Well—after all this lifetime I am writing to you! not to recall
myself to your mind, but to tell you what you ought to be
told—not merely officially, but with some words of sympathy
and detail.

George—*your* George Rennie and *my* George Rennie is
dead! died yesterday morning at six o'clock,—having been
insensible from the previous Sunday. By a strange fatality it was
I who watched by him thro' his last night on earth! I, his first
love, who received his last breath and closed his eyes! Was it
not a strange, sad thing! after so many separations—so many
tossings up and down this weary weary earth! His wife wrote
to me on Tuesday that he was at the point of death and I,'as
his oldest friend should know it.' God bless her for that
thought—death abolishes all forms and ceremonies; so I went
to her at once, and begged to be let stay. She granted my
petition; indeed, she was quite worn out with sleeplessness
and anxiety, and was needing the help of one [who] could give
it with such fellow feeling as I could. After that I never left him
till all was over— He never was conscious for an instant—but
still it was a satisfaction to have *been with him* at the last. Mrs
Rennie begged me to stay with *her*, she was so desolate! tho'
she bears up bravely, and I was willing for his sake to be of any
Earthly use to her, so long as my husband will spare me from
my own house.

    If I saw you I could tell you much about George, that you
would like to hear—but just now I am so sorrowful and tired;
that I must content myself with saying, tho' he kept up no
intercourse with his relations it was not from a cold or
changed heart. A few weeks before his death I spoke to him
about that part of his conduct which displeased me, and
found that *pride, reserve*, his soured temper about the world
was at the bottom of it all . . . . Never was there a man, as I told
him, then, who did himself more injustice. I believe he had
the *warmest*, truest heart, but it was incased in pride and
distrust of others' affection for him making it of no use to
them or himself. / God bless you / Yours affectionately / Jane
Welsh Carlyle

*A second letter to Mrs Dinning, 31 March, tells how when she
returned to the widowed Jane Rennie, she found that she was not
needed; her 'mood had turned round ... from soft to hard.... So having
helped her put on her weeds (a strange service from me to her! As
strange as all the rest of this sad business!) I left'. The former Isabella
McTurk, now married to a McTurk, was her old friend dating back to
childhood and Jane's time at Craigenputtoch.*

ISABELLA McTURK
Dumfriesshire

NLS Acc. 12039

...21st April [1860]

Alas, alas, my dear Isabella, to think that the first news that I
should have of you after so many years, should be that
sorrowful announcement!

It has not been want of care about you, nor of sympathy in
your affliction that has withheld me from writing sooner— I
have only waited that you might be more familiarized to your
loss, and more composed, before I intruded on you with
expressions of my affectionate interest, knowing by experience
so sadly well how little all the sy[m]pathy in the world can do
towards cheering ones heart at such times.

I never saw your Husband but once, and still I perfectly
remember his appearance and manner, and when I heard of
your marriage I thought you fortunate in having won the
affection of *that* man. I heard after that you had a child and that
you looked very happy—and then I heard no more—till now!—

Will you write to me and tell me how it all is with you, and
if this calamity came suddenly on you, or if you were long
prepared for it? Dear Isabella! I never *forget* those I have lived in
friendship with, however widely I may be parted from them—
Much both of joy and sorrow I have know along side of *you*—in
some of the *now* saddest as well as dearest recollections of my
past your image is mixed up— The scene in which we knew
one another is now for both of us made into a place of graves—
but you and I who still live, is it not natural that we should say
to one another; 'God help you'—and even at this distance
exchange a kind grasp of the hand?— Write to me then
frankly—as you would have done twenty years ago—twenty
years just think of that! Tell me what you are meaning to do—of
your child or children.— In short you can write nothing of
yourself that I shall not be interested to learn. God comfort
you— / Ever affectionately your / Jane Carlyle

In 1864 Jane was to meet again 'poor white little Mrs Robert McTurk;
who they say ... carries on the Farm with more money-result than her
Husband did!' (JWC to TC, 19 Aug. 1862). Though in poor health, Ellen
Twisleton continued to see Jane regularly as her diary for 1859 shows.
She briefly notes calling on her, taking her for a drive and going to see
her with her sister.

ELLEN TWISLETON   Houghton bMS Am 1408 (60)
3 Rutland Gate, London
                                                [1860]

Darling
...I have a gloomy presentiment that some dreadful Bore will
drop in to tea....
     My little Charlotte is come back, and dancing about the
House like a burst of living Sunshine! It is a sight to see—the
happiness of that girl! And *already* she had quite humanized my
young Housemaid!—and the House no longer feels to me a
Lodging-house, but *Home* again! To say nothing of 'Bread
Pudding' being insurpassable!
     God bless you Darling. I hope to see you very soon. / ever
affectionately yours / Jane Baillie Welsh Carlyle.

A daughter, Mary Florence, was born to the Ashburtons, 26 June 1860.

LOUISA LADY ASHBURTON   NLS Acc. 11388.28
The Grange

                           5 Cheyne Row Chelsea
                            Friday [29 June 1860]

...When I got Lord A's announcement I ran with it to M*r* C,
and what do you think were his next words after the; 'Well!
Thank God it is all safely over'! his next words were, 'Is your
note *from the Lady herself?*—!!' — 'My gracious! I cried, how
can you be so absurd as to imagine her *up* to writing notes
the instant after her confinement?' — 'Well my Dear! said he, I
dont pretend to know *what* people are up to in these cases.
The Lady seems to have all along been up to more than most
women who *have nothing of the sort the matter with
them*—and how could I know that she would *break down at
the last?*'!!! What a wonderful thing a Man of Genius is to be
sure! ...

*Amalie Bölte had anonymously collected and published Varnhagen
von Ense's letters to her as* **Briefe an Eine Freundin** *(Hamburg 1860),
which had been noticed in the* **Saturday Review**, *25 August, which
declared that she gossiped about the Carlyles like a 'police spy'. Possibly
expurgated, they are still surprisingly frank.*

RICHARD MONCKTON MILNES   Trinity College,Cambridge
Upper Brook St, London

[August 1860]

...I dont know the particular gossip to which you allude. I have
not read Varnhagen's correspondence; having no patience to
spare from domestic purposes, and being deeply impressed
with an idea that I should find it twaddle! For it has always been
born in on me that Varnhagen was a vain finical, pasteboard-
and-varnish sort of make-believe Man.

But *this 'Freundin'* who exhibits 'a particular dislike to
Miss Wynn' *can* be no other than a Miss Bölte.... She was in
frequent correspondence with Varnhagen, by force of flattery
on her part and flatterability on his.... She certainly was [as]
'much with me'—as *the old man of the mountain* was much
with *Sinbad the Sailor!*—Of course it is she! ...

*Carlyle stayed with Sir George Sinclair in Thurso Castle, in the north
of Scotland, for his summer holiday.*

LADY STANLEY   Duke
Dover St, London

5 Cheyne Row Chelsea [Aug. 1860]

...I venture to hope that my mistake in supposing you still
here is ascribable to Mr C's confusion of speech that day, rather
than to my own dullness of understanding! He *did* tell me he
had called at Dover Street, and found 'a cab or rather cabs at
the door, taking away *certain maids and such like things'*—
but *you* (as I understood him) were not going—'not just yet.'
Certainly he didn't know too well what he was saying that day,
or for several days, before his departure in the Aberdeen
Steamer! I never saw him in such a state of nervous
excitement—which is much to say!

But he seems to be getting calmed down at Thurso
Castle. Old Sir George writes to me that his 'dear and valued
friend and Guest' sleeps much better, and is 'the delight of all
their hearts' (Oh *my!*) So, it is hoped I will 'lend him to them
till the beginning of October'!— And Mr C himself expresses
mild contentment with his lot up there....As for me, I have
been feeling very much like a flock of Turkeys, at a dead halt,
for want of dangling a bit of red clout before them! ...

I trust there is nothing materially wrong with the *brain*

of 'the Ashburton baby.' I saw it the day before yesterday, sucking most vigourously, with its long dark hair '*all about*'! a most queer little creature to look at! picturesque to a degree!—but with every appearance of health. . . .

If the Baby's brain *were* a little 'irritable' as yet, it would be a very natural result of that Baby's fatalities! The first monthly nurse proved a disgrace to humanity, put (only think!) some six or seven napkins to the Baby-posteriors all at once, in the morning, and left them unchanged till night! So that the poor little Posteriors became 'all inflamed and sore,' and my *Lord* (!) (not my Lady) turned her off at a moments notice! a new Monthly Nurse had to be fetched from the Grange and a wet nurse—the Lady's milk having been frightened away by the row. One hoped the affairs of the nursery were settled in permanence. But what was my astonishment to find the day before yesterday every face changed! three perfectly new women! one of whom was in the act of being sucked! As Lady A was out I did not learn what had happened—only, asking the man who showed me down; was the former nurse gone for good? he answered; 'Oh dear yes! a *new* lot came in last night'! Poor wee Baby!—who can say what irritating effects all these new faces may have on its bit brain! I declare I could have found in my heart to undertake the suckling of it myself! were the giving of milk, as Dr Livingston and others make out, a pure act of *volition*!! . . .

WILLIAM DODS   NLS 1797.207
Haddington

Cheshire / Saturday
[25 Aug. 1860]

. . . So to Alderley Park I came, and have been leading a delightfully quiet Life: things going on here in a most *human* and simple manner, in the absence of the Lord of the Manor, who has been busied with his new Postoffice-Generalship in London. I was to have gone on to Annandale next Wednesday, and was quite in heart for the journey; having improved every day here;— felt to be *growing a new skin* over my nervous system! . . .

But, alas for 'best laid schemes of mice and men'! Yesterday came a letter from my Husband, whom I was fondly imagining fixed at Thurso Castle till the beginning of October; telling me he could not get on with his work at a distance from his reservoir of

Books; and might possibly be home next week! Home!—and the curtains of his bed at the Dyer's!—and all the spoons and silver things hidden away from *possible* thieves, where only myself could find them!—and all the Keys locked up in—the Piano!—unlabelled! No body to *do for* him but an old Cook of 71 whom every thing like an emergence reduces to absolute idiocy!— And *he* the most 'particular' and most impatient of men! and I the most self-bothering and excitable of women!— ...

THOMAS WOOLNER　　　　　　　Woolner, *Life* 201–2
Hampstead, London

[22 Nov. 1860]

... I am sorry for your cat's Influenza ... but it would have been worse if she had given way to passion, as her mother has just done, and done no end of mischief in attempting a great crime! For several days there had been *that* in her eyes when raised to my canary, which filled my heart with alarm. I sent express for a carpenter, and had the cage attached to the drawing-room ceiling, with an elaborate apparatus of chain and pulley and weight. 'MOST EXPENSIVE!' (as my Scotch servant exclaimed with clasped hands over a Picture of the *Virgin and Child* in the National Gallery!) and there had it swung for two days, to Mr. C's intense disgust, who regards thy pet as *'the most inanely chimerical of all'*—the cat meanwhile spending all its spare time in gazing up at the bird with eyes aflame! But it was safe *now*—I thought! and went out for a walk. On my return Charlotte met me with 'Oh! whatever *do* you think the cat has gone and done?' 'Eaten my canary?'— 'No, *far worse!*—pulled down the cage and the weight, and broke the chain and upset the little table and broken everything on it!'— 'And not eaten the canary?'— 'Oh, I suppose the dreadful crash she made frightened *herself*; for I met *her* running down stairs as I ran up—tho' the cage was on the floor, and the door open and the canary in *such* a way!' You never saw such a scene of devastation. The carpet was covered with fragments of a pretty terra cotta basket given me by Lady Airlie—and fragments of the glass which covered it, and with the earth and ferns that had been growing in it and with birdseed, and bits of brass chain, and I can't tell what all! That is what one gets by breeding up a cat!— She had rushed right out the back door and didn't show her face for twenty-four hours after!— And now I don't know where the poor bird will be safe. ...

Jane's 'dear beautiful' and newly-married Kate Ross, once Sterling, her best-loved young friend, had died of consumption.

JULIA STERLING   NLS 3823.191
Bath Hotel, Bournemouth
                                                      ... [3 Dec. 1860]

My dear kind Julia—There is not a minute of my life just now that Katie is out of my head. Her face seems to float between me and everything I set myself to try and do, or say, or think of! her *living* face,—as it looked when we parted at Brighton,— wasted, and wan, and wistful; but with all the old love and truth shining out of it! ...

As for the so-called *consolations*, which some people would 'feel it their duty' to offer you, and have the face to offer you; I hate the very sound of them! People, who can so much as dream of *consoling* under a loss like this, have never known a great grief; for the very first lesson real grief teaches, is that 'the heart knoweth its own bitterness and the stranger intermeddleth not therewith'!— Even I, who loved Katie as much as any one unless those of her own blood, and her Husband, *could possibly* love her, even I should feel it an impertinence to suggest to you and him any ground of comfort in this heavy calamity.

For myself I feel in no haste to be comforted! It has often struck me as the saddest part of our poor human bereavements, that the pain which so identifies itself with the Love, and which feels at first so infinite and eternal, gets blunted, whether we will or no, and finally effaced, by the mere friction of the Hours! It may take longer or shorter to do it, but if one live long enough it will be done! ... your ever affectionate Jane Carlyle

Margaret Oliphant was as yet a minor novelist, who, having decided to write Edward Irving's life, put to use her new friendship with Jane Carlyle. It was done with discretion. She elicited from Jane only a single letter of 1822, addressed by Irving to his 'dear and lovely Pupil'. Jane wanted her to leave out 'lovely', which Thomas wanted kept. Oliphant was to call Froude's account of their marriage that of a 'brilliant prosecuting counsel' who gave 'a false and odious impression' (J. A. Haythornthwaite, **Carlyle Newsletter** *3:25-6).*

MARGARET OLIPHANT   NLS 23210.42
Fettes Row, Edinburgh

... [18 Dec. 1860]

Dear Mrs Oliphant
        First and foremost let me give you a hearty kiss! Never
mind about our having met only once '*here down*' (as Mazzini
translates *quà giù*); there is no saying but we may have met
plenty of times in a previous state of existence! and I certainly
didn't feel to be seeing you that day, at Bayswater, for the first
time! Besides; you know the old saying 'Kissing goes by
favour'!—not by the length of people's acquaintance! There are
women with whom I have been what is called *intimate* these
dozen years whom it never entered my head to *kiss*!—never!
        Next, I have to thank you for your Book—'*forwarded by
desire of the Author*'—your Book which I like best of all your
Books for perhaps no better reason than this same; that it is
come to me from yourself.... But I waited till I should have read
the Book; so that I might thank you for the pleasure of *reading*
it, as well as for that of receiving it. I knew that in the case of a
Book of *yours* I was *safe* in risking the delay!
        Now, I will just tell you what happened, and if *that* does
not convey the highest praise of your Book, to your own ears;
then you cannot hold the same opinion as Jeffrey, 'that first of
critics,' who said to myself, some five and twenty years ago, 'The
first and last question to be asked about a novel is; '*Does it
make the heart beat?*' — If that can be answered in the
affirmative then has the book the highest merit a novel is
susceptible of, and is certain of success'! Not only did *The
House on the Moor make my heart beat*; but made it bang
against my ribs in such a thundering way, that when I lay down
in my bed at three in the morning,—(having sat up like an idiot
to see out Mr Scarsedale!) I couldn't go to sleep—couldn't
even lie still—for the thump-thumping! Had to get up and take
cold water; then try again!—then had to get up and take brandy
on a lump of sugar! That also failing to quieten me, had to try
something else, and decided on treating myself
homeopathically—that is; vulgarly speaking, on taking 'a hair of
the dog that bit me!' — So I drew a little table to my bedside,
placed two lighted candles on it, threw my fur-cloak round my
shoulders, and sat up in bed to read out the third volume! It
had struck *six* before the *Dramatis Personae* being all settled

in Life, I subsided into brief 'Dog-sleep'!—Ach!— And please to
take along with you the *age* of the 'Party' thus acted upon!—
and not my age only but all I had gone thro from what my
Scotch servant called 'just *rale* mental A—gony in my ain
inside!'— Yes Dear! not a doubt of it! your novel is a most
successful novel—and now I should like to know what you are
doing with the Biography?

I have often reflected, since that drive with you in the
'*neat Fly*,' what a distracted *mess* I made of the business in
hand! You were seeking information about Edward Irving *to put
in a Book*, and almost everything I told you about him was
'betwixt woman and woman'—under seven seals of secrecy!
And yet I pique myself on being a practical woman—I do
indeed!— Well—if I have the pleasure of meeting you again
while the Biography is being written, I shall endeavour to avoid
that Sancho-Panza-dinner style of thing! and draw upon my
recollections of Edward Irving to better purpose....

Chapter Ten

Spiritual Magnetism, 1861–63

The Carlyles had spent a few days at the Grange, and left because Thomas was restless, and a new visit was arranged.

LOUISA LADY ASHBURTON   NLS Acc.11388.28
The Grange
         5 Cheyne Row / Chelsea / Wednesday [9 Jan. 1861]

... I even refused myself the gratification of going with Mr C
to dine at Lady Sandwich's on New-years day; for fear of
bringing back my cold, so that the 15*th* might find *me* unfit
for travelling. And I had my D*r*'s leave to go—with certain
precautions!— He has an extravagant idea, my D*r*, of the
agony of mind it must be to a female patient to be denied
what he calls 'a little sociality.' So he 'really thought I might
risk dining out on New-years-day; provided I ordered a wax
candle to be burnt in the carriage for half an hour before
getting into it—and kept it burning all the way!' I tell you this
invention, (on the authority of a clever quite matter-of-fact
man) in case you may have some occasion to turn it to
account—not for yourself, who seem perfectly inaccessible to
Colds but for some less happily constituted friend.— As for
me; I confess, such a style of *driving*—boxed in along with
one wax candle! has something quite Ghastly and funereal in
it! not to be tried till one's impatience of confinement was
passing into mania!
    They were skating on the Serpentine last night with
torches, and a Band of music; little canvas booths dotting the
ice, with flags flying; where one could have *'roast-taties'* and
other solid and liquid condiments! The Londeners beat the
world for being able to do *nothing* without *'refreshments'*!
Mr C walked past the *'festive scene'* towards midnight; and
came home with a strong desire, at least a desire strongly
expressed, that 'somebody would take *him* out, and teach him
to *skate'* ... Good morning Baby! I continue to love you very
much Baby! ...

MARY RUSSELL   NLS 605.426
Thornhill

[early Feb. 1861]

...We staid at the Grange only *four* days!!— Alas Yes! All my
lookings forward to a pleasant time there, and all my
preparations of suitable *toilets* and my lockings up of silver
spoons &c at home ended in a visit of four days!—— It really
looks as if I were never to be allowed to go *thro'* with
anything pleasant again in this world!— I was feeling such a
different creature in these four days! The people were almost
without exception such agreeable people! Lady A so adorably
kind! the Weather so propitious! above all, the escape from
the valley of the shadow of Frederick the Great such a
happiness!— A *fortnight* of all that would brace me up; I
thought, to hold out against the worries of life for months to
come! And behold on the fourth night Mr C was pleased to
smoke and *talk* with some young officers in the Conservatory
till two of the morning—all about the *Crimea*—always a too
exciting subject for him! and, naturally, he couldnt sleep after.
And instead of just being more careful the next night, what
does he do but rush into my room whilst I was dressing in the
morning; and looking like an incarnation of the Gunpowder
plot, tell me that he '*would* and *must*' and the whole world
shouldn't prevent him returning home that day!—sleep being
impossible *there!*' —

Nothing that anybody could say or do, or imagine was of
the least use in altering his resolve, so there was nothing for it
but to fling my elaborately prepared *toilets* by armfuls into the
large Box (new-bought for that visit)—and go home—to a
house never dreaming of us!—not a fire in any room of it!—stair
carpets up, and stairs giving damp evidence of having been
newly washed!— Of course I caught a fine rheumatism in my
head and back by the job, and never got a wink of sleep the
night after this horrid homecoming. And *of course* Mr C had 'a
capital nights sleep—the best sleep he remembered to have had
for weeks!'—a man always sleeps *capitally* when he has had his
humour out! and the more provoking his humour the more
capitally he sleeps!—

It was ten days before I got over the effects of that *chill* in
the cold damp house—...

Walter Mantell had returned to New Zealand where, about 1834, Carlyle had once thought of emigrating with Jane to edit a newspaper. Both he and Jane liked Mantell, when, as Jane wrote, he was 'out of the valley of the shadow of Geraldine', while Carlyle saw him 'as far too clever and substantial a man to be thrown away on a flimsy tatter of a creature like Geraldine' (NLS 606.628).

WALTER MANTELL　　　　Turnbull Library, Wellington, qMS-0393
New Zealand

22*d* Feby / 61

...Mr C was *really* glad to hear from you and bade me say, with his kind regards, that '*anything* an intelligent man like yourself (!) liked to tell him about New Zealand would be read with interest and thankfulness here, where human information on *any* subject was so rare!'— For the rest; he (Mr C) is much overworked with his Book, almost frantic with impatience to have done with it; but, I think, not radically worse in health than when you saw him— Yes! it *is* to be lamented there are none of those swift and commodious means of transit still extant, which used to be so common in *The Arabian Nights!* If Mr C could awake tomorrow morning and find himself in New Zealand, it would be new life to him,—*for a while!* the mere sense of being so far from London would do him incalculable good.

What I would have you write to *me* about is yourself; *you* interest me more than New Zealand does. Begin, please, by *doing* one a sketch of your house; (You can draw better or worse? if *worse* it will make no difference). Then, describe to me the furniture of your rooms,—how many chairs you have? if you sleep in a bed?—or— roost?—what you are clothed with,—linen, or woolen, or skin and what is your '*natural food*'? My *second sight* doesn't take in these particulars, and, without them, my picture of you out there is vague as a latter-day *Turner*....

MARGARET OLIPHANT　　　　　　　　　　　NLS 23210.47
Fettes Row, Edinburgh

[27 April 1861]

...When I recognised your miniature handwriting the other morning, my heart gave a little jump for joy. For the '*notion*' I took of you at our first and only meeting hasn't died out, nor

got rubbed out in all these months! I am heartily glad that you
are coming to London, to stay. I thought you would! that Edin*r*
couldn't suit you in permanence; *me* it makes feel poorly—
even a few days of it!—Not because of its dulness. It is '*meant
to be* dull' (as are the Royal dinner parties)....I could stand
the dulness there; but I can't stand its narrowness, its
paltriness, its prejudicedness, its self-conceit, and above all its
religious cant....

But it wasn't my opinion of Edin*r* you asked me for, it
was for 'details' about Edward Irving. And to tell the Gods
Truth, I have written the above not out of any grudge against
the poor old Place, but just to stave off a minute longer the
business in hand. It is mildly and modestly that you ask for
these 'details,' But nevertheless—the effect produced on my
Imagination is that of——a loaded pistol at my breast and the
words '*details* or your Life'!! I lose all presence of mind! When
trying to recollect things thus *to order* (as it were); the blood
gets into my head; my heart falls to beating; my memory
becomes blank; It is very absurd! and if this nervousness in me
could have been overcome by force of Logic, it would have
been long ago, but I am so made there is no helping it! I have
sometimes imputed this mental nervousness in myself to
having been born prematurely *thro' a fright*! — The Author of
Elsie Venner would say, 'not a doubt of it'! If you haven't read
that Book, pray get it.—

If you were here—beside me—I dare say I might give you
some of the details you want—your questions would suggest
them—or they would suggest themselves in the natural course
of conversation. But to *write* them down—*to order*—all in a
row—with 'the reciprocity all on one side'—the idea of '*to be
printed*' lowering over me.— Oh my Dear! I can't indeed! the
thought makes me like to *scream!*—and makes me *tingle* from
head to foot!

But look here! I will direct you to a person from whom I
have no doubt you could elicit many details very interesting of
their kind. There is an old servant of my Mothers—*your own
sort of old servant*—to whom the name of Edward Irving is a
dear household name, and who will tell you all she recollects
about him—if I bid her do so. Independently of Edward Irving
this old Betty is a woman to make whose acquaintance will do
you good— There is now no woman on Earth whom I love so
dearly—or who so dearly loves me....

On 28 August Jane met her deeply admiring Charlotte Cushman, the great American actress, who had long wished to know her. She had been thrilled to hear about Jane from Geraldine Jewsbury, who had first taken her up—as Jane thought—in 'a blaze of enthusiasm' and fit of jealousy 'of me and Mrs. Paulet' (19 Jan. 1846; CL 20:109). A little later she had written of Charlotte as a liar (CL 24:38). Now, at last, they were brought together by the young actress Sarah Dilberoglue, wife of Stauros; see the Introduction, xxvi–xxvii. Charlotte told her partner Emma Stebbins that Jane 'came at one o'clock and stayed until eight.... Clever, witty, calm, cool, unsmiling, unsparing, a raconteur *unparalleled, a manner unimitable, a behavior scrupulous, and a power invincible,— a combination rare and strange exists in that plain, keen, unattractive, yet unescapable woman!'* (**Charlotte Cushman: Letters and Memories of Her Life**, ed. Emma Stebbins, New York, 1878, 84). *Grapes and flowers were despatched at once, with an accompanying note.*

CHARLOTTE CUSHMAN   Library of Congress, CCP
London

5 Cheyne Row Chelsea
Friday / [early Sept. 1861]

If I believe in one human will having power over another even thro' some miles of other human beings?— if I believe in Spiritual Mag[n]etism?— Most assuredly! I believe in it absolutely and entirely! It is the great Central Fact of the Universe for me! The concentrated Essence of Life!—I wouldn't say as much in 'mixed company'; knaves and idiots have so taken the name of *Magnetism* in vain—so disgraced and disecrated it with their Clairvoyant Champaign Breakfasts— their after-dinner table-turnings—all their brutal nonsenses, that to declare oneself a firm believer in Magnetism—*and in little else*—were to expose oneself uselessly to the misconception of the greater number: but it suits my humour to begin my correspondence with *you* by a *confidence*!

For the rest; I *do* wish to see you; *do* wish to hear from you; *do* love you; (you know that; why make me *say* it?) And, further I mean, deliberately and imperatively, that we Two should be friends for the rest of our lives,—and *good* ones—to make up for lost time. That is my modest meaning; understand!— Set yourself against it *if you can*!

In reading your programme I thought for a few moments of asking Mrs Dilberoglue to let me meet you once more in her dear little *Temple of Concord*, on Sunday evening; or asking yourself to *make* Time to come here again one morning before our departure— But the idea was quickly rejected. The impression left on my mind by our Parting the other evening was so good! so exactly the sort of impression of you I wished to keep till your return next June, and suppose I managed to arrange another—*parting*; how easily, in the prosaic unsettledness and bustle of the next days, might there arise something from without or from within to make the second parting less satisfactory to think of than that other! and to disturb or mar the impression of that other, which I wished to keep intact!

A cowardly apprehension you may think! at least a nervous one! But, anyhow it came to me with the impressiveness of a Monition of Nature; and having no 'principles of conduct' 'to speak of,' the more need I should give heed to my *Instincts*!!

You will write to me when you are settled—? I mean when you have leisure of mind and body— I dont want a letter written, as I am writing this one, in a worry of Things!

I have the strangest thing to tell you about your flowers! The moment I set my eyes on them, and before setting my eyes on the note, and in face of the glaring improbability that grapes and flowers should be sent from the same person, on the same day by *two different messengers* (!) I *knew* somehow—knew as assuredly as if I had taken them out of your hand—that those flowers were from *you*! My maid, in entering the room with them said—'not from Mr Ruskin I think mam'!—at least it isn't *his* man that brought them.' 'No' I said as if I had known of their coming 'they are from Miss Cushman.' And I knew the note was from *you*, before I had looked at the signature or read a word of it! I did not know the handwriting yet I knew it was *yours*!

I *must* stop— I have to go up to Piccadilly to arrange about—about— Oh Dear me about something much above my capacity! viz *placing Mr C's horse out at grass for a few weeks*!! He has gone and got himself bitten, (the horse not Mr C) on the neck by another horse, and Mr C who calls himself or is called a *Philosopher* is so ashamed of the trifling disfigurement to his Horse's beauty, that he declines taking him on a visit to an Aristocratic Stable!—and *I* (!) must find him a month's grazing somewhere!— My Dear! Men are—what shall

I say?—*strange* upon *my* honour!
God Bless you—kind regards to Miss Stebbins with the
clear fine eyes and gentle smile—your / affectionate Jane

*Cushman left for Rome, and on 16 November wrote from her
mansion there a letter which demands to be taken into account:'The
note which came to me on the 8th of Septr has made a part of my every
day since then.You who believe in the most subtle magnetism, will credit
this, for you willed it to be so when you said* "I do love you, I do want to
hear from you." *You know you were then buckling me to you with firm
clasp of a strong & loving nature....To possess the assurance under your
hand as well as your Eyes that you cared for me made & makes me very
rich indeed! But now comes the difficulty.This same precious note which
makes me just as proud and happy when I read it today, as I did the
day I received it—said* "You will WRITE to me when you are settled!" *I
mean when you have* "leisure of mind & body!" *I don't want a letter
written in a* "worry of things!" *Alas, if I wait for this Utopia you will
never hear from me, save from those who knowing from all time my
almost necessitated life of unsettled unrest &* "worry of things" *recognize
the fitness of the destiny & accept the unworthy droppings from my pen,
for just what they are worth....I cannot write to you.I love you but I fear
you & my sad blushes as I recognise the fear within the fear that it may
be more my self love which fears you than my heart. You are so
wonderful to me.I think of you ever—and of all that you said & did on
that first & only day I saw you when a new heaven & a new Earth was
revealed to me. I remember all your looks all your tones all your
unchecked flow of marvellous fitting words—all your far seeings—all
your subtle fancies—your facile dissection—your graphic description—
your inimitable behaviour—your perfect knowledge of & yet
indifference to what you were doing—your self possession—your
Evident indwelling sense of power to have and to hold. Even that which
was ridiculous to you through its unfitness & the indomitable frankness
with which you held it up to my view—all, all, all, are stamped upon
my memory—with an electric fire which burns me yet! I find you
marvellous! What have I to do with Communion with such! What
though I am kindly bidden can I offer in Exchange? Oh point of soul &
nature why should I think of barter—can I not accept the bounty &
be thankful. Offer that I am without this miserable self rising up to
refuse an obligation.There is but one of you—none other in the world
like you! I cannot hope to speak or think or write like you.Why should
I not minister in my own poor way? Because I want your respect—I
want your care for me—your thoughts of me to be as good as my*

*admiration of you & I fear to lose all through my desire to possess all.
But I cannot bear not to hear from you. . . . To hear of Cheyne Row
through Barnsbury Park [the Dilberoglues] is very dear to me—but I
want more the crumbs which fell from your table [which] will make
high Carnival for me and I cannot wait any longer in the hope that I
shall Ever be "settled." Ever have "leisure of mind or body." Ever be less
occupied with the "worry of things.". . . Dear Soul, I will not misjudge you,
I will not misdoubt you. . . . I will beg you to write me when you can. Let
me hear from you be it Ever so little. Tell me of yourself if you are well—
if you have Enjoyed your Summer-if you have Ever thought of me and
to know of me!'—And so on, for there is a good deal more, including a
description of a visit to the studio of the artist, Rosa Bonheur, near
Fontainebleau, and about Charlotte's travels, ending with the wish that
Jane would come to Rome:'Will that time ever come I wonder! What a
pleasure that would be to me. Do you dream how happy it could be to
me?' She asks about Mrs Venturi, who it seems made 'you see me. . . . Will
you* WRITE *to me. . . . Commend me in all humility unto his high
highness!'—presumably Thomas—and 'with loving sincerity to you
faithfully affectionately / Charlotte Cushman' (NLS 1774).*

*How Jane took this we have to infer from her silence and replies. She
was presumably interested, flattered and in a cooler way ready to meet
her friend when the chance arose, but there were to be delays, only
partly explained by her ill health.*

LADY SANDWICH   NLS Adv. Ms.19.3.52.47
Grosvenor Sq.
                                        [24 Sept. 1861]

. . . My young maids had every thing scrubbed and scowered to
'look as good as new'; and ran out to receive me after the
manner of Rose and Julia! And behind them, with more
deliberation and less vivacity, came Mr C! who had arrived a few
minutes before me, 'in spite of having fed and rested his horse
by the way' (perhaps in virtue of that!) and in spite of having
had a strange encounter—with a Being not often met on english
highways at the present day— An adder! no less! and no
contemptible one, for it was 'certainly more than a yard in
length, and of a horrid dark green colour,' and it 'crumpled itself
all up *as it saw* HIM! (no wonder, the wonder is that HE didn't
crumple HIMself up too!) and it 'quickened its pace accross the
road, and disappeared amongst some long grass.' I should like to
hear Fritz's ideas of the stranger-creature, which passed 'within

a foot of his head.' What a mercy he didn't take a notion of setting his foot on it! It was near Blacknest Gate that the meeting occurred. Some people go coasting over the whole world without ever having an adventure; but Mr C, born under a luckier star, can't make an innocent little journey of twenty miles without an adventure with 'a *french* Cook' in going, and with a yard-long *adder* in coming *back*! . . .

ANN CHAMBERLAYNE   Duke
[25 Dec. 1861]

. . . I cannot tell you how it *went to my heart* when Maria [her servant?] came up to the Drawing-room yesterday, carrying a tray piled with her own boots and little presents, and the cake and the ketchup &c &c for *me!* her face perfectly radiant with good-child happiness!— With the memory of my own good Mother *ever* fresh in my mind, I could enter so profoundly into her feelings—(happy girl who has still a Mother to care for her, and send her tokens of Motherly love!)—and could see in the contents of your parcel, spread out there so proudly, a more interesting, more beautiful sight, than I should have seen in a trayful of the finest diamonds, unsanctified by Mother-love!

I am often telling Maria how thankful she should be for her good Mother; not that I think she needs any telling—but as a sort of spoken sigh over the loss of my own Mother. . . . I hope to see you face to face, if we go to the Grange this winter—as is probable—if my health mend enough . . . .

LOUISA LADY ASHBURTON   NLS Acc.11388.28
The Grange

31*st* Decer—[1861]

. . . 'A good new year' to you dear Lady. 'and many of them'! And a good—a perfectly exquisite new year to Baby! *The only Child in the World*! Or, what comes to the same thing, the only Child that ever touched my Heart, or kindled my Imagination, or was distinguishable for me from other Children *of the Period*! I have often wondered that Babies didn't (so far as one knows) get *mixed*, and misappropriated! that Mothers and nurses seemed able to tell their own particular Baby from the general flood of Babies! It must be *by the* CLOTHES (I thought) or some private mark, such as Gentlemen put inside their hats! for, in point of fact, the little creatures were all alike as peas!

and equally uninteresting!— But *now!*—were all the Babies in
Middlesex and Hampshire collected in one place; *in puris
naturalibus* (if you can imagine anything so shocking!); and I
should be asked to point out 'the Grange Baby' among them all;
I venture to modestly affirm, that as soon as my eye found her, I
should say; *'that is she*! the Darling'!

Mercy! what a thing it would have been, had she been
spillt, thro' sheer stupidity and carelessness! I am afraid *I* should
have pitched that nurse *into* the Lake; by way of curing her
fancy for wandering by it in winter evenings, with *the only
Baby in the World* in her arms!

Now that is a nurse whom *Dr Francia* would have
ordered to be 'walked three times beneath the gallows! with
intimation, that if she didn't mind what she was about, she
should certainly be *hanged*'! ...

Mr C would be right glad to go to the Grange on the 14*th*
or when you please—... to stay a whole fortnight—if *that* does
not frighten you. Oh I shall be so glad! God bless *you* Baby! I am
coming to play with you, faithfully Jane Carlyle

*At the start of January, Jane heard from the newly married Emilie
Venturi, who was pleased that Jane 'liked Charlotte Cushman. She is a
dear good soul with far less of the actress in her than most actresses, &
worth loving which to my thinking few artists are' (NLS 1774.288). Jane
roused herself to write.*

CHARLOTTE CUSHMAN   Library of Congress, CCP
Rome

5 Cheyne Row—Chelsea
January [31 1862]

My Dear! My Dear! I want to put my arms round your neck, and
give you—oh! such a good kiss And then, if you can stand that
sort of thing, once in a way,—I should like to lay my head on
your shoulder and take a good cry! *That* is how nature prompts
me to acknowledge your dear letter, and dear newyear's
tokens,—with a good kiss and a good cry; rather than with any
written sentences that my poor nearly extinct Brain can cobble
together in these Hard Times! (I am so worn out and
disheartened with long illness and confinement to two rooms!)
But alas Dear! The 'gods', however entreated, will *not* 'annihilate
Time and Space, to make two Lovers happy'! That has been

clearly ascertained some time since! And so, *faute de mieux*, I
must have recourse to *writing* 'under difficulties', and that
without further delay, on penalty of passing for both fickle and
ungrateful; when—God bless you!—I am far as possible from
being either! and as unwilling as possible that such an idea
should be entertained of me—by *you*!

Mrs Dilberoglue, being the precisest and faithfulest of
dear little 'Goods', would do infallibly what she promised, nay
volunteered to do, namely '*explain* to Miss Cushman all about
it'—'*It*' meaning my happiness at having a letter from you,—
my true Scotch woman impatience to make '*a suitable
return*,'—and then my illness—the extreme weakness and
nervousness which made any—the least—use of my *head*
intolerably irksome besides being especially prohibited by my
Doctor;—*all that* the little *Good* was to 'explain'! and trusting
that she did so with her accustomed accuracy and lucidity, I
will not go back upon the causes of my long silence. It is
enough to have been *four months ill* and shut up in two
rooms; without 'renewing grief' by details of one's fit-for-
nothingness; so soon as ever one has recovered *a certain* use
of one's tongue and pen!

But if I shut down the lid and turn the key on my sick
room tribulations; what is there left out of these weary four
months to tell you? This—first and foremost; that I am not a bit
cooled on the sudden affection I took for you; and believe it to
be one of those Elective Affinities on which one does not
cool—ever! I have seen you twice—that's all! and already you
are mixed up with my life like an old friend! Something new
and good *in* my life—not outside it! I look forward with
pleasure to seeing you again; but, without seeing you without
interchanging words with you, it is a pleasure to know of you
in the same world with me. The influence of a strong, brave,
loving true woman may be felt at any distance, I firmly believe,
without outward visible sign. And then, Dear, you are come to
me just at the right time—to be a consolation as well as a
possession! For, of late years, it had been all loss, loss with me!
never gain! One Friend after another out of 'dear old Long
ago,' that had cared for me and that I had cared for all my Life,
had gone to their rest, leaving me so lonely on the Earth!
Playing at Friendship with the new people I was thrown
amongst; and so discouraged in my secret heart that I
despaired of both my chances and my ability to ever make

myself a *new real* Friend!—My Heavens! when I went to Barnsbury Park that day to see *you*; how very very little I dreamt of jumping into your arms! and 'swearing eternal Friendship,' like any Boarding-school Girl! But it was all right! After so many months and after a *severe fit of illness* (which I take to be the best possible test of realities and shams) I feel no misgivings about that somewhat German-looking transaction! rather compliment myself on having so much *Life* left in me after all! and on having turned it to such account!

My *Life* has been making another *pronunciomento* with which I could throw you into fits of laughter if I had you beside me! My Dear! I have had a fearful row with Geraldine Jewsbury! which has made 'pigs and whistles' of *that* everlasting friendship! and 'Like cliffs that have been rent asunder

A dreary sea now flows between!'

I should be more overpowered with grief than I am (in fact I have shown an insensibility unexampled!) had the cliffs been rent by *one* explosion; but the rent has been the gradual work of many years. And the cliffs were only of *Land* or some very loose Material to begin with! I do think that sort of emotional woman, all 'finer sensibilities' and no feeling, all smoke and no flame is one of the most intolerable inventions of Civilization, should be put down by act of Parliament, and prayed against in all Churches!

You asked for Mrs Hawks's (Madame Venturi's) address after the 1st of January (she wrote to me) I was to address *Emelia Venturi nata Ashurst poste restante Milan*—She had been living up to that date in some rooms of an old château, near Bresica [Brescia], dismantled and unfurnished, in the midst of all sorts of inconveniences and discomforts; waited on by a girl of the Country whom she named *Bare* legs (as Mr Carlyle would say) 'significative of much!' But caring for none of these things! very fond of her new Husband (I think, and very happy with him)— happy as a young girl!—and with a touching air of consciousness that not *being* a young girl she has no claim to that sort of happiness and no sure hold of it! She writes to me 'I am so glad you like Charlotte Cushman. She is a dear good noble soul!'

Aren't you glad that we are not to be natural enemies? It would have been so absurd that war as well as so vexatious!! When will you come? And how long will you stay?

I cannot put into words how touched I was by your new years bouquet, and the little scarfs! I took them not only as tokens from *you* but as omens of a fortunate year; and—next day I had a relapse and was thrown into bed again for a fortnight!!

Does your friend remember me? I do her—and offer her my kind regards and just one word more and the paper is full. Please love me ever so much but *don't* flatter me for it makes me '*think shame*'! Yours faithfully and affectionately / Jane Carlyle

It is, perhaps, of this letter that Sarah Dilberoglue wrote on 19 December that 'the note for Mrs Carlyle, too, came at a good time; she was confined to her room by illness, and it was quite comforting to her to receive it, indeed, she has been ill for more than a month: during part of the time in her bed'. Charlotte Cushman then wrote, 28 January 1862: 'How shall I tell you, dear, that I have been sad to death over your illness— that I have wanted to write to you, but could not for many reasons? ... Tell me how can I serve you? Mrs. Dilberoglue says that you have been ill— too ill to send me a note & I have been longing for some word.... & I have the Sorrow to love you, & not be able to help you.' She mentions having sent 'a little Roman scarf' as a new year gift, Emilie Ashhurst, the Italian question and English sympathy with the South in the civil war. Feeling was running high.'When we do come to blows I shall choose my English for fighting with you & shall be first. Could I be content to be whipped by you & kiss your hands. Oh how long before I shall see you' (NLS 1774.227). According to Stebbins, Charlotte seems also to have written to a friend on 8 February, mentioning Jane's letter of 31 January in which she said that they had met 'just at the right time' (Letters and Memories 181-2). Charlotte adds that there comes a time when nations and individuals must recognize and meet their 'real needs'. Sarah Dilberoglue reported, on 4 March, that she and her husband had recently had tea with Jane, 'who was much better—I found she had written to you the very day before she got the note ... and she had your answer before I saw her—I must get to see her this week for I know she is feeling me a recreant'. Of the same visit, she adds that the Carlyles were 'going out at night to Lord Ashburton's, and Mrs. C. was more like herself than I have seen her for months'.

Jane clearly liked her new friend, but it is not clear who could claim the 'conquest' of the other, and Charlotte was to grow discouraged. As noted in the Introduction (xxvii), she told her niece (19 February 1863) that she was wrong to think that she was 'prevented from writing' to Jane 'by any outward influence.... My not writing is purely in interior difficulty'.

MARTHA LAMONT   EUL Gen.1730 (Carlyle 28)
Liverpool

[mid-Feb. 1862]

...Just two lines to keep you from *speculating*; I am not *up to* a
letter; being only half recovered from a long and fatiguing illness....

Neither must you be angry that I say only the absolutely
needful; for I am so worn out with suffering and confinement to
the house—three months of it; that I have as great a horror of
pen and ink as a mad dog has of water....

MARY RUSSELL   NLS 607.606
Thornhill

[13 Feb. 1862]

...The last day I was out, I went to see *two* of my most
intimate friends here who are both, I fear, *dying* the one a
beautiful bright little M*rs* Twisleton, who, after having been
treated for two years by all the first Doctors for Neuralgia, is
discovered to have a far advanced *tumour* in her left side!
Locock says it 'is not absolutely incurable' which means, I
suppose, that he has *no* hope of her. She has next to none of
herself! but is lying there as calm (when out of agony) and
heroic, and loving as an angel! The other is Countess Pepoli,
who has been shut up in her room for six months with a
cough and difficult breathing *alone* having left her husband
and own family in Italy, and refusing to let any of them come
to her, 'because, she says, when one can be no *pleasure* to
ones friends it is much best to be without them!! and anyone
in the house with her would only give her the fret and
trouble of thinking about their dinners &c'!!! there is
Stoicism in *that* but not heroism—not lovingness She has a
dreadfully sharp haggard look that freezes one's sympathy.
When I saw her after so many months of mutual illness she
asked me after two minutes if I 'had read *Mrs Delany's
memoirs* and what I thought of the Book'!!! ...Oh the
difference between these two women! and yet they are both
brave in their several ways! Count Pepoli is made something
important in his native Bolognia, 'Governor' or something, and
one of her servants told me 'the Countess was fretting
dreadfully, she thought, that she wasn't well enough to be
with him now, *when she would have been of use at the head
of his house*'! Her vanity about 'Carlo's' greatness was the

only human trait I found in her the other day.

What a melancholy letter! Well! It is a melancholy world! ...

MARY DODS   NLS 1797.63
Haddington

8*th* March 1862

... If it was *you*, then, dear woman, who sent the Good Words;
accept my warm thanks and a good kiss! If it was Mrs Davidson,
do please, write and tell me, that I may send her grateful words
for her *good* ones!

For the rest; I had ten days in bed after my last note to you;
and more weeks on the sofa; and had to give up my usual winter
visit in Hampshire. All along of my Housemaid's 'Hysterical
Tendencies' and my own 'Excitability'; which between them
caused me more fatigue, and exposure, and fright, than I had
strength to bear. But the weather grew mild as milk; and one
evening, when a Lady who had been acting as Honorary sick
nurse to me all winter came in, on the points of her toes, to ask
how I was she found me dressed in black velvet and pearls, just
going out to dinner!! The poor Lady's face expressed exactly
what the man Nicholson said to me, at Haddington, when I had
scaled the Church yard wall; *'Weel then! I declare! there's* NO
end o' ye!' — ...

My Doctors little Daughter was getting herself married;
and it had been a promise for two years that I should witness
the Ceremony. And our *Rector* ordered the fires lighted in St
Lukes on the Sunday to be kept in till Tuesday (the day of the
Wedding) 'that I might run no risk of a chill'!! It was the most
astounding 'delicate attention' ever paid me in my Life!— And
me a *Presbyterian* too!—

I had heard much of the '*impressiveness*' of the English-
Church-Marriage-Service, but never before seen it
'*performed*' — What *did* I think of it? ... If I had doubted still
about my descent from John Knox, I should have been
satisfied of it, there and then; by the natural, genuine, burning
desire I felt to sweep all that so called—'religious' Play-
acting—white-surplices, crimson Altar and all the rest of it! out
of Creation!

Since then, we have had again a fortnight of cutting East
wind; during which I have again personalised the Bairns 'lying a
dead'—but since yesterday that the wind turned to West I have

been the Bairns 'all sitting laughing'! Isn't it humiliating to be
acted upon by Wind, as if one were no better than a tin
weathercock? . . .

Oliphant's **Life** *of Irving had just been published, and Carlyle's
considered opinion was critical: 'more or less romantic,* pictorial, *and
'"not like"'* (**Reminiscences** 346).

MARGARET OLIPHANT   NLS 23210.183
Fettes Row, Edinburgh
                                                        [early May 1862]

Darling woman! . . . I do long to see you to tell you, not what *I*
think of your Book, but what M*r* C thinks, which is much more
to the purpose! I never heard him praise a *womans* Book,
hardly any man's as cordially as he praises this of yours! You are
'worth whole cart-loads of Mulochs and Brontes and THINGS of
that sort'— You are 'full of geniality and genius even'!—
'Nothing has so taken him by the heart for years as this
biography'!— You are really 'a fine, clear, loyal, sympathetic,
delicate female Being.' The only fault he finds in you is '*a
certain dimness about dates: and arrangements of Time*!' In
short I never heard as much praise out of his head at one rush!
And I am so glad!
        For *me*, I am not in a state to express an opinion yet, having
read only 'here a little and there a little' in whichever volume M*r* C
was not occupied with; and amidst 'a pressure of things'!—all the
worse for being trivial things; But tomorrow I shall begin at the
beginning. M*r* C got to the end last night, and the last part is the
best of all; he says— And that he is 'very glad—very glad indeed
that such a biography of Edward Irving exists'! . . . believe me that I
love you very much, and try to love me a little / J. W. Carlyle

TC   NLS 607.589C, 591B
Cheyne Row
                        West Cliff Hotel Folkestone / Wednesday
                                                        [2 July 1862]

Thanks Dear! especially for telling me about M*rs* Forster. I
had been so vexed at myself for not begging you to go again and
send me word.
        Lady A came and sat in my room awhile last night, and
speaking of Miss Bromley's departure, I took occasion to say;

that as *she* and I *came* on the same day, I felt as if I [ought] to
have also *gone* on the same day. The answer to which was a
very cordial 'Nonsense! my dear friend!' . . . And then came up
the old question as a new one; '*did* I think *He* would come?' 'It
would be such a pleasure to Bingham [Lord Ashburton], now
that he could move about' I said you might perhaps be
persuaded to come for a very short visit; but &c &' — . . . .

Now *that* is just what you *must* do! Even two days of Sea
will benifit you, and it can be had at little sacrifice of anything.

You dont need to trouble about clothes—what you could
bring in your carpet bag would be enough, there is no
elaborate dressing for dinner *here*; and the tide is convenient;
and there is a horse! . . .

If you don't come, I will stay away as long as ever they
will keep me, just to *spite* you! . . . There is here too a Review
of *Frederick* in *The Corn Hill* which would amuse you!
adoring your genius; but absolutely horror struck at your
'*scorn*' which 'is become normal'!— How you *dare* to utter
such blasphemies against les respectables Messr Leibnitz and
Maupertuis!! I couldnt help bursting out laughing at the man's
sacred horror as if he had been speaking of Milton's Devil! /
Yours ever / JWC . . .

*

Holme Hill / Thornhill
Tuesday / morning [12 Aug. 1862]

. . . It is a lovely place and House they have made of old Holme
Hill!— . . . Above, there are plenty of bedrooms—one fine one—
but Mrs Russell put me into the ground floor room; and I *know*
why—because the up stairs windows MUST, some of them, look
towards Templand. Oh how kind they are, and I feel *that*
kindness, partly out of love for my Mother and Aunt Jeanie, so
much more keenly than kindness I derive from Lion-worship—
even tho' the Lion be you my Dear!— (Good Heaven one might
as well write with a skewer as this pen!)

I had a famous tea, and went to a most comfortable Bed in
deepest privacy— But, of course, tho' feeling no tiredness, I
couldn't go to sleep with my mind in such a tumult, and the
idea of Templand half a mile off!— But between four and five I
at last fell into what you call a *doze* (*is* it *s* or *z*?) and today I am
'better than I deserve'! . . .

At Carlisle, when I was rushing madly after my Box, which couldnt be found; but finally was perceived to have 'cam *haim* with its tail behind it,' into the Thornhill van! I noticed a dark Gentleman turn in passing, and look after me— and then I saw him, with the tail of my eye, trying to look at my face, fancying the proceeding some delusion (arising out of the spicy little hat). . . . I turned resolutely away when a voice said at my back; 'surely it *is* Mrs. Carlyle that I see'! I wheeled round and found the dark gentlemans face 'quite familiar to me,' but couldnt for my life identify him till he named himself. '*Huxley*' [T.H. Huxley]!— He was going to Edin*r* and we did a good deal of Portmanteau hunting together amidst distracted Pointer-dogs and more distracted Sportsmen!— I never saw such a lively representation of 'Confusion worse confounded'. . . .

I have not read the Ladys letter yet. it takes time to decipher but I am very glad of *your* few lines and the fact of there being a letter from you already has raised you to the stars in M*rs* Russells opinion 'as attentive a Husband as *mine*' (she says) . . . .

MARIA CHAMBERLAYNE   Duke
Holme Hill / Thursday
[21 Aug. 1862]

. . . Could you lay your hands on the Haddington newspaper I sent to Elizabeth? It had been at Cheyne-Row once already, and was redirected there by M*r* C, and I, having no leisure to read newspapers in a general way, returned it to Elizabeth; whom it might interest, and as a sign of remembrance from myself. Now comes a letter from Miss [Jackie] Welsh at Haddington, mentioning this newspaper as 'containing MORE *fun* about myself'—by which I have confirmed to me what somebody here said the other day, that 'not one but several 'articles' about my youth and childhood were going the round of all the newspapers!!! Pleasant!— Now, if you could send me back that Haddington paper, I should just look to see what 'the *fun*' is! as probably the reality would annoy me less than my imaginations about it! All this comes of M*rs* Oliphant's Life of *Irving*!— . . .

Charlotte Cushman had returned from Rome, and evidently sought Jane out, asking in July, 'May I come to you for a little while on Monday . . . just to look at you. . . . Ah you make me such a cormorant. How happy

I was with you on Thursday'.

And again, 'The Fates are cruel for I want to see you more than I dare tell you....I do not seem to belong to myself or be mistress of my time or actions. I am only sure of one thing, and that is my loving admiration for you—& my vexation and disappointment' (NLS 1774). They had trouble in meeting, but Jane wrote:

CHARLOTTE CUSHMAN   Library of Congress, CCP
The Gill (!) / Annan
Thursday [28 Aug. 1862]

My Darling!
    Your letter has just reached me here! I have a bad habit—I *know* it is a *bad* one—of putting off writing to those I love, till there comes an hour when I can do it with all the concentration of heart, and all the stillness from outward things, which they seem entitled to—and so all in wishing to express myself in the worthiest manner; I keep a silence which looks, at least, ungracious. I must try to break myself of this! were it only for *your* dear sake!
    Here is my first effort toward a better system! I have the daily letter to my Husband still to write—several letters which may be called 'of business'—letters about my goings and my *trains* &c—am 'surrounded by a' sister-in-law or *two*!—have a twelve-miles drive in a gig to execute—had next to no sleep last night—nor any night this fortnight back!—am busy, am wearied, and worried, am half delirious, am *on* my travels—and amidst all this I write!— But *well* or *much* you see clearly Dear, is impossible!
    When I told Stavros I was preparing for Edin*r*, it was an ELLIPTICAL expression. I had several visits to pay *on the road* there—did not expect to arrive there till the end of this week. And now, I am going back to Thornhill to make a fresh start for Edin*r*, *thence*, next Monday! My programme of route having been deranged by the illness of M*r* C's nieces!
    I had hoped to avoid going to Edin*r*—but my three aunts there were going to find 'such conduct *very* strange'—and after all, they are my Fathers sisters tho' little like him, and the only near relatives I have in the world; and one of them has been 'getting very frail'— Clearly it was my *duty* to go on—and there is a *certain*—not much—but a *certain* satisfaction in the discharge of one's duty!

Meanwhile the floods of sad and rather wild emotion that have been pouring thro' this excitable heart of mine have ruined my sleep—utterly—and I am grown nervous, cowardly and 'HORRID badly' (in the dialect of these Parts) I wish I were safe home again!

On Monday my address will be *Craigenvilla Morningside Edin*r—for a week.— I hope to be at Chelsea on the following Monday or Tuesday—and so to see you on your return from Paris.— I will write from Edin*r*— If I could write such a lovely hand as you do, I shouldnt hate so to send you a hurried letter— but my hand was spoiled in commencing to write at four years to [catch] the Post.(and Mr C's letter) Kindest regards to Miss S and M*rs* C Your loving / Jane Carlyle

LADY STANLEY   Duke
Alderley
                                                  ...23*d* Sept*r* [1862]

...Your letter affords a fresh example of a Rule in Human Life, not taught us at school, but which every one has to learn for him or herself—namely; '*The Wished for comes too late*'!— ...

Thus the announcement of your return, and your kind invitation to Alderley reaches us at oh such a perverse moment! the very day after M*r* C's holyday had EXPIRED, and he had set himself stiffly to 'work' again! Only one week's holyday had the infatuated man granted himself, made almost necessary by a slight derangement of his health, and falling in, as it happened, conveniently with a pause at the printers. And that week I know he would have gladly spent with you at Alderley. But tho' I have pleaded with him on my knees, with streaming eyes and flowing hair (figuratively speaking) to take another weeks idleness, which would be so good both the body and soul of him, no answer could I obtain but this;'my Dear! it is out of the question! I am up to the ears in a quagmire of Things again! Say every thing that is most kind from me to Lady Stanley; And—I say!— If you like—you can send her one of the little Photographs of me!'

My disappointment at not getting to you myself is great— for I was very happy at Alderley! But I may not say much about it! having just had a month's holyday in Scotland, *I*! I was feeling so ill and suicidal in London; that I had to fling over all conjugal delicacies and leave *him* to the tender mercies of the

Maids! merely writing to him a long letter every day to keep
him in heart.

It is amazing how well he seems to have done without me! ...

CHARLOTTE CUSHMAN   Library of Congress, CCP
London

5 Cheyne Row
Tuesday night [Sept. 1862]

Oh my dear dear Friend! Was there ever the like of this? What
cross purposes! What have I gone and done? Is it *I* who have
made a huge mistake, or *you* who have changed your
programme? It was clear in my mind, that you were not to start
for Rome till the middle of October! How I came by that
impression God knows; but there it was! And if it had only *been
there*! but—I have acted upon it! thought myself safe to engage
to spend a week at Dover, with a Lady whom I promisd to visit
in Derbyshire on my road home from Scotland; and I broke that
promise, and so *must* keep this one! I was to have gone today,
but put off till tomorrow being unwell. And now to day comes
your dear letter telling me you return the very day after I shall
have gone, and, far worse, that you leave for good before my
'week' is out! But *that* must never be! I *will* come back on
Monday, to get one look of you—will *try* to come back on
Saturday tho' of *that* I am doubtful. I will write which day I shall
be back, when I *see* what can be managed—without
ungraceness to the person concernd who is adorably kind to
me, tho' a *fine Lady*!

And *you*—can you—not stay in London till Wednesday
and spend Tuesday with *me*? all day Write to me directly to the
care of Miss Davenport Bromley, (Sidney Villa) Dover—one line
will do.

I have been too ill all this day to pack my things or do any
thing—so you *will* see why I write hastily and briefly now
about midnight? I will come in the forenoon of Monday at latest
and then couldn't you both come here for the evening / God
pity me, / Your JWC

*At present an account of their friendship remains incomplete, though
they seem to have continued to communicate, exchange gifts and call
when possible. Charlotte's friends helped to keep her informed, and
Sarah was to tell her promptly of Jane's death* (Markus, **Untried Sea** 227).

KATE STANLEY   NLS 1797.223

[30 Sept. 1862]

... Meanwhile Mr C wants a new coat and new trowsers! And
Oh! if you knew what a job *that* is for both the tailor, and *me*! I
have already been seeking vainly thro' the cloth-shops in
London for 'a piece of *honest* cloth, free from *devils dust*' that
may suit his ideas; and today I have to seek thro' the other half!
And I have various little matters to do for myself and the House!
and *five* letters that *must* be written before I go out ....

EMILY TENNYSON   Yale
Farringford, Isle of Wight

Dover / *4th* October [1862]

... Your kind note has reached me here, this morning;
forwarded, unopened by Mr C, and undivined!
      I will not put off answering it, till I shall have talked it
over with *him*. I shall not see him till Monday; and cannot reach
him by letter any sooner—tomorrow being Sunday— So I will
answer at once, what I *know* he would bid me answer, were I
beside him. That it is very beautiful and tempting what you
propose! but—*impossible!* at this time!— He has a great
pressure of work on him, he would throw over the visit to the
Grange; only that he had promised it, and put it off, and
promised again—and cannot *hither and thither* any more
about it this time; as the Ashburtons are going away to spend
the winter at Nice. It will be a very short visit however, and
having performed his engagement, he must rush back home to
his work—and not dream of prolonging his holyday, by going
on to Freshwater *just now*. He hopes another time—in happier
circumstances, that 'the Destinies' (his particular friends) will
permit him &c &c, I know as well that I should be bid say all
that, as if he were there saying it!
      I return on Monday, and shall then give him your note
without telling him what I have written. And if by possibility—
or rather, by *im*possibility, I have put wrong words in his mouth,
I shall be only too happy (I who am not writing Frederick) to
unsay them dear Mrs Tennyson—
      What a beautiful photograph of your Husband, that new
one! and there is as good a one of *My* Husband by the same
artist. Yours very truly / Jane Carlyle

Lord Ashburton's health improved enough for him to leave for Paris
but nothing would divert Carlyle from Frederick. Mazzini wrote to Emilie
Hawkes that he kept his old affection for Jane, but felt that he would
never renew his friendship with Thomas (Hansons, **Necessary Evil** 497).

LADY AIRLIE   NLS 20767.37, 41, 46
Cortachy Castle

24*th* October [1862]

. . . I saw your Mother and Sister at Dover Street, on their way to
Bath. . . . Mr Carlyle called the day after me, and what do you
think he said?— It was at night—hours after his return—he had
been lying on the sofa—asleep, I fancied. And he suddenly broke
out in a tenderly reproachful tone; 'These people dont like *me*
nearly as well as I do *them*!' 'What *people*? I said, what on Earth
are you talking about'?— 'The Stanleys I mean— I dont think
they care a bit about me!— I was far gladder to see them today
than they were to see me!'— 'Well, I said, I dare say Lord Stanley
cares nothing about you—but I am sure *Lady* Stanley does—she
has always professed to do so, and I am sure she is sincere in
whatever she says'— 'Ah——h——Well—I—I—I *used* to think
she liked me very well—but *today* she didn't seem to care
rigmarree for me!' —'and I am sure Miss Stanley likes you; only
she is very undemonstrative.' I went on comforting him!— But
he turned over on his side, and murmuring—'I dont believe
any of them like *me* half as well as I do *them*' —went to sleep
again! You can't appreciate the singularity of this *human*
outburst of M*r* C's unless you had had *my* opportunities of
observing how he never troubles his head whether people '*like*
him' or not! . . .

I am going off to lunch with Miss Farrer, and help her to
entertain Syme the Edin*r* Surgeon! In a moment of enthusiasm
she had begged of him to stop in London on his way to some
patient in Devonshire; that he might examine Lady Tierney,
about whom she was in a dreadful fright, poor Soul! And now
Lady Tierney declines being examined by *him*, and he is to have
luncheon instead. That poor woman has a dreadful life with
that idiot Husband of hers! And when he dies, as he is
expected to do 'this winter,' you will see, she will be an
inconsolable widow! Women always suffer more in losing a
husband who has wholly depended on them, and painfully
occupied every moment of their lives, than in losing one whom

they have been 'at ease in Zion' beside and had no bother at all
with— I have seen this more times than I can count! One of
the loveliest women I ever knew was promised at fifteen, by a
mercenary Brute of a Mother to a little fat vulgar rich man who
was taken by the poor childs Beauty. Bred up in a Scotch
Wilderness the girl had seen no men to compare him with,—
was grateful for the trinkets and 'sweeties' he gave her,—and,
when her Mother accepted him for her, hadn't courage to say
no. A year or two later, when transplanted to a Town, where
there were numerous men, she was claimed by her Betrothed
whom she had not seen in the interim, and was horror-struck at
his fatness and vulgarity—as for his riches, having taken, poor
girl to thinking and writing Poetry, they (the riches) were no
consolation whatever— So she wept, and remonstrated, and
postponed,—did everything except what she ought to have
viz: kick her foot thro' the whole '*burble*' [tangle].— She had a
very nice conscience *unfortunately*, and they persuaded her it
would be dishonourable to fling the man over, and moreover
he worked on her timidity by threatening to 'prosecute' her and
publish her child-letters to him!! So after some five years of
vain struggle to get out of the thing, she let herself be married
to the odious little man. And from the day she married the
brightness went out of her face for ever!— Well— (what a long
story I have got into!) She did all her duties of Wife,—obeyed
him at a word, studied his humours, was gently impassive to his
ill temper and vulgarity. But for the rest, she looked *dead* and
buried! Her voice sounded always as if it came from a great
distance—nothing seemed ever to amuse, or please; or pain or
excite her. . . .

*

[30 Oct. 1862]

It was very pleasant at the Grange. That Lady is adorably
kind! I never in all my life met with a more considerate,
unselfish Hostess. As for the caprice which I hear her frequently
accused of; *I* have never seen a trace of it! She seems wholly
occupied from morning till night in making her Husband and all
about her as happy as is possible in a conditional world. They
are going off to Nice next week—for *His* gout. Nice!— I wish
they were all safe back from that fatal place, which I should
have thought he would never have chosen. . . .

Oh such a photographing there was at the Grange! Vernon Heath was there doing 'views' and 'interiors' at the easy rate of five guineas a day and as much french cookery and champagne as he could stow into him. . . . Like all the artists . . . patronised by 'our lamented Prince Consort' he is pretty much of a Humbug, I think. Lady A made him photograph Lord A and Mr C sitting on the same bench under the Portico. It was hoped they would make a touching illustration of faithful friendship; but they have come out, she tells me, 'a pair of horrid criminals in the same *dock!* one (Lord A) as if he had already had sentence of death pronounced on him and was sinking away into deliquium; the other (Mr C) in the act of hearing *his* sentence, and glaring back anxious defiance!' But Mr Heath declared it to be one of his most successful efforts, and had 'made them into a transparency!'—and I am to have 'a *transparency.*' Won't it be nice? . . .

*

.. 10*th* / Novr [1862]

Darlingest of Ladyships! What a nice, dear letter you sent me! and so soon!— Decidedly, you are good!—good as gold, *when you follow just your own inspirations!*— And I should be a wretch if I were long of answering this time! should be (as Mr C might say) 'a vile off-scouring of Humanity, only fit to have a red-hot poker run thro' me, or a torrent of red hot shot poured into my belly'!!! Yes! *that* is the *style* Mr C is rioting in since the Novr fogs set in! I don't mean his style in addressing myself—better *not*; I can tell him!—but his style in speaking of the *greater* number of his contemporaries who have risen to 'office,' or power or distinction of any sort 'on the shoulders of a pack of braying jack asses (the Public)'— I don't know whether or not people *breakfast* in Pandemonium, but if they do; I think it must be very much like our breakfastings in Cheyne-Row—'the blackness of Darkness' outside; and inside, red-hot pokers, and red-hot shot, and every description of red-hot thing, flashed (figuratively) before ones eyes!— Ah you are happy who have not to pass in London 'that gloomy month of November, in which the People of England hang and drown themselves'! Still happier perhaps in having that blessed power of reaction which comes of Youth, and Health, and a whole Heart!

The last week has been a little enlivened for me by almost daily visits at Bath House; where the Lord and the Lady were going on like two buckets at a well in point of health—and their journey postponed until today. They were to start this morning at ten finally—but I shall not be sure, till I have been up and seen the gates closed.

They were very urgent that Mr C and I would go with them or to them for two or three months. I should have liked it so much! I who was never out of this Island! But until that weary Book is done; an invitation to spend three months in Paradise even would be declined by Mr C as an 'impossibility.' Oh what a dreary winter is before me! hardly a soul here that I care for! Countess Pepoli dead, dear clever little Mrs Twisleton dead, Lady Sandwich dead, almost all the rest gone away, not to return till the winter is past and gone. And the winter, it is inferred from premature Robin-red-breasts—multitudinous 'red-rowans' &c—will be a long and severe one. I begin to regret that I declined the offer of a certain Lady Holmes, wife of the Governor of Guiana, to present me with 'a pair of lovely green parrots' and 'a little monkey of a most affectionate disposition'! With such animal resources to fall back upon I might have fronted the winter with less apprehension. But if there is one thing on earth Mr C detests more than a parrot, it is exactly a——monkey!

Are you one of the prejudiced people who hate Mazzini? If not, I will send you, to read, a little book of his on *Duty*, which has just been translated into English. There was never a greater Fanatic than Mazzini! but also there was never a man more maligned! For example; *there* is a whole public of 'braying jack asses' accusing Mazzini of urging on the Mountebank Garibaldi to that mad expedition against Rome. And I *know*—knew it from Mazzini's own lips, *three weeks* BEFORE Garibaldi landed on the main land that Mazzini considered his enterprise 'perfectly ruinous'—had implored him to desist from it—and had written to him that he (Mazzini) would come and join him if he made the country rise—would come and join him because he was bound to him; but—that he would 'come, with A DEAD HEART'! All *that*, he said to me a month before Aspremonte and he wrote to me, in Scotland; 'I go in two days—KNOWING that I go, merely to involve myself in the ruin which Garibaldi has prepared for us all.' ... / Yours with true Love / Jane Carlyle

JULIE SCHWABE   NLS 1797.227
                                        5 Cheyne Row [10 Nov.1862]

. . . It is indeed very long since we met. How long and how
little you know of us at the present time is apparent from the
contents of your letter! Heaven bless you! M*r* Carlyle thinks of
nothing and cares for nothing just now, and for years back,
except just *Frederick the Great!*—whose Life he is writing—
Italy he doesnt take the slightest interest in—never did take
indeed in 'the emancipation of Italy'—even when the *personal*
influence of Mazzini—irresistible in most cases—was at work
on him!—— M*r* Carlyle's sympathies always have been, are,
and always will be with Austria!!! as for Garibaldi—! I really
couldn't help going off into fits of laughter at your applying to
M*r* C of all people in the world to give his voice to the lyrical
recognition of Garibaldi! It will seem incredible to you; but the
fact is, M*r* C doesn't admire Garibaldi at all! Has been bored to
death with all the talk of him, declares him to be 'the great
dramatic Mountebank of the Age.' I duly read your letter to M*r*
C and he told me to convey these his sentiments to you 'in
some *mild* form'— But as I dont know how to give them a
mild form and at the same time not impair their positiveness;
and as I have no talent for french-polishing, I tell you just the
plain truth. . . .

MARY AUSTIN   NLS Acc. 7864
The Gill

                                        . . . Thursday [11 Dec. 1862]

. . . Lord Ashburton, whom we had been led to suppose out of
danger, made no progress in convalescence and then began to
sink. Lady A who has had the news of her Mother's death since
his illness, was *alone* to nurse him day and night. . . . This
morning I had a few hurried lines from Her No—I was not to
come 'it could do *her* no good and would knock *me* up'— for
the rest she was 'past all human help' she said 'and past all
sympathy.' And the poor dear soul had drawn her pen thro' the
last words. So like her! that she mightn't seem unkind! even in
her agony of grief and dread, she thought of *that*!
      Their Doctor's last two letters to me were very
despondent; and neither today nor yesterday has there been
any word from *him*, as there would have surely been could he
have imparted a grain of hope! We dread now that the next

post will bring the news of our dear Lord Ashburtons death.
Carlyle will lose in him the *only friend* he has left in the world.
And the world will lose in him one of the purest hearted most
chivalrous men that it contained.

MARY DODS   NLS 1797.176
Haddington

[31 Dec. 1862]

...Oh my Dear! isn't it *Cold?!* In spite of having on *all* my
flannel petticoats at *once!* (*three* white, and *one* red) and a seal-
fur pelisse;—And piling up fires, till an untopographical stranger
might suppose, we lived within a mile of a coal pit, instead of
paying 28 shillings a cartload for our coals! And in spite of
taking *three* glasses of wine a-day (by order of my Doctor) I feel
from morning till night and from night till morning like a living
lump of ice! And then, while so many 'poor Gardners' are
bawling about the streets that they are '*froze out*,' I am
decidedly '*froze' in*! The first touch of frost set me off coughing,
and *then* I have to be what is called 'very careful,' and keep the
house till a warmer time comes.

Ach! and I am the same woman—at least I suppose I am—
who used to delight in fighting with snow-balls and skating on
the Tyne! Who would get up in the Dark of a Winter morning,
and, with our groom (James Robertson), carrying a stable
lantern and besom; trot off surreptitiously to the *Lang Kram*,
and get a space cleared of the snow that had fallen over night,
and have some skating 'all by myself' before breakfast.

I recollect once finding John Wilkie there before me,
similarly equipped with a lantern and besom; when the ice had
been swept it was slippery as glass, and your uncle advised me
to 'hold on' by *his* 'coat tails'—to 'steady' myself—(I needed a
good deal of *steadying* one would say!) It was hardly day-light
when we proceeded to shoot over the Lang Kram like the
'Gowk and the Tittlin' [Cuckoo and Hedge-sparrow]—I holding
fast by his coat-tail! But he had now and then a—what shall I
say?—*diabolic* inspiration, your Uncle John! and certainly he
had one that morning and acted on it! For in turning the figure
of 8 he suddenly jerked his 'tails' out my clutch, and down I
clashed on one side, like a ninepin! Ugh! I think I feel it
now!— I had to go my ways home ignominiously with a black
eye! and wouldn't *speak* to John Wilkie for weeks after! That is

the sort of things that come into one's head, when one sits
down to meditate a moment, beside another mile-stone in ones
life— It isn't over the *last* miles that ones mind runs; but away
to the far, far back ones!—God bless them! . . .

If you have read in the newspapers a startling Tale of the
Marquis of Downshire having found the Master of his Yacht
kneeling at the side of his young Daughter Lady Alice Hill, and
taking him by the neck and flinging him into the sea, and so
there was an end of *Him!* You needn't be wasting either horror
or sympathy on it: for it is a story of the '*six-black-Crows*' sort,
founded on next to nothing! . . .

LADY STANLEY   Duke
Alderley
                                              [15 Jan. 1863]

. . .Another instance of what I was telling your Daughter—that
I had degenerated from a woman into a sort of paper kite,
blown wherever the wind of Circumstance listed! . . . If I were
in good spirits I could make an amusing story for you out of
my last troubles. The materials are lying there invitingly. But I
am in the worst of spirits—I have just been deceived,
betrayed, made a fool of! and my present mood is more like
that of *Timon of Athens* (!) than anybody I could name! and
the individual who has converted me into a M*rs Timon of
Athens* for the time being is——a child! a small girl of
fourteen, whom I took some three months ago, to train into a
housemaid, and *attach to us while her heart was impres-
sionable*, and *that sort of thing*! . . . In fact she often reminded
me of the *Changeling* in old Fairy ballads.

But as little 'Flo' grew in favour, the Scotch Cook grew
out of favour. She had always been a Blockhead,—a
'Mooncalve,' M*r* C said—but now she exhibited a sulkiness, a
doggedness which coupled with dinners that looked (I quote
again from M*r* C) 'as if they had been cooked in The Infernal
Regions—' (so burnt and blackened every thing was!) became
unbearable, and tho' horrible the idea to me of changing in
the winter, I have her warning next! A new cook stept on the
scene, who had a good three years character and for the first
few days I augured well of her; but by the end of the first
fortnight, she had turned to be exactly like the Scotch one
translated into English! the same sullenness and

doggedness, and indifference whether Mr C was 'poisoned' or not!— I began to think the House was bewitched; and to wish myself any where else,—in a Model Prison, or a Private Mad House, or, say, in that Picturesque Hospital for Ideots! Meanwhile I told the new Cook she wouldn't suit, and lay awake all night wondering if any body ever *would* 'suit' again! But 'it is a long lane that has no turning'! Next morning the Cook came to me, to say; she 'was aware she had made herself disagreeable, but that it wasnt easy (with a sob) to be good tempered and to try to please, with Flo every time she came down stairs repeating dreadful things I said about her (the Cook) and her performances'! ... A 'searching cross examination' brought it clearly *out* that my paragon of a Child, that I was thinking of leaving a small annuity to when I died, and who had seemed ready to fly up the Chimney for me—or anything—while I yet lived, had occasioned the dismissal of the Scotch Cook, and all but done the same by the present one and was the most cold-blooded, systematic Imp of mischief I ever heard tell of in such small compass! When completely unmasked she turned on my a look that suggested arsenic, and said '*Well!* I have told a few lies, and I have been treacherous—very treacherous but that is ALL you have to say against me!!'— This explosion (with a strong smell of sulphur) of my ideotic dream, to attach a Servant to me while still a Child, occurred on the same day that I received your letter, and made me so ill ... that I could settle to nothing; not even to answering that kind letter of yours; but went mooning about, doing 'here a little and there a little' in the Housemaid line—to cover so far as Mr C was concerned the deficiency of service produced by the Changeling's sudden restoration to the bosom of her admiring Family. ...

... My last letter from *Dr* CHRISTISON, dated three weeks back, represented Lord Ashburton as still progressing tho' slowly towards recovery. He (Dr C) had no hope of Lord A's being able to reach Nice. The greatest change he contemplated for him, was removal to some sunnier part of Paris. ...
Yesterday I had a few lines from Lady A herself—chiefly to ask if I was ill, that I had not written—but without entering into any particulars, she said Lord A's state 'was not so satisfactory' and her 'hopes were *very* low'! ...

MARY DODS   NLS 1797.77
Haddington

                                        21 February [1863]

...Thanks, Dear! The new photograph has been done on a clear
day, and is much better printed than the former one; besides that
the additional eighth of an inch of head room enables me to
breath more freely in looking at it! But few I dare say, if any, of
your Husbands Friends have such a nervous Imagination, and such
intense physical sympathy as I have! *One* such woman, born with
no skin 'to speak of,' is enough to *have* among one's '*respectable*'
acquaintance! So the *lowness of the ceiling* will cause no
sensation of choking to those other friends of his and yours, one of
whom may be made happy by the photograph which I spoiled for
myself, and accordingly I place it at your disposal. And along with
it the *best* likeness of Garibaldi, and a tolerable likeness of
Mazzini—for your *Book*;—if it be set up on the usual principle of
receiving Celebrities, whether personally known or not. *My* Book
is the most exclusive I have ever seen; Besides that I admit
nobody that is not my own friend, I make the additional exaction
that the photograph should have been *given* me by the person's
self—and yet it has got filled! Fifty Friends! How nice! and the
photographed ones are a mere fraction! Don't you think in my
progress from the great original Oyster (according to Darwin) I
must number among my Ancestors '*The Hare with many
Friends*'?— But all that doesn't prevent me from feeling very
poorly in this unnaturally soft winter. I have been trying to muster
courage to go into a lodging, by myself, for a week, somewhere at
the sea-side. A breath of Sea-air being worth any number of my
Dr's bottles of '*Strengthening mixture*—for Mrs Carlyle'! But
strange to say; for all so many years as I have lived '*here down*' (as
Mazzini would say) *that* is a thing I never did—to go into a
lodging, alone! and flesh and blood recoils from the notion when I
try to 'carry it out'— The nearest approximation I ever made to it,
was once, going by myself 'for change of air,' to Hampstead and
dining on a horrid tough chop at a little wayside Inn; and taking a
ride on a——cuddy! with a Boy shouting and beating it on with a
stick; while the chop was being cooked; but I returned to my own
house to tea. There too, you see, the inconvenience of having no
skin to speak of comes out strong. How I admire my Aunt Ann,
who whenever she gets low at Morningside, packs a carpet bag
and trots off to Portobello or Bridge of Allan or somewhere, and

makes herself at home in a lodging that may be full of bugs for anything she knows, and whose Landlady she never before set eyes on!

Good night it has just struck midnight You will all be sound asleep in my little Birth-place and none of you dreaming of *me* I could swear. . . .

CHARLOTTE SOUTHAM   Chelsea Public Library
London

[9 or 13 March 1863]

. . .Yes, come and see me. I have no immediate prospect of going from home, tho' I much need a change of air and scene. The Influenza I am just recovering from has made me very weak and *low*.

But I left M*r* Carlyle alone last summer for five weeks, and I havn't the face to propose doing that sort of thing again, so soon!

Mrs Royston has got the beautifullest Baby, I ever set eyes on! after having been married and childless for fifteen years! I thought, when I went to see her and it, that I should find her in Paradise, lying on her sofa, in the Drawingroom, with the wax-work-looking baby in a pretty pink and white basket placed on a chair near her—*her* whose life looked always so lonely and empty! But when I said; 'Oh how happy you must be'! she answered in her old wailing tone, 'I suppose I *ought* to be! but the poor child causes me such unsupportable agony, with this bad breast, that I almost shudder when they bring him near me,'— I believe it *is* terrible business suckling a child, with a sore breast. Anyhow I couldn't help thinking; how good care is *always* taken that nobody should be in *Paradise*, in *this* Life! Whatever happiness is given one; there is ever some pain, or some sorrow, or some anxiety, or *something*, to set off against it, and keep one in mind, that Earth is not Heaven! and that no amount of wishing and hoping and striving can ever make a Heaven of it for us! . . .

GRACE WELSH   NLS 608.611B
Morningside, Edinburgh

[17 March 1863]

. . . I am writing with my pocket-handkerchief tied over my lower face, and my Imagination much overclouded by weary

gnawing pain there. Decidedly a case for trying your remedy.
and I mean TO .... It is a comfort to reflect anyhow, that I have
not brought these aches on myself, by rushing 'out for to see,'
the new Princess; as the rest of the world did; or to see the
Illuminations! I had an order sent me from Paris for seats for
myself and 'a friend' in the balcony errected at Bath House—the
best for *seeing* in the whole line of the procession. But first I
have no taste for crowds; and secondly I felt it would be so sad
sitting *there*, when the Host & Hostess were away in such
sickness and sorrow. and thirdly I was somewhat of Mr C's
opinion, that this marriage, the whole nation was running mad
after, was less really interesting to every individual of them than
setting a Hen of ones own on a nest of sound *eggs* would be!!

The only interest I take in the little new Princess is
founded on her previous poverty, and previous humble homely
life. I have heard some *touching* things about that, from people
connected with the Court. When she was on her visit to the
Queen after her engagement, she always wore a jacket. The
Queen said to her one day; 'I think you always wear a jacket;
how is that?' 'Oh, said little Alexandra, I wear it because it is so
economical! you can wear it with any sort of gown—and you
know I have always had to *make* my own gowns!— I have
never had a Ladysmaid—and my sisters and I all made our own
clothes—*I* even made my bonnet!' ... *That* interests me—and I
also feel a sympathy with her in the prospect of the bother she
will have by and by with that mean-natured, half-distracted
Queen. ...

Lady Ashburton found it difficult to get on with her husband's family.
Jane longed to see her again. Her gift of Carlyle's new horse was to
replace his old Fritz.

LOUISA LADY ASHBURTON   NLS Acc. 11388.28
The Grange

                                              1*st* May [1863]

Oh my Darling! my Darling! ... I cannot understand what these
others are made of, or *who* made them; that *knowing,—seeing*
how you are situated, and how you bear, and strive, and love,
and are more like an angel than a grand lady, they still cannot
put away their jealousy and envy of you. ... Don't think of them!
they are so small! Think just of what you are to *Him*, your

husband; you are his Consolation, his Hope, his Life! without you he *could* not have lived thro' all this! Would not have cared to live! and it may well comfort you, under worse than the coldness of these others, to feel that you are *all in all* to that man; who in nobleness, and unselfishness, and gentleness of heart is not surpassed, I firmly believe, in God's Earth! ...

I must leave it to Mr C to speak for himself, about that horse when he shall be told about it; for, indeed, I have more thanks to render you, already, on my own account, than power of putting them into words! I often wonder that I should not feel oppressed by your kindness, almost irritated by it; so being that I am without ability to repay it, or even to adequately express my sense of it!— Often wonder *what it is in you*, that makes it possible for me to be *always your debtor*, without fuming or winceing in the position! It is not enough to esteem or even love a person; something more, that I cannot define, is needed to make *gratitude* a pleasant, even a *bearable* feeling for me! ...

LADY TREVELYAN   Trevelyan Family Papers, Robinson
Wallington Hall,   Library, Newcastle University
Northumberland

                                          2*d* June [1863]

... It was a lovely thought in you, to write me a letter!— I was most agreeably surprised! having been told just a day or two before that you had 'hidden yourself among the Swiss mountains'! I should say however, in strict truth, the surprise became *agreeable* only after opening your letter and seeing *your* name to it! ... It was really very nice of you to write it— and I will tell Mr Ruskin.

Oh my Heavens! how do I wish that he maynt breakdown again on Friday evening: that the shadow of his last disastrous Lecture may not fall upon this one! I suppose there is no hope of Lady Eastlake or Mrs Millais, or both, being laid up with small-pox or scarlet fever!

Mr C thinks that your sword must be one of those swords that were made in great number, in 1741 at the grand Insurrection for Maria Theresa. Pandour is the generic name for a *Hungarian infantry soldier*—'a great, helpless, hulking, very ugly fellow,' Mr C says, who went swaggering about with a long gun, and numerous Butcher's knives stuck in his belt, and pistols, and a short sword, a sort of ——Garibaldi (!) of these days—and just as much of a swaggering ass, (Mr C ventures to say) as our Garibaldis of the present day!!' — The Hungarian Cavalry soldiers were called Hussars the Infantry Pandours—oh no! they didn't belong to Frederich they were the admiring subjects of Maria Theresa and Frederich was once very nearly belonging to *them!* they had very nearly taken him prisoner, An impertinence which Mr C cannot get over seemingly. . . . Yours very truly Jane Carlyle

Chapter Eleven

Like a Dim Nightmare, 1863-64

Early in October, seemingly on the 2nd, Jane was coming back from seeing a distant cousin connected with the General Post Office. She tried to catch a bus, tripped in dodging a cab, fell on her neuralgic arm and had to be conveyed home. Thomas tells the story in the **Reminiscences** *and her* **Letters and Memorials***: three days of intense pain, then at first three weeks of slow recovery and the hope of improvement, when, as she says, she even 'hitched' herself to her feet and managed to write:*

LADY AIRLIE   NLS 20767.60
Cortachy Castle

                           5 Cheyne Row / Chelsea
                                2*d* Novr [1863]

...Well! and what was it, the accident? you would like to know. I feel the less reluctance to 'renew grief' in telling you; as I am now so far recovered that I am past needing to be *condoled* with. . . .

    Just two or three days after I had that lucky glimpse of you in Piccadilly. I had occasion to be at the *General Post Office*. 'There is no such dangerous thoroughfare as *St Martin le Grand* in all London,' my D*r* says; so I may be excused for having been flurried in crossing, to get to a Cab; and in such a hurry to find myself safe on the Pavement, that I struck the side of my foot violently against the curb-stone, and was plashed down on my left side on the pavement. I tried to gather myself up, but the agony I was in wouldnt let me. So I had to resign myself to become the Centre of Attraction to a small crowd and to be lifted by two *Roughs* and a Policeman, and put into a cab. Then there was five miles of jolting over the stones, not knowing whether my leg and arm were *broken*, or what I had done to myself; only that I was in such agony as I had never known before! Then there was the getting me into the House, and up to my bed, which was accomplished by the ingenuity of the Gentleman next door, impeded rather than assisted by M*r* C, who was too nervous for anything! Then there was the Doctor—who found

no bones broken—considered it a case of 'lacerated sinews.'
Then there were days and nights when I couldnt move so much
as an inch on my bed, and couldnt sleep a wink for the terrible
pain! and was decidedly very ill off indeed!

After a fortnight I was lifted out of bed and set *on end* on
a sofa in my bedroom, reminding myself of Miss Biffin! After
another fortnight I was half-carried half-walked into the
Drawing-room. And now, at the end of six weeks since the
'*Accident*,' I can walk accross the floor, by myself, with a stick.

But I cannot sit up at a table to write with pen and ink. I
write with the paper on my knees, and cushions at my back—
ergo—in pencil. For while the leg has been gradually
mending—faster than could have been hoped; the sprained arm
has been tormented by rheumatism (*neuralgia* Dr Quain called
it. but no Dr nor 'plain human cratur' ever explained yet to my
satisfaction the difference between *Rheumatism* and
Neuralgia). *That* is now my worst grievance— But I have got a
new prescription for it, which I really think is doing it good.

Have you gone to sleep yet over this long story? Don't
please till I have told you further that nothing could exceed the
kindness of my friends! My servants too have been most kind
and attentive. . . .

What on earth is the meaning of this absurd scandal about
Lord Palmerston? Surely it must be either a political conspiracy
or an attempt to extort money! I have heard of nothing like it,
since the old Lord Buchan insisted on appearing before the
Kirksession and being '*rebuked*' for a child that some young
woman had laid to him!

Will you tell your Sister my lamed condition— I cannot be
writing about *that* to *her* too! When I get back into the regions of
pen and ink I will reply to her letter, which I thank her for. But
pencil writing is only for those one is on terms of ease and
confidence with—like presenting oneself in a loose wrapper,
without one's stays! I don't mind coming to *you* in—anything! . . .

ISABELLA SIMMONDS   NLS Acc. 9086.8
Oakley St, Chelsea

                                    5 Cheyne Row / 3*d* Novr [1863]

My Darling!
. . . I should be greatly pleased that *your* baby bore a name
of mine— But the 'godmother' hood? There seems to me *one*

objection to *that*, which is a fatal one—I dont belong to the
English Church and the Scotch Church which I do belong to
recognises no Godfathers and Godmothers! The *Father* takes all
the obligations on himself—(serves him right!)

I was present at a Church of England Christening for *the
first time* when the Blunts took me to see *their* Baby
Christened—and it looked to me a very solemn piece of
work!—and that Mr Maurice and Julia Blunt (the God Father
and God Mother) had to take upon themselves, before God and
man, very solemn engagements—which it was to be hoped they
meant to fulfil! *I* should not have liked to *bow* and *murmur* and
undertake all they did, *without* meaning to fulfil it according to
my best ability!— Now my Darling how *could I* dream of
binding myself to look after the spiritual welfare of any earthly
Baby. I who have no confidence in *my own* spiritual welfare? I
am not *wanted* TO! it may perhaps be answered—you mean to
look after *that* yourself—without interference!— What *are*
these spoken engagements then? A mere *form*? that is, a piece of
humbug!— How could I in cold blood go thro with a ceremony,
in a *Church*, to which neither the others nor myself attached a
grain of veracity?

If you can say anything to the purpose, I am very *willing*
to be proved mistaken—and in that case very willing to stand
Godmother to a Baby that on the third day is not at all *red*!!! ...

*In mid-November they enjoyed a pleasant evening with the Froudes,
and Jane even began going out by carriage, which may have led to a
cold and a renewal of the intensely painful 'neuralgia', or 'sea of agony'
as Thomas called it* (**Reminiscences** 175). *The house was in confusion,
though Maggie Welsh came to help from Liverpool. Carlyle persevered
at* **Frederick**, *while a succession of doctors, including Isabella
Simmonds' father, Dr Barnes, met complete failure. Eventually, as a
desperate measure, Jane was taken for some months to St Leonards on
the south coast, to stay with Dr and Mrs Blakiston. Even this failed. At
last she decided to return to London—to stay with the Forsters, where
one night was enough; and she set out, accompanied by Dr John
Carlyle, to stay with her much-loved sister-in-law Mary Austin, near
Dumfries. This lasted about ten days, enlivened by the breakdown of
her carriage, when she moved to Mary and Dr James Russell's at
Thornhill. The patchy letters of this time, notes Froude, show the
'touching ... affection' and trust which she now felt for Thomas* (**LM**
3:204). *It may even be, as Alexander Carlyle asserts, that the* **Letters**

and Memorials *give too despairing and gloomy an account; but it was clearly a time of deep misery and pain* (**NLM** 2:293).

MARY AUSTIN   NLS Acc.7864, a copy
The Gill
                                        [5 Cheyne Row, 20 Nov.1863]

... I am poorly today, having had a horrid bad night, in consequence of having listened to *the voice of wisdom* yesterday, and gone out with a stick, to try walking in the street! I did not stay above ten minutes, and the sun was shining; but I could not get along fast enough with my stick, to prevent me suffering from the change of temperature from my warm Drawing room to the open air, and the *fatigue* of the thing was very great, and so all my pains were aggravated for the rest of the day—and thro' the night I was in a fever....

ANN, GRACE, AND ELIZABETH WELSH   NLS 608.627
Clarence St, Edinburgh
                                        [St Leonard's, 24 March 1864]

My own dear Aunts,
        I take you to my heart and kiss you fondly one after another. God knows if we shall ever meet again! and *His* will be done!— My Dr has hopes of my recovery. but I myself am not hopeful, my sufferings are terrible— The malady is in my womb— You may fancy!— It is the consequence of that unlucky fall—no *disease* there the Drs say, but some nervous derangement— Oh what I have suffered my Aunts! What I may still have to suffer!— Pray for me that I may be enabled to endure!
        Dont write to myself reading letters excites me too much— And Maggie tells me all I should hear— I commend you to the Lords keeping—whether *I* live or die, Ah my Aunts I shall die, that is my belief....

TC   NLS 608.621, 624-6
Cheyne Row
                                        Friday [8 April 1864]

        Oh my own Darling— God have pity on us!— Ever since the day after you left—whatever flattering accounts may have been sent you,—the *truth* is, I have been wretched—perfectly wretched day and night—with that horrible malady—

Dr B[lakiston] *knows nothing* about it more than the other D*rs*— So God help me—for on earth is no help—

Lady A writes that Lord A left you two thousand pounds—not in his will—(to save the Duty) but to be given you as soon as possible—'The wished for come too late!' *Money* can do nothing for us now!— / Your loving and sore suffering / Jane W Carlyle

Today I am a *little* less tortured—only a *little*—but a letter having been promised I write. . . .

*

[25 April 1864]

Oh my Husband! I am suffering torments! each day I suffer more horribly

Oh I would like you beside me,—I am terribly *alone*— But I dont want to interrupt your work— I will wait till we are in our own hired house and—then if I am no better you must come for *a day* / Your own wretched J W C

*

Warrior Square/ 4 o'clock
[28 April 1864]

Maggie and Mary are gone with the luggage in a fly— leaving me to follow, after their fires are lighted. Oh me! me! What dismal work this is!

But thank God for *two days* of ease! I dare not hope the stilling of my torture will *last*. It has been obtained by rubbing *in* opium—and opium has never *continued* to help *me*— Dr B has no idea what that *agony is!* He has called it half a dozen different things—followed half a dozen different treatments— and when at his wits end he *ignores* the misery of the thing altogether.

I cannot think there can be any analogy between that Edin*r* case and mine—for mine is specially *female*.

Nevertheless I spoke to Dr B about the arsenic— *And he* said '*he never* used Arsenic it was a medecine he disapproved entirely'— That 'he would meet Dr Carlyle in consultation if he

pleased—but *random* suggestions founded on no knowledge of
the case were not worth listening to'—

He himself has made a good many 'random suggestions,' it
seems to me—

And I am to take 'patience'—and 'keep up my spirits.' Oh if
you felt for one five minutes, the *torture* I have been feeling for
months, without hope of relief except in the grave—you would
not *dare* to tell me about *patience*.

See what a long letter I have written!— Tomorrow it will
probably be the old story— I shall get no sleep in the *new*
bed—and the *rubbing in* will no longer avail! It is strange
that I can take no joy in my *present* ease—but I do not—I
dare not—I have been so often mocked with momentary
improvements. . . .

Oh you may understand my state, when wishing ardently
to live, for *your* sake and other sakes, I nevertheless pass no day
without wishing myself *dead*—out of my misery / Bless you /
Jane Carlyle. . . .

*

117 Marina / Friday [29 April 1864]

. . . What quantities of things I have to tell you—if I had my poor
soul freed from the pressure of physical torment.

Oh my Dear my Dear, shall I ever make fun for you
again?—Or is our life together indeed past and gone? I want so
much to *live*—to be to you more than I have ever been—but I
fear I fear!—As yet your / own affectionate / Jane Carlyle

MARY RUSSELL   NLS 608.629A
Thornhill

. . . [3 May 1864]

My darling Mary

You will be glad, I know, to see the poor old handwriting
again; and will infer from it, that I am given back to the living
world— — But you must not be too sanguine about my
recovery— I am still hanging between Life and death, only, for
the last few days I have been freed from the torture that has
distracted me these many months back— It may return—most
likely will return and be all the more intolerable by contrast
with this breath of ease—

So I make haste, while I can still do my own will, to write you these few lines, just to say I have thought of you and loved you always thro these dismal months of silence.... I have no strength for more....

LOUISA LADY ASHBURTON   NLS Acc. 11388.28
The Grange

[25 May 1864]

I do so want to write you a long letter dearest Lady Ashburton, and to thank you rightly for your two dear kind letters to me. But alas I cannot ....

I waited for you so anxiously yesterday Mr C went to meet you at the railway. Your letter did not come till four o'clock—

Shall I see you? I should give much to kiss your dear face again. They say I shall get well *in time* but I don't believe it— / Ever yours anyhow / living or dying Jane Carlyle

MARY RUSSELL   NLS 608.630
Thornhill

[31 May 1864]

... Oh my dearest Mary your kind invitations to Holmhill draw tears from my heart. Alas my Darling you have no idea I perceive of the critical, miserable state I am in .... You speak of my 'arm'—my *arm* is nothing in it now—for months my arm has been all right—the misery has been a more terrible thing, an everlasting torture in my womb—it is not a cancer or any such thing—the Drs say, only a nervous affection—but all the same the suffering attending it is beyond all words to tell ....

Oh *my* Mary shall I live to see your dear face again?— God only knows— I am *very* miserable ....

TC   NLS 608.635, 644
Cheyne Row

The Gill / Thursday
[21 July 1864]

Oh what a fool I was to dream that by putting myself on a railway I could get whirled away from my misery! or that there was any place quiet enough for *me* to sleep in but the grave! I *could* not write a line yesterday—and perhaps no news was better than the bad news I might have sent.

Not one wink of sleep all night and *the pain* raging! *that* was all I got by my long drive from Dumfries where John over-persuaded me to go to shake off my headache— I have put hundreds of miles between us—and am as ill and *need* you as much as ever.— Last night I got a little sleep towards morning all the animals are shut up on the premises but the railway screechs and roars all thro' the night, and other peoples dogs bark all about.

The porridge, like every thing else succeeded *once*— I have had to go back to my magnesia . . . .

*

Holme Hill, [Thornhill] / Wednesday [3 Aug. 1864]

Dearest / I write today less unwilling, for, thank God, I can report a *second* night with *some* sleep in it. not much; nor sound; but to have *slept at all* two nights running is a blessed novelty in my life. There had been grave consultation between Dr Russell and me, whether I should try that *Indian Hemp*— Dr Quain had given it me in the winter without result; but Dr Russell judged from its having been given twice or thrice during the *day*, that the trial had not been fairly made—it should be taken he says in *one* doze at bedtime. . . . Poor Mrs Russell is in raptures—I 'shall soon be all right now'—am 'getting like myself again'!— Ah! she has not seen enough of me yet, to know how soon these gleams of wellness fade away, and I am plunged again into torture and despair

These maids are perfectly disgusting—when I compare them with the servants *here* who wear no crinolines, and have heads that they *make use of*, I am impatient that I have no power to set all that to rights

One night it was windy and the open window of my dressing closet rattled—having no wedges I made it firm with four or five different bundles of paper—next day the papers had been removed, when the window was thrown up—but at night great was my admiration to find my paper-wedges all stuck back exactly as I had put them—and without a word said to, or by, the little housemaid! this has been done every night since!—the same attentive thoughtfulness marks her whole service.

I have a long lovely drive every day and when *the pain* is not too great I enjoy the sight of these old beautiful places—

Now I have written as much as I am up to—resting my

hand firmly on the paper to keep it sort of steady—which makes my writing more legible, I flatter myself— God help you and me. . . .

*

NLS 608.650
[11 Aug. 1864]

. . . John Carlyle appeared last evening to tea—he plays the part of *consulting Physician* here which I find a farce—When I needed his help—if he had had any, at the Gill, he only aggravated me with brutal impertinence. As I was more even than usually *ill* with my *pain* last evening, he kept assuring me I 'looked well—fuller in the face' —

Last night was bad, but not the worst sort—I tossed about—till two—then took my wine and after that, *waking sleep* till six. . . . / Now goodby—your own / Jane Carlyle

On a mild clear day, 1 October, John Carlyle came back with her to Cheyne Row: 'by far the gladdest sight', wrote Thomas, 'I shall ever see here. . . . Her life to the very end continued beautiful and hopeful to both of us,—to me more beautiful than I had ever seen it in her best days' (**LM** *2:215*). *At the end of January, with immense relief, he wrote the last sentence of* **Frederick***.*

Chapter Twelve

The Perfectly Extraordinary Woman, 1865-66

Early in March they went happily to stay for a month in Devon with Lady Ashburton.

[MARGARET OLIPHANT] Private MS

Seaforth Lodge / 29*th* March [1865]

...Oh, what a Place this is for lovers of the Picturesque! Such a sea! Such cliffs! the one so blue! the other so white! My head was quite turned at first, with all this 'beautiful nature'; and I had 'a moment of enthusiasm' in which I was near persuading Mr C to buy a Devonshire Craigenputtoch to be sold extraordinarily cheap! Pine-trees, and wild heaths, and black bog! a hundred acres of it! and in the midst, a charming House built in the style of a Convent! The speculation was wrecked by my answering to Mr C's fear I should 'die of the Solitude, in six months' — 'Oh no! for I will keep constant Company.' George 2*d's 'Non! J'aurai des maitresses!'* couldnt have given a greater shock!' — My chief indeed only discontents here, have been from my *Lady's Maid* who has put me in a rage at least once every day. Ever affly / your Jane Carlyle

Lord Ashburton had died, 23 March 1864.

LOUISA LADY ASHBURTON NLS Acc. 11388.28
The Grange

5 Cheyne Row, Chelsea [7 April 1865]

My Darling! My Darling! If I have not written it hasn't been for want of thought! God knows I have thought of you every hour of the day, and I may almost say every hour of the night too! I have lain awake so much! ...And I shall see you soon again? Oh my Dearest, my Beautifulest! my Best! I love you better than words can tell! And Mr C loves you or he wouldnt (don't I know his ways?) take the trouble of reading your letters (to *me*).

This morning, I thought I heard him go into the Drawing room just as I finished reading the last. (He breakfasts there while I am getting up in the adjoining bedroom). There is a door out of the one room into the other, thro' which I sometimes hand him a letter from *you*, while I am only half-dressed. So this morning, being in my petticoat, I opened this door, extending into the room a bare arm, with the letter, saying 'There is for you Dear'! Receiving no answer, I looked into the room, and so brought my *whole* petticoated person in evidence! And, my Heavens, it was not Mr C at all but George Cooke! Come to look at a Horse for me, that I was just about buying; my petticoat was *red* too! ... Will you give the Pet [her daughter Mary] my fondest remembrances / your loving and faithful / Henrietta Muff

TC   NLS 609.709, 737
Scotsbrig
                                    5 Cheyne Row / Wednesday
                                                [24 May 1865]

...And then I did the civil thing to Mrs Froude. Froude was in, and talked much of *your* 'gentleness and tenderness—of late'!— and the 'much greater *patience* you had in speaking of every body and every thing'— And I thought to myself 'if he had only *heard* you, a few hours after that walk with him in which you had made such a lamb-like impression.' He expressed a wish to read Mrs Paulets novel. And I have sent it to him. A very curious, clever, '*excessively ridiculous*, and *perfectly unnecessary*' Book is Mrs Paulets novel!—so far as I have read in the *first* volume! And Mrs Paulet herself I don't know what to make of! For I have seen her! In my saintly Forgiveness, and beautiful Pity, I left a card for her yesterday, and she came a few hours after, and Geraldine too came, and I was not left alone till half past ten; when it was too late to write....

One thing I have to say that I beg you will give ear to! I have not recovered yet the shock it was to me to find after six months all those weak wretched letters I wrote you from Holmhill, 'dadding [scattering] about' in the Diningroom!—and should you use my letters in that way again, I shall know it by instinct and not write to you at all! There! ...Your ever affectionate....

*

[27 July 1865]

...And Lady A did come last night Came at half after eleven! and
staid till near one! Mrs Anstruther was left sitting in the carriage
and sent up to say 'it was on the stroke of twelve'— And then
with Lady A's permission I invited her up—and if it had not been
for her I dont think Lady A would have gone *till* daylight! She
said in going 'My regards—my—*what* shall I send to *Him*
(you)—''Oh, I said send him a kiss!'— '*That is just what I should
like* she said but would he not think it forward'— 'Oh dear! not
at all' I said— So you are to consider yourself *kissed*....

*Lady Katherine Louise Russell (once Kate Stanley) was one of Lord
Edward J. Stanley's many daughters, of whom Jane was increasingly
fond.*

LADY AMBERLEY   NLS 1808.106
                                        5 Cheyne Row / Chelsea
                                           7*th* Novr [1865]

'Hope I don't mind your writing to me?!'— Oh you
bewitching little Darling! *I do* 'mind' it though!—very much!
Only— there are *two* ways of *minding*; and my way of
minding any token of kind remembrance from you is *not* to
be hoped *against*! ...The idea of a Baby Boy of *your own* is
an idea to stand amazed before, 'as in presence of the
Infinite'!— I must see Him before I shall be able to clearly
believe in Him, as an accomplished fact! And then—if He be
really so like his Mother—I think I should like to— eat Him.
He must be so nice!

What a mercy you *found out* that Ogresse before she had
done any irreperable mischief! Poor little Child! I can
especially sympathize with him under the *Gin*; for my own
Nurse used to put *me* into dead sleep with *whisky*, when she
had assignations outside! And my Mother was always of opinion
that my sleeplessness in after Life was owing to having been
drunk so often as a Baby!! *I* privately believed, it was owing
rather to the interminable lessons I had to learn! You won't
over-excite the Brain of your little one with 'Lessons,' will you?
when the time comes? There are more ways than one of
'making little Children pass thro' the fire to Moloch,' and that of
making them prodigies of Instruction at the cost of their bits of
nervous systems seems to me sadder than any other way; for is it

not a sort of 'seething of the kid in its mother's milk'?—And
after all, teach and teach what you will; what Gibbon said
remains true, that 'Instruction is hardly of any use except in
cases where it is almost superfluous'! ...

Where on Earth, or under it, do you imagine Mr Carlyle is
going this evening? First he is to dine with your Brother
(Colonel Stanley) at *The Travellers Club*, and then to be
conducted by him all thro' the *Slums*!! And no further gone than
last Friday (I think it was) He was dining with your Brother 'On
guard'!! People who hear of this intimacy predict from it
precious humanizing results for Mr C! ...

God bless you, Darling! / I am always affectionately / yours /
Jane W Carlyle

I went to the Study to ask Mr C if he had any message to
you— 'Well!— Oh— Yes—give Her my kindest regards.'—
'No!— I said—if a man of Genius like you has nothing more
original than *that* to say, it isn't worth sending!'— As I went
upstairs he opened his door and called after me— 'My Dear!—
I'll tell you what you can say! that she is a bonnie Woman'!

MARY CRAIK   Strouse
Belfast

28*th* Novr [1865]

... Oh my little Woman! my little Woman! Were it another than
you, I should't have the face to write you at all,—*now*,—at this
date!! ...

The fact is my Dear, I should need to be *born* over again,
into the Time of *Penny Post*! My actual Birth occurred when
postage was at a shilling and thereabouts, and it was a natural
consequence that people should make their letters long and
deliberate, to be worth the money they would cost. *Now*, one's
letter costs a penny and the penny paid by oneself; and the
nicest conscience neednt trouble itself how few lines, and
offhand the lines, that go to a letter on the present terms of
postage. Your modern Lady-letter may be written at any
moment under any distractions! but as I have said, I was born
too far back to adopt this free and easy little-note style—having
been early used to *filling* big square sheets when I wrote at all.
Now, I put off and put off always for 'some reasonably good
leisure' and *that* being a condition rarely vouchsafed me, with
one devilry and another; it happens—as it has happened in

your case, that I often give myself the airs of a Brute, without being brutal the least in the world!

But if anything is more stupid than leaving a dear friends letters unanswered; it is answering them with a cart load of apologies. . . .

MARY RUSSELL NLS 609.760A
Thornhill

24*th* Decemr [1865]

. . .When I told you I had been off my sleep; I told you did I not that I had been WORRIED off it? . . . But the grand worry of all— that which perfected my sleeplessness, was an importation of nine hens and a magnificent *Cock* (!!!) into the adjoining garden! For years back there has reigned over all these Gardens a heavenly quiet! thanks to my heroic exertions in exterminating nuisances of every description! But I no longer felt the hope or the energy in me requisite for such achievements! Figure then my horror, my despair, on being waked one dark morning with the crowing of a *Cock*—that seemed to issue from under my bed! I leapt up, and rushed to my dressing room window; but it was still all darkness! I lay with my heart in my mouth, listening *to* the Cock, crowing hoarsely from time to time, and listening *for* Mr C's foot stamping frantically, as of old, on the floor above!— But strangely enough, He gave no sign of having heard his Enemy!—his whole attentions, having been, ever since his visit to Mrs Aitkens, morbidly devoted to—*Railway whistles*!

So soon as it was daylight I looked out again, and *there* was a sight to see!— A ragged *irish* looking hen-house, run up over night; and, sauntering to and fro, nine goodly hens, and a *stunning* Cock!— I didn't know whether Mr C remained really deaf as well as blind to these new neighbours; or whether he was only magnanimously resolved to observe silence about them; but it is a fact, that for a whole week he said no word to enlighten me—while I expected and expected the crisis which would surely come! and shuddered at every Cock-Crow, and counted the number of times he crowed in a night! at two! at three! at four! at five! at six! at seven! Oh terribly at seven!— For a whole week I bore my hideous secret in my breast! and slept none to speak of! At the weeks end I fell into one of my old sick headaches. I used always to find a sick headache had a fine effect in clearing the wits! So, even this time, I rose from a day's agony with a scheme of operations in my head, and a sense of ability to 'carry it out'!

It would be too long to go into details, enough to say, my negociations with 'Nextdoor' ended in an agreement that the Cock should be shut up in a cellar inside the owner's own house—from three in the afternoon till ten in the morning! and in return I give the small boy of the house a lesson every morning in his *Reading Made Easy*!! The small Boy being 'too excitable' for being sent to school!— It is a house full of *Misteries No 6*! I have thoughts of writing a novel about it. Meanwhile Mr C declares me to be his *'Guardian Angel'*!— No sinecure I can tell him! ...

CHARLOTTE SOUTHAM   Chelsea Public Library
                                        ... 26*th* Decemr [1865]

Dear little Woman!

I have been literally *drowned* in letters; for some weeks back; and *off* my sleep at the same time, which makes my head not worth twopence for writing with.

This—and not neglectfulness of you, has been the reason I did not thank you sooner for that other and better photograph of yourself. Even this one does you no justice—at least does you no justice *when you* are GOOD. But— I HAVE SEEN you sufficiently like it when the Devil had got into you, and spread a sort of *cloud* of sullenness over your naturally kind and intelligent look! Oh yes! When I first knew you, and for long after, you were the nicest, brightest looking creature, one could wish to see!— Pity one can't keep always young!—

I am not *well*, ever, but I have not been positively *ill* this long time. . . .

Mr C is much in his usual health—taking his fill of idleness,—if *reading* all day long can be called idleness! He will have to go to Edinr to make a Speech the last week of March—if the weather keeps favourable and my health *ditto*, I shall perhaps accompany him. . . .

MARY DODS   NLS 1797.106
Haddington

                                        22*d* January / 1866

... I have written no letters that I could avoid since new year time, when I had a *surfeit* of letter writing, complicated with a cold in the head—lasting (the cold) I cant say how long; for it is not yet done with! Now, a cold in the head is hardly an indisposition '*to speak of*'! Nobody dies of it, and nobody pities it—much!—Nevertheless it makes one very sodden and abject!—gives one the feeling of being crammed full of *Wool*! especially one's head! ...

If this wonderful temperature would last a while, one might hope to bloom up again like the green things in the Garden. The Laburnum and Hawthorn which your Husband once sent me from Sunny Bank are actually budding! and all the bits of flowers and weeds brought from my different far away Homes are shooting out of the ground. Not one day since I returned from Folkstone in September have I failed to drive out for some three hours, except the two days of the Snow a fortnight ago, when the very Omnibuses stuck up. What the present fine weather may bode for the end of March; who can tell? ... But this much is certain, as far as anything *can* be certain under Heaven! *If* I go to Edin*r*, I will go to Haddington and, on the strength of your kind invitation, make your House my resting place for the brief time I may have to spare! I *should* like to look about in the dear old place again, and at the few known faces remaining to me! I used to feel, after Sunny-Bank fell desolate, that I *could not* face so many graves and empty Houses (empty for ME) ever more! But since my terrible, long, and painful illness, strange to say, my *nerves* are much *stronger* than they were before! Or is it, that they are only *deadened*? Any how, I feel *now* that I could look at my old Home without crying myself to Death.

It was a most provoking disappointment to me, missing you and your Husband when you called here. I say *provoking* because of the wilful mismanagement!! ...

I continued to be *vexed* and angry with you for ever so long! And would have put these sentiments in a letter, following you home; but for the good reason, that then, and for four or five months after, I had no use of my right hand and arm! Couldnt so much as feed myself therewith! My meat had to be cut for me as for a Baby! I had to learn to make strange writing with my *left* hand, and to do with my left hand everything that absolutely must not be left undone! This was the style of thing thro' out! [*Evidently writing with her left hand*]. The Doctors ordered me back to Dumfrieshire which had done me so much good the year before. I stayed

there six weeks without any perceptible benefit, and returned
home in the worst spirits. The night after my return, being
dead weary, I fell into such a long deep sleep, that, when I
awoke, I had not only forgotten *where* I was! but forgotten
utterly *who* I was!! I remember maundering to myself; 'It can't
be *me* who has had *this* nice long sleep! who am I, I
wonder'!! I had not had such a nights rest, poor wretch! for
two years! and to complete the miracle the neuralgia had
gone out of my hand and arm entirely and has never returned
to this hour! Yes! if it hadn't been for the pain in my arm you
would have got a thundering scold from me for that stupid
business....

*Servant problems still bothered her and, as Jessie Hiddlestone
recalled, her mistress often returned late from evening parties: what
Carlyle called her 'Career of Dissipation' helped her sleep. Jessie also
remembered how untroublesome Carlyle was, and how Jane 'spared
nobody in her talk' and 'was very jealous if he showed a liking for
anyone'* (Wilson, **Carlyle** 6:33, 35). *The time came round for Carlyle to
give his Inaugural Address as Rector of Edinburgh University, on Easter
Monday, 2 April. Though he at first accepted reluctantly, it was to receive
general approval and to mark the crown of his success. Professor John
Tyndall collected Carlyle on 29 March, and, as they parted, Jane 'kissed
me twice (she me once, I her a second time)'—his one hope 'to get back
to her again'* (**Reminiscences** 188). *They stopped at Milnes' home in
Yorkshire, met Thomas Huxley who was also to be honoured and
Carlyle gave time to preparing the address. At home a sleepless Jane was
joined by Maggie Welsh.*

TC   NLS 609.767
Edinburgh

                                        5 Cheyne Row / 2*d* April [1866]

...What I have been suffering, vicariously, of late days is not to
be told! If you had been to be *hanged*, I don't see that I could
have taken it more to heart. This morning, after about two
hours of off-and-on sleep, I awoke—long before daylight—to
sleep no more....

When the thing is *over* I shall be content—however it
have gone.... That you have made your 'address' and are
alive—that is what I long to hear, and please God *shall* hear in
a few hours! My 'Imagination' has gone the length of

representing you getting up to speak before an awful crowd of
people; and what with fuss and 'bad air' and confusion
dropping down dead!—

Why on Earth did you ever get into this galley? / JWC

LOUISA LADY ASHBURTON   NLS Acc. 11388.28
Seaton, Devon

[2 April 1866]

Dearest, Sweetest, Beautifullest! . . . You should have seen the
arrival of the Telegram. . . . You may conceive how my heart
leapt in my throat. . . . I read it to myself, then read it aloud to
my Cousin staying with me, & both the maids, who all waited
gaping for the contents, & forthwith fell to clapping their
hands & ejaculating like a Greek Chorus.'Eh, the Maister! Hear
to *that*! Hurrah—'! cried the Scotch Housemaid; '*I* told you
Mam! *I* knew how it would be'! cried the Cook; 'He, he, he, tee,
tee, tee, *how nice*'! cried the Cousin hopping round me—and
then the chorus combined in a cry for—*Brandy*! —'Where's
the brandy?'. . .'Don't you see the Mistress is *going* off'?'
'*Where* TO?' I asked in the midst of my outburst of weeping; all
my life I have so hated to be thought hysterical; but I
swallowed the Brandy. . . .

All these last letters were to Thomas, who stayed a short while in
Edinburgh before departing for Scotsbrig and Dumfries. They show
Jane's anxiety, quick ear for gossip and glow of pride in his success. 'I
haven't been so fond of everybody,' she wrote to Moncure Conway, 'and
so pleased with the world, since I was a girl as in these days when
reading the letters of his friends'. Carlyle then distinguished himself by
twisting his ankle.

TC   NLS 609.769, 771, 776, 778-80, 782-4
Edinburgh

[3 April 1866]

. . . Mrs Warren and Maggie were helping to dress me for
Forster's Birth-day when the Telegraph Boy gave his double
knock— 'There it is!' I said. 'I am afraid cousin, it is only the
Post-man' said Maggie. Jessie rushed up with the Telegram. I
tore it open and read '*From John Tyndall* (Oh God bless John
Tyndall in this world and the next!) *to Mrs Carlyle. A perfect*
triumph.' . . .

I went to Forsters nevertheless with my Telegram in my hand and 'John Tyndall' in the core of my heart! And it was pleasant to see with what hearty good will all there, Dickens, Wilkie Collins, as well as Fuzz [Forster], received the news. And we drank your health with great glee! Maggie came in the evening and Fuzz in his joy over you, sent out a glass of Brandy to Silvester!! Poor Silvester by the by showed as much glad *emotion* as anybody on my telling him that you had got well thro' it! ... I am *smashed* for the present / JWC

*

[4 April 1866]

...Well! I do think you might have sent me a *Scotsman* this morning; or ordered one to be sent! I was up and dressed at 7, and it seemed such an interminable time till a quarter after nine when the Postman came, bringing only a note about— Cheltenham, from Geraldine!

The letter I had from Tyndall yesterday might have satisfied any ordinary man—or woman; you would have said. But I dont pretend to be an ordinary man—or woman I am perfectly *extra*ordinary; especially in the power I possess of fretting and worrying myself into one fever after another, without any cause to speak of!

What do you suppose I am worrying about *now*, because of the Scotsman having *not* come?

That there may be in it something about your having FALLEN ILL—*which you wished me not to see*! *This* I am capable of fancying at moments. ... It was so kind of Macmillan to come to me—*before he had slept*. He had gone in the morning straight from the Railway to his Shop & work— He seemed still under the *Emotion* of the Thing— Tears starting to his black eyes every time he mentioned any *moving* part!!—

Now just look at that! If here isn't—at half after eleven, when nobody looks for the Edinr post—your letter—*two* newspapers, and letters from my Aunt Anne, Thomas Erskine, David Aitken besides.

I have only as yet read *your* letter. The rest will keep NOW— ...What pleases me most in this business—I mean the business of your *success* is the hearty *personal affection towards you* that comes out on all hands. These men at Forsters, with there cheering, our own people; even old

Silvester turning as white as a sheet, and his lips quivering when he tried to express his gladness over the telegraph, *all that* is positively delightful, and makes the success 'a good joy' to me. No appearance of envy or grudging in anybody, but one general, loving, heartfelt throwing up of caps with young and old, male and female! If we could only *Sleep* Dear, and what you call '*digest*'; wouldn't it be nice? ...

Oh Dear I wish you had been coming straight back....
Affly / Jane W Carlyle

A sharp exchange broke out between Jane and Abraham Hayward about Governor Eyre, at Lady William Russell's. Hayward, a barrister, writer and translator of **Faust**, *took a humanitarian stand about Eyre's fierce suppression of a black revolt in Jamaica, which a government report had just declared excessive if vigorous. Jane's loyalty to Carlyle was equally prompt.*

Scotsbrig

[10 April 1866]

... Frederick Elliot, and—Hayward!—were at Lady Williams. Hayward was raging against the Jamaica business—would have had Eyre cut into *small pieces* and eaten him raw.— He told me *women* might patronize Eyre—that women were naturally cruel, and rather *liked* to look *on while horrors* were perpetrated. But no MAN living could stand up for Eyre *now*! 'I hope Mr Carlyle does, I said. I haven't had an opportunity of asking him—but I should be surprised and grieved if I found HIM sentimentalizing over a pack of black brutes'!— After staring at me a moment, 'Mr *Carlyle*! said Hayward— Oh yes! Mr CARLYLE! one cannot indeed swear what *he* will *not* say! *His* great aim and philosophy of Life being '*the smallest happiness of the fewest number*!' ... Yours ever / Jane Carlyle

Send me a proof as soon as you can—

*

[12 April 1866]

... Well! there only wanted, to complete your celebrity, that you should be in the chief place of Punch! And there you are, cape & wideawake, making a really creditable appearance.... From *Punch* to Terry, the green grocer, is a good step; but let me tell you he (Terry) asked Mrs Warren; *was* Mr Carlyle the person they wrote of as *Lord Rector*, and Mrs Warren having answered in her stage voice 'the *very* same'! Terry shouted out—'(quite *shouted* it Mam!)' 'I never was so glad of anything—by George!—I *am* glad!' Both Mrs. Warren and Jessy rushed out and bought *Punches* to send to their families; and in the fervour of their mutual enthusiasm they have actually ceased hostilities—for *the* PRESENT. It seems to me that on every new compliment paid you, these women run and *fry something*, such savoury smells reach me up stairs! . . .

Don't forget about my oatmeal!— Edgar Yorstoun *died* . . . of having her oat cakes stopt when she went on a visit to Bath. . . .

Congratulations poured in, including John Mill's letter in reply to a copy of the Rectorial Address Jane had sent him as their old friend and adversary.

[13 April 1866]

. . . There came a note for you last night, that will surprise you at this date, as much as it did me, tho' I dare say it wont make you start and give a little scream as it did me. It—such a note—is hardly more friendly than silence, but it is more polite— I wish I hadn't sent him that kind message. Virtue (forgiveness of wrongs, 'milk of human kindness,' and all that sort of 'damned thing') being 'ever its own reward,'—'unless something particular occurs to prevent,'—'*which* is, almost invariably'!— . . .

There—I must get ready for that blessed carriage.— I have been *redding up* all morning / Ever yours / J W Carlyle

It would be good to send back Mills letter. . . .

If Thomas was missed, there was much to occupy her, though Sarah Dilberoglue wrote to Charlotte Cushman on 19 December that she had called on Jane about a week before, and that as usual she was too exhausted to write. Sarah had been much impressed with the extemporaneity of the Rectorial Address, and says that Jane told her how Carlyle found that prepared notes 'only impeded the free flow of speech—he would have no more of them—that in fact he seemed to ignore the idea of having to go to Scotland at all'.

[15 April 1866]

... It seems to me, in a vague way, that I have a good many things to tell you; if I could only bring my mind to bear on them; but my mind, I regret to say, is all 'dadded abreed,' at the present writing, by a horrid fit of sickness and headache which took me so soon as I rose this morning. I hadnt slept worse than usual—nay, for the last hour my sleep had been the sleep of a stone—but so soon as I began to dress, I turned oh so deadly sick! and as *you* were not there to force 'some breakfast' on me, I went on retching and fainting, till midday. But I went for my drive, all the same, at one; and having engaged to *lunch* with Lady Airlie, I turned it into *breakfasting* with her.... After luncheon ... Blanche conducted me to her conservatory to see 'poor Lady Giffords Monkey.' A weezened little Devil that Huxley would take to his heart! 'Significant of *much*'!— But why do you say *poor* Lady Gifford' I asked. The answer was sad enough; 'Don't you know? She has just had an operation for *cancer*; one of her breasts taken off.'—and Lady Elsmere underwent the same operation two weeks ago, they were saying at Lady William's— *Dying* one's hair with a cancer in one's breast! If *that* isn't a kind of Spartanism; *what* is it?—

I drove from Airlie Lodge to Lady William's, to inquire for Arthur, who had been two days in bed with Influenza. Arthur hearing my voice came out of his room, and made me come in, and sent for 'Madame.' If I found in Madame *a dash of Acrobate* before today I found her all acrobate with only *a dash of Lady*! She looked coarse, hard, comfortless! hands that seemed to have done much dirty work, and to have remained unwashed! hair all *toozy* [ruffled] like a Byremaid's! face that reminded me of hoeing turnips! A gown in the worst taste, of a sort of dirty brown, neither loose nor fitting, without a morsel of white collar or frill round the neck! Nor was her countenance such as made one overlook her details— Believe me she had the bored, somewhat ill tempered look of an acrobate *out of an engagement*. She will *flirt* that woman; and come to grief—at least Arthur will!

I had a nice little teaparty the night before last; and it 'passed over' like a breakfast in Deerbrook 'pleasantly'!— Miss Bromley, Saffi and Madame Saffi, Geraldine, Mr Twislton, and George Cooke. Mr Twisleton 'was meant' to *take to* Miss Bromley; but, instead, he took—very decidedly too—to the bright little Patriot-Wife! ...

Ruskin is going off to the Continent with the Trevelyans. I called for his mother on Friday / Now good night / JWC

Did you hear that Fryston Hall was *on fire* two days after you left?

*

[17 April 1866]

... Oh my Dear! These *women* are too tiresome! Time after time I have sworn to send on none of their nonsense but to burn it or let it lie; as I do all about '*Christ*'! ...

I called at the Royal Institution yesterday to ask if Tyndall had returned. He was there; and I sat some time with him in his room, hearing the minutest details of your doings and sufferings on the journey. It is *the* event of Tyndalls Life! ... I called at Miss Bromleys after. She had dined at the Marochetti's on Saturday, being to go with them to some Spectacle after.— the *Spectacle* she saw without any *going*, was a GREAT FIRE of Marochetti's Studio— Furnaces overheated in casting Landseers '*Great* Lion.'

I do entreat you not to cramm your foot into a shoe, till the swelling is quite fallen. Sprains are one of many things that cant and wont be made well *par vive force*.

How dreadful that poor womans suicide! What a deal of misery it must take to drive a working [woman] to make away with her life! What does Dr [John] Carlyle make of such a case as that? No idleness nor luxury nor novel-reading to make it all plain. / Ever yours / JWC

*

[19 April 1866]

... I read the *Memoir* 'first' yesterday morning; having indeed read the 'Address' the evening before, and read it some three times in different Newspapers. If you call THAT 'Laudatory' you must be easily pleased! I never read such stupid vulgar *janners* [foolish talk; TC adds 'capital Scotch word']. The last of calumnies that I should ever have expected to hear uttered about you, was this of your going about 'filling the laps of dirty children with comfits'!— Idiot! *My* half pound of barley-sugar made into such a Legend! ...

I didnt write yesterday because in the first place I was very sick, and in the second place I got a moral shock [TC adds: 'What? I could never guess'] that stunned me *pro tempore* [for the time being]! No time to tell you about that just now—but another day

I have put the women to sleep in your bed to air it! It seems so long since you went away!

Imagine the tea party I am to have on *Saturday* NIGHT. Mrs Oliphant, Principal Tulloch and wife and two grown up daughters! Mr & Mrs Froude Mr and Mrs Spottiswood!!!! Did you give Jane the things I sent—when one sends a thing one likes to know if it have been received safe; Yours ever JWC [TC adds: 'I did; & told her so in the letter *she* never recd.— —Why shd I ever read this ag*n*!]

*

[21 April 1866]

... Dearest—it seems 'just a consuming of Time' to write today, when you are coming the day after tomorrow. But—'if there were nothing else in it' (*your* phrase) such a piece of liberality, as letting one have letters on Sunday if called for, should be honoured, at least by availing oneself of it! All *long* stories however may be postponed till next week.

Indeed, I have neither long stories nor short ones to tell this morning. Tomorrow, after the Teaparty, I may have more to say; provided I survive it! Tho', how I am to entertain on 'my own BASE,' eleven people, in a hot night '*without refreshment*' (to speak of) is more than I 'see *my way*' thro'! Even as to *cups*!— There *is* only *ten* cups of company-china, and *eleven* are coming; myself making 12! 'After all,' said Jessie; you had *once eight* at tea! *three* mair won't kill us'!— I'm not so sure of *that*!— Let us hope the motive will sanctify the end, being 'the welfare of others'!—an unselfish desire to 'make two *Baiings* happy'! Principal Tulloch and Froude who have a great liking for one another! The Spottiswoods were added in the same philanthropic spirit. We met in a shop, and they begged permission to come again; so I thought it would be clever to get them over (handsomely,—with Froude and Mrs Oliphant) before *you* came. They couldn't '*ask for more*' for a long time! Miss Wynn offered herself, by accident, for that same night. . . .

I saw in an old furniture shop window at Richmond a copy of the Frederick picture that was lent you. *not* bad— coarsly painted; but the likeness well preserved. Would you like to have it? I will, if so, make you a present of it—being to be had 'very equal'— I 'descended from' the carriage, and asked:'What was *that*?' (meaning what price was it)— The Broker told me impressively;'*that*, Mam, is *Peter the Great*.'Indeed! and what is the price?'—'seven & sixpence' I offered five *shillings* on the spot. but he would only come down to six shillings. I will go back for it if you like— and can find a place for it on my wall.— Yours ever JWC

The tea party never took place. Frederick's portrait now hangs in the dining room at Cheyne Row. That afternoon Jane left for an airing in Hyde Park taking her little pug dog Tiny. Set down for a run, he was grazed by a passing carriage, and taken back into the brougham, which drove on. Shortly after she was found dead. When she was taken home, the penitential candles (once bought by her mother) were lit, Carlyle was told and her last letter to him was delivered in Dumfries. As long agreed, she was buried in her father's grave in St Mary's Abbey, Haddington, on 26 April. It has Thomas's inscription:'She had more sorrows than are common; but also a soft invincibility, a clearness of discernment and a noble loyalty of heart, which are rare. For forty years she was the true and everloving helpmate of her husband; and by act and word unweariedly forwarded him, as none else could, in all of worthy that he did or attempted. She died at London, 21st April 1866; suddenly snatched away from him, and the light of his life as if gone out'.

Index

1. Index of Correspondents

Names are listed in their correct form where they differ from JWC's spelling, and are repeated in capital letters in the General Index. For complete reference use should be made of both indices.

Airlie, Lady, 227, 244, 281, 282, 283, 294
Aitken, Eliza (Stodart), 78
Allingham, William, 177, 190
Amberley, Lady, 305
Ashburton, Lady Harriet, 189
Ashburton, Louisa, Lady, 246, 248, 252, 259, 267, 291, 300, 303, 311
Austin, Mary, 285, 297

Baring, Lady Harriet, 135
Braid, Betty, 232, 240

Carlyle, Isabella, 181, 195, 231
Carlyle, James, 243
Carlyle, John Aitken, 155, 173, 177
Carlyle, Margaret (Aitken), 28, 56, 62
Carlyle, Thomas, 3, 5, 6, 7, 9, 10, 11, 12, 14, 16, 17, 22, 33, 45, 47, 49, 51, 64, 92, 93, 96, 105, 116, 122, 123, 144, 157, 171, 173, 176, 184, 187, 192, 227, 233, 234, 235, 274, 275, 297, 298, 299, 300, 301, 302, 304, 305, 310, 311, 312, 313, 314, 315, 316, 317, 318
Chamberlayne, Anne, 267
Chamberlayne, Maria, 276
Craik, George Lillie, 224
Craik, Mary, 306
'Cry from Craigenputtoch, The,' 198
Cushman, Charlotte, 263, 268, 277, 279

Davidson, David, 236
Dinning, Grace, 249
Dods, Mary, 273, 286, 289, 308
Dods, William, 254
Donaldson, Jessie, 183
Duffy, Charles Gavan, 118
Dwight, Elisabeth, 196

Eliot, George, 230, 238

Forster, John, 66, 136, 137

Inglis, Henry, 31

Jewsbury, Geraldine, 102, 241
Journal (1855-56), 205

Lamont, Martha, 99, 145, 272
Lytton, Lady Bulwer, 161

McTurk, Isabella, 25, 245, 251
Mantell, Walter, 261
Miles, Eliza, 26, 29
Milnes, Richard Monckton, 253
'Much ado about Nothing', 146

Neuberg, Joseph, 179
Notebook (1845-1852), 129

Oliphant, Margaret, 257, 261, 274, 303

Redwood, Charles, 175
Russell, Mary, 119, 179, 182, 192, 193, 194, 195, 223, 226, 228, 229, 232, 237, 246, 260, 272, 299, 300, 307

Sandwich, Lady, 266
Schwabe, Julie, 285
Simmonds, Isabella, 295
Smith, Mary, 221
Southam, Charlotte, 237, 290, 308
Stanley, Henrietta Maria, Lady, 242, 253, 278, 287
Stanley, Kate, 280
Sterling, John, 38, 41, 75
Sterling, Julia, 256

Sterling, Kate, 166, 170, 186
Stirling, Susan, 97, 243
Stodart, Eliza, 1, 2, 4, 8, 20, 21, 30, 35, 40
Stodart, John Riddell, 151, 169

Tait, Robert Scott, 249
Tennyson, Emily, 280
Trevelyan, Lady, 292
Twisleton, Ellen, 191, 252

Wedgwood, Frances, 86
Welsh, Anne, Grace & Elizabeth, 297

Welsh, Grace (aunt), 290
Welsh, Grace (JWC's mother), 52, 55, 58, 61, 67, 68, 69, 70, 71, 72, 73, 74, 77
Welsh, Helen, 23, 59, 67, 83, 106, 112, 120, 125, 131, 137, 138, 155, 158, 164, 168, 174
Welsh, Jeannie, 81, 84, 85, 87, 89, 99, 113, 140, 142, 154, 163, 165
Welsh, John, 43, 91, 109, 161
Welsh, Margaret (Kissock), 18
Welsh, Margaret (cousin Maggie), 80, 127
Woolner, Thomas, 255

2. General Index

As a help to identification dates are given for some figures in the Carlyles' circle. Authors' works and characters are usually given under the authors' names. Maiden and other names are also given in brackets.

Aberdeen, 92–3
Aberdour, 241–2
Addiscombe (Farm), 89–90, 120, 154, 156, 179–80, 191–2, 219, 227, 232
AIRLIE, Lady Henrietta Blanche (Stanley, 1829–1921), xvii–xviii, 255, 315
Aitken, Rev. David (1796–1875), 37, 152, 312
AITKEN, Eliza (Stodart; d. 1869), 45, 144, 152
Aitken, James, 5
Aitken, Jean (Carlyle; 1810–88), xviii, 307
Albert, Prince Consort, 283
Alderley, 254, 278
Alexandra, Princess, 291
Allen, Dr Matthew (1783–1845), 24
Allen, Sarah (mother of drowned children, William and Arthur), 209–10, 212–3
ALLINGHAM, William (1824–89), 176
Alsdorf, Baron, 51
AMBERLEY, Lady (Kate; formerly Stanley), 281, 295, 305
America, Americans, 61, 94, 189, 196, 206–7, 271
    visitors, 42, 89–90, 97, 99–100, 133
    proposed visit, 59

Angus, Robby, 5
Animal Magnetism; see also mesmerism, xxvii, 108–11
Anstruther, Mrs Mary F. (Louisa, Lady Ashburton's sister), 305
Ariosto, 30
ASHBURTON, Lady Harriet (formerly Baring; Montagu; 1805–57), xiii–xiv, xxxi, 51, 88–90, 113–4, 117, 119–21, 125–6, 137, 140–4, 154, 156–8, 165–8, 179, 184, 186, 192–5, 204–5, 208, 212–3, 219, 225–6, 232, 237–8, 246
ASHBURTON, Louisa, Lady (Stewart Mackenzie; 1827–1903), xv–xvi, xix, xxxi, 237–8, 242, 244–8, 252, 254, 260, 274, 280, 282–5, 288, 291, 298, 303, 305
Ashburton, William Bingham Baring (1799–1864), 2nd Lord, xv, xviii, 51, 125–6, 140, 158, 165, 175, 179, 191–2, 216, 227, 232, 235, 238, 242, 244, 248, 252, 271, 275, 280–6, 288, 291–2, 298
Athenaeum, 108–9
Ashurst, Emily, see Venturi
Auchtertool (Fife), 144, 174, 192, 220, 241

AUSTIN, Mary (Carlyle, TC's sister at the Gill; 1808-88), 132, 220, 232, 245, 296
Austin, Sarah (1793-1867), 34-35, 37, 203, 208
Austria, Austrians, 96, 137, 285

Badams, Dr John (d. 1833) and wife, 14, 24
Bagley, William, xxiv
Baillie, Capt. James (JWC's cousin), 102, 215-6
Baird, Gen., 100
Baird, James, 5
Balfour, David (temperance worker), 129-31
Ballantyne, Thomas (1806-71), 188
Ballencrieff ball, 241
Balzac, H. de, 161
Bamford, Samuel (1788-1872), 124
Bancroft, Elizabeth, 135
Baring relatives, 242, 291-2
Baring, Emily, 235
Baring, Rev. Frederick, 244
BARING, Lady Harriet, see Ashburton
Baring, Mary Florence (1860-1902), 252-4, 259, 267-8, 304
Baring, William Bingham, see Ashburton
Barjarg library, 30, 33
Barlow, Rev. John (1799?-1869), 217
Barnes, Dr A., 273, 296
Barnsbury Park, 266, 270
Bath House, 189, 205-6, 208, 216, 218, 284, 291
ball at, 155-6
Bay House, 119
'Bear, the', see Ellice
Beethoven, 6
beggar prosecuted by A. Sterling, 160
Belfast, 145
Berlin, 224
Biffin, Sarah (1784-1850), 295
Blair, Prof. Hugh, 4
Blakiston, Mrs Bessie (Barnet), 296
Blakiston, Dr Peyton (1801-78), 296-9
Blanc, Louis, 141-2
Blessington, Marguerite, Countess of (1789-1849), 58
'blue marks' on wrists incident, xvi, xxxi, 220

Blunt, Rev. Dr Gerald Wilson, 273, 296
Bodleian Library, 45, 47-8
Bölte, Amalie C.E.M. (1811-91), xxiii-xxiv, 108-10, 113, 122, 137, 252-3
Bologna, 96, 170-1, 272
Bonheur, Rosa, 266
Botkin, Vassily P., 233-4
Bradford, 144-6
Bradfute, John, 37, 50
BRAID, Betty, 4, 127, 144, 163, 262
Brescia, 270
Brighton, 187-9, 256
Broke (or Brooke), Lady E.-Z. Capell, 208
Bromley, Catherine Davenport, 274-5, 279, 315-6
Brontë, Charlotte, xxi, 5, 157, 224-5, 274
Brontë, P. Branwell, 225
Brontë, Patrick (father), xxi
Brookfield, Jane Octavia (Elton; 1821-96), 204, 225
Brown (the Sterlings' servant), 73
Brown, Anne, 132-3, 138, 207, 223
Browning, Elizabeth Barrett, xxiv, 165
Browning, Robert, 70, 111, 165, 204, 220
Bryden (spirit dealer), 34
Buchan, Henry David (1783-1857), 12th Earl, 295
Buddha, 194
'Budget of a Femme incomprise', xxv, 184-6
Buller, Charles, Snr (1774-1848), xxiii, 9, 80-1, 89-90
Buller, Charles (1806-48), 9, 89, 126, 137, 141, 206
Buller, Isabella (d. 1849), xxiii, 80-1, 89, 110, 132, 137, 140
Burns, Robert, 15, 254
Burns, Tommy, 45
Butler, Mrs Pierce (Fanny Kemble), 42
Byron, Lord George, 4, 10

Caldesi, L. (photographer), 249
Campan, Jeanne L.H., 31
canaries, 195-6, 232, 255
Carlton Club, 49, 88
Carlyle, Alexander (TC's brother; 1797-1876), xviii, 2, 20-1, 200-1

Carlyle, Alexander (nephew; 1843–1931),
    xiv, xvi, xviii, xxx, 220, 296
CARLYLE, Isabella (Calvert; d. 1859), 181
Carlyle, James (TC's father; 1758–1832),
    23
CARLYLE, James (TC's brother Jamie;
    1807–90), 193
Carlyle, Jane Baillie Welsh; see also
    Chronology, Editors' Introduction
    and Thomas Carlyle
    (1815–26): birth, and father's death 1;
    early studies, 2, 5; tutored by
    Irving who visits with TC, 2;
    friendship with George Rennie,
    3–4; discusses reading, 4–7; TC's
    guidance and her father's
    influence, 6–8; her wish to guide
    'genius,' 8; refuses Irving's
    invitation to London, 9; her
    mother's supervision, 10; advises
    TC against translating Schiller,
    11–12; refuses to think of living at
    Craigenputtoch, 12–13; admits
    former love for Irving, 15–17;
    declares love for TC, and marriage,
    17–19
    (1828–34): daily life at
    Craigenputtoch, 20–22; writes to
    TC in London, 22–3; joins him,
    23–4; friends and excursions, 24;
    lodgings in Ampton St, 25–6;
    return to Craigenputtoch, 26–7;
    various difficulties, servant
    troubles and cholera, 27–8; books
    from Barjarg, 30–1; Emerson's
    visit, 32; leaves for London, 33–4
    (1834–42): Cheyne Row, 35–7; Rennie
    again, 36–7; John Sterling on
    Sartor, 38–9; the elder Sterlings,
    40–1; Carlyle's reputation, 42;
    lecturing, 44; reception of French
    Revolution, 45–6; at Oxford, 47–8;
    Malvern, 49–50; a reading at Leigh
    Hunt's, 51–2; D'Orsay and others,
    53–5, 58; lectures (1839), 55–7;
    her health, and a railway journey,
    59–60; Christmas (1839), 58–9;
    Helen Mitchell drunk, 62–4;
    Mazzini on TC, 65; at Newby, 67–8;
    concern for her mother, 68–75;
    Macready's acting, 71–5; Christmas
    (1842), 72–3; recruits Sterling for
    Foreign Review, 75–6; mother's
    death, 77
    (1842–45): loss of mother, 78–80;
    birthday presents, 80; at Troston,
    81; Mazzini, 82; recommends Mrs
    Paulet, 83; MS of Zoe, 85; a
    domestic scene, 86; old Edward
    Sterling, 87–8; first meets Lady
    Harriet, 88–90; home decorating,
    91–2; David Masson, 92–3; meets
    Fr Mathew, 93–5; risings in Italy,
    96–7; refurbishing Cheyne Row,
    97–8; women's position, 99;
    American visitors, 99–100, and
    Elisabeth Jesser Reid, 101; Mazzini,
    101; promoting Zoe, 103–4;
    support for Mrs Fraser, 104–5; at
    Maryland St, 105–6; Charlotte
    Sterling's insane jealousy, 106–8;
    mesmerism, 108–11; Tennyson, 112
    (1845–47): Amalie Bölte and John
    May Welsh, 113–4; Geraldine
    Jewsbury, 115; at the Paulets, 116;
    at the Martineaus, 116–7; troubles
    with TC, 117; ballads from Gavan
    Duffy, 118; Lady Harriet at
    Addiscombe, 119; delayed
    birthday letter, 122–3; at
    Manchester, 122–4; at Bay House,
    124–6; servant problems, 127–8
    (1847–49): John Dunlop's tales from
    Notebook (1845–52), 129–31; the
    heir-apparent to Grand Duke of
    Weimar, 131–4; on Emerson,
    135–6; Geraldine's The Half
    Sisters, 136; dining with Mrs
    Norton and the Procters, and
    Chopin's playing, 137–8;
    entertains godchild, 138–40; Lady
    Harriet, the Sterlings, Cavaignac's
    death, 140–2; dinner at the
    Dickenses, Samuel Rogers, and
    Mazzini, 143–4; at Bradford, 144–5;
    Martha Lamont, 145–6; 'Much ado'
    at Haddington, 146–51; reply to
    John Stodart, 151–3

(1850-56): a pimple, 154-5; Helen Mitchell's attempted suicide, 155; Bath House ball, 155-6; Peel's death, 156-7; the Grange, 157-8; a painful accident and TC's lack of sympathy, 158-60; A. Sterling prosecutes a beggar, 160; concern for Lady Lytton, 161; Pentonville prison, 161-2; Great Exhibition, 163; Malvern water-cure, 164-5; TC and Lady Harriet, 165-6; at the Grange, 167-8; Christmas, 168-9; replies to John Stodart, 169-70; rising at Milan, 170-1; dangerous visit to Grey Mare's Tail, 171-2; Liverpool Unitarians, 173; making the attic room, 173-4; death of uncle John Welsh, 174; next door cocks, 175; death of TC's mother, 176; Allingham's poems, 177; old Mrs Montagu, 177-8; the Ruskins, 178; Neuberg's gift, 179; Geraldine a neighbour, 180; Phoebe Carlyle's death, 181-3; photos and sketches, 183; 'Budget of a *Femme* incomprise', 184-6; unhappiness, 186; failed attempt to rent seaside cottage, 187-9; invitation to Grange, 189-90; Lord John Russell, 190; Ruskin and Tennyson, 190-1; to Ellen Twisleton, 191-2; visit to Auchtertool, 192; TC at Kinloch Luichart, 192-3; JWC's breakdown, 193-5; thanks Elisabeth Dwight for chair, 196-7

(1855-56): record of JWC's early married life at Craigenputtoch, 198-204; JWC's *Journal* (1855-56), 205-20

(1857-60): advises Mary Smith and tells about life at Craigenputtoch, 221-3; the Thackeray girls, 223; Gaskell's life of Brontë, 224-5; death of Lady Ashburton, 225-6; proofs of *Frederick*, 227; Tait's *A Chelsea Interior*, 228; Geraldine and Mantell, 229-30; letters to G. Eliot (1858), 230-1, (1859),

238-40; the Gilchrists' maid, 231; TC's Russian admirer, 233-4; Lady Lytton, 234-5; 'Skittles,' 236; TC revisits Germany, 236; Lord Ashburton to re-marry, 237-8; George Rennie again, 240-1; at Humbie farm, 241-2; photos, 243-4; Nero injured, 244-5; Isabella McTurk, 245, 250-1; new friendship with Louisa Ashburton, 246-7; no truck with evolution, 247-8; death of Nero, 248-9; Rennie's death, 249-50; the Ashburtons' new baby, 252; Varnhagen's gossip, 252-3; friendship with the Stanleys, 253; death of Kate Ross (Sterling), 256; Margaret Oliphant and Irving, 256-8

(1861-63): her health, and winter in London, 259; TC upsets arrangements, 260; Mantell in New Zealand, 261; Oliphant on Irving, 261-2; Charlotte Cushman, 263-6; TC meets an adder, 266-7; mother love, 267; baby Baring, 267-8; Cushman, 268-71; deaths of Ellen Twisleton and Elizabeth Pepoli, 272; marriage ceremony, 273; Irving's biography, 274; staying at Holme Hill, 275; meets T.H. Huxley, 276; Haddington news, 276; Cushman, 277-8; no visit to Alderley, 278; Cushman, 279; no visiting the Tennysons, 279; TC and the Stanleys, 281; a 'forced' marriage, 282; photography at the Grange, 283; going nowhere, 283-4; TC dislikes Garibaldi, 285; Lord Ashburton ill, 286-7; Haddington memories, 287-8; servant troubles, 287-8; photos, 289; Mrs Royston, 290; Princess Alexandra, 291; new horse (Noggs) for TC, 292; Hungarian sword, 292-3

(1863-64): JWC's accident and illness, 294-5; refuses to be godmother, 295-6; taken to St Leonards, 296-9; to the Gill, 300;

to Holme Hill, 301-2; home, 302
(1864-66): in Devon, 303; friendship
with Louisa Ashburton, 305, and
Lady Amberley, 305-6; suppressing
cocks, 307-8; catching up with
letters, 308-9; the Edinburgh
Rectorial, 310-12; Governor Eyre,
313; socializing and tea-parties,
314-7; death and memorial, 318
childhood, xix, 40, 48, 147-50, 159,
199, 202, 205, 239-40, 286-7, 305
letters; see also Editors' Introduction,
passim, and general entry for
letter-writing, 84, 116, 243-4, 272,
277-8, 304, 306, 308-9
portrait, 134
religious views, xxix, 39, 47, 117, 127,
173, 183, 186, 219, 273, 296
Writings: 'Budget of a Femme
incomprise', xxv, 184-6; 'Life at
Craigenputtoch', 'The Cry from
Craigenputtoch', see xviii, xxxi,
198-204; Journal (1855-56), xvi,
xxii, xxxi, 198, 205-20; 'Much ado
about Nothing', xv, 146-51;
Notebook (1834-1850s), xx-xxi;
Notebook (1845-52), xx, 129-31;
The School for Husbands volume,
xx; The Simple Story of My Own
First Love, xix-xx, xxix; 'The
Wish', xxx, 6.
Carlyle, Jean (TC's sister; later Aitken;
1810-88), xviii, 201-2
Carlyle, Jenny or Janet (Clow; Alexander's
wife; 1808-91), 62
CARLYLE, Dr John Aitken (TC's brother;
1801-79), xxiii, 30, 60, 72-3,
104-5, 108, 132, 158, 171-2,
179-83, 214, 296, 298, 301-2, 316
CARLYLE, Margaret (Aitken; TC's mother;
1771-1853), 154, 175-6
Carlyle, Mary Aitken (TC's niece;
1848-95), xviii, xxxi, 220
Carlyle, Phoebe E.H. (John's wife; d.
1854), 154, 179-83
CARLYLE, Thomas; see also Editors'
Introduction, and passim
(1821-26): meets JWC, 2; early
courtship and advice on reading,
5-7; advised by JWC, 10-12; told 'I
love you,' 12; continued courtship,
13-14; 'forgives' her confession
about Irving, 15-16; events
leading to marriage, 17-19
(1826-34): Craigenputtoch, 19-20; in
London, 22-6; father's death, 23;
London friends, 24-5; turns to
French Revolution, 30; Barjarg
library, 30-1; visit by Emerson, 32;
moves to London, 33-4
(1834-42): in London, 35-8; Sterling
and Sartor, 38-9; his 'admirers',
42; French Revolution almost
finished, 44-5; reviewed, 45-6, 52;
lectures, 55-6; meets D'Orsay,
54-5, 58; Christmas (1839), 61;
Mazzini's essay on, 65; plans for
Newby disappointing, 66-8;
Macready, 71; starts new work, 72;
ashamed of giving insignificant
presents, 72; trouble with
neighbour, 77
(1842-5): clears up Mrs Welsh's
affairs, 78; gives birthday present,
80; portrait by Gambardella, 82-3;
writing Past and Present, 84;
dinner-party problems, 86; old
Sterling, 87-8; first meets Lady
Harriet, 88; in Wales, 92; needs
soundproof room, 98; problems
with Cromwell, 98; on women, 99;
recommends Zoe, 103; Mrs Fraser,
104-5; Mrs Charlotte Sterling, 108;
not at home for Tennyson, 112
(1845-47): tolerates John May Welsh,
112; grim at JWC's idea of visiting
her uncle, 115; JWC tells TC not to
trifle with her 'rights of women',
116; their strained relations,
117-8; both at Addiscombe, 119;
works on second edition of
Cromwell, 121; restless, 121;
JWC's birthday letter delayed,
122-3; with Lady Harriet and her
parrot, 126
(1847-50): unimpressed by 'scum of
creation', 131; visited by Grand
Duke of Weimar's heir apparent,

131-4; with Emerson, 135; on women, 137; Rogers comments on TC and Lady Harriet, 143; visits Ireland, 144; admirer at Bradford, 145

(1850-56): turns to work on Frederick, 154; determined to attend Bath House ball, 155-6; mourns Peel, 157; invitation to Grange, 157-8; unsympathetic, 158; goes to Great Exhibition, 163; at water cure, 164; at Paris, 165; attitude to Lady Harriet, 166; present from Christmas tree, 168; JWC gives report from Moffat, 171; construction of attic study, 173, 175; sends JWC to deal with cocks, 175; last visit to dying mother, 176; kind to John on Phoebe's death, 182; Budget of a 'Femme incomprise,' 184-6; rejects Brighton cottage, 187-9; last invitation to Grange from Lady Harriet, 189; blamed for poor letter, 192-3; gloomy journeys to and from Scotland, 193; exasperated by Martin, 196; referred to in 'Cry from Craigenputtoch', 198-204; and in Journal (1855-56), 205-20

(1857-60): approves Mary Smith's verses, 223; considers second German visit, 224; Lady Harriet's death, 225-6; to Addiscombe with Lady Sandwich, 227; JWC praises proofs of Frederick, 227; George Eliot hopes he will read her novels, 230, 240; admired by Botkin, 233-4; interest in Lady Lytton, 234-5; German visit, 236; how to treat him, 237; on Lord Ashburton's marriage, 238; at Humbie farm, 241-2; on Lady Ashburton's expected child, 244, 247, 252; the shadow of Frederick, 246; Dr Henry Duncan, 247; regret for Nero, 248-9; confusion about return from Thurso, 254

(1861-63): wishes to skate, 259; cannot settle at Grange, 260; Walter Mantell, 261; encounters adder, 266-7; glad to visit Grange, 268; on Oliphant's life of Irving, 271; Frederick reviewed, 275; will not go to the Stanleys, 278; or Tennysons, 280; photo by Heath, 283; irascible gloom, 283; dislike of Garibaldi, 285; Lord Ashburton his 'only friend', 286; no interest in royal wedding, 291; given horse (Noggs), 292; a Pandour's sword, 292-3

(1863-64): during JWC's illness, 294; bequeathed gift by Lord Ashburton, 298; JWC wants to be with him, 299; their re-union, and finishes Frederick, 302

(1864-66): rejects idea of Devon cottage, 303; rebuked for leaving letters lying about, 304; Louisa sends kiss, 305; dines with Col Stanley, 306; ignores cocks, 307; Edinburgh Rectorship, 310; news of triumph, 311-2; disagreement about Gov. Eyre, 313; Mill's letter, 314; JWC's last letter and Frederick's portrait, 317-8; TC's memorial for Jane, 318

Works: Chartism, 62; Critical Miscellanies, 61; 'Dr Francia', 268; Frederick the Great, 154, 169, 187, 224, 226-7, 246, 260-1, 275, 280-1, 285, 296, 302; French Revolution, 39, 41-2, 44-6, 227; Heroes and Hero-Worship, 65, 233; Latter-Day Pamphlets, 154; Lectures, 44-5, 55-7; Life of Cromwell and Oliver Cromwell's Letters and Speeches, 64, 71-2, 74, 98, 102-3, 117-8, 121, 227; Life of John Sterling, 38, 154; Past and Present, 84, 95; 'Phallus Worship', xxiii; Sartor Resartus, 22, 35, 38-9, 42, 52, 93, 202, 240.

Catchpool, Elizabeth or A. (dressmakers), 212

Cavaignac, E.L. Godefroy (1801-45), 35, 39, 46, 51, 53-4, 60, 64-5, 137-8 141-2
Cavaignac, Gen. Louis E. (1802-52), 137, 142, 167-8
Cellini, Benvenuto, 222
Chadwick, Edwin (1800-90), 112
CHAMBERLAYNE, Anne, 267
CHAMBERLAYNE, Maria, 267
Chambers, Dr W.F., 69
Chapman & Hall (Edward Chapman and William Hall), 75-6, 102-4, 136
Chardonell, Mme, 61
Charteris, Lady Anne, 125-6
Chelsea, 36, 155
Cheyne Row (no 4), 57
Cheyne Row (no 5), 35-40, 68, 283
    alterations, 97-8, 169-70, 173, 185
    burst water tank, 207
    cat, 243, 255
    decorating, cleaning, 65, 91, 97-8, 119
    garden, garden tent, 36, 91-2, 309
    soundproof attic room, 173, 175
Cheyne Row (no 6), 77, 98, 173, 175, 307-8
Chopin, 138
Chorley, Henry Fothergill (1808-72), 54, 93
Chorley, John F. (1807-67), 93, 173
Christison, Dr D. (Ashburtons' doctor), 288
Christmas, 61, 168-9, 175
Chrystal family, one of, 33
Clubbe, John, xii-xiv
Cobbett, William, 222
Coleridge, S.T., 15
Collins, Wilkie, 312
Colman, Henry, 100
Comely Bank (Edinburgh), xviii, 17-18, 35-6, 199
Conway, Rev. Daniel Moncure (1832-1907), xvi, 311
Cooke, John George, 304, 315
Cooke, T.P. (actor), 31
Cooper (Haddington), 148-50
Copenhagen, 163
Cornhill Magazine, 275
Correggio, 245

Craigenputtoch, xviii, 12-13, 17, 20-3, 25-33, 35-7, 183-4, 198-204, 221-2
    leaving it, 33-4
    barrister at, xxix, 32
Craigenvilla, 278
CRAIK, Prof. George Lillie (1798-1866), 69, 100, 104, 205
CRAIK, Mary, 306
Crimean war, 260
Cromwell, Oliver, 45, 48, 66, 117
CUSHMAN, Charlotte Saunders (1816-76), xxv-xxviii, xxxii, 134, 263, 271, 276-7, 279, 314
Cunningham, Allan (1784-1842), 24

Daily Telegraph, 234
Dante, 76
Darwin, Emma (Wedgwood), 69
Darwin, Charles R. (1809-82), 247-8, 289
Darwin, Erasmus Alvey (1804-81), 35, 46, 60, 62, 69, 73-4, 109, 208, 219
Davidson, Mrs (David's aunt), 273
DAVIDSON, Major David (1811-1900), 236
'Deed' or Will, 17
Delane, John Thaddeus (1817-79), 216
Delany, Mrs Mary, 272
Dickens, Charles, xxi, xxxi, 100-1, 143, 312
Dickson, Frank, 96
Dilberoglue, Sarah (Anderton), xxvi-xxviii, xxxii, 263-4, 266, 269, 271, 279, 314
Dilberoglue, Stauros (1821?-78), xxvi, xxxii, 123-4, 263, 266, 277
DINNING, Grace (Rennie), 249-50
D'Israeli, Isaac, xiii
DODS, Mary, 273
DODS, William, 309
Donaldson, Helen, 183
Donaldson, Jean (1770-1860; JWC's godmother), 149, 183
DONALDSON, Jessie (1774-1860), 183
Donovan, Cornelius (phrenologist), 146
D'Orsay, Count Alfred (1801-52), 54-5, 58, 137
Downshire, Marquis of (1812-68), 287
Drowned children, see Sarah Allen
Drumpark, 34

Drury Lane, and Theatre Royal, 23-4, 72, 130-1
Duff Gordon, Lady, 137
Dufferin, Frederick T.H.M. Blackwood, 5th Lord, 138
DUFFY, Charles Gavan (1816-1903), xxvii, 117, 144
Dumfries, 34, 64, 200
Duncan & Flockhart, 68
Duncan, Dr Henry (1774-1846), 247
Duncan, Isabella (d. 1878), 247-8
Dunlop, Capt. John, 69, 129-30
DWIGHT, Elisabeth (1830-1901), xix, 186, 191-2, 196, 204

Eastlake, Lady Elizabeth (Rigby), 292
Ecclefechan, 182
Eddisbury, Lady, see Lady Stanley
Edinburgh, 18, 20-1, 29, 38, 69, 192, 262, 276-8
    Chair of Universal History, 69
    Rectorial installation of TC, 308, 310-14
Elgin, James Bruce, 8th Earl and mother, 208
ELIOT, George (Marian Evans), xxiv-xxv, 5, 230, 238-40
Elizabeth I, Queen, 48
Ellesmere, Harriet C., Lady, 315
Ellice, Edward (the 'Bear'; 1781-1863), 216
Elliots, family of, 37
Elliot, Thomas Frederick (1808-80), and family, 313
Ellis, Sarah Stickney (d. 1872), xxi, 153, 169, 213
Eloisa and Abelard, 4
Elsie Venner (Oliver Wendell Holmes), 256
Emerson, Ralph Waldo (1803-82), xxix, 32, 81, 125, 133-6
Erskine, Rev. Thomas (1788-1870), xxix, 312
Espinasse, F., xxxii
Euclid, 208
Eyre, Gov. Edward J. (1815-1901), 313
Examiner, 57, 93, 96, 163

Faderman, Lillian, xxv
Farie, Robert (1813-82), 208
Farrer, Annie Louisa and family, 206, 213, 281
Fawkes, Guy, 47
Fergus, Elizabeth, see Pepoli
Fielding, Henry, 93
Fisher, Dr A., 30
FitzGerald, Edward, 187
Flo', little (servant), 287-8
Foreign Review, 21
Foreign Quarterly Review, 75-6
Foreman, Mrs, 183
Forster, Eliza, 274, 296
FORSTER, John (1812-76), 59, 71, 75-6, 134, 143, 154, 163, 234-5, 296, 311-2
Forster, W.E. (1818-86), 134, 140, 144, 146, 166, 212
Fortnum & Mason, 208
France, the French; see also place and personal names, 30, 143-4
Fraser, James (d. 1841), 46, 61
Fraser's Magazine, 65
Fraser, Mrs William (Vivian, formerly Blair), xxiv, 102, 104-5
Fraser, William (c. 1805-52), xxiv, 102, 104-5
Frederick William II (Friedrich Wilhelm II; the Great), 187, 293
    portrait, 318
Fritz (horse), 241, 264, 266
Froude, Henrietta (Warre), 296, 304, 317
Froude, James Anthony (1818-94), see Editors' Introduction, passim, 205, 220, 256, 296, 304, 317
Fryston Hall, 310, 316

Gambardella, Spiridione, 80, 82-3, 101, 115
Garibaldi, Guiseppe, 146, 284-5, 289, 292-3
Garnier, Joseph, 35
Gaskell, Elizabeth C. (Stevenson; 1810-65), xxiv, 143, 218, 224-5
'Genius', xiii, xxiv, 8-10, 12, 14, 17, 35, 48-9, 54, 57, 66, 71, 76, 78, 116, 134, 170, 194, 242, 252, 306
Geology, 247-8
George II, 303

Germany,TC's visits, (1852) 169, (1858) 224, 236
Gibbon, Edward, 306
Gifford, Helena, Countess (Sheridan; formerly Countess of Dufferin) and her monkey, 315
Gilchrist,Anne, 231
Gilchrist, Catherine, 15
Gillies, Margaret (1803-87) and Mary (d. 1870), 51-2
Glasgow, alcoholic physician, 130
Glen Eslin (Glenessland), 25
Glenshimmel (Shinnel water), 245
Goethe, Johann Wolfgang von, 20, 23, 26, 131, 133
   Faustus, 3, 313
   Wilhelm Meister, 9, 38
Goldsmith, Oliver, 93
Graham, Sir James, 138
Graham, Mabel Violet, 138
Grange, the, 119, 157-8, 165, 167-8, 175, 189, 195, 204, 212-3, 226, 229, 245-6, 248, 259-60, 267-8, 280, 282-3
Great Exhibition, 162-3, 166
Greig, John (1779-1858), 100
Grey Mare's Tail, 171-2
Grisi sisters, 138
Grote, Harriet (1792-1878), 51
Gully, Dr James (1808-83) and sisters, 164
Guy's Hospital, 75

Haddington; *see also* 'Much ado about Nothing', xxix, 1, 17, 19, 40, 183, 217, 244, 273, 290, 309
Haddingtonshire Courier, 276
Hamilton, Capt. George, 235
Hampstead, 220, 289
Handel's *Messiah*, 219
Harris, Frank (1856-1931), xix
Harry (horse), 33, 200
Hawkes, Emily (Ashurst, later Venturi; d. 1893), 170, 270
Hayward, Abraham (1801-84), 313
Headley Farm, 141
Heath, Vernon (1820-95), 283
Helps, Arthur (1813-75), 97, 100, 108, 124
Helps, Bessie (Fuller), 100, 102, 108

Hiddlestone, Jessie, 310-11, 314, 317
Herzen, A., 233
Hill, Lady Alice, 287
Hill, Rowland, 69
Holcroft, Thomas (1745-1809), 24
Holme Hill, 275, 300-2
Holmes, Lady, 284
Howden, Christina, 2
Howell & James (haberdashers), 43
Humbie Farm, Aberdour, 241-2
Hungary, Hungarians, 146, 292-3
Hunt, Leigh (1784-1859) and family, 31, 36, 50-1, 56-7
Hunt, Thornton Leigh (1810-73), xxi
Hunter, Dr J., 181
Hunter, Rev. John (1788-1866), 30
Hunter, Susan, *see* Stirling
Huxley, T.H. (1825-95), 275, 310, 315

Illustrated London News, 228
Income Tax Commissioners, 211
Indian hemp (hashish), 301
INGLIS, Henry (1806-86), 31
Inglis, Sir Robert H. (1786-1855), 69
Iphigenia, xiii-xiv, xviii, xxiv
Ireland, 117, 134, 144-5
Ireland, Mrs Alexander (1809-93), xxi
Irving, Rev. Edward (1792-1834), xxix, 2, 6, 9-10, 15-16, 23-24, 27, 35, 176, 178, 203, 217, 256, 258, 262, 274
Irving, George, 25
Isle of Wight, 88
Italy, Italians; *see also* Mazzini, place names, etc., 30, 41, 80, 90, 96, 271-2
Italian Free School, 80-2

Jacobson, Rev. William (1803-84), 47
Jamaica, 313
James, Henry (1811-82), 97, 99-100, 206
Jameson, Anna Brownell (1794-1860), xxiv, 70
Jay, Hannah A., 137-8
Jeffrey, Francis, Lord (1773-1850), 20-1, 25-8, 116, 257
Jersey, Sarah S. Child-Villiers, Countess of (1785-1867), 236
JEWSBURY Geraldine Ensor (1812-80), xiii, xvi, xxi-xxvi, 5, 59, 81, 83-5,

89, 102, 113-6, 122-5, 134, 136,
157, 160, 180-1, 186-7, 191,
193-5, 197, 208-10, 212, 214,
217-20, 227, 229-30, 261, 263,
270, 304, 312, 315
letter to Froude (1876), xxi-xxii
The Half Sisters, xxiii, 134, 136, 180,
187, 195
Zoe, 81, 84-5, 102-4, 114, 136
Jewsbury, Frank, xxxii, 125, 180
Jewsbury, Maria (1800-33), 103, 219
Jewsbury, Thomas, 125, 140
Johnson, Dr Samuel, 64,
Journal (1855-56), xvi, xxii, xxxi, 198,
205-20

Kelty, Mary Ann (1789-1873), 219
Kemble (or Sartoris), Adelaide
(1814-79), 138
Kemble, John (1807-57), 65
Kemptown, 189
Kinloch, Lady Isabella (1773-1861), 37
Kirkpatrick, Catherine Aurora (Kitty, later
Phillips; 1802-89), 9
Knox, John, 1, 56-7, 217, 221, 273
Koh-i-Noor diamond, 163
Kossuth, Lajos, 170

LAMONT, Martha M., xxiii, xxv, 97
Landor, Walter Savage (1775-1864), 58-9
Landseer, Sir Edwin, (1802-73), 316
Latrade, Louis C. de (1811-83), 51, 53-4
Laurence, Samuel (1812-84), 52
Leader, xxiv
Leader, John T., 65
Ledru-Rollin, A.A. (1808-74), 168
Leibnitz, G.W., 275
Lesbianism, xxvi-xxvii
letter-writing; *see also* Jane Carlyle, 58,
66, 192-4
Lewald, Fanny (1811-89), 157
Lewes, Agnes (Jervis), xxi
Lewes, G.H. (1817-78), xxi, xxiv, 230
Liverpool, 71, 73, 102, 113, 121, 123, 174,
216
Livingston, Dr, 254
Loch Luichart, 227
Locock, Sir Charles, 272

London, 23-5, 27, 35-6, 124, 127, 157-8,
169, 194, 218, 232, 246, 259, 283,
294
London Library, 208
Lytton, Sir Edward G.E. Bulwer
(1803-73), xxiv, 161, 234-5
LYTTON, Lady (Rosina) Bulwer
(1802-82), xxiv, 161, 234-5
Lytton, Robert, 234

Mackenzie, Louisa Stewart, *see* Ashburton
Macmillan, Alexander (1818-96), 312
Macqueen, John, 33
Macqueen, Margaret, 79
Macqueen, Nanny, 36
Macready, Catherine F. (Atkins; 1806-52),
54, 72, 97, 137, 139
Macready, Letitia, 54
Macready, Lydia Jane (1842-58), 138-40
Macready, William Charles (1793-1873),
51-2, 55, 71-2, 97
McTURK, Isabella, 23, 245, 250-51
McTurk, Robert, 5, 245, 251
Macveagh family, 60
Madeira, 62
Magpie public house, 210
Malakoff, Duke of, 235-6
Malvern, 49-50, 164-5
Manchester, 122-5
Town Clerk (James Heron), 125
Manderson, Marion, 241
MANTELL, Walter (1820-95), 229-30,
261
Maria Theresa, Empress, 292-3
Marianne (Phoebe Carlyle's servant),
181-2
Marie Antoinette, 31
Markus, Julia, xxv
Marochetti, Carlo (1805-67), 316
Marrast, Armand, 46
Married Women's Property Act, xxiv
Marsh, Anne (Caldwell; 1798-1874), 42
Marshall, Georgiana Hibbert and child,
70
Martin, Frederick, 196
Martineau, Harriet (1802-76), xxiv, 35,
42, 87, 108-11, 315
Martineau, Helen and children, 116-7

Martineau, James (1805-1900), 105,
    116-7, 173
Masson, David (1822-1907), 90, 92-3
Mathew, Fr Theobald, (1790-1856), 90,
    93-5, 129
Maupertuis, P.M.L. de, 275
Maurice, Rev. John F. Denison (1805-72),
    43, 75, 296
Mazzini, Giuseppe (1805-72), xxx, 59,
    65, 69, 73, 76-7, 80, 82, 87-8, 90,
    96-8, 101, 104, 117-8, 135, 143-4,
    146, 168, 170-1, 174, 221, 281,
    284-5
Mesmerism, 108-11
Merrill, Lisa, xxv
Milan, 137, 170
Mildmay, Mrs H., 235
Mile End, 93
MILES, Eliza, 23
Mill, Harriet (Taylor; 1807-58), xxi, 39,
    43, 51, 117
Mill, James (1773-1836), 24
Mill, John Stuart (1806-73), xxi, 24, 31-2,
    35, 37, 39, 43, 59, 89, 117, 314
Millais, Euphemia (Gray), see Ruskin
Millais, John Everett (1829-96), 190-1, 292
Mills, Mary, 68, 182
MILNES, Richard Monckton (1809-85),
    59, 187, 216, 310
Milton, John, 27, 36, 59, 73, 248, 275
Mitchell, Helen, 50, 53, 55, 60, 62-4, 66,
    73, 75, 84, 93, 127, 154, 161, 227
Montagu, Anna Dorothea (Benson),
    15-16, 24, 26, 28, 69, 176-8, 203,
    220
Monteagle, Thomas Spring Rice, Lord
    (1790-1866), 70
Monthly Magazine, 52
Moore, Thomas (1779-1852), 115
Morgan, Lady Sydney (1783-1859), 137
Morpeth, 146
Morphia, xxi, 172, 194, 207
Moscheles, Ignaz (1794-1870), 26
Moxon, Edward (1801-58), 112
'Much ado about Nothing', xxi, xxv,
    146-51
Mulock, Dinah Maria (1826-87), 274
Mundell, Rev. Robert, 60
Murray, John (1778-1843), 22

Napoleon I, 86, 99
Napoleon III, 144, 167
National, Le, 46
Nero (dog) 154, 170-2, 179, 186, 190,
    207, 215, 217, 227-8, 231, 235,
    241, 244-5, 248-9
NEUBERG, Joseph (1806-67), xxvii, 144,
    178, 188
Newby, 64, 67-8
New Zealand, 261
Nice, 195, 280, 282, 288
Nicholson (Haddington sexton), 147-8,
    150, 273
Noggs, Newman (TC's horse), 291-2
Norton, Caroline (Sheridan; 1808-77),
    xxiv, 137-8
Norton, Charles Eliot (1827-1908), xxxi
Notebook (1834-1850s), xx
Notebook (1845-52), xx-xxi, 129-31

Oakley Hall, 208
Oedipus, xii-xv
'Oh little did my mother think' (trad.),
    209
OLIPHANT, Margaret (1828-97), 256-57,
    276, 317
Oxford, 47-8

Page, Mrs, 30
Paley, Rev. William, 4
Palmer, William (1824-56), 194
Palmerston, Lord, 295
Pandours, 292-3
Paris, 12, 140, 157-8, 165, 225, 281, 288,
    291
Parkman, Mary (Dwight), 198
Parrots, 57, 126, 175, 284
Paulet, Elizabeth (Newton; 1806-79),
    xxiii, 81, 83-4, 93, 102, 117, 121-2,
    134, 140, 145, 263, 304
Paulet, Etienne (d. 1850), 81, 83
Paulet, Julia (daughter), 123
Pease Bridge, 146-7
Peel, Sir Robert, 156-7
Penpont, 28
Pentonville prison, 161-2
Pepoli, Count Carlo (1796-1881), 35, 39,
    41, 60, 75, 272

Pepoli, Countess Elizabeth (Fergus; 1792-1867), 60-1, 75, 84, 87, 99, 101, 171, 206, 272, 284
Photographs, 183, 204, 234, 243-4, 248-9, 278, 280, 283, 289, 308
Pimlico, 209
Pistrucci, Filipo (1779-1857), 82
Pistrucci, Scipione (ca.1814-54), 171
Plato, 48
Plattnauer, Richard, 102, 133, 173-4, 217
Plutarch, 168
Pope, Alexander, 86, 114, 174
Portal, Lady Charlotte, 219-20
Praslin, Duchess of, 206
Procter, Anne Benson (Skepper; b.1799), 24, 138, 176-7
Procter, Bryan Waller ('Barry Cornwall'; 1787-1874), 24, 138, 176-7
Pullar, Philippa, xix
Punch, 313-4

Quain, Dr Richard (1800-87), xix, 295, 301

Ramage, Mr, 70
Rankin, Isabella, 167
Rawdon, 146
Récamier, Mme Jeanne F.J.A.B., 183
REDWOOD, Charles (solicitor; 1802-54), 92, 175
Reid, Elizabeth J., 97, 101
Rennie, George (1802-60), xxii, 3-6, 35-7, 40, 217-9, 240-1, 249-50
Rennie, Jane (Cockerell), 37, 217-8, 240-1, 250
Richardson, John (1780-1864), 224
Rigby, Dr E., 181-2
Rio, Alexis François (1797-1874), 51, 53-4
Robert (Paulets' servant), 123
Robertson, James (groom), 150, 286
Robertson, John, 90, 92-3, 115, 141-2, 214
Rogers, Samuel (1763-1855), 115, 135, 143
Roland de la Platière, Jean-Marie, (Phlipon; 1734-93), 31
Rome, 141, 144, 146, 170, 225, 284
Ross, Rev. A.J. (1819-97), 214, 256

Ross, Kate (Sterling; 1834-60), 255-6
Rottingdean, 188
Rousseau, J.-J., 4-5, 8
Royal Institution, 316
Royston, Mrs, 290
Ruskin, Euphemia (Gray, later Millais), 176, 178, 190-1, 207, 292
Ruskin, John (1814-1900), xxx, 176, 178, 190-1, 207, 218, 264, 292, 316
Ruskin, Margaret, xxx, 178, 190
Russell, Arthur, 315
Russell, Dr James, 70, 73-4, 77, 78-9, 193-4, 275, 296, 301
Russell, Lord John, 189-90
Russell, Lady Katherine L., *see* Amberley
RUSSELL, Mary, 78, 117, 119, 225, 275-6, 296, 301
Russell, Lady William (1794?-1874), 313, 315
Russia, Russians; *see also* personal names, 233-5

Saffi, Count Aurelio (1819-90), 167, 171, 315
St Edmunds Bury, 84
St Leonards, 296-99
St Luke's (Chelsea), 273
St Martin le Grand, 294
St Mary's Abbey, Haddington, l, 147-9, 183, 244, 318
St Mary's Loch, 171
Salmon, Rev. Henry, 167-8
Samson, Abbot, 84
Sand, George (1804-76), xxiii, 5, 85, 157, 210
SANDWICH, Dowager Lady (Lowry-Corry; 1781-1862), 88, 140, 166-8, 208, 226-7, 232, 238, 259, 284
Sarah (E. Darwin's servant), 74
Sartoris, Edward J., 138
Saturday Review, xxiii, 252
Saxe-Weimar, heir apparent to Grand Duke of, 131-4
SCHWABE, Julie, 285
Schiller, Friedrich von, 7, 11-12
School for Husbands, xx
Scotland, 14, 45, 59-60, 79-80, 121, 145, 174, 176, 187, 192, 194, 239

Scotsbrig, 45, 176, 193

Scotsman, 312

Scott, Miss (unidentified), 164

Scott, Lady (formerly Robinson), 224-5

Scott, Rev. Alexander J. (1805-66), and
Ann Scott, 69

Scott, Sir Walter, 63

Seaforth Hall, 83, 121, 134

Seaforth Lodge (Devon), 303

Sedgwick, Catharine Maria (1789-1867),
197

Senior, Nassau W. (1790-1864), 164

Serpentine, 259

servants; *see also* Betty Braid, Anne
Brown, Little Flo', Helen Mitchell,
Charlotte Southam etc., 27-8,
63-4, 70, 73-4, 126-8, 163, 200-1,
231, 237, 244, 287-8, 301, 303,
310-11, 317

Seven Dials, 129-30

Shakespeare, 10
Macbeth, 34
Merchant of Venice, 71
Timon of Athens, 287

Shandy (dog), 217

Shelley, Mary (Wollstonecraft;
1797-1851), 5

Shelley, Percy B., 4, 55

Silvester (coachman), 312-3

SIMMONDS, Isabella (Barnes), 273, 296

Simple Story of My Own First Love, The,
xix-xx, xxix

Sinclair, Sir George (1790-1868), 253

Sketchley, Penelope, 83

'Skittles,' *see* Catherine Walters

Smith, Goldwin (1823-1910), 216

SMITH, Mary (1822-89), xxi, 221

Smith, Dr Thomas Southwood
(1788-1861), 50-2

Somerville, Mary F. (1780-1872), 35-6

SOUTHAM, Charlotte, 233, 241-3, 248-9,
252, 255

Spaniards Inn, 220

Sparrow, Lady Olivia, 208

speaking with tongues, 23-4

Spedding, James (1808-81), 43

Spenser (as used by Froude), xiv-xv

Spiritualism, 207

Spiritual Magnetism, 263

Spottiswoode, Mr and Mrs W., 317

Staal, Marguerite de Launay
(1684-1750), 31

Staël, Anne Louise, Baronne de
(1766-1817), xx, 5-6, 31, 219

Stanley, Col John C., 306

STANLEY, Lady Henrietta Maria (Dillon;
1807-95), 67, 138, 281

STANLEY, Kate (later Lady Katherine
Russell), 281

Stanley, Lord Edward J. (1802-69), 254,
281

Stebbins, Emma (sculptor; 1815-82),
xxviii, 263-5, 271, 278

Stephen (Sterlings' servant), 48

Stephen, Sir George, 225

Sterling, Anthony Coningham (1805-71),
43, 88, 102, 107-8, 134, 139-41,
154, 160

Sterling, Charlotte (Baird; Anthony's wife;
d. 1863), 88, 106-8, 141

Sterling, Edward (father; 1773-1847),
39-41, 47-50, 60, 87-8, 90-1,
102-4, 134

Sterling, Hester (Coningham; d. 1843),
41, 43, 45-50, 73, 75, 87, 203

STERLING, John (1806-44), xxvii, 35, 38,
41, 53, 62, 65, 76, 87, 93, 102

STERLING, Julia, 256

STERLING, Kate; *see also* Ross, xviii, 214

Sterling, Susannah (Barton; John's wife; d.
1843), 40, 43, 87

STIRLING, Susan (Hunter; 1799-1877),
xxiii, 41

STODART, Eliza , *see* Aitken

STODART, John R., 144, 151, 169

Sunnybank, 149, 183, 309

Syme, Prof. James (1799-1870), 281

Tacitus, 48

TAIT, Robert Scott (1816-97), 187-8,
213, 228, 248-9

Taylor, Harriet, *see* Mill

Taylor, Henry (1800-86), 43, 86

Taylor, Jeremy, 4

Temperance movement; *see also* Fr
Mathew, 129-131

Templand (Thornhill), 17, 58-60, 68, 70,
182-3, 245, 275

Tennyson, Alfred (1809-82), xxix, 111-2, 191, 280
TENNYSON, Emily (1813-96), 280
Terrot, Very Rev. Charles H. (1790-1872), xxix, 37-8, 93
Terry (greengrocer), 313-4
Thackeray, Anne Isabella (1837-1919), 223-4
Thackeray, W.M. (1811-63), xix-xx, 45-6, 69, 157, 186, 204, 223
Thirlwall, Very Rev. Connop (St David's), 92
Thornhill, 61, 78, 245, 275, 296
Thurso Castle, 253-4
Tierney, Lady, 281
Times, xv, 45, 75, 89, 126, 224-5
Tiny (dog), 318
Tippoo, Sultan, 48
Toulmin, Camilla (1812-95), 124
TREVELYAN, Lady, 292, 316
Tulloch, Rev. John (1823-86), and wife, 317
Turgenev, Ivan, 233
Turner, Joseph M.W., xxx, 190
Twisleton, Hon. Edward T.B. (1809-74), xviii, 164, 179, 189, 191-2, 198, 204, 208, 216, 225, 315
TWISLETON, Ellen (Dwight; 1828-62), xviii-xix, 179, 186, 189, 191, 195, 197-8, 203-4, 208, 212, 216, 224-6, 229, 252, 272, 284
  'The Cry from Craigenputtoch', 'Life at Craigenputtoch', xviii, xxxi, 198-204
Tyndall, Prof. John (1820-93), 310-12, 316

Unitarians, 50, 113, 116, 167

Van Dyck, Sir Anthony, 228
Varnhagen von Ense, Karl August (1785-1858), xxiii, 108-9, 252-3
Venturi, Emilie (Ashurst; formerly Hawkes), 266, 268, 270-1, 281
Victoria, Queen, 55, 70, 87, 291

Wales, 92
Wallace, Sir William, 1
Walters, Catherine ('Skittles'), 235-6

Warren, Mrs (housekeeper), 311, 313
WEDGWOOD, Frances (Mackintosh; 1800-1899), 35, 62, 69, 86, 189, 208, 218
Wedgwood, Henry and wife, 69
Wedgwood, Hensleigh, 69, 218
wee Eppie Daidle, 36
Wellington, Duke of, xx, 156
Welsh, Ann (JWC's paternal aunt; d. 1877), 127, 151, 223, 276, 289-90, 312
Welsh, Elizabeth (paternal aunt; d. 1877), 183, 276
WELSH, Grace (paternal aunt; d. 1867), 276
WELSH, Grace (mother; Welsh; 1782-1842), xxii, xxv, 1-3, 10, 14-15, 17-18, 21-2, 28-9, 33, 38, 41, 51, 57, 59-60, 64, 66, 76-9, 119, 148, 159-60, 174, 176, 182-4, 186, 199-203, 209, 267, 275, 305, 318
WELSH, Helen (cousin; 1813-53), 23, 56, 70, 83, 85, 163, 174, 180
Welsh, Jackie (illegitimate paternal cousin), 276
Welsh, Jeannie (maternal aunt; 1798?-1828), 159-60, 275
WELSH, Jeannie (Babbie; later Chrystal), 56, 70, 78, 80, 83, 91, 106, 151, 158, 160, 180
Welsh, John (John Knox's son-in-law; 1568?-1622), 221
Welsh, John (JWC's paternal grandfather, of Penfillan; 1757-1823), 44, 198-9
Welsh, Dr John (JWC's father; 1776-1819), xxii, 1-3, 7, 17, 146-9, 159, 186, 193, 199, 228-9, 244, 318
WELSH, John (uncle; d. 1853), 52, 71, 79-80, 105, 174, 180
Welsh, John May (cousin), 113-5
WELSH, Margaret (Kissock; 1803-88), 17-18
WELSH, Margaret (cousin Maggie, b. 1821), 192, 216, 296-8, 310-12
Welsh, Mary (aunt), 159-60
Welsh, Mary (cousin), 70, 287

Welsh, Robert (uncle; 1784–1841), 113

Welsh, Walter (JWC's maternal grandfather; d. 1832), 22, 29

Welsh, Rev. Walter (cousin; 1799–1879), 33, 79, 146, 174, 192, 220, 241

'When I think on what I is', 208

Whitworth, Joseph (1803–87), 123–5, 210

Wilkie, John, 286

William (E. Darwin's servant), 74

Wilson, Jane, 41, 212

Wilson, John (Scotch songs), 86

Winyard, Mrs, 111

'Wish, The', xxx, 6

Women, nature, position, and rights of, xx–xxi, xxiii–xxiv, 26–7, 31, 62, 99, 106, 137, 145–6, 161, 221, 232, 281–2

WOOLNER, Thomas (1825–1892), xxxii, 255

Worthington, Dr James W. (1799–1879), 76

Wynn, Charlotte Williams (1807–69), 158, 160, 187, 253, 317

Yorstoun, Edward, 314